D1457493

Volume 5

Garland Folkore Casebooks

General Editor
Alan Dundes
University of California, Berkeley

ORAL-FORMULAIC THEORY
A Folklore Casebook

Edited by
John Miles Foley

GARLAND PUBLISHING, INC. • NEW YORK & LONDON
1990

Library of Congress Cataloging-in-Publication Data

Oral-formulaic theory : a folklore casebook / [compiled by] John Miles
Foley.
    p. cm. — (Garland folklore casebooks ; v. 5) (Garland
reference library of the humanities ; vol. 739)
  Includes bibliographical references.
  ISBN 0–8240–8485–3 (alk. paper)
  1. Oral-formulaic analysis. I. Foley, John Miles. II. Series.
III. Series: Garland reference library of the humanities ; vol. 739.
GR44.072073   1990   _L7879_
398.2—dc20   89–16911
                                  CIP

Printed on acid-free, 250-year-life paper
Manufactured in the United States of America

This volume is for
Frances Foley Kelly

In loco matris

Folklore Casebook Series

The materials of folklore demonstrate remarkable variation. Each of the cultures which share a particular item of folklore, for example, a myth, a folktale, a custom, a folk belief, has its own special version of that item. Sometimes individuals within a given culture will have their own idiosyncratic variations within the larger culturewide tradition. Students of folklore who study the folklore of only their own group may fail to appreciate the range of variation in folklore. By bringing together different studies of the same item of folklore, I hope to provide a means of demonstrating both the ways in which folklore remains constant across cultures and the ways in which folklore is inevitably localized in different cultural contexts.

With respect to the distribution of an item of folklore, there are two all too common erroneous assumptions. The first assumption is that the item of folklore is peculiar to one culture. Those anthropologists, for example, who are unwilling to be comparative, typically assume or assert that a given folktale is unique to "their" people, meaning the people among whom they have carried out their fieldwork. The critical theoretical point is that one cannot tell whether or how a folktale is really unique to one culture without knowing if the same tale is found in other cultures. Once one has examined other versions of the tale, then and only then can one comment intelligently on just how a particular version of that tale reflects the culturally relative characteristics of a given society.

The second erroneous assumption, equally irritating to professional folklorists, is that a given item of folklore is universal. This is the opposite extreme from the first assumption. Rather than presuming that the item is unique to one culture, the universalist (typically a literary or psychologically oriented student) simply posits the existence of the item in all cultures. Yet the facts do not support the position any more than the other. Most items of folklore have limited areas of distribution. For example, there are Indo-European folktales reported

vii

from India to Ireland, but most of these tales are *not* found among Australian aborigines, the peoples of Melanesia and Polynesia, South American Indians, etc. Similarly, there are folktales found in North and South American Indian tradition which are not found in Europe. If one takes the trouble to check the sources cited by universalists, he or she will normally find little if any reference to the traditions of the people of New Guinea, native South America, sub-Saharan Africa among other areas.

One cannot say a priori what the distribution of a particular item of folklore might be. One needs to consult the scholarship devoted to that item before venturing an informed opinion. Chances are great, however, that the item will not be limited to a single culture nor will it be worldwide. One aim of the Folklore Casebook series then is to show by example something about the range and spread of individual items of folklore.

Questions about the geographical distribution of an item of folklore are not the only ones worth asking. Even more important are questions about meaning and interpretation. Far too often, students of folklore simply collect and report. Pure descriptions of data are surely a precondition for serious study, but they do not offer a substitute for significant analysis. Unfortunately, the majority of writings about a particular item of folklore never attempts anything more than mere description. The discipline of folklore began several centuries ago with the collection of antiquities and presumed "survivals" from earlier periods. It was not until the late nineteenth century and especially the twentieth century that the crucial study of how folklore functions in context may be said to have begun. In most cases, the application of sociological, anthropological, psychological and other theories and methods to folkloristic data has yet to be undertaken. One reason for this is that most theorists in the social sciences are just as unaware of the nature of folklore data as folklorists are unaware of the theories and methods of the social sciences. One intent of the Folklore Casebook series is to bring data and theory together—at least for students of folklore.

Folklore has always fascinated members of many academic disciplines, e.g., scholars in classics, comparative literature, Bible studies, psychiatry, sociology, but despite its interdisciplinary appeal, the study of folklore has rarely been interdisciplinary. One can find lip service to the notion of interdisciplinary study, but scholars and their work for the most part tend to be parochial. Anthropologists cite only the work of fellow anthropologists, psychiatrists only the work of other psychiatrists. Similarly, folklorists too are not always open to considering studies of folklore made by nonfolklorists. Accordingly, students who come upon a specific problem in folklore are commonly restricted by the limited disciplinary bias and knowledge of their instructors.

One difficulty in being truly interdisciplinary involves a mechanical problem in locating the previous scholarship devoted to a problem. Folklore studies appear in an incredible and often bewildering variety of books, monographs, and professional periodicals. One needs sometimes to be a virtual bibliographical sleuth to discover what other scholars have said about the subject one has chosen to research. Yet the credo of the true scholar should be that he should begin *his* work where other scholars have ended theirs. With this in mind, one other aim of the Folklore Casebook series is to bring together under one cover a representative sampling of the scholarship relevant to a single item or problem. I hope it will encourage students of folklore not to be parochial in outlook but rather to be willing if not anxious to explore all possibilities in investigating the folklore research topic they have selected.

The topics covered in the Folklore Casebook series are of sufficient general interest to have received the critical attention of numerous scholars. Topics such as the evil eye, the flood myth, the bullfight, Christmas, the custom of couvade, or the folktale of Oedipus would be examples of topics appropriate for casebook treatment. In most instances, whole books or monographs have been devoted to the topics. However, for the most part, the selections chosen for the Casebook have been taken from periodicals. Assembling representative essays from a variety of sources seemed to be the best means of achieving the various goals of the Casebook series. Students who wish to explore further the topic of one of the Casebooks would be well advised to consult the book-length treatments available. In each Casebook, the editor will provide some bibliographical references for the student who wishes to go beyond the necessarily limited materials contained in the volume.

The selections included in the casebooks will be presented as they originally appeared, wherever possible. To be sure, essays written in foreign languages will be translated for the Casebook, but individual words or phrases in foreign languages may be left untranslated. It is important for students of folklore to be aware of the necessity for learning to read foreign languages. Because the different selections were written independently, it is inevitable that some repetition will occur. Students must realize that such repetition in scholarship is not unusual. In folklore in particular, the repetition of data is often desirable. As indicated above, folklorists are often concerned with the question to what extent is an item of folklore in one culture similar to or different from an apparently comparable item in another culture.

The scholarly apparatus including footnote and bibliographical reference style has also been left intact wherever possible. Differences between the humanities and the social sciences exist with respect to reference techniques as any scholar who has had occasion to rewrite or recast an essay to conform to the requirements of another discipline can very well attest. Leaving the footnotes in their original form also serves to demonstrate the partial nature of scholarship. Probably no one scholar ever controls all the relevant data and has read all the books and essays pertaining to his subject. For one thing, few scholars can read all those languages of the world in which germane material has been written. For another, there remains the perennial information retrieval problem which normally precludes even locating all the possible sources. Still granting the unavoidably incomplete nature of most scholarship, the student can still see differences in how well an individual scholar succeeded in finding source materials. Some writers make little or no attempt to consult sources—almost pretending that they are the first to ever contemplate the issue under consideration. Others seem to make a pedantic fetish out of citing esoteric and fugitive sources. In the final analysis, the criteria for the inclusion of an essay in a casebook did not include counting the number of references contained in an author's footnotes. Rather the criteria concerned the clarity of the description of the data and the degree of insight attained in the analysis of the data. It should be understood that not every important essay written about the topic or theme of a casebook could be included. Some essays were simply too long while others may have been superseded by later studies.

Despite limitations, it is hoped that the sampling of scholarship presented in the Folklore Casebook series will assist students of folklore in undertaking research of their own. Whether they are stimulated to continue the study of the particular topic treated in a casebook or whether they use one or more of the essays as a model for the investigation of some other topic, the ultimate goal is the upgrading of the quality of folklore research. As the discipline of folkloristics continues to grow, its success and its achievements will unquestionably depend upon how well future students study the materials of folklore.

Alan Dundes, General Editor
University of California, Berkeley

Contents

Introduction

Oral-formulaic theory, also known as the Parry-Lord theory after its founders Milman Parry and Albert B. Lord, is concerned with the interpretation of style and structure as evidence of a work's oral traditional provenance.[1] Its central premise holds that such works, whether recorded from the mouths of informants or filtered through a textual medium, will exhibit recognizable patterning at the levels of phraseology (*formula*), narrative scene (*theme*), and the tale as a whole (*story-pattern*). On the basis of identifying these typical kinds of multiform structure, scholars subscribing to the theory pronounce a text oral traditional or at least derived from an oral tradition.

Parry's brilliant first steps were taken in the late 1920s and early 1930s, as he offered a new solution to the ages-old Homeric problem. In his 1928 French dissertation he was able to show that ancient Greek epic phraseology was uniquely plastic in its structure, that the noun-epithet formulas like "swift-footed Achilles," for example, obeyed certain rules of combination and position. From these and other observations he went on to posit a *traditional* Homer, a bard who inherited the poetic idiom fashioned over generations and who depended on that idiom for composing the *Iliad* and *Odyssey*. In his 1930 and 1932 essays in *Harvard Studies in Classical Philology*, he made the leap of imagination from a traditional to a necessarily *oral* Homer, having been inspired to think comparatively by his mentor Antoine Meillet as well as by studies of oral poetry then available.

Just as Parry's textual analysis drew on the philological methods of German linguists like J.-E. Ellendt and Heinrich Düntzer, so his and Lord's fieldwork was influenced significantly by the prior field research

xiii

of anthropologists like V. V. Radlov on the Central Asian Kara-Kirghiz and particularly M. Murko on the South Slavs. In 1933-1935 Parry and Lord journeyed to Yugoslavia to test the insights gleaned from Homeric texts on the oral epic tradition that remained alive among the *guslari*. The hundreds of epics they collected during those years, to which Lord has added in later trips with David Bynum, make up the greatest part of the Milman Parry Collection of Oral Literature at Harvard University.

The pivotal next step was to be taken by Lord, with the publication of his comparative manifesto, *The Singer of Tales*, in 1960. Here he brought together Serbo-Croatian oral epics, the living comparand, with a variety of oral-derived works: the ancient Greek epics, the Old English *Beowulf*, the Old French *Song of Roland*, and the Byzantine Greek *Digenes Akritas*. This landmark book provided the impetus for the emergence of an interdisciplinary scholarly enterprise; from 1960 onward the comparative investigation widened rapidly in scope until, by the present day, more than one hundred separate traditions have been approached via the oral-formulaic theory.

This casebook is not the place to attempt to recount how such an explosion of research and scholarship took place or to try to assess its implications for our understanding of oral, oral-derived, and literary art. Two of my earlier books present a history and a bibliography to which the present collection may be considered a companion: they are, respectively, *The Oral Theory of Composition: History and Methodology* (Indiana U. P., 1988) and *Oral-Formulaic Theory and Research* (Garland, 1985; with updates in the journal *Oral Tradition*).[2]

What this casebook can do, however, is to present samples of relevant work that touches in some important way on the origin, evolution, or response to oral-formulaic theory. In each case a short headnote introduces the selection, helping to place it in the larger context of the theory as a whole. Thus it is that the volume begins with an excerpt from Matija Murko's 1929 *La Poésie populaire épique en Yougoslavie au début du XXe siècle*, a slim work that had a major influence on Parry; I have translated the first chapter for this purpose. Albert Lord's two "Perspectives" essays, originally published in 1974 and 1986, form the bookends for the rest of the collection; together they not only refine his own ideas but also present a broad overview of contemporary research on oral literature.[3]

With the Murko and first Lord essay constituting the opening section, the second part is given over to "Classic Statements and

Summaries." Although many other candidates presented themselves, I have chosen—as a pars pro toto selection—seven papers or book excerpts that illustrate or summarize some of the most significant insights and problems associated with oral-formulaic theory across a variety of traditions. The first two, by Robert P. Creed and Donald K. Fry, treat Old English poetry, which, after ancient Greek, has seen more activity than any other tradition. Medieval French and Spanish are represented in selections from work by, respectively, Joseph J. Duggan and Ruth H. Webber, thus adding to the perspective on the medieval world. Robert Culley next offers an excellent survey of oral tradition and the Bible, while Walter J. Ong studies the oral-formulaic nature of African talking drums and Bruce Rosenberg discusses the art of the American folk-preacher.

Since oral-formulaic theory has from the start attracted a healthy share of controversy, it seemed important to include in the casebook a sampling of opposing opinion in a "Challenges" section. Larry D. Benson's essay certainly suits this purpose, seeking as it did to counter Francis P. Magoun's seminal 1953 article that introduced the work of Parry and Lord to Old English studies.[4] Another natural entry in this category is Ruth Finnegan's 1976 query asking "What Is Oral Literature Anyway?"—an intriguing counterstatement based on her research on African traditions.

The final section, "New Directions," has been the most difficult to put together, and for at least two reasons: not only do we lack the historical perspective that limits the number of essays that can confidently be labeled "classics," but we also run the risk of dating the collection rather quickly in a field that has developed, and continues to develop, so rapidly. What is "new," in short, cannot be "classic"; nor is it likely to remain "new" for very long. These caveats issued, I acknowledge the choice of Michael Nagler's extremely influential work on Homer, Alain Renoir's pioneering consideration of aesthetics and oral-formulaic structure, and my own attempt toward a more finely honed poetics of what we too crudely lump together as "oral literature."

Some readers may find these fifteen selections merely a partial reflection of what has become a complicated and many-faceted theory (and in many cases much more than is usually implied by the term "theory")—and I would have to agree. If, however, they collectively give some appreciation of that complexity and in the process convey some of the excitement involved in rediscovering the oral traditional roots of some of our most cherished works, then the casebook will have served its admittedly introductory purpose. Perhaps it is not completely irresponsible to hope that readers will want to venture well beyond the necessarily limited resources of this volume, or even that at some time in the future a sequel casebook might be warranted. No theory worth the name could be tidily contained within two covers, nor could even such a forced prisoner be kept under lock and key for any period of time.

For the present, however, this collection must suffice, and I am grateful to those editors and publishing firms who authorized reprinting its contents.

The editorial assistant on this project, Sarah J. Feeny, has been of enormous aid, bringing expertise, precision, and a lively wit to all aspects of the process. I also thank Michelle Mitchell-Foust of our Center for Studies in Oral Tradition, who helped with encoding the essays, and Lee Edgar Tyler, who smoothed the rocky road of computer typesetting. The editor for this series, Gary Kuris, and the computer specialist at Garland, Chuck Bartelt, have been both patient and encouraging. Finally, I express my gratitude to Alan Dundes, general editor of the Garland Casebooks, who urged this project as a companion to other reference works. My debt to my family—to Anne-Marie, Joshua, Lizzie, and little John—remains unpaid.

John Miles Foley

NOTES

[1]The most fundamental works are Parry, *The Making of Homeric Verse* (see note 3 below), and Lord, *The Singer of Tales* (Cambridge, Mass.: Harvard University Press, 1960 et seq.). For a complete survey of the origins and development of this field of inquiry, see Foley, *The Theory of Oral Composition: History and Methodology* (Bloomington: Indiana University Press, 1988). For bibliography, see Foley, *Oral-Formulaic Theory and Research* (New York: Garland, 1985), with updates in the journal *Oral Tradition*.

[2]For further information on structure, see Foley, *Traditional Oral Epic: The Odyssey, Beowulf, and the Serbo-Croatian Return Song* (Berkeley: Univ. of California Press, 1990); the implications of structure for aesthetics are the subject of a study entitled *Immanent Art* (to be published by Indiana University Press).

[3]Readers will note that no sample of Parry's own writings is included herein. In addition to their being readily available in a standard collection, *The Making of Homeric Verse* (Oxford: Clarendon Press, 1971; rpt. New York: Arno Press, 1980), his analyses are highly technical and therefore of use principally to classicists. Since Lord and others employ his general definitions, applying the chief insights of the 1928 doctoral theses and the 1930 and 1932 essays to a wide range of works in less technical fashion, I have thought it best to let Parry's fundamental ideas be communicated through them. On Parry's achievement see further Foley, *The Theory of Oral Composition*, Ch. 2.

[4]Magoun, "The Oral-Formulaic Character of Anglo-Saxon Narrative Poetry," *Speculum*, 28 (1953), 446-467.

Oral-Formulaic Theory

The Singers and their Epic Songs[1]

Matija Murko

Matija Murko, a Slovenian ethnographer who taught at Prague but spent his summers documenting oral traditional epic in Yugoslavia (see especially his posthumous masterwork, Tragom srpskohrvatske narodne epike, *1951), was one of the primary influences on Milman Parry as he made the leap from Homer's* traditional *diction to the conclusion that such a phraseology must also have been* oral. *Murko happened to be lecturing in Paris a week or so before Parry's* soutenance *in 1928; although the young classicist apparently did not attend the talks which were the next year to be published as* La Poésie populaire épique en Yougoslavie au début du XXe siècle, *his mentor Antoine Meillet saw that Murko was present at Parry's defense of the theses. Meillet's criticism that his student had not taken into account the necessary orality of the Homeric poems, along with the firsthand evidence which Murko's fieldwork provided for an oral tradition of epic, helped Parry toward the portrait of an oral and traditional Homer as realized in his monumental* Harvard Studies in Classical Philology *essays of 1930 and 1932. Indeed, as Parry put it in his own field notes of 1933-35, "it was the writings of Professor Murko more than those of any other which in the following years led me to the study of oral poetry in itself and to*

Reprinted from *La Poésie populaire épique en Yougoslavie au début du XXe siècle* (Paris: Librairie Ancienne Honoré Champion, 1929), pp. 1-31.

3

the heroic poems of the South Slavs" (from "Ćor Huso," The Making of Homeric Verse, p. 439). What follows, then, is an excerpt from Murko's La Poésie populaire of 1929, the work that Parry most often cited.

One finds mention of the folk poetry of the South Slavs beginning with the seventh, then in the tenth century, and, in relation to the epic songs in particular, from the thirteenth century forward. Documents of any length bearing on the epic songs become more and more numerous among all South Slavic peoples from the fifteenth century, and they are printed for the first time in *Fishing (Ribanje)* by the Dalmatian author P[etar] Hektorović. From the first half of the eighteenth century, there already exist ample manuscript collections as well as numerous enough imitations of epic songs: among the latter the *Pleasant Conversation of the Slavic People (Razgovor ugodni naroda slovinskoga)* by the Franciscan Croatian monk Andrija Kačić-Miošić, originally of the Makarska region in Dalmatia, stands out; this poem dates from 1756 and eventually became the single most widespread Croatian book. Kačić-Miošić sang episodes from the history of all the South Slavic peoples, and especially of their battles against the Turks, in the spirit of the true folk epic poetry, and he included in his work a considerable number of actual folk songs. It was through the Latin translation of this work that for the first time the world heard the "Illyrian bards" speak. Nevertheless, the principal architect of their glory was an Italian naturalist, the abbot Alberto Fortis, who in his *Viaggio in Dalmazzia* (1774) devoted an entire chapter to the music and poetry of the mountain folk of Dalmatia, the "Morlaks," and published the original as well as an Italian translation of one of the finest folk epic songs, the *Sad Ballad of the Noble Spouse of Hasanaga*. Through the translation made by Goethe, which was printed for the first time in the *Volkslieder* of Herder (1778), where some translations of Kačić-Miošić are also to be found, this ballad became an integral part of world literature; it was also translated five times into French. Fortis had compared the Illyrian national epic songs to Ossian; the comparison to Homer was made in principle as early as the end of the eighteenth century by a physician from Split named Bajamonti, and by a poet from Ragusa writing in Latin, Ferić (*Ad clarissimum virum Julium Bajamontium Georgii Ferich Ragusini epistola*, Ragusa, 1799).

It was from these sources, as well as through his personal relations with the Serbs and Croats, that a Viennese Slavist, the Slovenian B. Kopitar, would learn of the great richness of their national songs. He sought to insure that these songs were collected. The unhappy outcome of the First Serbian Revolt in 1813 brought to Vienna Vuk Stefanović Karadžić, descendant of a Hercegovinian family, a talented and self-educated peasant whom Kopitar would make the reviser of the orthography and written language of the Serbs, an excellent grammarian, a remarkable lexicographer, and the celebrated collector of Serbian folk songs, proverbs, and tales. In the period of romantic enthusiasm for folk poetry and the national ethos, the first edition of Karadžić's Serbian national songs (1814-1815) was to be received with correspondingly great enthusiasm, notably by Jakob Grimm: the second edition (Leipzig, 1823-1824; Vienna 1833), in the wake of the excellent and musical translation by Miss Talvj (later to become Mrs. Robertson), provoked among the scientific critics[2] (once more above all Jakob Grimm), among Goethe and the poets, a veritable ecstasy that, thanks to other translations, won over all of Europe and even America.

This gave way in France to the famous hoax by Mérimée: *The Guslar, or a Selection of Illyrian Poems Collected in Dalmatia, Bosnia, Croatia, and Hercegovina* (Strasbourg, 1827). Goethe recognized that this collection was a fraud, and was greatly amused with it, but the Englishman Bowring, the German W. Gerhard, and even the great Russian poet Pushkin made translations of these supposed folk songs. Nevertheless, the French had also at hand a translation of the genuine national songs of Vuk Karadžić in the *Folk Songs of the Serbians Collected by Vuk Karadžić and Translated in the manner of Talvj*, by Miss Elise Voiart (Paris, 1834, 2 vols.).

The third edition, much enlarged, of folk songs collected by Vuk, called the "Vienna edition" (1841-1865), established their reputation and became the basis for scientific study as well as for new translations (of which the best was by S. Kapper, into German at first and then afterward into Czech). At the end of the last century there appeared in Belgrade a new standard edition, augmented by numerous epic songs found in Vuk's papers, songs which he had put aside for various reasons during his lifetime. Today the complete collection comprises nine substantial octavo volumes, of which only two, the first and the fifth, contain lyric songs, all of the others being completely composed of epic songs, a fact that characterizes well the richness of the Yugoslav folk epic poetry.[3]

Even during Vuk's lifetime, as well as after his death, the Serbs and Croats published a whole series of collections of folk songs, enough to fill a library. And one should mention the collections of songs from the seventeenth and first half of the eighteenth centuries from all along the southern Adriatic coast, those of Miklosich and B. Bogišić, member of the Institute, as well as the songs from the first half of the eighteenth century from the northwestern regions that were found in Erlangen in Bavaria and recently published by G. Gesemann. The collection of the Croatian Society (Matica Hrvatska) of Zagreb, whose rich resources furnished numerous variants—notably in volumes V and VI—and a selection of Moslem folk songs from the northwest of Bosnia— volumes II and IV (1898, 1899)—whose introduction, which we owe to Luka Marjanović, constitutes the finest study of the folk epic poetry that has been written since Vuk Karadžić. Ten years previously, Kosta Hörmann had published in Sarajevo a first anthology of Moslem folk songs from the entire Bosnia-Hercegovina area.

In the period of the Turkish invasions, the Slovenians also had an abundant epic literature, and many magnificent ballads were transcribed at the end of the eighteenth century and during the first half of the nineteenth. The first critical edition of these folk songs was that of K. Štrekelj. This collection was at the same time the finest made in any Slavic tongue.

The example of the Serbs and Croats was followed by the Bulgarians; for them folk epic poetry did not exist except in the western regions, and that poetry was comparable—in an earlier period—to that of the Serbs and Croats but with less artistic finish in the form. Mostly after their liberation, the Bulgarians published numerous documents [recording this tradition], in large part in the *Sbornik za narodni umotvorenija* [*Anthology of Folklore*].

Among the South Slavs, the best known folk epic poetry is that of the Serbs; Vuk Karadžić was the first to study it in his great and classic collection, where from the start none but the finest songs played a part, edited in conformity with his linguistic and aesthetic principles: the official edition put together in Belgrade nearly doubled the size of the original. It is on Vuk's collection, which appeared precisely during the period of romantic enthusiasm for the folk song, that the greater part (and the best) of subsequent translations was based.[4]

Nevertheless, today one merges the epic poetry of the Serbs and that of the Croatians under the single heading of Serbo-Croatian epic poetry, just as one does with the language of these two branches of the same people; this poetry was and remains equally alive among both groups, it has traveled from east to west and from north to south and back, and it has been equally collected, imitated, and celebrated in both regions. Since a significant part of the poetic oeuvre stems from Moslems who were often neither Serbs nor Croatians, it is better to apply the more general term "Yugoslav."

This Serbo-Croatian, or Yugoslav, folk poetry, in particular the epic poetry, became an important element of the national literature; for some time it was considered the only form of modern literature among the Serbs, the necessary basis for the written language reformed by Vuk Karadžić. That was why the national poetry was excessively praised not only by romantic authors and patriots but also by rigorous philologists; on the other hand, in more recent times it has gone unacknowledged, and today the popular epic poetry is much less familiar to the Yugoslav intellectuals themselves.

Among the Slavic peoples, the Russians, far to the north, have an abundant folk epic poetry, very ancient and very interesting in its imaginative character. The name of these national songs, *byliny* or *stariny*, corresponds to that of the French *chansons de geste*. The Ukrainians have preserved only a small number of moving and more lyrico-epic *dumy*, related to battles undertaken against the Tatars and the Turks. The richest, the most perfect from an artistic point of view, the most realistic and the most humane of the Slavic folk epic poetries is the Serbo-Croatian, which is further distinguished again by the fact that it has remained alive to our time and has preserved its creative power. This epic poetry, which even before being universally known was compared to that of Ossian and Homer, offers analogies with the ancient works and sheds light on Greek folk epic poetry and on that of the Romance and Germanic peoples. It presents in one respect an advantage over Old French and medieval Spanish epic: whereas the Romance traditions often allude to the battles against the Saracens and the Arabs, without our having any songs from the enemy featuring Christian heroes [in a different light], among the Yugoslavs there exist at the present time anti-Christian songs, often celebrating the same heroes as do the Christian poems, since the Turks, with whom the Yugoslavs were perpetually at battle, were for the greater part of the time Moslems in the same country (in Serbo-Croatian *musliman*).

These Moslems ordinarily showed more fanaticism than real Turks, although they might have spoken the Serbo-Croatian language. The Bosnian beys had a great influence in Turkey, and they long dominated not only Bosnia, Serbia, and Montenegro but also the greatest part of Dalmatia and Croatia, all of Slovenia, and most of Hungary. It will suffice merely to cast a glance over a religious map of Bosnia-Hercegovina[5] to determine how complicated the region still is today, even after the emigration of a great number of Moslems. In the villages, Moslems are usually in the majority relative to Orthodox, Catholics, and Jews.

The Moslem epic songs attracted my attention because of their interest in innovation [*nouveauté*] against the background of their importance for the history of the civilization. I drew up a report on these songs at the international congress held in Berlin in 1908.[6] In 1909, 1912, and 1913 I made trips of some duration through Bosnia and Hercegovina, as well as neighboring regions of Croatia and Dalmatia, with the intention of studying the folk epic poetry *in situ*. I quickly realized that I would not be able to, nor should I, limit myself to consideration of Moslem epic poetry, which was intimately connected in all respects to the epic poetry of the Catholic and Orthodox peoples. An example will make the point. In the course of my second field trip, I entered a café one day during Ramadan (in Serbo-Croatian *ramazan*), the month of fasting for Moslems, where every night a Catholic singer performed songs for Moslems. Surprised, I inquired how this situation was possible. They answered: "We live in harmony: *onda bilo, sad se spominjalo* (that which was, one evokes its memory now)."[7] From this moment on, I was no longer amazed to see Christian singers performing for the beys and pashas of Bosnia for weeks and entire months. Among the people, Moslems listen to Christian singers just as Christians listen to Moslem singers. It can happen that the songs are selected or adapted, but on the whole there is no need for this, because each *junak* (hero) is universally honored, with whatever acknowledgment is fitting.

I have furnished preliminary, detailed reviews in the publications of the Viennese Academy of Sciences[8] on the principal results of these field trips and on the phonographic transcription of songs from Bosnia and Hercegovina. I could not then write a work of more depth on the folk epic poetry, the [First World] War and the unstable situation of the Yugoslav territories having prevented me from resuming my fieldwork for some time.[9] It was not until 1924 that I could travel within the ancient *sandžak* of Novi Pazar, which up to 1913 had been under Turkish domination and was linked historically and administratively with Bosnia-Hercegovina until the occupation of these provinces by Austria-Hungary. I found in Novi Pazar a situation analogous to that which could have prevailed in Bosnia-Hercegovina before the occupation of 1878, and I made acquaintance with a patriarchal way of life that was truly epic, extremely idiosyncratic but very durable.[10]

In 1927 I wished to see the land of the famous ballad about Hasanaga's wife; to my delight I found the folk epic poetry still alive in that Croatian region near the small village of Imotski in Dalmatia (which continued under Turkish domination until 1717), but it was in vain that I sought stories about Hasanaga and Pintorović bey; nonetheless, I believe that one could, with the aid of documents drawn from Dalmatian and Bosnian archives, put together a survey of the properties owned by their descendants. On the other hand, the tragic conflict of this "sad ballad" now became clear to me for the first time. It is because she had been raised so strictly according to Moslem customs that Hasanaga's wife was not able, for modesty's sake, to go see her ill husband, even though he longed for her visit, having himself already acquired more humanistic, more Western attitudes in the course of frequent travels to the cities of great civilization along the nearby Adriatic coast. I also went to see the homeland of A[ndrija] Kačić[-Miošić], but there the folk epic poetry is already dead.

During my trips I did not seek new songs, and I did not transcribe any, except in fragments—such recording being a difficult task at best, and, at the time of harvest and the other labors associated with agriculture, almost impossible. But I gladly compared written and sung texts when the songs were printed; in addition, one day I studied two songs that the same singer had dictated twenty years previously in Zagreb and which had gone through important and instructive changes.

The essential purpose of my observations was to come to know the manner in which the folk epic poetry lives; who the singers are; for whom, when, and how they sing; whether folk songs are still being created; and why the folk poetry is disappearing and dying. Many of my observations confirm, complete, or clarify facts already known, but I have also gathered a fair amount of new material. My reports [note 8 above], which appeared during the Balkan Wars and World War I, were not circulated widely enough, but they did attract the attention of specialists on folk epic poetry. Engelbert Drerup showed how one could use my remarks for comparative studies in his work entitled *Homerische Epik (I, Das Homerproblem in der Gegenwart).*

*   *   *

Where does narrative epic poetry still live in the mouths of its people? In the Vojvodina, that is to say in the southern part of ancient Hungary, and in Syrmia (western Slovenia), where it admitted to a certain poverty from the time before Vuk Karadžić, the poetry has died out completely; the same is true for Serbia, with the exception of the mountainous area in the southwest (the Russian Hilferding had already found nothing there in 1868-69). In Slovenia, where toward the end of the eighteenth century epic songs were still often sung and imitated, there are none today. In southwest Croatia, from which region came a number of Vuk Karadžić's fine songs, they are in the process of disappearing. On the other hand, they are still sung frequently enough in the mountainous areas of Dalmatia, which were neglected by their Venetian and Austrian governments, and which preserved a character as patriarchal as certain other Balkan lands. Where the national epic poetry is very well conserved is in Bosnia, and better yet in Hercegovina and Montenegro, chiefly on the ancient border between these latter two provinces, where Christians and Moslems did not cease from continuous battles until the occupation of Bosnia-Hercegovina in 1878, and in the *sandžak* of Novi Pazar situated between Montenegro and Serbia before the Balkan Wars. These are in general lands of plateaus, inhabited by the people of the Dinaric Alps—strong, heroic, and at the same time possessed of a delicate sensibility and endowed with a natural rapport between imagination and intelligence, as well as with a sense for language and form.[11]

Vuk Karadžić called these epic songs "heroic" *(junačke)*, but he likewise represents among them mythological songs, legends, stories, and ballads. The people themselves employ the term "heroic" *(pjesme junačke, o junacima, o junaštvu)* or "ancient" *(starinske,* cp. Russian *stariny)* to designate those songs that celebrate heroes or personages of more or less historical character. These songs constitute the greater part of the popular epic poetry; they are much enjoyed and renowned.

The song itself, which is usually a species of recitation mixed with music, is performed with accompaniment on a primitive instrument, the *gusle* (in Hercegovina and in Montenegro the ancient form *gusli* is customarily preserved), a sort of violin with horse-hair strings, more often one but two in the northwest regions. In northwest Bosnia, the Moslems exclusively employ—and the Christians also make some use of—the *tambura* or *tamburica*, a type of small guitar or mandolin with two metal strings which is likewise known in the north of Dalmatia and in the district of the Lika in Croatia, and which was formerly used in Slovenia.

Scholars have long spoken, in the spirit of romanticism, of the people-as-singer [*peuple-chanteur*] or of the people-as-bard [*peuple aède*] (in German *das singende Volk*), and have truly believed that it was the people as a whole in a nation who sang. Today it is known that the representatives of the folk epic poetry are certain gifted individuals, spread in more or less great numbers through the lands and the villages of a patriarchal civilization. Among the people, these representatives are called simply the "singers" (*pjevač, piva*); their literary name of *guslar* (player of a *gusle*, in ordinary speech *guslač* among the people) is in less common use and is less exact, since a large percentage of singers do not accompany themselves on the *gusle*. There is no condition or profession one would find unrepresented among them. In the countryside the singers are for the most part farmers; in the towns they are artisans. In the mountainous regions they are mostly shepherds who delight in singing the epic songs, and these songs were naturally cultivated by the *hajduks* ["outlaws, brigands"], common during the revolts in Turkey and also in the Christian lands, against the public order, ordinarily for the sake of idealism. Among the singers were also found, and are still found today, the noblest Moslem lords, the beys, as well as priests of all faiths up to and including an Orthodox archbishop. The epic song was especially honored among the native monks of the Franciscan order, and the devotion which they showed it went so far that in 1909 in a seminary in the Mostar district I saw a *gusle* hanging on a hook above the bed of every novice.

Besides these amateurs, one also encounters professional singers, especially among the Moslems, in northwest Bosnia and further south. Even those who in most recent times ordinarily sang in Turkish coffeehouses, usually in winter and during the month of Ramadan, had and customarily still have some occupation, but formerly there existed among them true professionals who travelled in the orbit of Moslem nobility from one to the next, staying in one place for weeks and months to entertain the master and his guests. Many nobles supported their own particular singers, who were occasionally even Christian. This position was equivalent to that of servants of an elevated rank or of soldiers, more exactly non-commissioned officers such as commanders of squads and standard-bearers (*bajraktar[i]*); at the court of Dedaga Čengić, son of Smailaga Čengić, the tale of whose death was sung by the Croatian poet Ivan Mažuranić in a celebrated epic, there was, during the second half of the last century, a singer of this type who held the rank of commandant. These traces of Moslem traditions would allow us to formulate an idea of the way in which the oral epic poetry lived in centuries past, even if we were to ignore the fact that it had been cultivated among the Serbian, Bosnian, and Croatian nobility. There is no doubt in my mind that the real folk epic poetry springs, in the same way as does folk art in general (the costumes, for example), from the most elevated Christian and Moslem social milieus, but, in the course of centuries, has evolved along its own lines.

I must also address myself to another assumption. The legendary Homer is represented as blind, and some indications given by Vuk Karadžić himself have encouraged the erroneous impression that many of the singers, and especially the best of them, are blind. In reality, in the lands where the national epic poetry is still flourishing, blind singers are extremely rare, and these unhappy individuals usually lost their sight at an advanced age, most of the time as the result of smallpox. It is only in the regions where the folk epic poetry is in the process of disappearing or is already dead that one sees blind and crippled beggars depending on singing for a way to exist.

I was surprised to observe that Moslem women know how to recite the epic songs, but not to sing them, and that among the Christian women singers are found, in the present day always as rare exceptions other than in the north of Dalmatia.

The singers begin to learn to play the *gusle* and to pick up the epic tradition from early childhood—on the knees of a father or grandfather, or of other relatives or friends, then in public—the greater part of the time between ten and twelve years of age, but always in general while young, "while they still have nothing else on their minds," up until the age of perhaps twenty-five. It is ordinarily sufficient for them to hear a song sung a single time, though they may need to hear it more than once when they grow older. Yet in Gacko, the aged Janko Ceramić, sixty-eight years old, assured me that he could repeat the next day an entire song heard the preceding evening. Nevertheless, the songs that make up this poetry called "oral" or "traditional" are not always transmitted from one mouth to the next; they are very often, and more and more, taken from books and pamphlets, and this practice goes on even in Hercegovina, the classical territory of the epic song. One can by no means dismiss the possibility that even the blind singers themselves might not have learned their songs from the mouths of other singers, since someone may have read the songs to them, [or] they could have learned from another singer whom a priest, schoolmaster, or some other person had instructed. It is among the Moslems that the oral tradition is best preserved, because they are more traditional in spirit and think better of illiterates. The singer who learns a song that is read to him must have it repeated more times in order to know it.

The Moslem singers know how to evaluate those from whom they have learned their songs, and who are customarily found among their kin. The Christian singers acquire material everywhere that people sing but often also at home or among their relatives. When they hear of a fine singer, they may travel many hours seeking him. A certain number of songs are spread about by travellers or by wagon-drivers and laborers who move around from place to place.

People sing during the long winter nights around the hearth and during gatherings (*sijelo, silo* [lit., "village"]) in the houses of well-to-do peasants, throughout the evenings, at the time of ritual and familial celebrations, and in general on all joyous occasions, especially weddings, which until recently lasted an entire week when they took place in the parents' household, and longer still when the bride was brought from a distance. Thus it was that the singer Janko Ceramić of Gacko accompanied the guests of the Ljubušak beys for 34 days, when all three of them were married at a single time. In certain regions the groom's family and that of the bride each has its own singer, and these two compete to see who will perform better and longer: it is a disgrace if another singer leaves the bride's house victorious in such a competition. One also sings publicly in the coffeehouses, principally among the Moslems, at the time of *zbori* (masters' assemblies or celebrations), [or] near the monasteries and churches, as at the markets. People would also often sing while traveling on horseback, mostly at night, but in this case without the *gusle*. Among Moslems in the north and northwest of Bosnia, there are singers who during the winter spend entire months journeying from territory to territory; in the season of Ramadan certain villages and their coffeehouses engage these singers for all or a part of the thirty-day duration. The pashas and feudal lords summoned such singers for Ramadan and for other occasions in order to entertain themselves and their guests. The women, too, were allowed to listen to the singers—but from behind a curtain, unless the singer were a parent to one of them, a person before whom they had no need to veil themselves. The nobles especially desired singers who would come for a stay of some length in their domain to settle down, to work there or collect taxes. Naturally, in the Christian villages they most often summoned singers who were also Christian. In a word, the national epic poetry was and is—for the nobility, the middle class, and peasantry—what concerts, theater, and other amusements are for us. In Dalmatia a peasant told me this: "You people in the city, you have your music, and we have our songs."

*   *   *

It is therefore not surprising that these songs may be extremely long and may last many hours, an entire night and even, among the Moslems, two and three nights. Among the songs collected by Vuk Karadžić, there is one whose length some found astonishing: *The Wedding of Maksim Crnojević (Ženidba Maksima Crnojevića)*, which comprised 1225 verses of ten syllables and filled 42 pages of printed text in a grand-octavo volume, that is, a length greater than that of any book of the *Iliad* or *Odyssey*. In 1891 *The Wedding of Senjanin Tadija* was published, a song by an Orthodox singer of Travnik in Bosnia which runs 3412 decasyllabic verses. The Moslem songs are particularly long; the Croatian Society (Matica Hrvatska) in Zagreb has in its archives eleven songs from two to three thousand lines and four between three and four thousand lines; such length caused them to be set aside by the editor, and the longest published song [from this collection] has no more than 1862 lines.

First of all I make the observation that the singer can shorten or lengthen his songs at will according to his artistic personality; for example, there are singers who are famous for knowing better than anyone else how to portray a young girl or woman, a hero (*junak*), his horse or armament, while others do not occupy themselves at all with such things. A singer can also modify songs as he goes, according to the time available, his own mood, the audience before whom he is performing, and the payment he has reason to expect. Moreover, the audience can directly influence him, and, when a song lasts too long, someone may cry out to him: *Goni, goni!* (faster, faster! [lit. get going, get going!]). I cite the example of a certain prisoner from Lepoglava in Croatia, from whose dictation songs of 2500 and 4400 verses were transcribed, even though the same songs had no more than 1200 and 1500 verses when sung by the man in Bosnia who had taught him. One comes to realize that these songs are not sung continuously, but with pauses. Each session usually lasts a half-hour to an hour. In 1911, at a wedding in Hercegovina, a singer fifty years old sang for an hour and a half consecutively in a competition, from which he emerged victorious.

The singers are not prepared to specify exactly the number of songs that they know. They commonly say that they know 30 or 40, or a hundred, or better yet that they can sing a new one every night for three months, or even for a year. They do not usually exaggerate, and I would estimate that their repertoires might be even more considerable than they themselves indicate. To give an idea of the richness, I recall that between January 2 and February 17, 1887, in Zagreb the Moslem Salko Vojniković from Bosnia sang, or, to be more precise, dictated 90 songs comprising a total of 80,000 verses, about double the combined length of the *Iliad* and *Odyssey*, given that the decasyllabic verses are shorter than hexameters and the number of verses three times greater. And there have been philologists who doubted that a single singer could know all of Homer by heart! Such a memory is all the more astonishing in that the singer had no prompter.

People have long believed, and believe still, that the singers do not change their songs. Even John Meier, who remarked that the [Homeric] rhapsodes were improvisers, remained convinced by the accounts he had received of Russian and Yugoslav epic poetry that the singer would adhere closely to the text and would not change one iota. I have already said that, on the contrary, he can shorten or lengthen his songs at will, and that the same poem can be very different in content in the versions of different singers. It is absolutely certain that under such conditions a text cannot remain unchanged. I have demonstrated this experimentally. On two occasions I brought with me a phonographic apparatus perfected by the Viennese Academy. I could not record the long epic songs on this machine, but it did suffice for fragments of less than 30 verses to

verify something unexpected. Since it was necessary to write down each
text before phonographic recording, I asked the singer first of all to
practice outside the tent while a stenographer transcribed the text. I thus
had three texts at the same time from a single session, and even four in
one case.[12] The comparison showed that not only isolated words or
word-sequences but entire verses appeared in a wholly new form or
simply disappeared, so that of 15 dictated lines [in one version], for
example, there might remain [in the next version] no more than 8 sung
lines. A fine singer from northwest Bosnia himself modified the first
line on each occasion.

He said the first time:

> Beg Osman beg rano podranio (etymological
> figure)
> "Osmanbeg arose early";

then while practicing:

> Beg Osman beg na bedem izidje
> "Osmanbeg mounted the ramparts";

and afterward he sang:

> Beg Osman beg niz Posavlje gleda.
> "Osmanbeg gazed out over the Sava plain."

Professor Vladimir Ćorović of Belgrade, originally a native of
Hercegovina who therefore well understands the national epic poetry,
has declared in a critical evaluation that the singer, embarrassed, made
an error. There can be no question of such a thing with a professional
singer. Accordingly, I paid particular attention to this issue the
following year. In the Orthodox monastery of Duži near Trebinje in
Hercegovina, we listened to the songs of a peasant associated with the
monastery (*kmet* [a landless peasant]) and much beloved by the monks
and the abbot. Earlier one of these monks and a schoolmaster had
written down the beginning of one of his songs from dictation. I now
requested that they transcribe the variants throughout the present song,
but they were forced to give up at the second verse. I repeated the
experience with a teacher and a student near Bijelo Polje in the *sandžak*
with similar success. It is thus very clear to me that the songs we

possess today in printed form were not all sung only a single time or, more exactly, dictated only a single time before being committed to writing. This is also why all of the attempts to reconstruct a song in its "original" form are futile. The comparison of different variants cannot enable us to determine the primitive content of a song or even parts or single verses. Having had the kind of experience described above, I was able to show[13] that Vuk Karadžić had not written down the song *Jakšići kušaju ljube* (*The Jakšići Test their Wives*), which appears in his *Srpske narodne pjesme* of 1845 (the Belgrade edition, vol. 2, pp. 624-627), from dictation by a young man of eighteen years from Užica in Serbia, as he himself affirms—although the event is inherently possible,—but that he simply borrowed it from the Croatian poet A. Reljković, who had published it in his *Satir* in 1779 to instruct the men of Slovenia not to place trust in their women. Vuk Karadžić reprinted it verse for verse, even though identity between texts from the eighteenth and nineteenth centuries would be impossible, and according to his usual custom made changes in the song-text which are solely of a phonetic, morphological, and lexicographical order.

Most Moslem singers sang in expectation of reward. The beys gave them grain, horses, oxen, even pairs of oxen as in the case of the Hindu singer of the Rigveda, cows, sheep, clothing, and ducats, and even, as late as the last century in Hercegovina, land. In the course of recent years, people from these regions have passed from a natural economy to a cash economy, but, as for the singers, collections made with saucers in the coffeehouses yield less and less money, and the singers are "honored" today more often with coffee, tea, lemonade, cigarettes, and tobacco. In the case of the Christian singers, when they are not expressly hired, there is no question of payment; the custom is to give them only something to drink and to smoke. The singers all like to drink, chiefly the aqua vitae (*rakija* [highly distilled plum brandy]), since beer and wine do not have a salutary effect on the voice. Nevertheless, the Christian singers do not disdain these latter beverages. Such drinks do not adversely affect a singer, says one man, because for him "it passes while he is shouting."[14]

The singers retain their songs as long as they do thanks to the well-known epic repetitions, utilized for example for messages, and to the various clichés reserved to celebrate aspects of feminine beauty, heroes, costumes, horses, arms, duels, and so on. I knew a Moslem singer, already affected by civilization, who sang these commonplaces, but who narrated the real action. Many singers recite one part while singing, another part while narrating. There are those who narrate better than they sing, but also those who do not know how to narrate at all. The Montenegrin Marko Miljanev, from the Vojvodina and self-taught, related to us the entire history of his clan (the clan of the *Kuči*) by alternating between recitation, for the old traditions, and verse. Poetry and prose can thus co-exist perfectly side by side, a fact which is not without importance for the study of analogous conditions in the ancient oral literature of other peoples.

The singer, seated, begins with an instrumental prelude on the *gusle* or on the *tamburica* (when he accompanies himself on the *tamburica*, he can also remain standing); then comes a short prologue during which he speaks about his art and assures [those present] that he is about to sing a "true" song about "the old times" or "the old heroes."[15] Often he also gives voice to his patriotic sentiments and offers greetings to the audience, in particular to those of an elevated social rank.

Of the musical aspect of the song, I can say nothing, not being a specialist. I merely make the observation that the song is on the whole a monotone recitation that produces a non-musical impression, and which is likewise incomprehensible to the cultivated people of the region, especially when they have lost contact with the common people.[16] In any case, for the admirers of beautiful poems related to ancient Serbian history, it is better not to hear them sung. The Russian Rovinskij, author of a classic book on Montenegro, tells that a Frenchman, an admirer of Serbian folk poetry, having gone to Cetinje expressly to hear the songs, could not listen to them for very long and quickly departed. This is also why Serbian emigrants, throughout the Great War, were wrong to make an exhibition of the singing of epic poems with *gusle* accompaniment. In America, Serbian and Croatian laborers would sing behind closed doors, for fear of mockery. Before a public who do not understand the language, people would not sing the poems, even short ones, or excerpts longer than what is sufficient to give an idea of the character of the national epic poetry after a brief introduction; there is also an opportunity to give such an idea before beginning the text.

The essence is the content or subject matter, with its poetic form. The language, rich in tropes and figures and infinitely plastic, resounds magnificently on the lips of fine singers. In the end the melody also pleases those who understand the spoken words, when they have listened long, and especially when they see the singer—caught up with enthusiasm for his heroes and their exploits—adapt himself to the flow of the action, express his feelings through his mimicry, and wax truly dramatic. He starts slowly, but he accelerates the rhythm and can achieve a remarkable speed [of delivery]; he ceases to play his instrument at these times. During such moments even a parliamentary stenographer would be helpless to follow him.

There are different kinds of songs; in many places, people distinguish songs reserved for peasants from those reserved for the cultivated classes. In a general way, a song is darker and more indistinct in the northwest region of Bosnia, and much livelier and clearer in Hercegovina and in Montenegro. It is not that the playing of the *gusle* may not be able to engage interest; one cannot believe that such beautiful sounds could emanate from such a primitive instrument. That will always be for me a memory as imperishable as the music to which the Archimandrite Nicephore Šimonović of the Montenegrin monastery of Kosijerevo had me listen.

One may also be amazed at the physical exertion of the singers, who sing, according to my observations, from 13 to 28, or on the average 16 to 20, decasyllabic verses per minute for whole hours and even all night, often in cramped quarters and before a large audience, so that they become bathed in perspiration.

What struck me the most is the magnificent delivery of the singers. Can one picture for himself what it is to sing long poems, without error in subject matter, in irreproachable poetic verses, with the greatest of speed? This is not possible except among singers who do not learn the poems by heart, or word for word, but who re-create them anew each time in brilliant improvisation, thanks to their "science" of language and of poetry. A fine singer can make a mediocre poem remarkable, and a poor singer can spoil the best poem. It was not in error that Vuk Karadžić often sought a singer of quality to dictate a certain song that had not pleased him. The listeners also appreciate this art of the singer. A bey one day expressed to me his admiration in these terms: "Myself, I would not attempt a composition of even three words." In Hercegovina people told me of peasants who would give the best ox from their stable to know how to sing one certain song.

The singers are artists, a fact shown by their extreme jealousy of one another. One day in Sarajevo, after having collected recordings of three singers, I gave the same payment to all three. One among them refused to accept it. I sensed immediately that I had bruised his ego in some way. The people present in effect warned me that he considered himself a much better singer than the other two, an observation which he confirmed himself the next day. In Hercegovina a young man nineteen years old said to me: "As many as we are here, we are all enemies to one another. It is painful for me when I meet another who knows more about [singing] than I do." And he went on to explain, with reference to me: "You also, Mr. Professor, you travel more widely than do other professors in order to gain an understanding of things, and so you would consider yourself much better than your fellows." In fact he had a point: this took place in a village where there was not even an inn, so that I was obliged to resort to the hospitality of the local constabulary.

The audience listens to the singer with maximum attention, interest, and sympathy for the heroes and is sometimes extremely moved by the whole of a poem or by certain episodes. During the pauses for rest, the members of the audience make various remarks, question the singer, and critique him, to which criticism he does not fail to respond. One time I reproached a singer for having given a favorite Moslem hero, Hrnjica Mujo, four brothers instead of the two he is credited with elsewhere; he retorted in a bitter tone: "That's how another told it to me; I wasn't there when they were born." There is one process of criticism which does not lack originality: when the singer is absent during a pause for rest, someone greases the strings and the bow of his instrument with tallow, which makes it impossible for him to continue.

*   *   *

We know, by virtue of the existing collections of folk songs, that only a very small number of them celebrate events that took place before the Turkish occupation. The overwhelming majority of Serbo-Croatian epic songs treat the battles against the Turks, which begin in Macedonia, reach their climax with the great disaster at Kosovo, are transported across the Danube and then into Croatia, Dalmatia, and Montenegro, lead into the liberation of Serbia, and which, at the beginning of the nineteenth century, crop up unceasingly on the borders of Montenegro, and reach their end at the time of the Balkan Wars and the Great War. Nonetheless, the greatest battles and their consequences form the subject of but few of the poems; for the majority are devoted to the deeds and actions of favorite heroes—such as Prince Marko from the Christian side, and from the Moslem sector of Bosnia, Djerdjelez Alija and Mustajbey of the Lika—and in the same way to small struggles fought along the Turkish-Christian border, chiefly in the sixteenth and seventeenth centuries. The Christians who had escaped from Turkey (*uskoci*) could gain distinction for themselves there, in the service of the Viennese emperor in the vicinity of Senj (Zengg) on the Croatian seaboard, or in service to the Venetian doge in the Kotar plains around Zara; but it was very common to see them attacking the Turks on their own initiative, in the same way as did other leaders of such bands and various hajduks (in the poems these bands ordinarily numbered 30 men). Likewise, the Moslems were little concerned with the official peace, as witnessed by their songs about Hungary and the Lika district in Croatia. It was chiefly this kind of guerilla operation which offered occasions for personal heroism, duels, adventures, acquisition of rich booty and beautiful women and girls, who often willingly fled the Christians for the Turks and vice versa, romantic marriages, attacks at weddings, freeing of women and imprisoned heroes, distant trips on horseback (*obdulja*), various knightly sports, feasts during which the Turks drink a great deal of wine, and so forth. In the Christian quarter various heroes are distinguished: Ivo and Tadija Senjanin, Ilija Smiljanić, Stojan Janković; on the Turkish side Mustajbeg of the Lika, Hrnjica Mujo and Halil, whose renown spread from northwest Bosnia to the north of Albania.

People say that the Moslems, a traditional group, live more in the past, and that they especially evoke the era of their domination in Hungary and the Lika in Croatia. Yet they also possess poems on their battles with Austria in the eighteenth century, on their occupation of Bosnia-Hercegovina, and on the continual skirmishes along the Montenegrin border; but these poems are little known. Those of the most recent epoch, in particular, have not even been collected, much less published. Likewise, the Bosnian and Hercegovinian Catholics are to an extent traditionalists, and the poems they sing the most are those of Kačić[-Miošić] and the recent collections (above all that of Jukić). Philologists were formerly astonished to encounter this or that song by Kačić[-Miošić] among the people, but in Hercegovina I made the acquaintance of Catholic singers who knew by heart all of Kačić[-

Miošić]. The songs of this Franciscan had also spread among the Orthodox people, especially in Montenegro, and were even encountered in Macedonia (Galičnik). I was surprised that the Bosnian and Hercegovinian Orthodox did not know the magnificent songs relating to the ancient history of Serbia as well as I expected, any more than did the Orthodox people of Montenegro. When I collected recordings in Sarajevo, the intellectual Serbs present asked a singer from the region if he knew the poems about Prince Lazar, Miloš Obilić, and Vuk Branković. He answered: "No, I'm illiterate."[17]

Nowhere except in Hercegovina did the sense of these words become entirely clear to me: people sang for me chiefly poems on the recent and modern battles fought by Hercegovina and Montenegro against the Turks, and I learned that these poems came mostly from *published* collections. One of them, the *Kosovska Osveta (The Revenge for Kosovo)* is particularly widespread. It is by Maksim Šobajić, and it reports the battles of the Hercegovinians, Montenegrins, Serbs, and Russians in the period 1875-1878. But there are in addition the Greco-Turkish, Russo-Japanese, Italo-Turkish, Balkan, and World Wars, which are also celebrated in the poems of known and unknown singers. In a poem dating from 1912, the sultan already makes use of the telephone:

Telefonu care doletio,
na telefon zove Enverbega.[18]

"The tsar hastened to pick up the telephone,
on the telephone he called Enverbey."

In a word, the singers wish to and indeed must show themselves modern in all respects; the public requires songs relating to actual events, although such poems do not generally attain the beauty of the ancient songs and although they often are no more than mere accounts, just as the Russian P. Rovinskij called the Montenegrin poems modern, or indeed like newspaper articles, as some would say of certain Montenegrin poems in Vuk Karadžić's collection. What is most surprising is that the epic poem of Hercegovina and Montenegro, provinces where it is flourishing the most, is, for the most part, of literary origin. In the second half of the last century, Orthodox and Catholic priests, schoolmasters, and other literate persons recited and sang to singers and to other people poems drawn from books, and today the singers very often know how to read the texts themselves; there are even some among them who learned to read only for the sake of learning the epic poems, which are spread abroad in innumerable printed reproductions, books or pamphlets, in Cyrillic or Latin characters. I devoted a good part of my effort to determining whether more folk songs were coming into existence, and if so in what manner. I collected 13 expressions that designate the creation of a poem, but the one most current in Hercegovina, the term *isknaditi, knaditi*, is almost unknown in literature and is treated as "obscure" in the great historical dictionary of the Yugoslav Academy. I also often heard it said that the singers knew how to "put back to back" (*nasloniti*) one poem with another, that they knew how to condense many poems into one and how to modify, correct, and complete poems. One singer declared that a poem could not be good "if the singer knows nothing to add from his own ornamentation [ajouter son crû]." In a general way one can say (see above what was said on the delivery of the songs) that at least in our own day all singers of any quality are improvisers. Also it is superfluous to debate, as have the classical philologists, the question of whether the pre-Homeric bards were followed by rhapsodes or by mere reciters, since there are bards, that is singers who themselves compose the poems [they perform], still today among the rhapsodes. I have myself seen many of these singer-poets, and I have reliable accounts testifying to others.

Among the singers are people of every social rank capable of immediately composing a poem on some martial deed or on any other interesting event. Many unremarkable singers told me that they could even narrate my meeting with them in a poem, and I received a poem of this type from a blind female singer from Dalmatia. A 75-year-old bey from Bosnia also claimed the same ability. The exploits of leaders in small battles were frequently celebrated by the men in their bands. In the same way, among the poems relating to the death of Smailaga Čengić there is one which was sung by his *bajraktar* (standard-bearer), on horseback, even as he returned from the field of battle. Rare are the leaders who sang of themselves. The most curious of these in recent years is Jusuf Mehonjić of the *sandžak* of Novi Pazar, who fought against Serbia after the Balkan Wars, against Montenegro and the Austrians, and even against the new kingdom of the Serbs, Croats, and Slovenes, and who recorded his campaigns in decasyllabic verse in a log of his travels which is to be found at the Ministry of the Interior in

Belgrade, its author having lost it during his flight. Other people also, for example shepherds and shepherdesses, who did not observe an action except from far away or even had no connection other than hearing it being described, occasionally composed a poem on the subject. Songs of this type were composed collaboratively by many different authors, whose verses were adopted, corrected, or rejected. This was the way it was done in the Montenegrin army, where, after the battles, reports were carefully edited in this manner, distributed in manuscript copies among the military singers, and finally published. To be cited and placed in the action of a poem was, in Montenegro, the greatest mark of distinction, the equivalent of medals and decorations in other armies.

I was very surprised to hear it often said that battles of some importance could not be celebrated except by those "who had studied," who "had been at school," pursued their studies "for twenty years," or even who are "like you," said one person, indicating me. Effectively, an ordinary folk singer would not be capable of describing in its entirety a battle in which many Montenegrin troops had participated. This is also the reason why one does not find in the Yugoslav epic poetry full accounts of great battles but only episodes and events that bear some relation to those battles and only rarely an action like the siege of a town. One sees that the people themselves conceive of the poets, authors of epic poems, as individuals who are very gifted and at the same time very cultivated. It is nonetheless the epic poetry of Hercegovina that for the most part inspired Jakob Grimm and the Slavists to believe in a kind of origin, a mystical genesis of folk epic songs, works which were created, so they said, by an entire people—[a theory] in which, for example, the great Slavic philologist Miklosich believed until his death (1891).

Nevertheless, the narrative epic song can also be subjective, even while being composed by many authors. In addition, certain poems and collections can offend or displease. People have criticized a poem as widely known as Maksim Šobajić's *Kosovska osveta* (*The Revenge for Kosovo*) for being partial to the Montenegrins and for assessing too lightly the services performed by the Hercegovinians. National tribunals looked into the matter, and the poem was even burned! Analogous disputes have arisen in Montenegro, where each clan has its own epic poetry.

I have already said that the epic poems can border on newspaper articles. I had confirmation of this from the singers themselves. When I asked a revolutionary who had fought against Turkey and Austria and who was in some vague way a hajduk in the Balkans, why he did not sing about his own exploits, he responded: "It's not worth the trouble; that's a job for journalists, men of learning." And, just as one can pay to insert personal news in the press, so one can, through financial means, secure an appearance in a folk song. In Nevesinje the singer Alexis Ivanovit recounted to me that after the Battle of Vučji Do (1876) his uncle saw two such "men of learning" approaching him. They asked two *pleta* (about two francs) to describe him as a *junak* (hero) who mowed down the Turks, but the penniless man could not afford such glory.

Besides the events of war, people also celebrated other bloody encounters through the songs as well as all interesting goings-on such as weddings and elections. In Bosnia and Dalmatia, proclamations are distributed in decasyllabic verses; in this way one celebrates popular political leaders, for example Etienne Radić. Last year in Dalmatia, I myself saw the program of the popular Catholic party explained via the same medium in a pamphlet of respectable dimensions. The ancient provincial government of Bosnia-Hercegovina received [legal] complaints and appeals in decasyllabic verses. In a word, the epic verse continues to live among the people, in the manner of all of the apparatus of epic poetry. Thus it is that a singer from the vicinity of Gacko began a poem on our meeting in the following manner:

> *Poletiše dva sokola siva*
> "Two [grey] falcons rushed together,"

meaning the two constables whom the sub-prefect of the district had sent to find him so that he and I could be introduced. Attention has recently been drawn to these introductions and other heroic-epic processes by G. Gesemann (*Studien zur südslavischen Volksepik*, pp. 65-96). This kind of imitation can also be transformed into parody: in Bosnia, an attendant in a coffeehouse told me that along with his friends he had composed, in the style of the epic poems, a song celebrating the wedding of a proud bey, one who was in reality a poor peasant.

*   *   *

According to the claims of singers and the belief of the people, the epic songs had to be true. The same is not the case with the most recent songs, which do not allow anything but an understanding of the idea that the people formulated from various repeated events; all the more reason to doubt the truth of the older songs.

There was a lively dispute among Serbian historians—between the romantics and the critics—over the relative historical truth of the national songs. It has been proven, for example, that the last tsar of Serbia, Uroš, survived his assassin by many months; that Miloš Obilić was not the son-in-law of Prince Lazar, and that there could therefore not have been any dispute between the sisters-in-law; and that the real son-in-law of Lazar, Vuk Branković, was not the traitor—the Ganelon—indispensable to this passage in the national poem. In general, the entire cycle of the Battle of Kosovo in 1389 is a myth, although a magnificent myth. Every poet, the folk epic poet like all others, has the right to handle his subject as he sees fit, and to modify the facts and the characters according to his needs. Nevertheless, the essence of numerous poems, even the older ones, is historical. What is above all remarkable is the veracity of the songs from the point of view of the history of the civilization, and, from this perspective, many folk epic songs deserve rehabilitation. In them one sees perfectly reflected the feudal life of the Yugoslav noblemen of the Middle Ages, which the Moslems of Bosnia and Hercegovina have preserved into the second half of the nineteenth century. One understands what opposition, going as far as insurrection, the feudal lords of Bosnia showed against the reforms of the Turkish sultans themselves, until their dominion had been shattered (1850-1854) by Omer pasha, former sergeant-major of cadets in Austria, and originally a Serb. Until that date these lords warred among themselves, and they maintained in their troops singers whose duty it was to celebrate their glory, to entertain and incite their soldiers. This is one altogether faithful way in which the epic songs describe life as it was on the Turko-Austrian and Venetian borders up to the peace of Karlovci (1699), and then later on the same borders and on the Montenegrin frontiers as well as in the interior of ancient Turkey.

The national epic poetry is dying in all regions because it has ceased to be reflective of reality. The feudal aristocracy is no longer interested in the poetry, since its military glory was annihilated by Omer pasha and by the occupation of Bosnia-Hercegovina. The songs on the battles along the frontiers in the sixteenth and seventeenth centuries today constitute a perfect anachronism. A modern state would not know how to lend an interested ear even to the heroism of hajduks. Small skirmishes are no longer the order of the day; the *handžar* or Yataghan (cutlass) has given way to the magazine-rifle, to the machine gun, less epic weapons. In contemporary war it is not possible to challenge an adversary to single combat; what prevails today is not heroism but, as my singers said to me, "discipline"—one of them added, "and politics." A person would not any longer know how to teach the strategy and tactics employed in the folk songs. The circumstances of the professional singers are more and more difficult, and the people themselves sing less and less in accordance with the complete transformation of the economic situation. One aga (great landholder) from northern Bosnia explained it to me in the following terms: "People sang when they had nothing to do (*od besposlice* [as a result of unemployment]), but at present the "Swabian" (the German, in the pejorative sense of *Welche* for the French in Germany, but in fact any man who crossed the Sava river and was wearing a hat or a military cap) requires that they work." Having asked a Hercegovinian Catholic on another occasion whether it was also the "Swabian" who had compelled him not to sing any more, he responded: "No, it is my wife and children." The Christian intellectuals reacted against long wedding ceremonies and other inauspicious amusements, which were one of the prime occasions for singing. The people themselves do not find as much pleasure in the epic songs because they have lost faith in their truth and utility, and the youth prefer the lyric songs and other games and diversions. The choral song and the musical societies with folk instruments (*tamburaši*) contribute equally to the disappearance of the epic songs. In Plevlje, in the *sandžak* of Novi Pazar, I was struck in 1924 to see that a choral group of Serbian singers had wished to surprise me with their choirs directed by the pope (Orthodox priest) of the area, and that the public paid very little attention to the *guslar* who was summoned on my behalf. The singer was whisked away to the Moslem lecture hall, where a large audience listened to him with attention and lively interest. But the greatest enemy of the singer is modern instruction. The collections have caused people to lose interest in the folk songs (I could not gain the confidence of numerous singers without assuring them that I would not make a transcription of their poems). Today any child can amuse the nobility, the citizens, and the rural population by giving them a reading of the folk songs, a practice already carried on in the coffeehouses. The poems are in themselves still interesting, and children carry to school large collections published by the Croatian Society (Matica Hrvatska) and others, in order to read them in secret.

Finally, the folk epic poetry has lost its principal support, the five-century resistance against the Turks. Turkey is today far away, and as for the Moslems within the country, they have reconciled themselves to modern civilization. They have so well adapted themselves to the situation that the Yugoslav Moslem organization is today[19] a governmental party in Belgrade, and a Moslem is Minister of Commerce and Industry and actually a substitute for the Minister of Finance. Let us mention in passing that this amounts to proof that Yugoslavia, or the realm of the Serbs, Croats, and Slovenes, is not practicing Balkanization but rather organization—social, national, and political progress. Soon one will be able to shout: "Yugoslav epic poetry, folk and oral, has died, long live Yugoslav epic poetry!" It will continue to live through its magnificent poems as an important element of the literature and of national civilization, it will provide yet more inspiration—and with greater success than before—to epic and dramatic poets and other artists, as it has to the great sculptor Meštrović, and it will nourish the national opera, all of which influences were foreseen a century ago by B. Kopitar, master and friend of Vuk Karadžić. Nevertheless, the national Yugoslav epic poetry will always remain a fertile field for study by native and foreign scholars. We hope that French scholarship as well will devote to the poetry the same attention it has given its own national oeuvre, bringing to such study the experience of brilliant work with their *chansons de geste* and their epic poetry of the Middle Ages.

Translated by John Miles Foley

NOTES

[1]Text enlarged and completed from the lectures given at the Sorbonne the 23rd, 24th, and 25th of May 1928, at the invitation of the Institute for Slavic Studies. The first part appeared in *Le Monde slave*, 5, VI (1928), 321-351.

[2]That is, the practitioners of the "scientific" approach to literature and language—philology [Ed.].

[3]But see now the songs published posthumously from Vuk's manuscripts: *Srpske narodne pjesme iz neobjavljenih rukopisa Vuka Stef. Karadžića*, 4 vols., ed. Živomir Mladenović and Vladan Nedić (Beograd: Srpska Akademija Nauka i Umetnosti, 1973-1974) [Ed.].

[4]In France: A. d'Avril, *La Bataille de Kossovo* (an attempt to gather together all of the poems on Kosovo into a single unique collection); Auguste Dozon, *L'Epopée serbe: Poésies populaires serbes*; F. Funck-Brentano, *Chants populaires des Serbes*.

[5]See *Razdioba konfesija u Bosni i Hercegovini po rezultatima popisa žiteljstva g. 1910*, supplement to *Die Ergebnisse der Volkszahlung in Bosnien und der Herzegowina* (Sarajevo, 1912).

[6]See *Zeitschrift des Vereins für Volkskunde in Berlin*, 19 (1909), 13-30.

[7]This decasyllabic phrase is a very common formula in Serbo-Croatian epic, especially Moslem epic; it occurs almost exclusively during the *pripjev* (or proem) to songs, as the singer is describing the process of traditional oral performance in preparation for the start of his narrative. [Ed.]

[8]*Bericht über phonografische Aufnahmen epischer, meist mohammedanischer Volkslieder im nordwestlichen Bosnien im Sommer 1912*, Berichte der Phonogramm-Archivs-Kommission der Kaiserlichen Akademie der Wissenschaften in Wien, 30 (Vienna: Alfred Hölder, 1912); *Bericht über eine Bereisung von Nordwestbosnien und der angrenzenden Gebiete von Kroatien und Dalmatien behufs Erforschung der Volksepik der bosnischen Mohammedaner*, Sitzungberichte der Kaiserlichen Akademie der Wissenschaften in Wien, philosophisch-historische Klasse, Band 173, Abhandlung 3 (Vienna: Alfred Hölder, 1913); *Bericht über eine Reise zum Studium der Volksepik in Bosnien und Hercegowina im Jahre 1913*, Sitzungberichte der Kaiserlichen Akademie der Wissenschaften in Wien, philosophisch-historische Klasse, Band 176, Abhandlung 2 (Vienna: Alfred Hölder, 1915); *Bericht über phonografische Aufnahmen epischer Volkslieder im mittleren Bosnien und in der Hercegowina im Sommer 1913*, Mitteilung der Phonogramm-Archivs-Kommission, 37, Sitzungberichte der Kaiserlichen Akademie der Wissenschaften in Wien, philosophisch-historische Klasse, Band 179, Abhandlung 1 (Vienna: Alfred Hölder, 1915).

I have furnished an abstract of my remarks, from the perspective of literary history, in my study "Neues über südslavische Volksepik," *Neue Jahrbücher für das klassische Altertum*, 22 (1919), 273-296.

[9]But see his posthumous work, *Tragom srpsko-hrvatske narodne epike: Putovanja u godinama 1930-32*, 2 vols., Djela Jugoslavenske Akademije Znanosti i Umjetnosti, knjige 41-42 (Zagreb: Jugoslavenska Akademija Znanosti i Umjetnosti, 1951) [Ed.].

[10]See *Prager Presse*, 11 January and 25 January, 1925.

[11]J. Cvijić, *Govori i članci*, II, pp. 80ff.; Branko Lazarević, *Tři jihoslovanské nejvyšší hodnoty*, p. 6.

[12]Although the language is inexplicit, Murko is describing a process whereby he obtained at least three *different* texts of the same material, one or two of them recorded and one or two taken (sometimes without the singer's knowledge) from dictation. Milman Parry and Albert Lord followed a similar procedure in their fieldwork, asking a *guslar* to repeat the opening of a song (called the "Proba" technique in Nikola Vujnović's notes) or to perform the same song again a day or more later. Both the Murko and Parry-Lord experiments amounted to strategies through which they could obtain variant texts of the same material for comparative evaluation. See Murko's deductions immediately below. [Ed.]

[13]*Sbornik prof. Jana Máchala*, pp. 329-335.

[14]This explanation may seem problematical to those who have never heard or seen a *guslar* perform. As indicated by the singers' own use of the verb *turiti* ("to drive out, impel") to denote the actual singing of a song, oral performance is a very strenuous exercise that requires a good deal of physical exertion. Songs are not sung *sotto voce*, but in full voice in a manner approximating "shouting" (*criant*). [Ed.]

[15]I reproduced for my lecture [see note 1 above] a phonograph disk which had recorded on it the beginning of the song *The Wedding of Banović Mihajlo*, which tells of the vicissitudes attending a marriage between a Christian and a Turk.

[16]The premier collector of Yugoslav tunes, Kuhač, has declared with respect to the best Moslem singer, Mehmed Kolaković, who was in Zagreb, that his recitations did not at all deserve the term "song." He did not as yet have a sense of historical evolution. When, at the start of the year 1928, a very fine Montenegrin singer, T. Vučić, was brought to Berlin so that he could establish phonograph recordings of some of his songs, many experts in the history of music declared that people probably sang in more or less the same manner in Germany in about the tenth to twelfth centuries.

[17]In early 1928 the singer T. Vučić, having been invited by me to sing the poem *Majka Jugovića* for the Seminar for Slavic Philology in Prague, asked for the text collected by Vuk Karadžić, which he studied assiduously before appearing in public.

[18]Transcribed in Hercegovina in 1913.

[19]That is, in May 1928.

Perspectives on Recent Work on Oral Literature [excerpted]

Albert B. Lord

The present excerpted study, originally published in full form in 1974, serves as one of the bookends for this collection of classic essays on oral-formulaic theory, the other being its 1986 sequel (see p. 379ff.). In surveying the current state of affairs in the field as of the early 1970s, Albert Lord chronicles advances in scholarship on ancient and Byzantine Greek, Serbo-Croatian, Old English, Old Irish, Old French, African, Chinese, Russian, Albanian, Sanskrit, Sumerian, Ugaritic, and other traditions, adding notes on fieldwork where available. Special attention is paid to the ancient and medieval traditions, and particularly to the questions of what constitutes a formula and a theme, how one distinguishes between formulaic phraseology and repeated phrases, and what are the characteristics of "transitional" texts. Lord's first of two surveys thus provides an extremely valuable companion to his more analytical work, as well as glosses the most important, and the most hotly debated, issues raised in his landmark volume, The Singer of Tales *(1960).*

Reprinted from *Oral Tradition*, 1 (1986), 467–503.

During the last ten or fifteen years the study of oral literature has been enriched by many books and articles representing research and criticism in a wide variety of fields. The recently published *Haymes Bibliography of the Oral Theory*, Publications of the Milman Parry Collection (Cambridge, Mass., 1973) is a most welcome guide and *sine qua non*, yet already a supplement is being prepared for the numerous works that have appeared later or that its compiler and editors have since discovered or had brought to their attention. Generally speaking, while comparatively little work has been done on analysis of living oral tradition, much has been written on applying oral theory to ancient and medieval texts. The application has outdistanced the new presentation of an exact description of an oral traditional poetry. I say new, because we tend to forget that before Parry's time at least three oral poetries had been well described. There was W. Radloff's classic description of Turkish epic songs (*Proben der Volkslitteratur der nördlichen Türkischen Stämme*, V, St Petersburg, 1885), D. Comparetti's book on the Finnish *Kalevala* (Domenico Comparetti, *The Traditional Poetry of the Finns*, London, 1898: the Italian original was published in Rome in 1891, *Il Kalevala o la poesia tradizionale dei Finni*), and the several collections of Russian epic songs, such as those of Hilferding and Rybnikov (A. F. Hilferding, *Onežskija byliny*, St. Petersburg, 1873; P. N. Rybnikov, *Pjesni*, 4 volumes, Moscow and St. Petersburg, 1861-1867), with descriptions of singers and singing, including versions of songs from a number of singers. These collections still merit our attention. We are extremely fortunate to have F. P. Magoun, Jr.'s, recent translation of the *Kalevala* (1963) and of the *Old Kalevala* (1969) and pertinent material, both publications of the Harvard University Press. We still need English translations of the Turkish and Russian songs.

Aside from a small number of articles, the first main step in this century in describing an oral lyric and epic tradition with as great accuracy as modern methods of collecting can afford was Milman Parry's collection of South Slavic songs, the publication of which began with *Serbo-Croatian Folk Songs* (Columbia University Press, 1951) by Bela Bartók and Albert B. Lord, and continued in 1953-1954 with volumes I and II of *Serbo-Croatian Heroic Songs* (Harvard University Press). Here were presented real oral traditional texts without editorial changes, a microcosm of an oral tradition. The seeds of the answers to most of the questions of scholars were, and are, at hand in those volumes. The results of my own research on Serbo-Croatian poetry appeared in 1960 in *The Singer of Tales* (Harvard U.P.). It set forth the processes of composition and transmission of that oral traditional poetry. The scene was thus nearly all set for the next act in this scholarly drama. The first volumes of *Serbo-Croatian Heroic Songs* had provided textual materials and *The Singer of Tales* had presented the description of the processes. There was, however, one major piece of evidence still lacking. When it was forthcoming, all else would, one hopes, be modification, improvement, refinement. The missing publication was that of one of the long songs of Avdo Medjedović, "The Wedding of Smailagić Meho," and it is now in press [publ.1974].

.   *   *   *

Of the older literatures, ancient or medieval, that have been approached as oral, or possibly oral, three have been the focus of most of the writing before the nineteen sixties: Ancient Greek, Old English, and Old French. Let me turn now to an overview of recent work in these literatures, because it is here that most controversy has been engendered and most, though not by any means all, theoretical problems have been aired.

Ancient Greek

By and large, I believe it is true in Ancient Greek scholarship that Homer's place as an oral poet has been accepted, sometimes a bit grudgingly, and that Hesiod, too, after the work of series of careful scholars, has been accorded a place in oral tradition. In Hesiod's case the earlier writings of J. A. Notopoulos have been followed more recently by those of G. P. Edwards, A. Hoekstra, W. W. Minton, and most recently Berkley Peabody. With the exception of Peabody, much of the concern of scholars is with his relationship to the Homeric poems. It is usually assumed that Homer represents "the" tradition and that differences between Homer and Hesiod are departures, whether development or decline, from "the" tradition. One sees a Hesiod who knew the *Iliad* and the *Odyssey* and proceeded from them as the tradition. What seems to be lacking is a broader concept of oral tradition, such as, indeed, is reflected in an admirable recent article by Geoffrey Kirk, "The Search for the Real Homer," *Greece and Rome*, Second Series, XX, No. 2, (October, 1973), 124-139. The Homeric poems are only two performances by a single singer, or by two different singers, in the ancient Greek tradition of narrative song. Homer in his lifetime performed many times over a long period of time not only those songs, if they are both his, but probably many others as well. There were other singers before him, contemporary with him, and after him, also with many performances of many songs. One must also take geographic range into consideration. The singers in the ancient Greek tradition were not all located in one town or city or region. Thus one must realize that if Homer and Hesiod were oral poets the differences between them, other than those connected with a difference of subject matter, may be simply those between individuals in different places as well as different times. From that point of view neither of them is more "the" tradition than the other. As Geoffrey Kirk's article indicates, a realization of this aspect of tradition is becoming clearer in Greek scholarship.

From the standpoint of oral literature the most difficult problem with Hesiod concerns the *Works and Days* rather than the *Theogony*. The latter is not an anomaly in an oral tradition. Songs of the gods and of the creation and ordering of the universe and the establishment of the base of power are common enough and play a highly significant role in oral narrative traditions in many places. But what kind of song is the *Works and Days*? When would such a song be sung in a traditional society? With these questions, of course, is associated that of the unity of the composition. Is it a series of separate songs or a single one? If one accepts Hesiod as an oral traditional poet, then these questions clamor even more for an answer. In a book entitled "The Winged Word" published by the State University of New York at Albany Press (1975), Professor Berkley Peabody has an ingenious answer to these questions. Part of the book deals with the history of the hexameter, and I shall return to that shortly, but part is concerned with a complicated, yet methodologically, I believe, quite correct analysis of the structure of the poem, which leaves one with a clear concept of a unified composition. By noting thematic and acoustic responsions and echoes that are characteristic of oral composition, Peabody leads the reader from the beginning of the *Works and Days* through to the end. I found it both an exciting and a convincing adventure. His suggestion about the kind of poem which the *Works and Days* is, or might be, is equally ingenious, if somewhat less convincing, although I believe it is the best so far; namely, it is a song used, presumably by Hesiod, in a contest with another singer. I leave the argument for the reader of "The Winged Word" to follow, but I might give a hint that the parallel situation is to be found in one of the songs of the *Kalevala* in which Väinäimöinen contests in song with a younger challenger Joukahäinen.

It is no easy task to assess Homeric scholarship at the present time, because there is so much of it and because of its variety. The late Adam Parry's Introduction to his edition of his father's works, *The Making of Homeric Verse* (Oxford U.P., 1971) is very useful for this purpose. Thanks to the astuteness of a number of scholars we know more about the Homeric formula and formula systems than ever before, and the hexameter has come under very careful and imaginative scrutiny. In these regards the work of J. B. Hainsworth, A. Hoekstra, Michael Nagler, Gregory Nagy, and Berkley Peabody have been outstanding. We know the flexibility of the formula from Hainsworth and Hoekstra, and the latter has attempted to reconstruct an older layer of formulas, although this is a very difficult task and some may doubt his results. Nagler has led us into a more abstract realm along the lines of generative-transformational grammar; his work is challenging, but I sometimes feel that the individual composing poet is lost in its rarified atmosphere. His most recent work, published by the University of California Press in 1974, I have not yet seen, but it promises to be an important contribution to Homeric scholarship. In short, the formulaic weave of Ancient Greek oral narrative song is emerging ever more clearly as the product of generations of singers who composed in it, as did Homer, with the ease that others compose the sentences and paragraphs of everyday speech.

The forthcoming books of Berkley Peabody, of which I have already spoken, and of Professor Gregory Nagy deserve special mention when one turns to the hexameter. Nagy's book, "Comparative Studies in Greek and Indic Meter," will soon appear in the Comparative Literature series published by Harvard University Press [1974]. Nagy centers his work on a single formula, *kleos andrôn*, found in Homer and Sappho, and its Sanskrit equivalent, from which he reconstructs an Indo-European formula. He is led thus to Greek lyric poetry as well as epic, and with the help of the Indic parallels derives the hexameter from a pherecratic with the internal expansion of three dactyls. Peabody, on the other hand, while also using Indic parallels, makes larger use of the Avesta with the stanzaic form that it shares, in part at least, with Indic, and derives the hexameter from a fusion of a dimeter with a trimeter. He thus accounts for the various caesuras in the line differently from Nagy. I feel that both these books will be richly discussed; for they both add much to our knowledge of the metrical context and depth of the Ancient Greek tradition.

In an appendix Nagy presents an explanation of the meaning of the word *kleos*. The argument is involved, and some scholars will surely disagree with it, but I note that both Peabody and Nagy conclude their extraordinarily fine books with a reference to the magic or sacred power of song. Nagy writes: "I propose, then, that *klewos* was the word used to designate the hieratic art of song which ensured unfailing streams of water, light, vegetal sap, etc. Since these streams were unfailing, the art of song itself could be idealized and self-servingly glorified by the Singer as 'unfailing.'"

Thus the search for special meaning and contextual relevance of formulas moves forward. A number of Nagy's students at Harvard have been working in this vineyard and several challenging doctoral dissertations have resulted. Here, too, special mention should be made of Professor William Whallon's book *Formula, Character, and Context: Studies in Homeric, Old English, and Old Testament Poetry*, Center for Hellenic Studies, 1969. In the first chapter he says that he simply wishes to discuss cases that Parry neglected to mention where "epithets describe the essential and unchanging character of the men whose names they augment." His examples are worthy of attention, as are those in his second chapter on epithets and characterization. In short his book is a reasonable and moderate attempt to counteract what is often thought of as Parry's too mechanical explanation of epithets and other formulas, namely, their use for filling a line, or for fitting a given noun into a given metrical space. Once again, in closing this section, I would like to refer to Geoffrey Kirk's discussion of formulas in the article in *Greece and Rome* referred to above.

Although classicists and medievalists have not on the whole been inclined to use the Serbo-Croatian (or other oral traditional) materials themselves for comparative research, there are at least two studies of theme in Homer which have been introduced by an investigation of theme in *Serbocroatian Heroic Songs* and thus deserve special mention. William F. Hansen, Jr.'s, doctoral dissertation at Berkeley in 1970, recently (1972) published, scrutinized *The Conference Sequence, Patterned Narration and Narrative Inconsistency in the Odyssey*. David M. Gunn of the University of Newcastle upon Tyne published an article in *Harvard Studies in Classical Philology*, 75 (1971) investigating "Thematic Composition and Homeric Authorship," in which he first looked at the same theme in the songs of several singers in *SCHS*, noting the individual differences. From a similar consideration of passages in the Homeric poems Gunn concluded that the two songs were indeed by the same singer. Although the investigation should be carried much further than Mr. Gunn did in his article, the general method employed seems to me to be acceptable.

Other studies of themes in the Homeric poems include Joseph A. Russo's "Homer Against His Tradition," *Arion*, 7 (1968), 275-295, in which he attempts to see Homer's hand in the more elaborate forms of any given theme. He considers the short forms of a theme, such as that of arming, to be traditional, whereas the longer examples are Homer's own use of tradition. While there is something, to be sure, to be said for ascribing to Homer the fact of expansion of themes, it does not follow that the material used by him to expand is any less traditional than that in the unexplained instances. G. S. Kirk's brief discussion of Homer's handling of traditional themes is more successful in "The Search for the Real Homer," *Greece and Rome*, 2nd Series, Vol. XX, No. 2 (October, 1973), 124-139. But the fullest study of any Homeric theme is that of Bernard Fenik, *Typical Battle Scenes in the Iliad: Studies in the Narrative Techniques of Homeric Battle Description, Hermes*, Einzelschriften Heft 21, Wiesbaden, 1968. This is very fine and significant work, and I am tempted to quote a few sentences from his conclusion:

> The technique of composing a battle scene was therefore related to that of composing a single phrase or line. The poet had certain ready-made compositional elements at his disposal; dictional formula, formulaic lines, typical details, typical groupings of details, recurrent situations. He created his battle scenes out of pre-formed, standardized material that had been used before, probably by himself as well as by other poets. . . .
> Thus far there is no method to distinguish between the type scenes, patterns and all their particular variations which Homer may have invented himself, and those which he inherited from

the tradition. It is, however, as unlikely that one man invented
all the typical details and type scenes in the battle narrative as
that one man created the formulaic diction of the *Iliad* and
Odyssey. Both these stylistic features are at home only in a
learned, inherited style—what we might call a stylistic
tradition—formed and shared by many poets over many
generations. (p. 229)

And from his introduction:

It has become fashionable in certain quarters to emphasize the
atypical or unique features in the *Iliad* on the ground that this
is, after all, where Homer's particular excellence lies. A study of
Homer's poetic technique must have as its goal the discovery of
his variations on formular material and the special effects that
he achieves with them. Some eminently worthwhile work has
already been done along this line. An especially fine example is
J. Armstrong's study of the arming scenes, in which he shows
the effect that is achieved by a slight change in a typical
arming sequence ("The Arming Motif in the Iliad," *AJPh*, 79
(1958), 337-354). But it is one thing to do this for a relatively
small homogeneous group of scenes, and quite another to
attempt it amid the welter of small incidents in the rest of the
fighting. . . . We cannot pick out the unique element in a
passage, the significant variation, unless we have some means
of identifying it, and we can do this only if we have first
established, at least so far as is possible, what is typical. (p. 8)

It would be less than fair of me not to quote something of Fenik's
opinion about the orality of the Homeric poems and about the value of
the comparison of compositional techniques in Homer and Serbo-
Croatian oral narrative song:

The existence of a "typical style" of battle description has
certain clear, but limited, implications for the theory of oral
poetry. The nature of this style, like the nature of the diction,
indicates that it was created under the pressure of oral recitation,
in which the poet had no time to stop and ponder each new
phrase or each new incident of the battlefield. But it does need
to be emphasized that the typical style of the battle scenes does
not prove, any more than does the formulaic language, that the
Iliad is a purely oral composition. Only that the diction and

style of the poem grew out of an oral tradition is certain. The exact nature of the poetic inheritance, the way it was handed down, as well as the particular set of circumstances which produced the *Iliad* still remain largely unclear. (pp. 229-230)

Finally, in speaking of the *Iliad* vis-à-vis the Serbo-Croatian songs Fenik writes:

> The formidable differences between the poems imply equally considerable differences in the poetic traditions and specific circumstances out of which they grew. The modern parallels doubtless illuminate a great deal in the Homeric poems, and in this respect they are most valuable, but they leave even more unexplained—particularly the overwhelming excellence of the *Iliad* and *Odyssey*.
>
> ...for an outstanding poet to achieve anything approaching the quality of a poem like the *Iliad* he must have had the benefit of a tradition and training, in whatever form, far superior to anything which prevails among, say, the Yugoslav oral poets today. Many important pieces to the puzzle are still missing. (p. 230)

Fenik is not the only scholar, of course, who has found it difficult to see the relevance of the Serbo-Croatian songs to Homer. Geoffrey Kirk's reservations in this regard are well known and were voiced in *The Songs of Homer* (1962) and elsewhere. They agree that the Serbo-Croatian tradition can show us the importance of formulas and themes as the pragmatic basic composition of oral story verse. I do not think that this much has really ever been denied; its validity is actually demonstrable. It was precisely in order to learn something of the processes of composition and transmission that the study of the living oral traditions of the Balkans was undertaken. To this extent it can be said that the comparison with the Serbo-Croatian material has already had an impact. The South Slavic singers have taught us a great deal about the mechanics of oral composition of traditional narrative verse or song, and we should be willing to acknowledge, as Fenik has, at least that much of a debt to them. To do otherwise would seem to me to be unjust. They have, however, shown us more than the mechanics of the style. We have been able to see in the modern Balkans the *whole* of a tradition and that over a long period of time—not just two songs from one singer but many songs from many singers, some good, some mediocre, some bad. We have seen young singers and old singers, and middle-aged singers. The lesson for us in this is that we should realize that the Ancient Greek tradition, if it was a real living dynamic organism, and the Homeric poems prove that it certainly was just that, also had good, bad, and mediocre singers, young, old and middle-aged singers in addition to Homer, and probably some other superb singers, standing head and shoulders above even the good ones.

As a matter of fact, we do not really have the means as objective scholars to judge Homer's relationship to his own tradition, because, except for the Hesiodic poems, which are on different subjects, even different kinds of subjects, we have no other poems from ancient Greece with which to compare them. We do the best we can with late summaries, with fragments, with whatever clues have survived, but our best evidence is Homer's reputation, the reverence with which he was treated. The fact is that we do not have enough of the tradition outside of Homer's poems to judge, on our own, pragmatically, Homer's relationship to his tradition. We know next to nothing, therefore, about the quality of other ancient Greek songs, although we know that such songs existed. We do not know whether they used formulas and themes in the ways in which Homer is alleged to use them. We do not know whether Homer was unique in this or whether this was a characteristic of his tradition.

Moreover, although we have materials for the study of the Serbo-Croatian songs, the actual study of them from this point of view has not been made. The publication of Medjedović's "The Wedding of Smailagić Meho" and of other songs as well, will give us even more and better texts and will enable us to make such a study. This is the task of those who know the languages involved. There is clearly much to be done. But until it is done it is premature to condemn the South Slavic poets out of hand. They deserve a more sympathetic hearing. While we can tell much about basic compositional techniques from the published songs—and there is still much for us yet to learn from them in this regard—we can also see in them, if we will, the seeds of expansion and variation of themes and of the possibility of the adjustment of themes to song context, to mention only two phenomena that have a bearing on Homeric practice.

I have already in *The Singer of Tales* pointed out briefly the intricate balances by various types of parataxis in line and passage construction in Salih Ugljanin's singing. We have noted also a similar tendency in themes to chiastic arrangements, as when a series of questions is answered in reverse order, a simple form of ring composition. Singers whose minds work in this orderly way cannot be said to be devoid of any aesthetic sense. Their poetics must be more fully studied before judgment is passed on the quality of their poems.

Old French

Ramón Menéndez-Pidal's work (French translation, 1960) in the field of Romance epic stands as the fullest review of Roland scholarship to its time and itself presents a statement of a form of traditionalism. It includes discussion of Jean Rychner's *La Chanson de Geste* (Geneva, 1955), a seminal work, which it takes to task for considering the *Roland* as atypical. For a bibliography of the problems of oral literature in the *chansons de geste* Menéndez-Pidal's book, plus Joseph J. Duggan's *The Song of Roland: Formulaic Style and Poetic Craft* (Berkeley, 1973) and C. W. Aspland's *A Syntactical Study of Epic Formulas and Formulaic Expressions Containing the -ant Forms in Twelfth Century French Verse* (Queensland, 1970) are most helpful. Rychner's fine study of the style of the *chansons de geste* was marred only by the fact that he could not bring himself to include the *Roland* among those he was sure were oral traditional songs. It is from this point that Duggan takes his departure.

Duggan's published work in the field of formula study is the most valuable contribution so far in all three of the fields being considered here. Duggan has demonstrated in his analyses of formulas in the *chansons de geste* that density study is still very worthwhile. By means of it he has been able to mark off distinct groups of poems, to differentiate the earlier *chansons* from the romances. I see no reason why this distinction, in the case of the *chansons de geste*, should not be understood as a distinction between oral and written.

Duggan's book contains an excellent general discussion of formula and theme, reviewing and commenting on the work of E. Villela de Chasca, R. Hitze, and others. But it goes far beyond the formula in its treatment of *Roland*. In illustrating why the *Roland* is greater than the other *chansons de geste*, Duggan has taken several planctus of the *Roland*, compared them with the planctus in other *chansons de geste*, and thus shown the superiority of the former. In this way he has demonstrated that one judges a traditional poet by comparison with other poets in the same tradition. Such a method, of course, depends on having enough of the tradition itself to use as a control of the themes involved. In this, Old French with its many texts is in a far better situation than any other medieval field. Duggan has also pointed out that in the *Roland* the similar laisses of the dramatic moments of the song are not found, for example, in the Baligant episode and in later *chansons*. This technique for similar laisses used to underscore heightened drama seems to have been developed in the *Roland* and appears to be a characteristic of an earlier period of the *chansons de geste*, a characteristic which was lost in time. These examples are of judgments of quality made in terms of oral traditional song itself, made from the point of view of the tradition, from the inside out, within the parameters of traditional composition. Duggan's book is a model of this type of scholarship.

One of the most valuable recent doctoral dissertations in Old French epic studies is that of Tod N. Luethans, "*Gormont et Isembart*: A Description of the Epic as Seen in Light of the Oral Theory" (Harvard, 1972). Luethans's analysis of the battle themes in this rare octosyllabic Old French epic, together with its formulaic content, is a significant contribution to the study of oral literature.

Old English

In 1953 Francis Peabody Magoun, Jr.'s well-known article on *Beowulf* was published in *Speculum*, 28 (1953), 446-467, "The Oral Formulaic Character of Anglo-Saxon Narrative Poetry." Its impact was felt widely in Anglo-Saxon studies and to some extent elsewhere as well. A number of important doctoral dissertations were written under its influence. It was challenged in an article by Professor Larry D. Benson, "The Literary Character of Anglo-Saxon Formulaic Poetry," *PMLA*, 81 (1966), 334-341, in which he demonstrated that there were many formulas in Anglo-Saxon poems that could not be oral traditional compositions but must be literary, even learned works, and thus he maintained that analyses of formulaic density are not necessarily a proof of oral composition. While formulas are characteristic, he stated, of oral poetry, and probably derived from it, they existed also in Anglo-Saxon literary poetry.

In her book *The Lyre and the Harp*, Ann Chalmers Watts in 1969 surveyed the situation of the oral-formulaic theory in respect to its application to Old English Poetry. In her conclusion she says:

> Unsatisfactory as it is, there seems to be no better evidence for the oral composition of ancient poetry than a high degree of formular phraseology. The degree must vary from language to language, verse-form to verse-form, and must be determined in each case; but even though the untold loss of early poetical manuscripts must make the criterion of exactly repeated phraseology a rough gauge at best, still no other criterion comes as near to identifying for us the difference between phrases selected for their metrical efficacy and phrases not so selected. The rough gauge is hardly good enough to be useful. . . .
>
> The formulaic analysis of Old English texts may characterize what is on the page but not the means by which it got there. This distinction is of paramount importance to the study of any "old" poetry less formulaic than Homer—that is, all un-Homeric poetry. . . .
>
> According to the arguments set forth at length in this book, the degree of formular phraseology in *Beowulf* and *Elene* is small by Homeric standards. At what point does a small degree of formular content become conventional diction in a literary composition as opposed to formular phraseology in an oral composition?

In the opening of Professor Donald K. Fry's article, "Themes and Type-Scenes in *Elene*, 1-113," *Speculum*, XLIV, No. 1 (January, 1969), 35-45, the author makes the following assertion about the present state of formulaic studies in Anglo-Saxon:

> Formulaic studies of Old English poetry have come a long way since Francis P. Magoun's "Oral-Formulaic Character of Anglo-Saxon Narrative Poetry," published in 1953. Both opponents and proponents of the theory have found themselves moving closer together as the former survey the overwhelming body of evidence accumulating for formularity, and the latter begin to have serious doubts about the term "oral." Larry Benson's recent article, "The Literary Character of Anglo-Saxon Formulaic

Poetry," marks a nexus of the two viewpoints, acknowledging both the definitely formulaic character of the verse and the lack of evidence for oral composition. The current stance could perhaps be summarized as hypothesizing a survival of formulaic technique in written poetry from an earlier oral tradition. At any rate, proof of oral composition would make little difference in assessing artistic success.

It appears from these two quotations that the effect of Benson's article was to free formula study from oral composition or, rather, to emphasize the formula as being derived from oral composition but surviving to some degree into such work as the religious poems in Anglo-Saxon. The relationship of the style of such poems to the style of oral traditional poems or songs is a legitimate and worthwhile subject for investigation, as, indeed, is the study of the aesthetics of such poems, be they traditional or not.

There is, of course, in Anglo-Saxon only a small number of poems which from their subject matter could be traditional, even oral traditional. The most outstanding of these is, needless to say, *Beowulf*. We may have to leave it in limbo so far as the question of whether it is an oral traditional poem or not, because there simply is not enough possibly oral traditional material surviving in Anglo-Saxon for analysis. I might add that I must disagree with Fry on the final statement of the quotation above. I do believe that it is important "for assessing artistic success" to know whether a given text is part of an oral tradition or not. Otherwise the question of orality is not vital.

The basic concept of formulaic style is not complex, although its application in any given tradition or text or group of texts may present problems. For the sake of what follows, I should like to take a minute to recapitulate very briefly a view of oral composition. Language (at least, the Indo-European languages), especially spoken language (but also written language to the extent it follows the spoken language), is organized in substitution systems in repeated syntactic patterns. The formal language of law or religion has its set phrases, and the lawyer or priest thinks and speaks under the proper circumstances in those set phrases. In fact, every group of specialists has its own characteristic repeated phrases, so that when one of its members speaks or writes he uses the phrases of his speciality. The same is true for the story teller in a traditional society, modern, medieval, or ancient, rural or urban. The matter of his stories is repetitive, and when an idea is repeated it most frequently is repeated in the same or very similar words. When a story is sung in verse, the requirements of the medium limit the possible choices of phrases more than does prose, and the repeated phrases become more noticeable, more "visible." The formulas and the network of phrases like them are more numerous in traditional sung verse than in prose. They can be readily measured, particularly, as Duggan has well demonstrated, when computers are used.

From the narrowest point of view of text each performance is a new song, because the story is being told again without memorization of a non-existent fixed text, oral or written. The poet thus reconstructs his text each time, even as the story teller retells his story without concern for whether he uses the same words or not. The parallel is a useful one. On the other hand, the poet does not "improvise," that is to say, he does not make up consciously entirely new lines or entirely new passages. Just as a story teller, when he retells a story, will sometimes use the same sentences, or sentences very like the ones he has used before, so the singer in his story telling in verse will use lines he has used before, or lines like them. Neither of them consciously concerns himself or is even aware of whether he is using the same or slightly different or quite different phrases. Both of them are telling stories and are concentrating on that. What I am describing is that special kind of composition in verse that does not seek newness or originality, that is not afraid of using the old expressions—a special kind of "improvisation," if you will, but not improvising out of whole cloth. In my attempts in the past to combat the idea of a fixed text that was memorized, I have apparently given the impression that not only is the text different at each singing by a given singer (which is true, of course), but that it is *radically* different, entirely improvised. This is not true. South Slavic oral epic is not, nor, to the best of my knowledge, is any oral traditional epic, the result of "free improvisation."

Because, however, of the restrictions of the verse, there emerges a number of more or less fixed phrases, lines, or groups of lines, i.e., the formulas and formulaic expressions of the poetry. *Both* these elements (formulas and formulaic expressions) are characteristic of this style. It has already been noted by others who were seeking to define the formula that the complex substitution systems that appear in an in-depth formulaic analysis are really equally, if not more, significant than the exactly repeated formulas. I suspect that a writer trying to imitate the oral traditional style would fix first on the repeated phrases, since they, as I have said, are more "visible." The true weaving of the style is more difficult, perhaps impossible, to imitate. Such a weave, with its formulas and formulaic expressions, might be considered to be the actual "oral" part of the style, since it is the necessity of rapid telling in the confines of song that has produced it.

There is, however, another part, the "traditional," which has been little written about as such. This part is related directly to the subject matter of the songs, the ideas expressed by the story teller in song. That is to say, there is a specific given body of formulas and formulaic expressions, not just any phrases, but traditional phrases tied to the traditional ideas and subjects of the songs. Indeed, a tradition can be defined as the body of formulas, themes, and songs that has existed in the repertories of singers or story tellers in a given area over usually a long period of time.

Thus "oral" describes the weave of the style, and "traditional" defines the subject matter, the specific words and word combinations which express the ideas and set the specific patterns of the weave. It is, I believe, correct to speak of an "oral traditional" narrative song, using *both* terms. One should certainly not eliminate "oral" from this combination.

But do we find formulas outside of oral traditional sung verse? This question is the true thrust of Benson's article. It is clearly an important question, if we are to be able to use formulaic analysis for determining whether a text belongs to oral tradition or not, if the "rough gauge," as Dr. Watts says, is to be "good enough to be useful."

The first answer would be that one cannot have *formulas* outside of oral traditional verse, because it is the function of formulas to make composition easier under the necessities of rapid composition in performance, and if that necessity no longer exists, one no longer has formulas. If one discovers repeated phrases in texts known not to be oral traditional texts, then they should be called repeated phrases rather than formulas. I do not believe that this is quibbling about terms, because the distinction is functional. When one has said that, however, while one has clarified the terminology, one has not clarified the situation in the texts nor answered the question.

The fact of the matter is that the oral traditional style is easy to imitate by those who have heard much of it. Or, to put it another way, a person who has been brought up in an area, or lived long in one, in which he has listened to the singing and found an interest in it, can write verse using the general style and some of the formulas of the tradition. After all, the style was devised for rapid composition. If one wishes to compose rapidly in writing and comes from or has had much contact with an oral traditional poetry one not only can write in formulas, or something very like them, but normally does so. The style is natural to him. When the ideas are traditional the formulas may be those of the oral traditional poetry; when the ideas are not traditional, they will not.

One should not overlook the possibility that such written poetry may set up formulas of its own for those ideas that do not come from the oral traditional poetry. The situation is extremely complicated, because one must keep in mind (a) that within the oral tradition itself, that is, within the group of practicing singers in the tradition, new ideas enter the songs, and (b) the poems written in the style of the tradition sometimes may influence the tradition itself. The question is whether one can tell by formulaic analysis the differences between the various kinds of poems. It seems clear that in order to be able to do this one must consider not only repetitions as such but the specific formulas used or ideas expressed by them.

It is evident, therefore, that much more research will have to be done on texts of all kinds before any responsible answer to Benson's article can be given. In Anglo-Saxon research needs to be done not merely in numbers of formulas—although we could use still more definite statistics in this area—but also, and more particularly, in specific formulas. That is to say, it would be useful to know, for instance, what formulas are common to *Beowulf* and to the religious poems, with attention paid, of course, to the Cynewulf poems as a unit and to the seemingly special relationship of *Andreas* to *Beowulf*. It would be helpful to know what formulas occur only in the religious poems—and so forth. The purpose is to determine not only whether a tradition exists but what its content is. We should also hope to find out more about the "weave" in Anglo-Saxon poetry. We already know a great deal about Anglo-Saxon poetry in these regards and compiling the rest of the information should not be too difficult. The same kind of investigation should be undertaken in other medieval poetries as well, such as Old French, Byzantine, and Old Spanish, insofar as materials are available.

It is ironical that we know considerably more about formulas in the Homeric poems and in Anglo-Saxon poetry than we do about them in a living narrative tradition. We urgently need further research in the Serbo-Croatian poetry and/or in that of other living narrative traditions. I have long been acutely aware that to date my formulaic analysis of a few of Salih Ugljanin's verses in *The Singer of Tales* is the main one on which we base our knowledge of oral traditional formulas in Serbo-Croatian. Kenneth Goldman's computer studies of formulas and formulaic systems in the songs of a Hercegovinian singer collected by Parry will be very valuable, and it is to be hoped that other investigations of pure traditional narrative poetry will be undertaken.

But the Serbo-Croatian material is especially pertinent to the study of both pure traditional songs and of all the various types and mixtures of written poetry as well. We have concentrated on the purity of the oral tradition, because one cannot investigate the mixed forms until the unadulterated form is well understood. In Serbo-Croatian literary history there is a unique situation, as far as I know, in which collecting of the traditional songs, and interest in them in general, led to writing what was thought to be that kind of poem. No less unique is the fact that both the tradition and the various mixtures can be documented by collected and published written texts over a period of more than two hundred years. R. Spraycar's paper, "The Oral-formulaic Character of Serbo-Croatian Poetry: A Reassessment," read before the Old English section of the MLA convention in Chicago, December 27, 1973, contains formulaic analysis of some lines of the eighteenth-century Franciscan Andrija Kačić Miošić, who wrote a history of the South Slavs in prose and verse. His poetry is in the style of the traditional poems. We need many more analyses of such poems, including more of Kačić, as well as unpublished mixed texts in the Parry Collection. In the analyses attention should be given not only to the repetitions themselves, but even more importantly, to the weave of the style and to the specific formulas. What we seek is as full a description as possible of all facets of the style of an oral traditional narrative poetry and of its imitations and derivatives.

Benson's article has raised legitimate and vital questions which must be pursued fully until the whole truth of the several varieties of style involved and of their relationship to one another is clearly understood. It is certain that at the moment our knowledge of the facts is incomplete. We are fortunate that the material needed for such research is available in abundance.

Professor Fry's definitions of type-scene and theme are helpful in pointing up some of the difficulties in thematic study of oral traditional poetry. Here are his definitions as summarized in his 1969 article already mentioned above. They originally appeared in an earlier article, "Old English Oral-Formulaic Themes and Type-Scenes," *Neophilologus*, LII (1968), 48-54:

> Most studies of Anglo-Saxon formulaic poetry have focused on the level of diction, that is, on the formulas themselves with some attention to systems of formulas. In Homeric and Yugoslavian scholarship, however, the emphasis has been on the next level of formulaic structure, the composition of the plot in stereotyped units, variously called "motifs," "type-scenes," "action patterns," or "themes." . . .
>
> The definitions are as follows: A type-scene is a recurring stereotyped presentation of conventional details used to describe a certain narrative event, requiring neither verbatim repetition nor a specific formula content; and a theme is a recurring concatenation of details and ideas, not restricted to a specific event, verbatim repetition, or certain formulas, which forms an underlying structure for an action or description. Some typical type-scenes are sea-voyages, councils, and the arrival of a messenger. A series of such scenes connected by linking passages appropriate to the plot makes up the narrative; the poet might, for example, compose a series such as banquet, damnation, approach to a city, exhortation, approach to battle, and battle itself (the poem so composed, of course, is *Judith*). The poet can repeat the same type-scene in one poem as many times as necessary, such as sea-voyages and banquets in *Beowulf*; and he can insert one type-scene into another, such as a council held during a banquet. A theme, on the other hand, is not tied to a specific narrative situation; it provides a framework of imagery underlying the surface of narrative. So far only two themes have been isolated for study: the "Hero on the Beach". . . and "Exile."

Before discussing this passage from Fry, I should like to quote a condensed version of my comments on theme contained in a paper entitled, "The Marks of an Oral Style and their Significance," read at meetings of the International Comparative Literature Association in Belgrade in 1967:

Where shall we look on the story level for *narrative* criteria by which we can test whether any given text is from oral tradition or from literary tradition? Surely the theme is the answer. If, however, by theme one means *subject*, a narrative element, such as a catalogue, or a message, or equipping, or gathering of an army, then our definition is inadequate; for clearly we can find gatherings of armies, equippings, messages, and catalogues in written as well as in oral literature. The theme as *subject* alone is too general for our very special purposes. But if by theme one means a repeated narrative element together with its verbal expression, that portion of a poem, an aggregate of specific verses, that tells a certain repeated part of the narrative, measurable in terms of lines and even words and word combinations, then we find ourselves dealing with elements of truly oral traditional narrative style. . . . Only thus is theme parallel on a "higher" level with formula. . . .

Themes are useful as aids in composition because they can be employed in more than one place in a song or in more than one song and because the singer has a ready-made form for them, just as he has ready-made forms for formulas. He adjusts the formulas, to some extent, to a particular environment in the song. No literary composer would tolerate the repeated use of the same passage, even if there were some slight verbal changes in it. When we find a passage used over and over again, we know it to be a theme, in the very technical sense applicable only to oral literature.

Moreover, just as on the formula level in an oral poem almost everything is formula, so on the thematic level almost everything in a poem is theme. When one can analyze a kind of thematic density similar to the formulaic density of which we spoke earlier, this is another indication that the style of the poem involved is oral.

Although the repeated passages will not be word for word alike, there will be at least a sufficient degree of similarity of wording to show that the singer is using a unit of story that he holds already more or less formed in his mind. The closeness of text can be seen in the beginnings of three tellings of the same song by Salih Ugljanin. The song is "The Captivity of Djulić Ibrahim," and the three texts are published in *Serbocroatian Heroic Songs*, Volume II, Nos. 4, 5 and 6 (see chart p. 54).

There are some texts, of course, that show less verbal correspondence between occurrences of a theme, but the above demonstrates the kind of similarity in wording which is characteristic of what might be called a compositional theme. The chart also affords me the opportunity to remark that the kind of composition reflected in the three passages in it could not be described as "free improvisation." On the other hand, they could not be described as memorized passages either nor as the product of a writer seeking originality of expression.

To return to a discussion of the quotation from Fry given above, it seems to me that his definition of theme is somewhat unclear, and I shall concentrate on his comments on type-scene. It is noticeable in Anglo-Saxon and evident from Fry's treatment of type-scenes that there seems to be no, or at best very little, verbal correspondence between instances of type-scenes, and, therefore, it appears appropriate to differentiate them from the compositional themes with a reasonably high degree of verbal correspondence. The term "type-scene" performs this function very well.

Such type-scenes contain a given set of repeated elements or details, not all of which are always present, nor always in the same order, but enough of which are present to make the scene a recognizable one. David E. Bynum's doctoral dissertation in 1964 isolated the type-scenes (using the term "theme") in the songs about weddings in Serbo-Croatian oral epic. For each theme he listed the elements which were found in it. He examined some seventy-five songs and ascertained that all parts of the songs were themes, i.e., were repeated elsewhere in the tradition (or at least in the body of seventy-five songs which he investigated). Fry's method of identifying and describing type-scenes is generally the same as that used by Bynum in studying themes in Serbo-Croatian oral epic, and the results are similar. In both cases one finds a core of elements repeated within a frame. This kind of type-scene is characteristic of oral epic.

What distinguishes the type-scene from the theme (as I use the term) is the degree of verbal correspondence that makes the theme as such a distinctive feature of the oral compositional habit of a given singer. It (the theme) may also, although this has not been investigated, show regional differences, i.e., the habits of singers who listen to one another and belong to the same singing district.

In his analysis of type-scenes in *Elene* Fry has gone one step further, as have some Homerists as well, than defining and delimiting specific scenes. He has pointed out the way in which the poet shows his skill in composition and sensitivity by his handling of type-scenes. I find his analysis on the whole very convincing. He has, in short, moved into an aesthetics of thematic composition, a kind of composition that he is willing to call "traditional," but which he hesitates to call oral, probably because of the strictures in Benson's article.

I would like to present the following suggestion for consideration. The men who knew the religious and saints' legends seem also at some time to have known an oral traditional poetry and its style, to have known it well enough to compose in it or in something similar to it. On the verse level the style may be marginal, not quite as formulaic in its repeated hemistichs as one might expect an oral traditional style to be, yet containing many hemistichs known from the oral traditional poetry such as that surrounding or behind *Beowulf*, if not *Beowulf* itself. This would account for the repeated phrases in poems like *Elene*, *Andreas*, and others. Although the composers of these poems might have known the saints' legends from sermons, i.e., not necessarily in written form, yet it is normal to assume that they knew them from some written source, for example, the Latin versions that were to be found in the monasteries. I would also like to suggest the possibility that in these poems, namely, the religious ones, a new body of formulas to express the new ideas of the Christian poetry was beginning to be developed on the model of the oral traditional poetry. I am tempted to call the religious poetry "transitional" or perhaps "mixed." If that is the correct term, it applies not only to the formulas but to the themes as well.

If the religious poems were truly oral traditional songs, I would expect to find a higher degree of verbal correspondence among the various instances of a theme within a given poem, after making due allowance for adjustment to the specific position in the poem which it occupies. It may possibly be that the necessity that gave rise to themes with close verbal correspondence no longer existed or was felt. But the theme with its elements persists and is operative as a model for composition and as a base for multiforms. As Fry has demonstrated, in this respect the theme was still a living force in composition, and the audience for the poems must have been still enough of a traditional audience to feel that the working out of these models was right.

In sum, the increase in the last few years in the number of studies of oral literature is very encouraging. We are learning about many aspects of this phenomenon in many hitherto either unexplored or inadequately described traditions. Our analyses of medieval and ancient texts have somewhat outdistanced our knowledge of the processes of living traditions. But work in progress is slowly lessening that gap. There is emerging a degree of moderation in aesthetic studies of medieval and ancient texts in consideration of traditional and/or oral characteristics found in them. In this regard our greatest need is for further investigation of the aesthetics of oral traditional narrative poetries. Finally, although I have spoken almost exclusively of stylistic matters, because it is through style that we have tried to identify and characterize oral literature, one should not forget the many other aspects of oral literature, above all its function and its meaning.

Chart

No. 4
Ej! Dje sedimo, aj! da se veseljimo,
A da bi nas i Bog veseljijo,
Veseljijo, pa razgovorijo,
A lepšu ni sreću dijelijo
Na ovome mestu i svakome!
E! Sad veljimo da pesmu brojimo.
Davno nekad u zemanu bilo,
Davno bilo, sada pominjemo.

—

Jednom vaktu beše josvanulo,
E! U Zadaru pucaju topovi,
Dva zajedno ja trides' ujedno.
Stoji zemlje crne tutljavina.
Sve se svijet po čudi čudahu.
Šenluk čini jod Zadara bane.
Jufatijo slugu Radojicu,
E! Radojicu, tursku pridvoricu,
Pa ga tavnu bacilji zindanu.
Pa kad Rako ju tavnicu dodje,
E! Tu nadje trideset Turaka,
I medju nji' Djuljić bajraktara,
A do njega Velagić Seljima.

—

Pa kad Rako ju tamnici dodje,
Dodje, stade, te him pomoj dade.
Sve mu age ljepše prifatiše,
Sve mu redom dobrodošle daje.

No. 5
O starome vaktu i zemanu
Jedno jutro teke osamnulo,

No. 6
Jednom vaktu a starom zemanu
Jedno jutro beše osvanulo

U Zadaru pucaju topovi,

Dva zajedno, trideset ujedno.

—

Sve se zemlja i planina trese.

—   —

Šenluk čini od Zadara bane.

Ufatijo slugu Radojicu,	Ufatio uskok Radovana,

Radojicu, tursku pridvoricu,
Pa ga baci ljedenu zindanu.

Pa kad Rako u zindanu dodje,	Pa kad Rako u tamnicu dodje,

Tuna nadje trideset Turaka,

I medju nji' Djuljić Ibrahima,	A medju nji' Djuljić Ibrahima,
I kraj njega Velagić Seljima,	I kod njega Velagić Selima.
I njihovo trides' i dva druga.	—
—	—
Pa him Rako pomoj naturijo,	Dodje Rako, pa him pomoj dade,
A Turci mu bolje prifatilji.	I svi njemu bolje prifatiše,
—	Pa mu redom dobrodošle daju.

The Making of an Anglo-Saxon Poem

Robert P. Creed

Robert Payson Creed, student of both Francis P. Magoun, Jr., and Albert Lord, was one of the first to probe the implications of the comparative program introduced and developed by his mentors to the area of Old English poetry. In addition to studies applying oral-formulaic theory to manuscript cruces, critical methods, larger textual structures, sound-patterning, and other issues, Creed's 1959 study on "The Making of an Anglo-Saxon Poem" went so far as to actually illustrate the oral poet's method of formulaic composition. By remaking lines 356-359 of the Anglo-Saxon epic poem Beowulf *in different but "equivalent" formulaic language, he provided a classic example of the flexibility and multiformity of oral traditional phraseology. Responses by Robert Stevick (1962) and R. F. Lawrence (1966), answered by Creed in his 1968 version of the original essay, questioned the role of memory and memorization in oral composition as well as the nature of the formulaic repertoire of a traditional singer. But with the essays of Magoun, Benson, Fry, and Renoir found elsewhere in the present volume, Creed's "Making" remains a touchstone in the application of oral-formulaic theory to Old English poetry.*

Reprinted from *English Literary History*, 26 (1959), 445–454; also reprinted with "Additional Remarks" in *The Beowulf Poet*, ed. by Donald K. Fry (Englewood Cliffs, N.J.: Prentice-Hall, 1968), pp. 141-153.

I

The diction of *Beowulf* is schematized to an extraordinary degree.[1] Roughly every fifth verse is repeated intact at least once elsewhere in the poem. An essential part of about every second verse—such a part as a whole measure, or a phrase which straddles both measures, or one which encloses two measures of the verse—is repeated elsewhere in the poem. Many of these verses or essential parts of verses bear such a resemblance to certain others as to suggest that the singer "knew them"—in the late Milman Parry's words—"not only as single formulas, but also as formulas of a certain type."[2] In composing a line containing any one of these verses, therefore, he was guided by the rhythm, sound, and sense of other verses belonging to this type of "system."[3]

The degree of the schematization of his diction suggests that the singer of *Beowulf* did not need to pause in his reciting or writing to consider what word to put next. His diction was one which, in Goethe's words, did his thinking and poetizing for him, at least when he had completely mastered that diction and its ways. Precisely *how* that diction might have done his poetizing for the Anglo-Saxon singer is the subject of the present paper.

I cannot attempt to deal in so brief a study with the way in which the singer puts together the larger elements of his poem. I shall therefore take only a very small portion of *Beowulf*, eight verses (four lines), and attempt, by means of references to similar verses and lines in the rest of the poem and in other surviving Anglo-Saxon poems, to illustrate the thesis that the making of any Anglo-Saxon poem was a process of choosing rapidly and largely on the basis of alliterative needs *not* between individual words but between *formulas*.

A formula may be as large as those whole verses repeated intact to which I referred earlier, or even larger. There are whole lines and even lines-and-a-half repeated within *Beowulf*. At the other extreme a formula may be as small as those trisyllabic prepositional phrases which end certain A-verses, or even as small as a monosyllabic adverb, *if* the adverb makes the whole spoken portion[4] of the measures and thus makes it possible for the singer to compose rapidly.

This last fact is important. The essential quality of the formula is not its memorable sound—although some formulas are, even for us, memorable—but its *usefulness* to the singer. To be useful to a singer as he composes rapidly a phrase or word must suggest to him that it belongs only at one point, or possibly only two points, in his verse or line; that is, it must be a significant segment of his rhythm. To be useful to the singer every phrase or word which is metrically significant should also be a syntactic entity, that is, if it is not a polysyllable which by itself makes a whole verse or whole "crowded" measure, it should at least be a phrasal group or a clause. It should be, for example, an article and its noun, or a noun or pronoun and its verb, or a verb and its object, or a preposition and its noun, *not* such syntactically meaningless groups as, for example, an adverb and a preposition.

The formula in Anglo-Saxon poetry is, then, to paraphrase and somewhat emend Milman Parry's definition of the formula in Homer, a word or group of words regularly employed under certain strictly determined metrical conditions to express a given essential idea.[5]

In a formulaic or traditional poem we are frequently able, because of this schematization of the diction, not only to examine the formula which the singer chose, but also to guess at with some measure of assurance, and to examine, the system or entire group of formulas from *among* which he chose at a given point in his poem. When we have studied his tradition with care we are able to appreciate his poetry in a unique way, because we can perform in slow motion the very process which he of necessity formed rapidly: we can unmake, and make in new fashion, each line according to the rules of the game, and thus approximate what the singer himself might have done in a different performance of the same tale.

II

At line 356 of his poem the singer has got Beowulf safely across the sea from Geatland to Denmark, and has placed him outside the hall Heorot. Wulfgar, Hrothgar's herald, has just learned from Beowulf who he is and what his mission is at Hrothgar's court.

> Hwearf þa hrædlice þær Hroþgar sæt,
> eald and unhar, mid his eorla gedryht;
> eode ellen-rof þæt he for eaxlum gestod

Deniga frean; cuðe he duguðe þeaw.[6]

> Then he [that is, Wulfgar] turned quickly to where
> Hrothgar sat, old and very hoary, with his troop
> of men; famous for his courage [he, Wulfgar] went
> until he stood before the shoulders of the lord of
> the Danes; he knew the custom of the comitatus.

There are several different ways by which the singer could, in good formulas, have got Wulfgar or anyone else from one place to another. Not many lines before this passage the singer has got Beowulf out of Geatland with the following verse: *gewat þa ofer wæg-holm* [he departed then over the wave-sea]. At line 720 the singer will get Grendel to Heorot with the following verse: *com þa to recede* [he came then to the hall]. At line 1232 he will get Wealhtheow to her seat with *eode þa to setle* [she went then to the bench].

We can be sure that each one of the verb-adverb groups (*gewat þa, com þa, eode þa* [he departed then, he came then, she went then]) which begins these lines is a formula not only because it fits the conditions of usefulness and significance but also because the singer has used each of these phrases in this same position more than once.

But at our point in the story the singer chose to say *hwearf þa* [he turned then], like these other verb-adverb groups a demonstrable formula since it appears at the beginning of line 1188, 1210, and 1573. We can find good reasons for his choice of *hwearf þa* [he turned then] in this passage. *Gewat þa* [He departed then] suggests a journey longer than the length of a hall, *com þa* [he came then] suggests a new arrival rather than a return. The singer might then have said *eode þa* [went then] as he will do at 1232 and 1626 (*eodon . . . þa* [they went . . . then]), or simply *eode* [he went] as he does at eight other places in his poem. That he said *hwearf þa* [he turned then] here suggests that he had already thought ahead not only to the adverb with which *hwearf* [he turned] incidentally alliterates, but to *Hroþgar* in the second verse of the line, which is the excuse for the adverb itself. The singer had no particular need to get Wulfgar from Beowulf to Hrothgar with haste; he *did* need to get him to Hrothgar with alliteration.[7]

In *Beowulf* 356, then, the singer has correctly established his alliterative bridge-head with *hrædlice* [quickly] for an assault on the second verse of the line. That verse, *þær Hroþgar sæt* [where Hrothgar sat], does not divide neatly into two formulas each of which makes a single measure as does 356a. Verse 356b belongs to a type the pattern of which can be expressed by *þær x sæt* [where x sat], where *x* equals the subject of *sæt*. Eight hundred lines after this passage, at line 1190, the singer has composed another verse of this type, *þær se goda sæt* [where the good-one sat], in which the substitution for the sake of alliteration is perfectly straight-forward. Just seventy lines before our passage, however, the singer has apparently used the same container, *þær . . . sæt* [where . . . sat], with a different kind of alliterating content: *þær on wicge sæt* [there on his horse he sat]. Apparently the singer does not restrict himself to employing the same kind of substituting element within the framework of this simple substitution system. Or perhaps it would be more correct to say that he shows signs at such points as these of thinking in terms of two complementary types of formula which he can readily combine to make a single verse.

This verse, *þær Hroþgar sæt* [where Hrothgar sat], completes a line, and might, had the singer so chosen, have completed a thought. He does not so choose; he amplifies in the following line this brief mention of Hrothgar seated into a noble picture of the aged king surrounded by his retainers. But before we turn our attention to this picture in the next line of the passage, let us first observe how this line as a whole has helped to prepare the singer to make another whole line later in his poem.

Some eight hundred lines after this passage the singer moved Wealhtheow not into but across the hall with the following line: *hwearf þa be bence/þær hire byre wæron . . .* [she turned then along the bench/where her sons were . . .] (1188). The design of this line is very similar to that of the one we have just studied. Both lines begin with the same formula; the second verse of both lines is enclosed by a similar phrase (*þær . . . sæt, þær . . . wæron* [where . . . sat, where . . . were]). The singer requires, however, a different alliteration in each line: he wishes to name Hrothgar in the first and to refer to Wealhtheow's sons in the second, consequently he uses a different second measure (*hrædlice, be bence* [quickly, along the bench]). We shall return to this later passage in a moment to indicate how the earlier passage has influenced even further the construction of the later.

To sum up my rather extensive remarks on this single line: the singer appears to have composed his line of at least three separate formulas, *hwearf þa* [he turned then], *hrædlice* [quickly], and *þær x sæt* [where x sat]. He seems to have chosen the second formula, which carries the important alliteration of the first verse, in order that he might name Hrothgar in the second verse. He was, finally, guided in the shaping of the line as a whole by the *association* in his mind of these three formulas, as his later line 1188 seems to prove.

Line 357 presents fewer problems. The first verse, *eald and unhar* [old and very hoary], belongs to a type long recognized as a formula, the so-called *reim-formel* [rhyme-formula]. Formulas of this kind have sometimes been regarded as a particularly characteristic kind of formula in Anglo-Saxon poetry or elsewhere.[8] Such formulas are indeed distinctive and decidedly ornamental; in fact, so far as getting any real work done is concerned, they are more ornamental than useful. For this very reason they can hardly claim to be the type of formula *par excellence*.

In making this verse the singer was guided by its simple and rather pleasing A-rhythm. At three other places in his poem the singer was guided by the same play of sound and rhythm to link *eald* [old] with another alliterating word (*eald and infrod* [old and experienced], 2449 for example).

The vowel-alliteration of *eald* [old] gets him easily to the second verse of this line. Had he wished to name Hrothgar in the first verse of this line, or for any other reason to employ *h*-alliteration or even *s*-alliteration he would have been faced with no problem in making the second half of the line. *mid his eorla gedryht* [with his troop of earls] is an even better example than verse 356b of the simple substitution system. For *h*-alliteration the singer replaces *eorla* [earls] with *hæleða* [heroes], as he does at line 662; for *s*-alliteration he replaces *eorla* [earls] with *secga* [men] as he does in line 633 and 1672.

The noble picture is complete with this fourth verse; the singer pauses momentarily, and editors punctuate accordingly. If, during that pause, we turn again to that later picture of Wealhtheow at which we have already glanced, we shall see even further similarities between these two passages. Line 1188, like 356, is followed by a *reim*-formula, *Hroeþric and Hroþmund*, in this case a *reim*-formula which, like 357a, amplifies the alliterating core of the previous verse. Again like 357a, and probably to some degree because of 357a, 1189a is followed by the mention of the troop of warriors, "sons of heroes," seated around the two princes: *and hæleða bearn* [and sons of heroes]. But this later passage does not end with the fourth verse; *hæleða bearn* itself is amplified by the following verse, *geoguþ ætgædere* [young-warriors together]. Thus the two passages are alike but not identical. We can only with increasing difficulty deny, however, that the rhythms and ideas which governed the making of the first passage played some part in the making of the second when we note that *geoguþ ætgædere* [young-warriors together] is followed by the paradigm of 356b: *þær se goda sæt* [where the good-one sat]. *Se goda* [The good-one] in verse 1190b refers not to Hrothgar but to Beowulf, whose name and whose location *be þæm gebroðrum twæm* [by the two brothers] completes in eight verses a reflection of the noble picture we have seen condensed into four.

But perhaps it is not quite correct to say that the earlier picture is yet complete, since, in verse 358a, the singer returns to the idea contained in the first measure of 356a. The singer has made the second measure of the later verse not out of a single adverb but a single substantive, *ellen-rof* [famous for courage]. Eighteen lines before this he has made the entire second measure of a B-verse out of this word; twenty-eight hundred lines later in his poem he will again make *ellen-rof* [famous for courage] the second measure of a D-verse.

But to stop with these observations of the other appearances of this compound as a compound is to ignore an important and interesting point of the singer's technique. That point may be expressed as a kind of rule-of-thumb which runs something like this: the first element of any compound noun or adjective will more often than not exist for the sake of alliteration rather than for the sake of a more precise denotation. We can demonstrate the operation of this rule in the present case by noting that the singer has elsewhere combined *hige-* [mind-] with *rof* [famous] to mean something synonymous with *ellen-rof* [famous for courage] but having a different alliteration and a different metrical value. He has also combined *beadu-* [battle-], *brego-* [chief-], *guþ-* [war-], *heaðu-* [battle-], and *sige-* [victory-], with this same adjective *rof* [famous] to obtain only slightly different meanings and three more different alliterations.

Verse 358b, *þæt he for eaxlum gestod* [until he stood before the shoulders], appears to be made of two such complementary formulas as appear in 356b. The container, *þæt he . . . gestod* [until he . . . stood], is made in the same fashion as the container of 356b. Again, the container does the real work of the verse, that is, it functions syntactically as a complete clause with its subject pronoun and verb. The easily replaceable contained element, *for eaxlum* [before the shoulders], both carries the alliteration and delimits the action of the verb.

This verse might indeed be spoken of as a delimiting formula, or as a formula for indicating distance. Once the singer has learned to isolate the container from the alliterating content of the verse, as we have just done, he has learned a most useful technique. That the singer of *Beowulf had* so isolated the container is evident from the following verses in which he indicates, at various points in his poem, different distances travelled by inserting a different prepositional phrase into this same container:

> þæt he on heorðe gestod [until he stood on the
> hearth] (404)
> þæt hit on wealle ætstod [so that it stood fixed]
> (891)
> þæt hit on hafolan stod [so that it stood in the
> head] (2679)

Compare also

> þæt him on ealdre stod [so that in his vitals
> stuck] (1434).

The problem of indicating before whose shoulders it was that Wulfgar came to a stop caused the singer little difficulty. He knew several kinds of whole verse formulas for referring to Hrothgar. The most numerous group of these formulas, or, to express it properly, the most useful group, is the *x Scieldinga* [x of the Scildings] group, to which belong *wine Scieldinga* [friend of the Scildings], which he employs in the poem seven times, *frea Scieldinga* [lord of the Scildings], which he employs four times, *helm* [protector] (three times), *eodor* [prince], *leod* [prince], *þeoden* [prince] (each twice). This group alone provides him with six different alliterative possibilities.

But before speaking 359a, the singer must have thought ahead to the *duguðe* [retainers] with its *d*-alliteration in 359b. Hence he provided himself here with a *d*-alliterating epithet, *Deniga frean* [ruler of the Danes], as he had done at line 271 and was to do at 1680.

359b, *cuðe he duguðe þeaw* [he knew the custom of the comitatus], has no very close analogues in *Beowulf*. If, however, we compare it with verse 1940b, *ne biþ swelc cwoenlic þeaw* [such is not a queenly manner (to behave)], we can observe some similarity between the second measures of these two verses.

If the two second measures are derived from the same play of sounds and ideas, the first two measures which accompany them are not. *cuðe he* [he knew], which appears nowhere else in *Beowulf*, is quite unlike *ne biþ swelc* [such is not] in 1940b, which appears again in line 2541. It has been suggested that, in such lightly stressed first measures as these, the singer has a kind of escape valve, or a measure into which he can cram, without worrying about alliteration, needed but metrically annoying words and phrases. Perhaps this is so, but it is also true that the singer composed many of these lightly stressed measures out of formulas.[9]

III

At the beginning of this paper I noted that we can both unmake and make again each of the singer's lines if we are careful to follow the same rules which seem to have guided the singer. It might be amusing, and perhaps even instructive then, for such a novice singer as I—who have, however ridiculous this idea seems, been training myself and the careful reader to be a singer, and in a way not unlike that by which the singer trained himself—to attempt to do just that: to remake this passage from *Beowulf* which we have just unmade, attempting to say as closely as possible but with other formulas what the singer has said:

> Eode þa ofostlice   þær se ealdor sæt
> har and hige-frod   mid his hæleða gedryht;
> eode hilde-deor   þæt he on heorðe gestod
> frean Scieldinga;   cuðe he þæs folces þeaw.

> [He went then speedily where the prince sat hoary
> and mind-wise with his troop of heroes; he went
> battle-brave until he stood on the hearth the
> prince of the Scildings; he knew the custom of
> the people].

There is my poem. If you analyze it properly you will find every single formula elsewhere in *Beowulf* or in other poems in the Anglo-Saxon corpus, and used exactly as I have used it here. I must however claim credit for combining *har* [hoary] with *hige-frod* [mind-wise] and, I had thought, even for the manufacture of *hige-frod*. I needed a *reim*-formula with *h*-alliteration and hit upon *hige-frod* by following that rule-of-thumb I spoke of earlier. Only afterwards I discovered *Genesis* 1953, *halig and hige-frod*, [holy and mind-wise], along with marginal notes indicating that I had been reading this portion of that poem not very long ago.

I don't like my poem nearly so much as I like the singer's.[10] Yet my poem is composed of the same formulas out of which this singer and other Anglo-Saxon singers of ability created their poems. The diction of my poem is schematized to no greater degree than the diction of most other surviving Old English poems. What my experiment helps to prove, then, is that the simple use of formulaic diction is no guarantee of aesthetic success. Conversely, the use of a formulaic diction does not make success impossible. *Beowulf*, with its highly schematized diction yet continually marvelous subtlety, is sufficient proof to the contrary.

If my feeble attempt to compose formulaic poetry only serves to demonstrate once again the subtle art of the singer of *Beowulf* I shall be satisfied. I should be more than satisfied if the experiment should serve also to remind the reader that this subtle art is a traditional and formulaic art, and that it is possible to praise the four lines of *Beowulf* I have chosen to examine as, for their purposes, the best of all possible *combinations of formulas*.

Additional Remarks

In the years that have elapsed since the appearance of this article it has come under the scrutiny of a number of scholar-critics of Old English poetry. I should like to take the opportunity, generously offered by the editor of the present volume [D. K. Fry], to respond to some of these criticisms in the hope that by accepting and attempting to deal with just criticisms I can make the article somewhat more useful.

In "The Oral-Formulaic Analyses of Old English Verse," *Speculum*, XXXVII (1962), 382-89, Robert D. Stevick points out that "memory of past performances will have a very large effect on any further performance; any familiarity at all with successive jazz performances suggests strongly that performers (and particularly professional ones) repeat earlier performances as entities, subject only to such changes as faulty memory, momentary experiments, or effects of audience reaction may produce. They do not build each performance merely a phrase at a time" (p. 386). I am grateful for this reminder of the complexity of the forces impinging upon any traditional performance. I should therefore modify my description of the factors at work upon these eight lines from *Beowulf* to indicate the possibility that not *all* the singer-poet's "decisions" that produced the recorded performance were made at the same time, that is in a single performance. Yet some simplification of the complexity of the interaction of tradition and the traditional singer-poet may well be necessary if we are to try to understand something of the nature of the singer as artist, that is as *shaper* of the tradition, and not simply as performer, that is as *transmitter* of the tradition.

In "The Canons of Old English Criticism," *ELH*, XXXIV (1967), 141-155, Stanley B. Greenfield quotes with approval R. F. Lawrence's comment: "'If [Creed] can effectively use the oral techniques in the privacy of his study, then how much more effectively might the Anglo-Saxon monk have done like-wise?'" (R. F. Lawrence, "The Formulaic Theory and its Applications to English Alliterative Poetry," in Roger Fowler, ed., *Essays on Style and Language*, London, 1966, pp. 175-176.) I should point out that the "monk" who was as much concerned as I was about possible substitutions of the sort I have suggested above either performed the same elaborate and painstaking operations I performed with the aid of his version of Grein-Köhler-Holthausen's *Sprachschatz* or was a singer-poet thoroughly trained in the tradition.

Greenfield later quotes Lawrence again, though this time with only grudging approval: "it may well be, as Lawrence says, 'that a popular theme, or poem of several related themes, as it is progressively developed and refined by a succession of oral poets [or, we might add, by the same singer himself in successive performances] could achieve a perfection of form and a density of utterance perhaps even beyond the capacity of written literature'" (p. 143). Lawrence's suggestion, particularly as modified by Greenfield's bracketed insertion, seems to be worthy of ungrudging approval.

Greenfield's sharpest criticism focuses on my definitions of the formula and formulaic system in the article. (See his pp. 144-146, especially p. 145.) From another point of view Donald K. Fry has recently attacked my definitions in "Old English Formulas and Systems," *ES*, XLVIII (1967), 193-204. I am willing to announce my retreat from the position taken in the article that a formula can be as small as a measure to Fry's position that a formula can be no smaller than a whole verse (p. 203). Yet I must add that even under the new definition only two of the eight verses discussed in the article require special comment: verse 356a, I should now state, can be viewed as composed of the blending of the two formulaic systems *hwearf þa x* [turned then x] and *x hrædlice* [x quickly]. Similarly verse 358a appears to be composed of the blending of the two systems *eode x* [went x] and *x ellenrof* [x famous-for-courage].

NOTES

[1]The evidence for this statement is contained in Appendix A, "Supporting Evidence," of my *Studies in the Techniques of Composition of the Beowulf Poetry* . . ., Harvard University (unpublished doctoral dissertation), 1955, pp. 200-385.

[2]Milman Parry, "Studies in the Epic Technique of Oral Verse-Making. I. Homer and Homeric Style," *Harvard Studies in Classical Philology*, XLI (1930), 85.

[3]Parry uses the term *system* to designate a group of formulas of similar construction (pp. 85-89). For a discussion of certain systems of formulas in Anglo-Saxon poetry, see Francis P. Magoun, Jr., "Oral Formulaic Character of Anglo-Saxon Narrative Poetry," *Speculum*, XXVIII (July, 1953), especially pp. 450-453, and also my "The *andswarode*-System in Old English Poetry," *Speculum*, XXXII (July, 1957), 523-528.

[4]As opposed to that portion of the measure accounted for by a rest or harp-substitution. See John Collins Pope, *The Rhythm of Beowulf* (New Haven, 1942).

[5]See Parry, p. 80.

[6]Quotations from *Beowulf* and other Old English poems are cited in the normalized spelling proposed by Francis P. Magoun, Jr., in "A Brief Plea for a Normalization of Old-English Poetical Texts," *Les Langues Modernes*, XLV (1951), 63-69, and adopted in Magoun's own classroom edition of the poem, *Beowulf and Judith, Done in a Normalized Orthography* . . . (Cambridge, Mass., 1959). [This edition is based primarily upon Charles Leslie Wrenn, *Beowulf with the Finnesburg*

Fragment (London-Boston, 1953).] [Accents (macra) have been deleted—Ed.]

[7]Quite by accident the study of this passage (which, by the way, I chose at random) led me to what seems to be a rather dramatic demonstration of this principle. In my reflections on what the singer *might* have said here it seemed to me that, had he chosen not to mention but rather to allude to Hrothgar in his second verse, he might have substituted for *Hroþgar* a vowel-alliterating noun or phrase such as *se ealdor* [the prince]. In consequence he would probably have substituted for *hrædlice* [quickly] the adverb *ofostlice* [speedily] in the second measure of the first verse. The point is that the singer is likely to have regarded such synonymous and metrically equivalent polysyllables as interchangeable. As a matter of fact the singer of *Beowulf* uses at line 3130 *ofostlic[e]* [speedily] exactly as he uses *hrædlice* [quickly] here, that is, as the second measure of a C-verse which begins the line : *þæt hie ofostlic[e]/ut geferedon/diere maðmas* . . . [that they speedily carried out the precious treasures . . .]. But another singer, the singer of *Genesis*, at one point in his poem appears to have supplied *one* of these two adverbs where he intended the other. In *"Genesis 1316," Modern Language Notes*, LXXIII (May, 1958), 321-325, I discuss this fascinating slip of the singer more fully. Had I not been, in effect, performing the part of the apprentice singer by seeking here for a different polysyllabic adverb from *hrædlice* [quickly], I should not have stumbled so soon across this slip, nor so quickly have grasped what I found in *Genesis* 1316.

[8]Klaeber [Fr. Klaeber, *Beowulf* . . ., Third Ed., Boston, 1950] gives a prominent place to *reim*-formulas (which he more accurately but also more ponderously calls "copulative alliterative phrases") in his list of "formulas, set combinations of words, phrases of transition, and similar stereotyped elements" (p. lxvi). John S. P. Tatlock, in "Lagamon's Poetic Style and Its Relations," in *The Manly Anniversary Studies in Language and Literature*, Chicago, 1923, page 7, calls attention to these formulas in Lawman: "One *chief function* of his *shorter epic formulas* was as expletives to fill in a half-line [a whole verse in Old English poetry] for which he had no matter, that he might not be obliged to introduce a new theme." (My italics.)

[9]See my *Studies in . . . Beowulf* (note 1, above), Chapter VI, especially pp. 90-94, and the chart which accompanies this chapter on pp. 118-120.

[10]A close comparison of my poem with the *Beowulf* singer's seems to me to show a sharp contrast between the ceremonial slowness with which the Anglo-Saxon gets Wulfgar in the D-verse *eode ellen-rof* [he went famous-for-courage] before his lord and the rather discourteous bump

with which in the B-verse *eode hilde-deor* [he went battle-brave] I get him into the royal presence. Nor do I like for describing Hrothgar the jigging rhythm of my *har and hige-frod* [hoary and mind-wise] so well as the singer's *eald and unhar* [old and hoary]. My *eode þa* [he went then] is also a vaguer introduction to the passage than the singer's more precise suggestion of Wulfgar's turning *away* from Beowulf in order to move *towards* Hrothgar in *hwearf þa* [he turned then]. But then this is where I've got by *trying* to be different from a great singer.

The Memory of Cædmon*

Donald K. Fry

Donald K. Fry, Jr., has contributed a long series of insightful essays on the oral-formulaic theory and Old English poetry, including influential analyses of the formula and formulaic system (1967) and of the type-scene and theme (1968). The present article follows out his initial work (1974) on Cædmon's Hymn, *the brief panegyric poem whose oral-formulaic creation was described by the Anglo-Saxon historian Bede in his* History of the English Church and People. *Fry interprets the story of the divinely inspired cowherd Cædmon as a way of explaining how the Germanic tradition of unwritten verse-making was put to a Christian purpose, in the spirit of Pope Gregory's contemporary admonition to his English missionaries to convert pagan temples into Christian churches. Bringing Eric Havelock's work on oral poiesis and F. C. Bartlett's theories of memory to his explication, Fry concludes that the formulaic technique offered a way for Old English lettered poets to spread Christian learning through an imaginative harnessing of the native idiom. In addition to supporting this bold new hypothesis, Fry's essay also exemplifies the current scholarly consensus on orality and Old English poetry: most poems must have been composed in writing, but, as is evident in their use of formulaic diction and thematic narrative structures, they also retained firm roots in oral tradition.*

Reprinted from *Oral Traditional Literature: A Festschrift for Albert Bates Lord*, ed. by John Miles Foley (Columbus, Ohio: Slavica, 1981), pp. 282-293.

I am honored to contribute to a *Festschrift* for Professor Albert Lord, whose scholarship has influenced my thinking for the last fifteen years. This paper builds on the seminal insights of Lord, Milman Parry, and F. P. Magoun, attempting to propose a new model for Old English literary history on a formulaic basis. What do we mean by "formulaic"? I think we mean the typical traditionally expressed. We mean that traditional poets sound like the poets of their past, like their contemporaries, and like their own previous performances. They tell stories familiar to their audiences, organized in narrative and imagistic patterns familiar to their audiences, and expressed in diction familiar to their audiences. Even when they incorporate new stories and concepts requiring new vocabulary, they manipulate the old formal patterns to preserve the impression of traditional and familiar continuity. In short, they constantly play against their audiences' memory of poetry.

We all think we know how memory works: like a computer, of course, storing bits of data and recalling them in original form whenever we need them. In fact, psychologists generally reject that mode, preferring instead a reconstructive theory along lines suggested by F. C. Bartlett in his classic book, *Remembering, A Study in Experimental and Social Psychology.*[1] Bartlett divides memory into perception and recall, proposing that the process of perception itself organizes material to be memorized into general impressions accompanied by a few striking details, both then stored. Such perception patterns vary according to the individual, but with a counter-tendency towards standardized patterns determined by social groups. Memorizing proves quite simple when the memorizer's perception patterns fit the material closely, and difficult when they do not. Bartlett observes (p. 45):

> In certain cases of great structural simplicity, or of structural regularity, or of extreme familiarity, the immediate data are at once fitted to, or matched with, a perceptual pattern which appears to be pre-existent so far as the particular perceptual act is concerned. This pre-formed setting, scheme, or pattern is utilised in a completely unreflecting, unanalytical and unwitting manner. Because it is utilised the immediate perceptual data have meaning, can be dealt with, and are assimilated. In many other cases no such immediate match can be effected. Nevertheless, the subject . . . casts about for analogies with which to subdue the intractability of the perceptual data.

Bartlett also found that these perceptual grids group together through associations drawn from past experience (p. 197):

> A study of the actual facts of perceiving and recognizing suggests strongly that, in all relatively simple cases of determination by past experiences and reaction, the past operates as an organised mass rather than as a group of elements each of which retains its specific character.

In recall, we reconstruct the perceived material by combining the stored general patterns and some details, although we may not recognize the discrepancies between the original and this reconstruction. Bartlett comments (p. 175-176):

> Human remembering is normally exceedingly subject to error. It looks as if what is said to be reproduced is . . . really a construction, serving to justify whatever impression may have been left by the original. It is this "impression," rarely defined with much exactitude, which most readily persists. So long as the details which can be built up around it are such that they would give it a "reasonable" setting, most of us are fairly content, and are apt to think that what we build we have literally retained.

And Bartlett summarizes (p. 213):

> Remembering is not the re-excitation of innumerable fixed, lifeless and fragmentary traces. It is an imaginative reconstruction, built out of the relation of our attitude towards a whole active mass of organized past reactions or experience, and to a little outstanding detail which commonly appears in image or in language form. It is thus hardly ever really exact, even in the most rudimentary cases of rote recapitulation.[2]

The mind, according to Bartlett, consists of interconnected patterns of organization which control perception and recall. We might express his theory in a visual metaphor: the mind organizes itself in certain associated shapes. Perception is a screen pierced by holes shaped like the mind's forms, a screen we hold up to outside material. Data which fit enter easily through a hole; data which do not fit must be altered to the shape of an opening. In recall, we reconstruct the original material by means of these shapes. Put another way, we could say that perception compresses material into abstract patterns containing selected details; in recall, we supplement those selected details with reconstructed details sufficient to re-inflate the abstraction back into the full-blown shapes of external experience. If you are skeptical about this model, try a little experiment. Recall something you see every day: your own face. Got the picture? Did you forget the ears? Put them in. Are all the bumps and moles in place? Put them in. Did you remember to color the eyes? You see, Bartlett is right. We recall generalities and congratulate ourselves on our precise memory, and we can reconstruct the details if we want to. But the key word is "reconstruct."

Bartlett's model sounds familiar, for it parallels current notions of formulaic poetry. The stereotyped phrases we call formulas cluster into families, whose abstract structures we label "systems." These substitution systems are analogous to the grids of perception, abstract shells filled out with other words. At the narrative level, type-scenes function as the abstract patterns with plot details fleshing them out. Stories and themes tend toward the typical, toward general patterns of behavior modified for specific applications. These traditional organizations of formulaic material fit Bartlett's standards for easy memorizing: "great structural simplicity, . . . structural regularity, . . . extreme familiarity" (p. 45), allowing a simplified perception stage. The mind does not have to abstract perceived formulaic material because such material is already organized into familiar abstract patterns. To return to my visual metaphor, the formulaic phrases are already shaped like the holes in the perceptual grid.[3] Furthermore, just as material stored in the memory has an internal structure of associations, so do the formulaic wordhoard and scenehoard and storyhoard structure themselves around ties of association. Certain formulas and systems cluster thematically with others, certain ideas and images cohere, certain scenes tend to include certain details, etc. Material formulaically organized is easily memorized and easily recalled for members of a traditionally oriented culture. Hence traditional poets can recall millions of formulaic phrases and thousands of systems and hundreds of scenes and stories. And so can their audiences.

We profess astonishment at such memory feats, but in fact powerful memories characterize non-literate societies, indeed usually function as the primary device for education of the young and for ethical reinforcement in adults. Early Greek civilization proves a case in point.

The best evidence points toward the introduction of the Greek alphabet about 700 B.C.; Homer, who lived about this time or a generation earlier perhaps, probably composed his epic poems without the aid of writing, by formulaic means. Marcel Jousse characterizes Homeric man as a "mnemotechnician,"[4] whose practical and intellectual life turned on memorized cultural values, defined and reinforced by oral poetry. James Notopoulos puts it this way:

> The oral poet as a mnemotechnician preserved the useful by binding it in verse, by forging a metrical pattern which facilitated and guarded against mistakes in the information to be preserved. Memory therefore is equally important in conserving the useful as well as perpetuating the immortal in oral literature; the poet is the incarnate book of oral peoples.[5]

In a daring hypothetical reconstruction of early Greek culture, Eric Havelock differentiates the social function of oral verse from modern notions of art:

> Greek society before 700 B.C. was non-literate. In all such societies experience is stored in the individual memories of the members of the society and the remembered experience constitutes a verbal culture. The verbal forms utilized for this purpose have to be rhythmic to ensure accurate repetition, and the verbal syntax has to be such that statements, reports, and prescriptions are cast in the forms of events or acts. The Homeric poems, and to an equal degree the Hesiodic, exhibit these symptoms. They constitute not literature in the modern sense, but orally stored experience, the content of which incorporates the traditions of a culture group and the syntax of which obeys the mnemonic laws by which this kind of tradition is orally preserved and transmitted.[6]

The introduction of writing about 700 B.C. brought about changes, but probably not so drastic as we might expect. Writing remained a difficult art to master, a craft skill for the few, with widespread popular reading far in the future.[7] In fact, this transition period probably lasted until Socrates's lifetime (died 399 B.C.). Havelock believes that the first Greek texts written down were *The Iliad* and *The Odyssey*, as one of the measures taken by a non-literate culture to preserve its corporate tradition in an enclave of language existing apart from the vernacular, metrically contrived to preserve an extensive statement in the memories of the members of the culture. To transcribe this enclave became the first business to which the alphabet was put. And so we reach in the first instance the poems that pass under the name of Homer.[8]

The transition period involved authors such as Pindar, Hesiod, and even the Athenian dramatists, writing for essentially nonliterate audiences. Again, Havelock proposes:

For a long time after the resources of transcription became available, they would be used still to transcribe what had previously been orally composed, . . . the transcription would be made in the first instance for the benefit of the composers themselves rather than their public, and . . . the products of the Greek poets who followed Homer would be devised for memorization by listening audiences, not for readership by literates. ("Prologue," p. 362)

Conservative tendencies would prevail, both in style and in the social functions of poetry; as Havelock puts it,

Composers of the contrived word originally . . . allowed their compositions to be taken down by a listener. Later they took to writing them down themselves at dates which cannot easily be settled. But whichever they did, their initial proclivity would be to use the script now available only to record what was already previously composed according to real principles. That is, the oral habit would persist and would remain effective to a varying degree, even in the case of composers whom we would style writers. This habit, after all, had not been personally chosen by themselves; it was a conditioned response to the needs of an audience who still demanded of the compositions offered that they be memorisable. ("Prologue," p. 388)

Although these literate poets took advantage of the new writing techniques to modify their own compositional methods, they still lacked any significant reading public. So the authors probably produced only one copy of their works or at most just a few; families and authorities stored such copies in archives, even sometimes engraved the poems on temple walls.[9] Transmission and diffusion of the texts depended almost completely on memory and public recitation.

The Greeks memorized the early poets as a part of their education, and Homer emerged as "the Hellenic educational manual *par excellence*" (*Preface*, p. 28). Tutors recited Homer for their pupils to memorize. Poetry held a position, says Havelock,

> central in the educational theory . . . a position held apparently not on the grounds that we would offer, namely poetry's inspirational and imaginative effects, but on the ground that it provided a massive repository of useful knowledge, a sort of encyclopedia of ethics, politics, history and technology which the effective citizen was required to learn as the core of his educational equipment. Poetry represented not something we call by that name, but an indoctrination which today would be comprised in a shelf of text books and works of reference. (*Preface*, p. 27)

Memory and performance dominated education, both public and private:

> A purely poetic *paideia*, to be effectively transmitted, requires only regular occasions for performance, whether professional or amateur. The youth would be required to repeat and to match their memories against each other and against their leaders. Everything that was to be absorbed and remembered was communicated to them as the deeds and thoughts of their great ancestors. (*Preface*, p. 124)

In summary, after 700 B. C., Homer's poems were written down and memorized for educational purposes, and later writers composed in a form suitable for recitation and memorization. Thus oral poetry continued to exert its influence as a device for preserving cultural values throughout the semi-literate era of Greek history.

The Anglo-Saxons remained semi-literate, or more accurately nonliterate, both in English and in Latin, throughout their history, at all levels of society. For example, V. H. Galbraith counts exactly four literate Old English kings (Sigbert, Aldfrith, Alfred, and perhaps Ceolwulf);[10] Cædmon, although he became a monk, never seems to have learned to read or write. Even after Christian missionaries introduced writing in England in 597, no popular reading audience ever developed. Yet the Church faced the difficult twin problems of attaining and strengthening converts. I propose here that, after about 680, the English church used written poetry as an educational device, transmitted largely in memorized form.[11] And Cædmon and his memory began the whole process.

Cædmon extemporizes exactly once, creating the original hymn in his dream; after that moment, he becomes exclusively a memorial poet. In his *Ecclesiastical History*, IV, p. 24, Bede tells us:

> When [Cædmon] awoke, he remembered [*memoriter retenuit*] all that he had sung while asleep and soon added more verses in the same manner, praising God in fitting style.[12]

He recites these verses from memory the next morning to Abbess Hild and "a number of the more learned men." They read him "a passage of sacred history or doctrine, bidding him make a song out of it, if he could, in metrical form. He undertook the task and went away; on returning the next morning he repeated the passage he had been given, which he had put into excellent verse."[13] Cædmon memorized what the scholars read to him and also memorized his own resultant poem in order to recite it the following day. Later, Bede describes the poet's procedure explicitly:

> He learned all he could by listening to them and then, memorizing [*rememorando*] it and ruminating over it, like some clean animal chewing the cud, he turned it into the most melodious verse: and it sounded so sweet as he recited it that his teachers became in turn his audience. (Colgrave and Mynors, p. 419)

The Old English translator expands that last clause:

> and his song and his leoð wæron swa wynsume to gehyranne, þætte seolfan his lareowas æt his muðe wreoton and leornodon.
> [and his song and his music were so delightful to hear, that even his teachers wrote down the words from his lips and learnt them. (Miller, pp. 346-347)]

The scholars did not memorize the poems and then write them down. Rather they wrote them down from Cædmon's memory in order to memorize them for themselves. Abbess Hild, I believe, recognized immediately that Cædmon's invention of Christian vernacular verse had broad applications as an educational device. In Bede's narrative, before our very eyes, we see her turn Cædmon, as it were, into a teaching machine. The scholars feed Cædmon sacred narrative and/or doctrine, and he manufactures palatable verse, which they record and memorize. Bede tells us two subsequent effects of Cædmon's invention:

> By his songs the minds of many were often inspired to despise the world and to long for the heavenly life. It is true that after him other Englishmen attempted to compose [*facere*] religious poems, but none could compare with him. (Colgrave and Mynors, p. 415)

Cædmon's songs brought about conversions and started others writing such verse, including Bede himself. Elsewhere I have suggested that later Anglo-Saxon poets, whether they composed in writing or orally, used the forms of the inherited oral poetry, simply because no other poetic existed for them.[14] Now I wish to propose another reason for such conservative loyalty to tradition: Old English poets used formulaic techniques because, as I argued in the first section of this paper, formulaic poetry is easy to memorize. The pre-formed units (formula, type-scene, known story), already organized for easy memorization by poets, also aid the memory of the audience. I suggest that, as in early Greece, memorized poetry formed a large part of the education of an essentially nonliterate populace. Such poetry easily moved about, penetrating all classes of society, lay and clerical, spreading by word of mouth to remote areas. It promoted proper behavior, conveyed the basic Christian message for conversion, and strengthened the faith of new converts and old, all in entertaining, familiar form, requiring no elaborate training in Latin or theology. Such poetry also had the latitude to absorb new subject matter while making it sound like old familiar poetry; thus Christ becomes a warrior with a *comitatus* of apostles,[15] Adam talks like a thane, etc. So churchmen could inject doctrine into narrative, raising the theological sophistication not only of the laymen, but also of clerics, whose average formal learning never reached very high. Indeed, the Anglo-Saxon poetry we possess ranges from the simple paraphrase of the *Lord's Prayer* to the rich density of *Christ I*, from the flat piety of *Juliana* to the whirling allegories of *Phoenix*, from the astonishing Patristic virtuosity of *Exodus* to the inexpressible genius of *Beowulf*, a mirror for princes and Christians alike.

Much evidence exists for this memorial transmission and its educative function, but I shall confine myself here to a brief discussion of King Alfred. His contemporary biographer Asser tells us:

> Alas, by the unworthy carelessness of his parents and tutors, he remained ignorant of letters until his twelfth year, or even longer. But he listened attentively to Saxon poems day and night, and hearing them often recited by others committed them to his retentive memory. . . .
>
> When, therefore, his mother one day was showing him and his brothers a certain book of Saxon poetry which she held in her hand, she said: "I will give this book to whichever of you can learn it most quickly." And moved by these words, or rather by divine inspiration, and attracted by the beauty of the initial letter of the book, Alfred said in reply to his mother, forestalling his brothers, his elders in years though not in grace: "Will you really give this book to one of us, to the one who can soonest understand and repeat it to you?" And, smiling and rejoicing, she confirmed it, saying: "To him will I give it." Then taking the book from her hand he immediately went to his master, who read it. And when it was read, he went back to his mother and repeated it.[16]

Illiterate Alfred memorizes vernacular poems "recited by others" constantly. Alfred must have the book read to him by a tutor in order to memorize it. Since he did not learn to read until about the age of forty, he continued learning by memorizing vernacular books. Asser continues:

> Meanwhile the king, in the midst of wars and frequent hindrances of this present life, and also of the raids of the pagans and his daily infirmities of body, did not cease . . . to recite Saxon books, and especially to learn by heart Saxon poems, and command others to do so. (Asser, Chapter 76, p. 267)

Alfred took the church's educational technique, used it for his own continuing education, and later applied it to secular education as well.

In summary, the formulaic techniques explored by Parry, Lord, and Magoun allow us to account for the phenomena of the surviving Old English poetic material. Anglo-Saxon Christian poets, inspired by

Cædmon, wrote in the inherited formulaic style, whose familiarity and formal properties made the poems easy to memorize. Christian learning spread through an illiterate population by means of memory and recitation, all radiating from an author's original manuscript. The Vikings and Henry the Eighth no longer need to shoulder all the blame for our present scarcity of surviving Anglo-Saxon poetic manuscripts. There simply were not very many in the first place. Indeed, the manuscript of a traditional society, of the nonliterate Anglo-Saxons, was memory.

NOTES

*This paper serves as a prospectus for a book in progress, entitled *Cædmon's Memory*. My argument responds to the seminal work of Jeff Opland, published and unpublished, and I wish to express my appreciation here for his impressive scholarship. I also wish to thank John Foley, Bruce Rosenberg, Walter Scheps, and Leo Treitler for their helpful comments on this essay.

[1](Cambridge, 1932).

[2]He admits the presence of rote recall as well (pp. 203, 264).

[3]For similar imagery, see, for example, John Miles Foley, "Formula and Theme in Old English Poetry," in *Oral Literature and the Formula*, ed. by Benjamin A. Stolz and Richard S. Shannon (Ann Arbor, 1976), pp. 207-232; and Michael Nagler, *Spontaneity and Tradition: A Study in the Oral Art of Homer* (Berkeley, 1974).

[4]*Le Style oral rhythmique et mnémotechnique chez les Verbo-moteurs* (Paris, 1925).

[5]"Mnemosyne in Oral Literature," *Transactions of the American Philological Association*, 69 (1938), 469.

[6]"Pre-literacy and the Pre-Socratics," *University of London Classical Studies Bulletin*, 13 (1966), 50.

[7]*Preface to Plato* (rpt. New York, 1967), p. ix, hereafter cited as *Preface*.

[8]"Prologue to Greek Literacy," in *University of Cincinnati Classical Studies*, II (Norman, 1973), p. 361, hereafter cited as "Prologue."

[9]J. A. Davison, "Literature and Literacy in Ancient Greece," Chapter 4 of his *From Archilochus to Pindar* (New York, 1968), pp. 86-128.

[10]Galbraith, "The Literacy of the Medieval English Kings," in L. S. Sutherland, ed., *Studies in History* (London, 1966), pp. 78-111; Rosalind Hill, "Bede and the Boors," in G. Bonner, ed., *Famulus Christi* (London,

1976), pp. 93-105; C. P. Wormald, "The Uses of Literacy in Anglo-Saxon England and Its Neighbours," *Transactions of the Royal Historical Society*, 5th series, 27 (1977), 95-114.

[11]Alan Jabbour, "Memorial Transmission in Old English Poetry," *Chaucer Review*, 3 (1969), 174-190.

[12]All references to Bede's Latin version cite *Bede's Ecclesiastical History of the English People*, ed. and trans. by B. Colgrave and R. A. B. Mynors (Oxford, 1969). For the ninth-century Alfredian translation, I cite T. Miller, ed. and trans., *The Old English Version of Bede's Ecclesiastical History of the English People*, EETS 95-96 (London, rpt. 1959). This quotation appears on p. 417.

[13]Colgrave and Mynors, p. 419. Cp. "sacrae historiae *sive* doctrinae sermonem" with "sum halig spell *and* godcundre lare word" ("a holy narrative *and* some word of divine doctrine," my italics; Miller, pp. 344-345). The Old English translator substitutes "and" for "or," suggesting that Cædmon melded history and doctrine; see my "Cædmon as a Formulaic Poet," in *Oral Literature: Seven Essays*, ed. by Joseph J. Duggan (New York, 1975), p. 43.

[14]See my "Cædmon as a Formulaic Poet" and "Themes and Type-Scenes in *Elene* 1-113," *Speculum*, 44 (1969), 35-44.

[15]See C. J. Wolf, "Christ as Hero in *The Dream of the Rood*," *Neuphilologische Mitteilungen*, 71 (1970), 202-210.

[16]*Asser's Life of King Alfred*, trans. by Dorothy Whitelock, in her *English Historical Documents c. 500-1042* (New York, 1955), p. 266; quoted from W. H. Stevenson, ed., *Asser's Life of King Alfred* (Oxford, 1904), Chapters 22-23.

Formulaic Language and Mode of Creation [excerpted]

Joseph J. Duggan

In this selection from "Formulaic Language and Mode of Creation," the second chapter of his The Song of Roland: Formulaic Style and Poetic Craft *(1973), Joseph J. Duggan argues from quantitative evidence that the Oxford manuscript of the Old French epic poem is the product of an oral tradition. His position derives from the application of oral-formulaic theory and goes a step beyond the opinion of Jean Rychner, who in his 1955 study of the* chanson de geste *made the case for an oral genre but reserved literary status for its centerpiece, the* Song of Roland. *Operating on the assumption of a necessary link between formulaic density and oral provenance and basing his calculations on a computer-assisted analysis of thirteen* chansons de geste, *Duggan reaches a figure of 20 percent straight repetition as a threshold for orality. Since the* Roland *proves to be 15 percent over that minimum, in his eyes it qualifies unambiguously as an oral work. Duggan's contributions, including also his concordance to the* Roland *(1969), his collection* Oral Literature *(1974), his study of the* Poema de Mio Cid *(1989), and numerous essays on medieval French and Spanish poetry, have been of*

Reprinted from *The Song of Roland: Formulaic Style and Poetic Craft* (University of California Press, 1973), pp. 16-62.

*considerable influence both in his home fields and in other areas touched
by oral-formulaic theory.*

The three alternative modes of creation with which the critical
tradition presents us for the archetype of the Oxford manuscript are:
individual creation by a literate poet; fusion of a preexisting oral poem
into a composite creation; or direct oral dictation of the first written
version behind Oxford, which would then have been transmitted with
only slight scribal variations.

A starting point for discussion of these three possibilities is the
proposition that formulaic language and oral composition are
inseparably linked. This statement is meant not as an *a priori* postulate,
but rather as a conclusion based upon quantitative evidence. Before
describing the sequence of deductions from which it is drawn, however,
I would like to review previous comparisons made between long
narrative poems in regard to their relative repetitiousness.

Several scholars have attempted to determine the formulaic density
of whole poetic works, both oral and written, in differing national
traditions, through the method, initiated by Milman Parry, of choosing
short samples of the poems in question and underlining those phrases
verifiable as semantic and syntactic formulas on the basis of the whole
poetic material.[1] Since I am dealing mainly with semantic formulas in
this study, I will consider here the information available for this type of
formula and leave aside for the moment the question of syntactic
formulas, termed by Lord "formulaic expressions."

There has been general agreement that any group of words bounded
on either side by a natural pause or caesura and repeated in substantially
the same form (allowing for inversions, paradigmatic variations and a
few other admissible modifications) should be counted as a formula.[2]
Parry found that 50 and 54 percent of the first 25 lines of the *Iliad* and
the *Odyssey*, respectively, were made up of formulas.[3] To find
repetitions, he searched all 27,000 lines of the Homeric corpus as a
referent for each sample. Lord applied an analogous test to 15 lines of
the *Song of Bagdad*, recorded from the performance of Salih Ugljanin of
Novi Pazar, Yugoslavia, on the phonograph records of the Milman
Parry Collection of South Slavic Texts at Harvard University, and
uncovered formulas in 65 percent of the sample.[4] For verification he
used 11 different songs by the same performer, totaling 12,000 lines.
On the basis of the entire Anglo-Saxon Poetic Records, Francis P.
Magoun, Jr., found the first 25 lines of *Beowulf* to be 61 percent

formulas,[5] and with the same referent 20 lines of the *Meters of Boethius* and 153 lines of the *Metrical Psalms* were estimated to be 50 and 60 percent formulaic, respectively, by Larry D. Benson and Robert E. Diamond.

The evidence in other studies has been based only on the poem under consideration rather than on an entire corpus or on several pieces, but unfortunately this method has been followed only for works which were considered, on external evidence, *not* to belong to the oral tradition: the Middle English *Havelok the Dane* and *Sir Gawain and the Green Knight*, the Old English *Daniel*, the verse part of Andrija Kačić-Miošić's history of the South Slavs (*Razgovor ugodni naroda slovinskoga*, 1759), and Matija Antun Reljković's satirical poem *Satir*. *Havelok*'s two samples were 18 and 30 percent formulas, *Daniel*'s 22 line sample 19 percent, while in *Sir Gawain* only one formula appeared in 18 lines. Thirty lines of the Slavic historical work were 27 percent formulas, and nine verses of *Satir* yielded none.[6]

Two serious difficulties arise from the survey of previous quantitative formula analyses. The first derives from the length of the material upon which one bases the evidence for the sample. Obviously the more lines one searches for identical phrases, the more formulas one is likely to uncover in the sample: the difference in formula densities based upon evidence from 27,000 lines and 12,000 lines is substantial. The results have little meaning, then, *on a comparative basis*, unless one adjusts the larger figure by counting only those formulas discovered in the first 12,000 of the 27,000 lines. The purpose of the research we are considering here was to draw inferences about specific works on the basis of analogies with poems in various languages. There are three absolute figures involved in the proportions upon which the analogies are based: the length of the sample, the number of formulas in the sample, and the number of lines in the referent which was searched to find evidence for these formulas. That the third figure is not included in the actual calculation of percentage does not lessen its significance. If samples are to be dependable, then the number of lines upon which the evidence for formulas is based must be identical in each case. Otherwise inferences drawn from the relative densities of the samples have no meaning.

My second, more fundamental, objection is to the size and choice of samples. The shorter the random sample, the less chance that it will reflect the characteristics of the entire text under consideration, and random samples taken from one place in the poem and counted in two-digit amounts are hopelessly inadequate. Public opinion polls use samples and are more often than not astonishingly accurate, but this is precisely because only samples which are microcosms of the whole are chosen, so that they faithfully reflect its qualitative make-up. Random samples—and the beginning of a poem, chosen because it happens to come first and not on account of its subject matter, is a random sample—cannot be relied upon to the same degree unless the sampling is conducted upon statistically valid principles. In the research conducted on formula density to date, the samples have been random, concentrated, and small. Corroboration for their unreliability is not difficult to find. In the *Singer of Tales*, Albert B. Lord picked a sample of the first 10 lines of the *Roland*'s laisse 105, and found 12 formulas, or 60 percent of the hemistichs sampled.[7] He could just as easily have chosen the 27 verses of laisses 34 and 35, an even longer sample, in which case the percentage would have dropped to 15, or the 23 verses of laisses 99 to 101, where the result would have been 76 percent, five times higher. Lord at no time claimed that the *Roland* as a whole was 60 percent formulas; he prudently argued that the presence of a passage 60 percent formulaic is a strong indication that the whole contains many formulas. Nevertheless, it is desirable that whatever method is employed be capable of revealing the quantity of formulas in the poem, and Parry's, Lord's, and Magoun's figures have been interpreted by others as statements of formulaic density for the poems in question. For a random sample to be a realistic segment of the whole, it should be much longer than those previously employed, as the figures given below for hundred-line sections of the *Roland* demonstrate.[8] In the case of *Roland* only the results for four-hundred-line segments approach within five percentage points of the figure for the whole poem. Presumably this is also true for poems in other national traditions. If, on the other hand, one elects the alternative of a smaller sample carefully chosen on the basis of its subject matter and attempts to select a typical passage, a microcosm of the whole, the problem is no less thorny. Only 92 of *Roland*'s 290 laisses fall within the range of accuracy of the four-hundred-line segments.[9] Certainly the motif which, from the standpoint of subject matter, is most typical of the epic, the single combat, is on the average more formulaic than the entire poem. But if one then resigns oneself to taking a four-hundred-verse sample, the methodological difficulty changes but by no means disappears. It is, in fact, compounded beyond measure on the level of verification, since a single man cannot practically search for repetitions of four hundred separate lines (for the Old French epics this would mean 800 potential formulas) without mecanographic help. If electronic data processing equipment is employed, it is no more difficult to give up sampling altogether and determine the real percentage of verifiable formulas for the whole work. I have learned from frustrating experience that the computer-aided method is indeed the only practical and accurate way of accomplishing this task. When it is applied, the first difficulty discussed above, that of the varying number of lines searched in order to detect formulas, is also circumvented, for with this method the size of the population and the size of the referent are identical, both being equal to the entire poem. Statistics collected on this basis can be compared without adjustment, because the relationship between the referent and the population is always constant.

The results of sampling are summed up in Table 1:

TABLE 1

Poem	Length of Sample(s)	Referent	Length of Referent	Percentage of Formulas
Satir	8 lines		2203 lines	0
Sir Gawain	18 lines	entire poem	2530 lines	negligible
Havelok	?	entire poem	3001 lines	18, 30
Daniel	22 lines	entire poem	4019 lines	19
History of Slavs	30 lines	verse sections of part two	3208 lines	27
Metrical Psalms	153 lines	Anglo-Saxon Poetic Records	30,000 lines	50
Iliad	25 lines	Homeric corpus	27,000 lines	50
Odyssey	25 lines	Homeric corpus	27,000 lines	54
Meters of Boethius[10]	20 lines	Anglo-Saxon Poetic Records	30,000 lines	60

Roland	10 lines	entire poem	4002 lines	60
Beowulf	25 lines	Anglo-Saxon Poetic Records	30,000 lines	61
Song of Bagdad	15 lines	songs of the same singer	12,000 lines	65

In all these cases the actual formulaic density is unknown, although one is at liberty to assume that a poem whose random sample yields more than 50 percent formulas is more likely to be a product of the oral tradition than one for which the sample is 27 percent formulaic or less. Nonetheless the degree of probability for such an assumption is slight.

The computer-aided method of determining the formulaic content of an entire poem on the basis of repetitions within the poem itself has produced more consistent results. In addition to the *Couronnement de Louis*, to which I have devoted a previous study,[11] and *Roland*, I applied it to *Gormont et Isembart*, the *Chanson de Guillaume*, the *Charroi de Nîmes*, the *Prise d'Orange*, *Raoul de Cambrai*, the *Pèlerinage de Charlemagne à Jérusalem et à Constantinople*, the *Moniage Guillaume* (longer version, sometimes called *Moniage II*), the first 2700 verses of the *Siège de Barbastre*, *Buevon de Conmarchis*,[12] the first 2695 verses of the *Roman d'Enéas*,[13] and the decasyllabic *Roman d'Alexandre* from the Venice manuscript.[14] Most of these poems employ a ten-syllable line, the exceptions being *Gormont et Isembart* and *Enéas*, both octosyllabic, and the dodecasyllabic *Pèlerinage*, *Siège* and *Buevon*. The figures for the 13 poems are in Table 2:

TABLE 2

Poem	Hemistichs	Repeated Hemistichs	Percentage of Repeated Hemistichs	Approximate Date[15]	Versification
Buevon	7762	1187	15	1269-1285	dodecasyllabic
Enéas	5390	953	16	1150-1160	octosyllabic
Alexandre	1614	277	17	1150	decasyllabic
Pèlerinage	1740	402	23	1100	dodecasyllabic

Siège	5314	1221	23	1180	dodecasyllabic
Moniage	13258	3308	24	1180	decasyllabic
Gormont	1318	380	29	1068-1104	octosyllabic
Charroi	2972	851	29	1135-1165	decasyllabic
Guillaume	7108	2172	31	1075-1125	decasyllabic
Raoul	11110	3630	33	1190	decasyllabic
Couronne-ment	5390	2021	37	1131-1150	decasyllabic
Prise	3774	1464	39	1150-1165	decasyllabic

Only those hemistichs repeated within a given poem in substantially the same form have been counted as formulas. If all the hemistichs of all twelve poems were to be compared to each other (66,750 possible formulas), more formulas would be detected, but this is a task which, because of the expense it would entail and the difficulty of correlating the disparate orthographies and dialectal traits of the texts,[16] I am not prepared to undertake. It would, in addition, be a more artificial approach to the problem of formulaic language, since one would be considering resemblances between minute segments of texts composed as much as two centuries apart in widely separated geographical areas.[17] By confining the examination of each poem's formulas to those which can be distinguished through a scrutiny of the poem itself, we are at least assured of working with phrases which possessed an identity as formulas in the mind of the poet who uttered them. The possible objection that the material is incomplete, since it does not include formulas which occur only once in a given work but would be recognizable as formulas if other *chansons* were searched for them, is, in a sense, valid, but completeness is unattainable without a living oral tradition to provide the context within which the poet's formula-generating abilities develop and within which they can be judged as a totality. Students of medieval French literature consider themselves fortunate if they can date a text within ten or twenty years of its actual time of composition. It is asking too much, in all but a few cases, to attempt to find poems which we can be sure were sung in temporal and geographical proximity to those now extant in manuscript. The overriding consideration in a comparative study such as this is that the same criteria be applied rigorously to each poem. As long as this requirement is adhered to, analogies are valid. The formulas which are undistinguishable are undistinguishable in all the poems without discrepancy, and on this basis the data may be validly compared.

What conclusions can be drawn from them? There is no correlation between the percentage of formulas and either the dates or the lengths of poems. Thus it would be gratuitous to assume without further evidence that a gradual watering-down of the traditional style of *chansons de geste* took place through the course of the twelfth century. The most formulaic poem, *La Prise d'Orange*, is customarily dated around the middle of the century, while the early *Pèlerinage de Charlemagne* is near the lower limit of *chansons de geste*.[18] Neither does the type of versification appear to be significant, since the octosyllabic *Gormont et Isembart* is near the middle of the grouping, far from *Enéas*; the alexandrine *Siège de Barbastre* and *Pèlerinage de Charlemagne* both rank higher than *Alexandre* and *Enéas*, which separate them from *Buevon de Conmarchis*, also in alexandrines.

Only one consistent explanation for the rankings is plausible: there is a marked distinction between the *chansons de geste* and the *romans courtois Enéas* and *Alexandre*. *Buevon de Conmarchis*, which contains a lower proportion of repeated hemistichs than any other poem treated, would seem to invalidate this distinction. But *Buevon*, authored by the unquestionably literate Adenet le Roi, who is known to have written the courtly romance *Cléomades*, is as much a product of the written art as *Enéas* or *Alexandre*, since it is the creation of a learned author and reflects courtly conventions in many of its aspects.[19] *Buevon*, *Enéas* and *Alexandre*, taken together, have an average 16 percent density of repeated hemistichs, while the mean percentage for the nine *chansons de geste* is 29.8.

The three romances present a strikingly uniform profile. It has always been recognized that writers repeat themselves, and the cliché or *cheville* or filler has never been accorded more than universal disapproval in the annals of literary criticism. Although the repetitions are not here under qualitative judgment but rather under quantitative estimation, the two aspects are relevant to each other. A filler (functional aspect) is cliché (valuational aspect) because of its statistical characteristics, since frequent occurrence diminishes its value in the reader's eye. There is a continuum along which clichés can be ranged:

the less rare the occurrence, the less the semantic weight and literary value. The data for repeated hemistichs in the romances suggest, however, that in the overall view the proportion of repetitions in written poetry is relatively constant. Since only eleventh, twelfth and thirteenth-century texts are in question, this conclusion should be regarded as tentative until it has been tested against factual analyses of works composed in other periods and other languages, and by writers of differing stature as well.

The *chansons de geste*, on the other hand, differ widely in proportion of formulas. Another technique is evident behind this phenomenon, a technique in which recourse to formulas is permissible and even desirable. The scribes who took down the cyclical manuscripts in which so many works of the *geste de Guillaume* have survived— among them the *Siège de Barbastre*, the *Moniage Guillaume*, the *Charroi de Nîmes*, the *Couronnement de Louis*, the *Prise d'Orange*— presumably imposed a selectivity of their own. At the very least we cannot assume that they chose the worst versions of these poems for the *manuscrits de luxe* destined to be read to noble patrons. And yet the *Couronnement de Louis* and the *Prise d' Orange* are the most repetitious of our eleventh, twelfth, and thirteenth-century narratives. The terms cliché and stereotype, with their pejorative connotations, are applied with no regard to medieval taste when they are used to describe the formulaic style of these poems in which such a wide latitude of repetition was accepted.

The poems analysed here were not picked at random. Their choice reflected a desire to test the hypothesis whose formulation has colored Old French epic criticism for the last fifteen years: the conclusions to Jean Rychner's *La Chanson de geste: essai sur l'art épique des jongleurs*.[20] It may be put as follows: the early *chanson de geste* is the manuscript reflection of a genre which lived and flourished in the state of improvised performance before an audience; evidence for this oral existence is found in the highly stylized narrative on all its levels, but most of all on that of the standard scene (motif) and the standard phrase (formula), the very means through which improvisational performance was made possible. To check the hypothesis on the basic, formulaic, level, I chose to scrutinize the formula content of the nine *chansons de geste* which Professor Rychner had analysed in his book,[21] and I added the *Siège de Barbastre* so as to be able to compare differing realizations of the same narrative material, that poem being a close relative to the source of Adenet le Roi's *Buevon de Conmarchis*. As a test I applied the same criteria to the *Roman d'Alexandre*, an early romance in a versification with the same syllable count as that of the *chansons de geste*; the *Roman d'Enéas*, a typical octosyllabic romance; and *Buevon de Conmarchis*, a fairly late reworking of an epic legend, as representatives of a genre which, if Professor Rychner's hypothesis turned out to be true, would not be expected to have been composed through the medium of formulas. If they had encompassed as many repetitions as the *chansons de geste*, or even approached the same degree of repetitiveness, his theory would have been gravely weakened. Any repeated half-verse in the romances, allowing as always for paradigmatic variations, inversions, lexical changes involving function words, and, in these poems, rhyme, was considered to be analogous to the epic formula and counted in the tally.

The results tend to confirm the hypothesis. They indicate a quantitative difference of 16 percent against 29.8 percent between the number of repetitions in the works known to have been composed in writing and those deemed by Rychner to have been improvised orally and only later committed to writing. This fundamental difference is basic to any understanding of the nature of formulaic language. It is perceived not primarily through the comparison of one work to another, but above all through the analysis of works representative enough to stand, collectively, for the two genres. Henceforth these quantitative differences and all they imply should be taken into account in any definition of the *chanson de geste* in contradistinction to the romance.

Albert B. Lord has given his estimate of the threshold of formula density between oral and written works: "So far, I believe, we can conclude that a pattern of 50 or 60 percent formula or formulaic, with 10 to perhaps 25 percent straight formula, indicates clearly literary or written composition."[22] My quantitative examination of Old French narrative verse does not include figures for what Lord terms "formulaic expression" and what I call "syntactic formulas," some examples of which will be treated in Chapter 5. But that part of Lord's statement which is directly relevant here, namely, his estimate of "straight formula" density, closely parallels my own, in spite of the varying criteria by which his base statistics were collected. I would be more specific about the threshold and say that, in general, if an Old French narrative poem is less than 20 percent straight repetition, it probably derives from literary, or written, creation. When the formula density exceeds 20 percent, it is strong evidence of oral composition, and the probability rises as the figure increases over 20 percent. Conversely, as the formula density approaches the threshold of 20 percent, other factors, such as the presence of unrefined popular legends, formulas of oral narration, statements that the work is being sung, and so on, should be accorded more and more weight in the decision about the orality of the work in question. These general remarks apply to tests of individual poems. But taken as a whole, the set of figures reveals a distinction on the level of diction, between the two medieval modes of narration, *chanson de geste* and romance, long recognized as discrete in the tradition of scholarship and criticism. They differ not just in subject matter, versification, psychological content and thematic aspects, but in the most fundamental characteristic of all, the art of combining words. The 23 and 24 percent densities for the *Pèlerinage de Charlemagne*, the *Siège de Barbastre* and the *Moniage Guillaume* must be viewed with this in mind. One might not find 23 or 24 percent a convincing figure in itself, but it gathers credulity when one recalls that all the works traditionally called *chansons de geste* fall on one side of the threshold while those known as *romans* fall on the other. This combination of considerations convinces me personally of the oral nature of these three poems, which do not differ significantly from the more obviously formulaic *chansons de geste* in their qualitative aspects either. I invite comments on this interpretation, however, for I recognize that it is a delicate question, not to be settled lightly. Certainly for *Gourmont et Isembart*, the *Charroi de Nîmes*, the *Chanson de Guillaume*, *Raoul de Cambrai*, the *Couronnement de Louis* and the *Prise d'Orange*, the case is clear. These six, and, I believe, the three less formulaic *chansons de geste*, provide convincing evidence that formulaic style and oral composition are inseparably linked.

The mourning over the demise of the theory of oral composition which greeted publication of Larry D. Benson's 1966 article, "The Literary Character of Anglo-Saxon Formulaic Poetry,"[23] was, then, to say the least, premature. Lionel J. Friedman claimed that Benson's work "disprov[ed] the second half of the Parry-Lord axiom that 'oral poetry is composed entirely of formulas . . . while lettered poetry is never formulaic'" since "if formulaic diction characterizes both kinds of poetry, it is no touchstone."[24] Morton W. Bloomfield more cautiously called for a reexamination of the theory, remarking that the optimism of those convinced that it is being accepted more and more widely as it applies to Old English poetry "perhaps . . . reflects the climate of four years ago" [1965].[25] But Benson's evaluation, circumspect in other respects, is unfortunately based upon a formulaic analysis which does not hold up under scrutiny.

A large portion of his evidence comes from two studies by Robert E. Diamond, "The Diction of the Signed Poems of Cynewulf,"[26] and *The Diction of the Anglo-Saxon Metrical Psalms*.[27] In the first of these Diamond examined every line of Cynewulf's four poems, matching them up against the totality of the poems and against the entire Anglo-Saxon poetic corpus; in the second, he chose, at random, about fifteen lines every fifteen pages, eleven passages totaling 153 lines, and compared them to the Anglo-Saxon Poetic Records. The sampling method employed for the *Metrical Psalms* is superior to previous attempts in that the samples are gathered from throughout the work and together constitute a sizable body of poetic material. Cynewulf's formulas were examined not on the basis of samples at all, but on entire poems. The two studies are, then, statistically valid and much more homogeneous than any comparisons made previous to Diamond's work.

Benson also added two studies of his own, one of the *Phoenix* poem, the other of the *Meters of Boethius*, both based on samples checked against the Anglo-Saxon Poetic Records, and, as samples, of doubtful reliability.

But the crux of the matter is this: when Benson begins to draw conclusions from Diamond's statistically reliable material and his own counts, technical vocabulary obscures the true significance of his results. Thus he finds that "a full analysis of the 3500 verses (1750 lines) of the *Meters [of Boethius]* shows that they contain about 250 whole-verse formulas used around 700 times; one such formula, '*ealla gesceafta*,' is used at least twenty-two times. Diamond . . . found that this sort of 'whole-verse' formula accounts for 19.9 percent of Cynewulf's verses, 1037 out of 5194 (2598 lines)."[28] Obviously the term "verse" is being used here, as it commonly is in the discussion of Old English poetry, to mean the "A" or the "B" part of the line, equivalent to what I have termed, following usage, a "hemistich,"[29] and not to the Old French verse, which is a whole poetic line. The term "whole-verse formula" may be misleading when it is employed in the context of the theory of oral poetry, especially since the problem of whole formulaic verses, that is formulas which run from the beginning of the poetic line to the end, has already drawn the attention of scholars concerned with formulaic language.[30]

Therefore since Benson and Diamond found that 19.9 percent of Cynewulf's lines and approximately 20 percent of the *Meters of Boethius* are "whole-verse" formulas, these are the figures which should have been compared with the results of previous samplings and which should now be compared with the formulaic analyses of Old French narrative poetry—although obviously a truly accurate estimation would result only from a comparison of hypothetically oral Old English verse with learned Old English works—since what they call a "whole-verse" formula is what Lord and Parry termed simply a "formula."[31] The higher figures for their analyses, 43 percent for Cynewulf (restricting the evidence to Cynewulf's works themselves) and 60 percent for the sample of the *Meters*, really encompass what Lord calls "formulas and formulaic expressions"—my "semantic and syntactic formulas"—and are consequently not to be compared with my figures or with those cited from previous researchers. In conclusion, if the *Meters* and Cynewulf were counted in with the Old English narrative poems, they would represent marginal cases at 20 percent and slightly below, and could not be called oral from internal evidence. Even in the context of previous samplings, Cynewulf's poems and the *Meters* would be relatively thin in formulaic content, that is, close to the bottom of the list.

Benson's work shows not that the Anglo-Saxon poets in question, certainly learned and literate men, composed in the medium of formulaic language employed by oral poets, but merely that they had formulas in their poems, which is quite another state of affairs. There is nothing to prevent a learned author from using formulas, but as far as is now known no learned author has ever made formulaic language the ordinary medium of his writings. The question of whether or not a "transitional" text is possible is not yet closed by any means. But far from disproving the connection between formulaic language and orally improvised composition, Benson merely raises some interesting possibilities about the influence of traditional language on learned poetry which should be pursued with more rigorous method by scholars in the Old English area.

I have until this point omitted any account of the *Chanson de Roland*'s formula density, since this poem has, because of its literary excellence, been accorded a place apart from the body of *chansons de geste* in the critical literature.[32] It seemed desirable to establish the connection between formulaic language and oral composition without the *Roland* material so as to provide a context against which the formulaic aspects of the poem could be placed in perspective.

Using the guidelines set out above, one can verify 2814 formulas in the Oxford *Roland*,[33] or 35.2 percent of the 8004 hemistichs in the poem.[34] This figure was arrived at through a painstaking process of counting, recounting, and testing which leaves little room for error. Certainly if there is an error—that is by no means impossible—it has been on the conservative side, for certain hemistichs, although employed as formulas by the jongleur, may contain orthographic variations so diverse that they are not perceived in the concordance as formulas. If the possibility of error is set at 1 percent of the total number of hemistichs, this would allow for my overlooking 80 formulas, which I consider extremely unlikely, since that would amount to nearly 3 percent of the actual number of formulas uncovered. Most probably, then, the *Chanson de Roland* is formulaic to a degree of 35.2 percent, with the possible addition of one percent as an allowance for error.

Some critics, willing to concede oral composition for the earliest stages of the Old French epic (Menéndez Pidal's *état latent*) but reluctant to admit that its masterpiece could result from this process, have assumed that the *Roland* poet took previously existing poetic legends handed down by oral tradition and, pen in hand, reworked them into the predecessor of the Oxford version, ordering the material in such a way as to create a consummate work of art. But there is no reason to place the *Roland* in a different category from the other *chansons de geste* on the basis of formula density. Indeed *Roland* is one of the more formulaic works examined, its nearest neighbors in this respect being *Raoul de Cambrai*, slightly less formulaic at 33 percent, and the *Couronnement de Louis*, 37 percent. It contains proportionally more formulas than the *Chanson de Guillaume*, the *Charroi de Nîmes*, *Gormont et Isembart*, the *Moniage Guillaume II*, the *Siège de Barbastre* and the *Pèlerinage de Charlemagne*. Only the *Couronnement de Louis* and the *Prise d'Orange*, the latter occupying the maximum position, a mere two percentage points higher than the *Couronnement de Louis*— which Jean Rychner estimated, in a remarkably accurate intuitive judgment, to be the most formulaic of the twelfth-century works he treated[35]—surpass it in the relative abundance of repeated hemistichs. Since a high formula content is evidence of oral composition, the *Chanson de Roland* which we have in the Oxford version must be regarded as having descended in some way from the oral tradition, formulaic analysis having shown it to possess a typical formulaic profile.

We are now in a better position to consider the three alternatives for the *Roland*'s mode of creation. The method will consist, again, of taking each alternative as a hypothesis to be measured against quantitative evidence for formulaic composition.

If several hypotheses are available to explain the existence of a given phenomenon, then the one which exhibits the greatest simplicity is preferred. The supposition that *Roland* was created in writing does not have the advantage of simplicity, as it necessitates a double assumption which has never been proven and may well be unprovable: that a literate poet would and could author a poem by means of formulas. Parry argued that it would be more difficult to construct a formula system than to write a poem without formulas because of the complexity of possible metric patterns in the Greek hexameter and what he saw as the economy (one formula for every idea in a given metrical context) of the Homeric formula system. But this argument applies as well to other bodies of poetry: there is no reason to assume that a literate poet would wish to employ the same phrases many times over in his poem to the extent that fully one-third of his diction is repeated. The oral poet, we know from Lord's study of the Yugoslavian milieu, has a good motive for repeating himself with stylized phrases, namely the need to sing verses before a demanding audience at the rate of ten to twenty decasyllabic lines per minute,[36] a pace far too rapid to permit the constant generation of unique word combinations. The proponent of a hypothesis of written composition for *Roland*, then, merely substitutes one difficulty for another: having assumed that the poem derives from a process of composition in writing, he must show that extensive use of formulas is desirable and possible for a poet whose means of creating is the written word. His adversaries, on the other hand, have been provided by Lord and Parry with compelling proof that formulaic composition is the ordinary medium of contemporary Yugoslavian and ancient Greek oral poets, and that they use no other means of composing.

The second alternative, that the *Roland* is a composite creation, the result of a writer of genius coming into contact with the oral tradition and transforming a more or less primitive poem about Roncevaux into the magnificent version which comes down to us in the Oxford manuscript, deserves weighty consideration, all the more so now that concrete evidence for *Roland*'s formulas is available. For the skeletal hypothesis can now be fleshed out with additional information about the poem's style.

One is forced to speculate about the exact nature of the linguistic, stylistic, and aesthetic changes the *remanieur de génie* would have made in the poem during the course of his intervention. If he did not himself possess formulaic skill, the formulas found in Oxford would derive from the preexisting oral tradition into the course of which the literate poet is presumed to have intervened. A further look at formulaic density of *Roland* would, in this case, allow one to pick out those parts of the poem where the late *remanieur* reworked the formulaic text with literate, that is nonformulaic, additions of his own.

Distribution of formulas over the body of the poem is shown in Table 3. The Oxford manuscript has been broken down into groups of 100 verses, and the number and proportion of formulas within each group is noted.

TABLE 3

Verses	Formulas	Percentage
1-100	78	39
101-200	94	47
201-300	63	31.5
301-400	48	24
401-500	55	27.5
501-600	91	45.5
601-700	66	33
701-800	75	37.5
801-900	67	33.5
901-1000	74	37
1001-1100	75	37.5
1101-1200	78	39
1201-1300	104	52
1301-1400	70	35
1401-1500	64	32
1501-1600	83	41.5
1601-1700	76	38
1701-1800	67	33.5

Verses	Formulas	Percentage
1801-1900	73	36.5
1901-2000	77	38.5
2001-2100	56	28
2101-2200	70	35
2201-2300	62	31
2301-2400	69	34.5
2401-2500	63	31.5
2501-2600	44	22
2601-2700	56	28
2701-2800	72	36
2801-2900	67	33.5
2901-3000	64	32
3001-3100	76	38
3101-3200	54	27
3201-3300	79	39.5
3301-3400	86	43
3401-3500	80	40
3501-3600	68	34
3601-3700	51	25.5
3701-3800	60	30
3801-3900	52	26
3901-4002	63	30.9

No group of one hundred lines is less than 22 percent nor more than 52 percent formulas. While these extremes are far enough apart that, if viewed in isolation, they would appear to constitute a significant difference, when taken in the context of all 40 hundred-line segments, they merely indicate that the *Roland* is not sporadically, but uniformly, formulaic. All the segments are more formulaic than the 807 decasyllabic verses of the *Roman d'Alexandre*, the most repetitious of the romances tested at 17 percent.

Which passages are most likely to have been inserted or reworked by an intervening literate poet? For a clue to the percentage below which one might consider nonformulaic composition to be at work, let us turn to the table of relative formulaic density for Old French narrative poems. There it appears that the most repetitive romance is 17 percent repeated hemistichs, while the least formulaic epic is 23 percent. The mean percentage for all the *chansons de geste* is 29.7.[37] The *Pèlerinage de Charlemagne*, the *Siège de Barbastre* and the *Moniage Guillaume*, lowest among the epics on the list, are all within one percentage point of each other, at 23 to 24 percent formulaic. Since only one *Roland* passage is less than 23 percent formulas, one can identify little as the possible intervention of a literate poet in the text on this basis. All hundred-line segments except verses 2501 to 2600 are more formulaic than the least formulaic *chanson de gestes*; none are as little repetitive as the most repetitive romance, as we might have expected if the hypothesis of a learned use of previously existing oral materials were correct.

The one passage most likely to be literate, verse 2501 to 2600, tells of the evening following the French army's defeat of the pagan forces responsible for the destruction of Charlemagne's rearguard at Roncevaux. Of the 70 verses dedicated to this narration, 45 are given over to the emperor's two dreams of foreboding, one concerning his duel with Baligant, the other the trial of Ganelon. The remaining thirty verses show Bramimunde's lamentations before the ineffective pagan idols, which she helps to destroy, and her regrets over the mortally wounded Marsile. As interesting as these two scenes are, few would claim that they are on a literary level with the best *Roland* passages. It is difficult to conceive of them as improving the poem to any significant degree except that the two dreams, prefiguring the two remaining major episodes, contribute to cohesiveness of structure. But similar anticipations are scattered throughout the poem in more formulaic passages; nothing about this function of the two dreams strikes one as unique. Charlemagne, in fact, has two other dreams which fill an identical anticipatory role in verses 717 to 736, but the hundred-line segment which includes this passage is 37.5 percent formulaic, slightly above the figure of 35.2 percent for the poem as a whole.

On the basis of this examination of the hundred-line segments, then, there is no reason to suppose the intervention of a learned poet between the oral tradition and the archetype of Oxford.

*   *   *

If the literate poet whom we are hypothetically assuming intervened late in the *Roland* tradition added any passages to the poem, the best scenes, considered here [French council, first horn, second horn, leavetaking, Durendal and Roland's death scenes; see original publication (Ed.)], are plainly not among them, for they bear the hallmarks of the oral tradition. There is no need to assume that a learned poet had to intervene in Oxford or its archetype in order to improve the literary quality of the legend unless he were a singer versed in the oral-formulaic style who had learned to write, since those passages which, in the estimation of literary critics, assure the *Roland*'s right to a place among the world's great epics, reveal an oral technique at work. If a *remanieur* who composed in the style of writers rather than in the oral-formulaic language had a role in the formation of these scenes, his intervention must have dated from a period considerably before the archetype was committed to parchment—long enough before that event to allow oral tradition to efface stylistic traces of his craft. It is difficult to conceive how a *Roland* already endowed with these scenes would have required any substantial "improvement" from the hands of a late literate poet. The comparison of *Roland* with the twelfth and thirteenth-century *chansons de geste* and romances showed the Oxford text fitting perfectly into the formulaic spectrum while differing radically from the poems known to have been created in writing. A truly learned poet would have to be supposed to have endowed his work with a formulaic profile which is, in its extent and its uniformity, just what one would expect from an oral poet. The hypothesis of a significant learned intervention between the jongleurs and Oxford does not stand up under factual analysis.

One is at liberty to speculate about the early stages of the legend, during which a learned man, perhaps even several, may have had some hand in its formation and transformation. There is, however, no stylistic evidence for this in the text which has come down to us.

We are left with but one cogent possibility supported by concrete evidence: the *Roland* which we possess must be a very nearly unadulterated product of oral tradition, little changed, except for its orthography, from the form in which it was first taken down from the lips of a singer or written down by a singer who had acquired literacy. If verses were added by eleventh or twelfth-century scribes, they were not of such a nature as to have changed the poem significantly for the better. While entertaining the possibility of the archetype of Oxford having been created by a singer who learned how to write, one must bear in mind that the uniformity of formulaic density found throughout the poem and the highly formulaic character of its best scenes show that such a singer's style was that of oral poetry and not that of poets who create in writing.[46] It seems therefore more likely that the *Roland* is an oral-dictated text, taken down by a scribe, or perhaps by several scribes working in tandem, from the lips of a singing poet. This would best account for the fact that the prime method of poets who compose in writing, namely revision by afterthought, is nowhere in evidence.

The presence of so many formulas in *Roland's* key scenes poses an unexpected problem for the critic. Should we suppose a causal connection between the higher formula density of these passages and their literary excellence? The six key scenes I have examined contain on the average one-fourth more formulas than the poem as a whole. But I doubt that such a conclusion would be warranted were it based solely on the evidence I have presented. I do believe, however, that the figures point up the desirability of a new critical orientation. For too long it has been assumed that lasting poetry could only be created in one way, that is by poets working with the methods of literate creators. The extent to which the *Roland* poet used traditional, formulaic language does not differ significantly from that of other poets who came after him: it is what he made out of that traditional language that sets him apart from them. Obviously his genius does not lie in a capacity for juxtaposing individual words in striking combinations, but rather in an ability to combine whole blocks of words with other blocks, while employing the methods of oral improvisation. In his greatest moments he relied upon the formulaic language not less, but more. It is time for medievalists to cease treating formulas like the repetitions or clichés of the written language. Literary works can be composed in a highly stylised diction: the *Roland* alone is proof of that. Instead of admitting grudgingly that it is a worthy piece of literature *in spite of* its formulas, we should take our cue from the poet himself and recognize that formulas are the basic matter of his creation and that it is the effective use of formulas that generates effective scenes.

Critics of medieval French literature have shown an obvious reluctance to admit that an unlettered, improvising poet is capable of composing, in the act of singing, a work of high artistic quality. Not only is this assumption gratuitous: it is ultimately based upon a circular reasoning which might not at first be apparent. The establishment of a critical tradition involves evaluation of thousands of literary works, of which some attract more admiration than others. The very idea we hold of perfection in the epic is eventually the result of a filtering of epic production through the fine mesh of thousands of accumulated critical reactions. But if one goes to the most ancient epic models, those most admired by the first systematic literary critic but still revered above all others in this age of criticism, one finds, as Parry proved, two orally-composed poems, the *Iliad* and the *Odyssey*. To hold that the *Chanson de Roland* is too well organized to be an orally composed poem is ultimately to say that it is better constructed than Homer's masterpieces, and no critic has yet ventured this proposition. Further progress in medieval French epic criticism depends upon recognition that the assumption of the inferiority of oral poetry to written poetry is invalid.

NOTES

[1]Robert E. Diamond is, to my knowledge, the only scholar who has improved upon this method to date. His study of "The Diction of the Signed Poems of Cynewulf," *Philological Quarterly*, XXXVIII (1959), 228-241, is limited to *Elene, Juliana*, the *Fates of the Apostles*, and *Christ II*, they being both the subject of the study and the referent. This approach is, as we shall see, methodologically sound. In addition, he checked a random sample of 456 "verses" (two "verses" make up a line in the terminology of Old English metrics) against the whole Anglo-Saxon Poetic Records, and uncovered 62.7 percent formulas. Less happily he relied on random samples in his later study of *The Diction of the Anglo-Saxon Metrical Psalms* ("Janua Linguarum," Series Practica, X; The Hague: Mouton, 1963), discussed in greater detail below.

[2]The prime test of any formula is that it be useful to the poet in sustaining his narrative, and occurrence within the text even as infrequently as twice is proof of a hemistich's utility. Those occurring more often are even more useful. Lest the reader remain sceptical, when quantitative analysis is carried out for the purpose of comparing one poem's repetitions to another's, the practice of counting phrases occurring twice is methodologically justified as long as they are counted in all the works which enter into the comparison, as is the case with the present study.

[3]"Studies in the Epic Technique of Oral Verse-Making. I: Homer and Homeric Style," *Harvard Studies in Classical Philology*, XLI (1930), 73-147, esp. pp. 118-121; reprinted in *The Making of Homeric Verse: the*

Collected Papers of Milman Parry (Oxford: Clarendon Press, 1970), pp. 266-324.

[4]*The Singer of Tales* (Cambridge: Harvard University Press, 1960), p. 46.

[5]"The Oral-Formulaic Character of Anglo-Saxon Narrative Poetry," *Speculum,* XXVIII (1953), 446-467.

[6]Albert B. Lord, "Homer as Oral Poet," *Harvard Studies in Classical Philology,* LXXII (1968), 20-24.

[7]P. 202.

[8]See below.

[9]*Ibid.*

[10]For a discussion of the validity of the figures for this poem, see below.

[11]"Formulas in the *Couronnement de Louis,*" *Romania,* LXXXVII (1966), 315-344. The text used was E. Langlois, ed., *Le Couronnement de Louis* (2nd ed.; Paris: Champion, 1925).

[12]The method employed for the *Siège de Barbastre* and *Buevon de Conmarchis,* though just as effective as the word-group concordance method described in Chapter I, differed from it in its mechanics. It consisted in analysing each hemistich of the two poems into a code based on semantic fields and then concording on the basis of the code. I later abandoned this method for the present one because the latter requires no preliminary analysis. See my dissertation, "Formulaic Language in the Old French Epic Poems *Le Siège de Barbastre* and *Buevon de Conmarchis,*" Ohio State University, 1964.

[13]This number was chosen to provide a romance of equal length with the *Couronnement de Louis.* Likewise for the *Siège de Barbastre* I only tested the part which inspired Adenet's *Buevon de Conmarchis.* I realized only later that the size of the text is irrelevant if the population and the referent are identical.

[14]The following editions were employed: Alphonse Bayot, ed., *Gourmont et Isembart* (3rd ed., Classiques français du moyen âge, XIV; Paris: Champion, 1931); Duncan McMillan, ed., *La Chanson de Guillaume* (2 vols., Société des anciens textes français; Paris: Picard, 1949-1950); J.-L. Perrier, ed., *Le Charroi de Nîmes* (CFMA, LXVI; Paris: Champion, 1931); Blanche Katz, ed., *La Prise d'Orange* (New York: King's Crown Press, 1947); Paul Meyer and Auguste Longnon, eds., *Raoul de Cambrai, chanson de geste* (SATF; Paris: Firmin Didot, 1882); Eduard Koschwitz, *Karls des Grossen Reise nach Jerusalem und Constantinopel* (7th ed., Heilbronn: 1925); Wilhelm Cloetta, ed., *Les deux rédactions en vers du Moniage Guillaume* (2 vols., SATF; Paris: Champion, 1906-1911); J.-L. Perrier, ed., *Le Siège de Barbastre* (CFMA, LIV; Paris: Champion, 1926); Albert Henry, ed., *Les Œuvres d'Adenet le*

Roi, II, *Buevon de Conmarchis* (Bruges: "de Tempel," 1953); J.-J. Salverda de Grave, ed., *Enéas, roman du XIIe siècle* (2 vols., CFMA, XLIV, LXII; Paris: Champion, 1925-1931); Milan S. LaDu, ed., *The Medieval French Roman d'Alexandre*, I (Princeton University Press, 1937). The Aebischer and Favati editions of the *Pèlerinage de Charlemagne*, the Régnier edition of the *Prise d'Orange* and that of the *Charroi de Nîmes* by G. de Poerck *et al.* were all published after I had made the concordances to these poems.

¹⁵Dating is based on the following authorities: *Buevon*:Albert Henry, *Les Œuvres d'Adenet le Roi*, I, p. 47; *Enéas*: Salverda de Grave, *Enéas*, I, pp. xix-xx; *Alexandre*: E. C. Armstrong, ed., *The Medieval French Roman d'Alexandre*, II, p. x; *Pèlerinage*: Koschwitz, *Karls des Grossen Reise*, p. xxv; *Siège*: Raymond Weeks, "The *Siège de Barbastre*," *Romanic Review*, X (1919), 287; *Moniage*: Cloetta, *Les deux rédactions en vers*, II, p. 269; *Gormont*: Ferdinand Lot, "Encore *Gormond et Isembard*," *Romania*, LIII (1927), reprinted in Robert Boussat, ed., *Etudes sur les légendes épiques françaises* (Paris: Champion, n.d.), p. 342; *Charroi*: Jean Frappier, *Les Chansons de geste du cycle de Guillaume d'Orange*, II (Paris: SEDES, 1965), p. 186; *Guillaume*: Lot, *Etudes*, p. 242; *Raoul*: Paul Meyer and Ernest Longnon, *Raoul de Cambrai*, pp. lxx-lxxi; *Couronnement*: Frappier, *Cycle de Guillaume*, II, p. 59; *Prise d'Orange*: ibid., II, p. 258.

¹⁶In practical terms this would require the preparation of a standardized line, in, say, the *francien* dialect, for each of the thirty-three thousand lines in question. While admittedly a formidable undertaking, its achievement is not impossible: an analogous project has been begun for the relatively limited corpus of Anglo-Saxon verse by Francis P. Magoun and Jess B. Bessinger. See Bessinger's *Short Dictionary of Anglo-Saxon Poetry in a Normalized Early West-Saxon Orthography* (Toronto: University of Toronto Press, 1960). A computer-generated concordance could then be compiled based on the standardized lines but printing out the original text. A suitable program, called DISCON, has been developed by Sidney M. Lamb and Laura Gould, who describe it in *Type-Lists, Indexes and Concordances from Computers* (New Haven: Yale University Linguistics Automation Project, 1967).

¹⁷"Not only the quantity but also the provenance of the material is of importance for formula analysis. One must work with material of a single singer at a given time, and then outwards by concentric circles to his group, district, and so forth. Otherwise one uses material which is irrelevant to the song and singer under scrutiny."—Lord, *Singer of Tales*, p. 289, note 11.

¹⁸To date poems on internal evidence is always hazardous. As a check on the relationship of formula density to dating, here is another

set of dates taken from Raphael Levy, *Chronologie approximative de la littérature française du moyen âge* (Beihefte zur *Zeitschrift für romanische Philologie*, XCVIII; Tübingen: Niemeyer, 1957):

Poem	Date	Percentage of formulas
Gourmont	1125	29
Couronnement	1131	37
Guillaume	1140	31
Charroi	1144	29
Prise d'Orange	1148	39
Pèlerinage	1149	23
Alexandre	ca.1160	17
Enéas	1160	16
Raoul	1180	33
Moniage Guillaume	1185	24
Siège de Barbastre	1150-1200	23
Buevon	1275	15

Although Levy follows other authorities, there is no more correlation between formula density and date in his chronology than in the one I have adopted.

[19]Thus Albert Henry, Adenet's editor, compares *Buevon* to the *Siège de Barbastre*: "Avec le *Siège de Barbastre* nous avons affaire à un tout homogène: matière de chanson de geste, style de chanson de geste, style un peu mécanisé déjà, mais s'adaptant parfaitement à la matière qu'il revêt. Style carré, dominé par le vers dont l'indépendance, sinon l'absolue souveraineté, se marque, presque partout, par la fixité de la césure et l'ignorance de l'enjambement, style précis, brutal, dur et limité comme une cuirasse. L'adaptation d'Adenet a quelque chose d'hybride et de trouble: sa démarche manque de décision."—*Les Œuvres d'Adenet le Roi*, II, p. 28. For a detailed treatment of Adenet's versification and formulas, see my dissertation cited above, note 12.

[20]Geneva: Droz, 1955.

[21]Results of the analysis of the *Chanson de Roland* are given below.

[22]"Homer as Oral Poet," p. 24.

[23]*PMLA*, LXXXI (1966), 334-341.

[24]In his review of Renate Hitze's *Studien zu Sprache und Stil der Kampfschilderungen in den "chansons de geste"* in *Romance Philology*, XXII (1969), 334-336.

[25]Review of Robert Creed, *Old English Poetry, Fifteen Essays*, in *Comparative Literature*, XXI (1969), 285-286.

[26]*Philological Quarterly*, XXXVIII (1959), 228-241.

[27]The Hague: Mouton, 1963.

[28]P. 229, note 19.

[29]Strictly speaking, a poetic unit in the Old French decasyllabic epic, either 4 or 6 syllables, is either not quite or just more than half a line. This is often the case with Old English "verses," which are based on stress counting rather than on syllable count.

[30]See, for example, Milman Parry, "Whole Formulaic Verses in Greek and Southslavic Heroic Songs," *TAPA*, LXIV (1933), 179-197.

[31]Thus Lord, "Homer as Oral Poet," p. 26: "It is important to work from line break to line break rather than with simple repetition of words and phrases by themselves, because it is in terms of parts of a line, I believe, rather than words in themselves, that the singer thinks. A formula extends from one break to another. . . . I think that the repeated words or groups of words are significant only when they stretch from break to break."

[32]Maurice Delbouille saw Rychner's exception of the *Roland* from the orally composed genre as a weakness in his theory: "Que voilà une belle et grande exception aux règles du jeu et du genre! Et qui constitue, contre l'idée du jongleur-improvisateur et du poème oral, la plus redoutable des objections!" "Les Chansons de geste et le livre," *La Technique littéraire des Chansons de geste: Actes du Colloque de Liège (septembre 1957)* (Bibliothèque de la Faculté de Philosophie et Lettres de l'Université de Liège, CL; Paris: "Les Belles Lettres," 1959), p. 307n.

[33]The edition was that of Raoul Mortier, *Les Textes de la Chanson de Roland*: vol. I, *Le Manuscrit d'Oxford* (Paris: Editions de la Geste Francor, 1940), which follows Oxford closely. The reader is invited to check my figures through the use of the *Concordance to the Chanson de Roland* (Columbus: Ohio State University Press, 1970).

[34]In his *Formulaic Diction and Thematic Composition in the Chanson de Roland* (University of North Carolina Studies in the Romance Languages and Literatures, XXXVI; Chapel Hill: University of North Carolina Press, 1961), Stephen G. Nichols' conclusions on the formulaic density of *Roland* are curiously incomplete, as they concern only the first hemistichs of vv. 1-2000. He found 1157 "formulas" but it is obvious from the examples in the schematic appendix that he was counting syntactic as well as semantic patterns.

[35]*La Chanson de geste*, p. 149.

[36]*Singer of Tales*, p. 17.

[37]I am not eliminating the possibility of individual verses added to the poem sporadically. The statistical method which I employ could not

detect such verses, and each instance alleged would have to be judged on its merits. But obviously the poem was not transformed into a masterpiece by the addition of a few verses here and there.

[38-45For data, see original publication (Ed.)]

46Italo Siciliano's attempt, in *Les Chansons de geste et l'épopée*, Biblioteca di Studi Francesi, III (Turin: Società Editrice Internazionale, 1968), pp. 132-133, to prove the contrary is woefully insufficient. A few repetitions quoted at random from Virgil, the *Enéas*, and other poems do not prove anything. Beginning with Parry, researchers in this field have always admitted that repetitions are a fact of literary life. Orally composed poems are distinguishable not because they contain repetitions, but because semantic and syntactic repetitions are fundamental to their style.

African Talking Drums and Oral Noetics

Walter J. Ong

Walter J. Ong, S.J., has contributed a series of major studies on topics closely allied to oral-formulaic theory, including especially books and articles on Petrus Ramus and rhetoric as well as The Presence of the Word *(1967),* Interfaces of the Word *(1977), and* Orality and Literacy *(1982). These last three works have set forth his revolutionary ideas on the necessary relationship between communicative media and the structure of human consciousness, the psychodynamics of orality and literacy, and the implications of "noetic" structures for artistic expression. In the present essay Ong offers a uniquely illuminating perspective on the function of oral tradition by examining a medium that uses neither letters nor lexicons: the drums imitate words by imitating their sounds, "disambiguating" the tone sequences by recourse to longer, stereotyped, and thus formulaic expressions. Drummers "speaking" this language use the equivalent of Homer's noun-epithet formulas to convey their message, relying on repetition and redundancy to structure their idiom. Ong closes with some observations on the link between communication and time, adding the caveat that modern Africa is recapitulating the Western evolution from sound to letters, print, and word-processing at a relatively dizzying speed.*

Reprinted from *New Literary History*, 8 (1977), 411-429.

The primary orality in which human thought and verbal expression is initially and fundamentally lodged undergoes other metamorphoses besides those which lead through writing and print to the electronic management of thought and expression. Most of these metamorphoses have not been studied in detail. What effect, for example, did the Morse code have on the way news is formulated by journalists? Or how did use of the semaphore alphabet curtail normal oral redundancies or otherwise affect the way marine and military directives were formulated? How did nonalphabetic signaling, such as the use of varicolored flags, each the equivalent of a particular word or phrase displayed in accord with an explicitly devised "grammar," affect thought and expression where such signaling was operative? What did the sign language of the American Plains Indians do to their normal oral verbalization? How did its effects on verbalization compare with those of various sign languages for the deaf? Many other metamorphoses of primary orality could be enumerated, but in virtually every case, except for that of sign languages for the deaf, little or nothing is known of their effects on noetic processes.

The talking drums of Subsaharan Africa metamorphose primary oral processes in ways which are unique, at least in their sophistication and cultural importance. The last word has certainly not been said about all the ways the drum languages function in the hundreds of different cultures across the lower half of Africa—a vast area, since Africa is a continent some four times the size of the pre-Alaskan United States. But we do know enough to be able to compare some typical features of drum talk at least in certain African cultures with some of the features of primary oral verbalization. The present study undertakes such a comparison, in a limited, preliminary fashion. The comparison would appear to throw light not only upon the drumming processes but also upon the primary oral processes themselves out of which the drum languages have been developed.

I

For some time African talking drums or slit-gongs have been of considerable interest to anthropologists, linguists, and others, for on these instruments Africans have produced probably the most highly

developed acoustic speech surrogates known anywhere in the world.[1]
Various cultures have developed acoustic surrogates or sound substitutes
for ordinary spoken words, using gongs or drums or whistles or bells or
other instruments, as well as special sounds produced by the human
voice itself, to communicate verbalized messages, often at a distance
greater than that which articulate speech itself can cover. (Writing
systems or scripts are also speech surrogates, but visual rather than
acoustic, and we are concerned only with acoustic surrogates here.)
Sometimes an acoustic speech surrogate is a code, that is to say, a
system of sounds which essentially have no similarity to the sounds of
the speech they represent: the Morse code used on an old-style telegraph
is a standard example here, for the clicking buzz of a telegraph does not
sound at all like speech and is not intended to. An African drum
language is not such an abstract signaling code but rather is a way of
reproducing in a specially stylized form the sounds of the words of a
given spoken language.

Only recently have knowledgeable descriptions of various drum
languages been worked out, and our knowledge of most such languages
is still somewhat defective. To arrive at an understanding of how drums
operate, one must first have a command in depth of the normal spoken
language which the drums adapt and then discover the principles
governing the adaptation. That is to say, to understand African drum
talk one must know the spoken language being used—for one drummer
will drum his native Duala, another Yaounde, another Lokele—and, in
addition, one must discover the way in which the language is adapted or
styled for the drums. A drum language is not understood *ipso facto*
when one knows the spoken language it reproduces: drum language has
to be specially learned even when the drums speak one's own mother
tongue.

To the not inconsiderable literature about the drums, much of it
highly technical, there has just been added an invaluable small book
(121 pages) in French, partly a translation but also an updating and
magisterial streamlining of an earlier book in English by the same
author.[2] Although it honors existing linguistic, anthropological,
musicological, and other scientific work, this new little book is not in
itself highly technical. But its author, John F. Carrington, now
professor of botany at the Kisangani campus of the National University
of Zaire, has qualifications, technical and other, hard to top. He has
been in Africa, with only brief interruptions, since 1938 and has been

writing about the drums for at least twenty-five years—an article of his on the subject appeared in the *Scientific American* in 1971,[3] and he is cited regularly in anthropological and linguistic studies. Most significantly, however, he writes as one who talks on the drums himself. The title of his little volume bespeaks the confident expertise of one completely at home in his subject: *La Voix des tambours: Comment comprendre le langage tambouriné d'Afrique.*

Carrington drums chiefly in Lokele, a Bantu language which, with more meticulous regard for Bantu grammar, may also be called Kele, the language of the people known as Lokele. (I follow Carrington's later practice and English idiom in using the same form for people and language.) Carrington speaks Lokele, of course. Not all who know an African language are so advantageously equipped, for of the many hundreds of African languages (not dialects but mutually incomprehensible languages) in active use today, by no means all can readily be put onto drums—Swahili, for example, lends itself to drum talk only with great difficulty, Carrington notes (p. 21).

Carrington has the in-depth knowledge of his subject which comes from having lived for over twenty-five years as a Christian missionary in intimate association with the Lokele people in upper Zaire near Kisangani, in effect as one of the Lokele themselves. He drums often for practical purposes: for example, to have a boat come from the opposite bank of a river to ferry him across. "He is not really a European," one African explained to others (pp. 65-66) on an occasion when Carrington was at the drums, "despite the color of skin. He used to be from our village, one of us. After he died, the spirits made a mistake and sent him off far away to a village of whites to enter into the body of a little baby who was born of a white woman instead of one of ours. But because he belongs to us, he could not forget where he came from and so he came back. If he is a bit awkward on the drums, this is because of the poor education the whites gave him." It is clear—at least to his fellow Africans—that Carrington has enviable credentials. He is twice a native son.

II

The sophisticated drum languages of Africa have been developed within an oral economy of thought and expression. Recent studies have shown how oral noetic processes—ways of acquiring, formulating, storing, and retrieving knowledge in cultures unfamiliar with writing or print—have certain distinctive features as compared to the noetic processes of cultures possessed of writing and, a fortiori, of print, and how these distinctive features are related to what can be called an oral lifestyle. Because Carrington's book recreates, informally but quite substantially and circumstantially, the drum language world as a whole, a reader of the book who is familiar with oral noetics can hardly avoid being struck by the way in which the drums exemplify and often informingly exaggerate the characteristics of the oral lifeworld, or of primary orality (oral culture untouched by writing or print, as contrasted with secondary orality, the electronic orality of present-day technological cultures, implemented by telephone, radio, television, and other instruments dependent for their existence and use on writing and print). My intent here is to bring together what we know about oral noetics and about concomitant oral lifestyles on the one hand and on the other hand what is now known about the talking drums as explained by Carrington.

The latter subject is by no means so familiar to me as the former, which I have treated and documented elsewhere at length, most notably in *The Presence of the Word*.[4] Yet the alliance between drums and an oral economy of thought and expression kept asserting itself vigorously over and over again in the course of my recent month-long visit as Lincoln Lecturer in Equatorial and West African republics, where I spoke on some thirty occasions about orality, literacy, print, and electronics to and with African anthropologists, linguists, folklorists, literary scholars, journalists and other communications specialists, novelists, poets, and others, including many students—in Zaire, Cameroun, Nigeria, and Senegal, all in the heart of the drum country. The relationship of drums to orality came up always as a familiar close-to-home subject badly needing explanatory development rather than as a subject already well fitted with explanation. But there is ample explanation in Carrington's handbook to document the conclusion already forcing itself on me in Africa before his book appeared: the talking drum is not merely an element in some primary oral cultures but is also in fact a kind of paradigm of primary orality. Because African talking drums amplify and exaggerate—sometimes almost caricature—the most basic techniques of oral noetics as we have recently come to know these, they open new depths to our understanding of orality.

Carrington's work does not treat all talking drums but primarily those of the Lokele, with some reference to other Central and West African peoples. He does not discuss every aspect of drum talk treated by other scholars, such as special ways of securing emphasis or the use of more than two tones for some languages. But the Lokele drumming is at least typical and Carrington discusses it not only in its essentials but also in rich human detail. This is all the present study requires, for it undertakes to establish merely some landmarks.

III

Not all drums that transmit information are talking drums. The Jibaro Indians, for example, as reported on by Rafael Karsten, have certain drum rhythms for signaling narcotic ceremonies, others for manioc beer ceremonies, still others for deaths and attacks by enemies, the rhythms being differentiated much as those of a dirge and of wedding music might be in Western culture.[5] Many cultures, including that of the present-day United States, use drum beats or gong beats or church bells in this way. African talking drums work differently. To make subsequent discussion here intelligible, it will be well to highlight certain points in Carrington's account of the drums.

As explained by Carrington, talking drums among the Lokele and generally through Africa imitate words by imitating their tones. Hence, for these talking drums a tonal language is needed. A tonal language uses pitch to distinguish words. Many African languages are tonal. English is not a tonal language. It is true that English uses tone or pitch to distinguish between the several possible senses in which a word or a group of words may be used in a given case. For example, in the following group of words the speaker raises the pitch of the word "good" to identify a question: "It is good?" If he wishes the same words to be understood as a declaration, he can lower the pitch of "good": "It is good." Or, to counter a denial, he can raise the pitch of "is": "It *is* good." But English does not normally use pitch to distinguish from each other words otherwise homonymic. Lokele does. In one of Carrington's instances (p. 19), the syllables represented in writing or print as *lisaka* can have three meanings: if the syllables are pronounced all on the same pitch (...) the resulting word means pond; if the final syllable is raised in tone (..·) the resulting word means promise (the noun); if the last two syllables are raised in tone (.··) the resulting word means poison (the noun). Words keep their tone independently of the sense of an utterance in which they occur. One result that Carrington points out is that a tonal language cannot be effectively whispered—the meaning will not always come clear. Tonal languages are known in many places other than Africa, and not all African languages are tonal. In a given linguistic family, some languages may be tonal and others not.

What African talking drums do, as exemplified among the Lokele, is reproduce the tones of words, not the vowel or consonant sounds as such. To reproduce two tones (which suffice for Lokele), one drum with two tones is commonly used. Carrington wisely notes that the term "drum" is derived from other cultures and applied, not with complete success, to the African instruments. A typical two-toned wooden "drum" might be styled more properly, a wooden gong or a slit-gong—an "idiophone," the whole of which vibrates when struck, like a metal gong or a xylophone bar or a tuning fork or a bell. The African wooden slit-gong is typically, though not always, a section of tree trunk, and thus a cylinder, some two to six feet or so in length, hollowed out with a slit an inch or so in width running almost its entire length. The hollowing can be done, laboriously, through the slit, but more commonly the log is opened at the ends, which are then plugged up again afterwards.

The hollowing is done in such a way that the two lips of the slit produce two different tones. Generally the low tone is considered the male "voice" and the high tone the female "voice." But the Lokele conceive of the contrast in terms not of the common Western metaphor "low" and "high" but in terms of "stronger" and "weaker," so that if in a given case the high note of a drum carries farther, it is considered the "male" (p. 25). Some wooden "gong" drums are structured differently from the simple cylinder models, and some are even carved in the shapes of animals, but they all work in essentially the same way, with "lips" of different tones. The word *lisaka* (...), pond, can be signaled by striking the male lip three times; *lisaka* (..·), promise, by striking first the male lip twice and then the female once; *lisaka* (.··), poison, by striking the male lip once, the female twice.

This kind of tonal differentiation can be and is effected also with African stretched-skin drums, "membranophones," in which a vibrating membrane is stretched over a resonator, like the drums common in Western orchestras. For "talking" two such true drums are used, a "husband" (lower pitch) and a "wife" (higher pitch). In fact, the same drum language can be "spoken" by contrasting two pitches produced by almost anything. It is actually "spoken" by using two differently pitched whistled notes (produced with the lips or with instruments), or by using horns or string instruments, or by two contrasting spoken syllables—the Lokele thus use the syllable "ki" and "li" (Carrington's transcription, p. 98, in French spelling) for the female voice, "ke" and "le" for the male. Compared to other instruments, however, drums have the advantage of carrying farther—perhaps a normal maximum of around four or five miles under favorable conditions (usually along a quiet river, and at night), though Carrington reports (p. 34) from his own experience an exceptional case of a gong, the largest he has ever seen, which carried twenty-five kilometers (about fifteen miles) along a quiet river at night. Longer distances can be covered by relays of drums. Stories one hears of individual drums carrying sixty miles are based, at best, on ignorance.

Obviously, gong or drum "talk" of this sort can be understood at great distances even though heard faintly because all that need be distinguished in it are two different tones or pitches. But the fact that drum language is based only on the tones of words creates problems. *Lisaka* (...) is not the only three-syllable word in Lokele pronounced with three low tones, nor are *lisaka* (..·) or *lisaka* (.··) the only three-syllable words with their sequence of tones. A given sequence of tones does not signal a very determined meaning at all but remains quite ambiguous. If, however, a set of tones is put into a context, the context can eliminate many or all of the ambiguities, can "disambiguate" a given tone pattern, especially if the supplied context is a stereotyped one.

So the "words" on the drums are set into stereotyped contexts or patterns. To say "moon" the drummer does not simply strike the tones for the Lokele word for moon, *songe* (··), for two high tones could mean many things besides moon (p. 39). Rather, he strikes the tones for the stereotyped phrase meaning "moon look toward the earth" (··.·....). The tones of "look toward the earth," also themselves ambiguous, limit and are limited by the tones of the "moon." "Moon look toward the earth" is beat out on the drum every time the drummer wants to say "moon." And so with the rest of the drum lexicon. For each simple word of ordinary speech, the drum language substitutes a much longer expression. These expressions moreover are stereotyped, fixed in the drumming tradition, and must be learned by each novice drummer: a drummer cannot make up his own stereotyped expression at whim. For "cadaver," the Lokele drummer must say "cadaver which lies on its back upon clods of earth." For "war," the stereotyped phrase is "war which calls attention to ambushes." And so on through the drummer's entire drum vocabulary.

It takes much longer to say something on a drum than *viva voce*, on the average eight times as long. The insertion of an ambiguous drum word into a standard context in order to "disambiguate" the word suggests a similar practice, not mentioned by Carrington, *lien-hsi* or "joining," in Chinese, a language having many homonyms. Spoken Chinese has more such problems with ambiguities than written Chinese, since in a set of written homonyms each will often be represented by a different character, though they may sound the same.[6]

The expanded or stereotyped expression on the drums, however, never becomes an abstract code of high and low tones: the drummers think of it as consisting not of tones alone but of words represented by the tones. However, when the drummers are asked to say what the words in their drummed phrases are, it is found that some of the words they say have lost their significance in the spoken language. In the stereotyped phrase for a young girl (pp. 41-42), *boseka botilakende linginda*," the young girl will not go to the '*linginda*,'" the Lokele drummers are sure that the last word is *linginda* but they are no longer agreed as to what *linginda* means—perhaps a kind of fishing net (tabu to young girls, thought to bring users of this net bad luck by their presence) or perhaps a council of the elders of the clan (obviously not frequented by young girls). It is obvious that drummed Lokele is a very special form of Lokele, which even native Lokele speakers can learn only with some effort.

IV

This brief summary of relevant portions of Carrington's account will perhaps suffice to identify some of the connections between the noetic economy of the drums and that of oral cultures as such when these are contrasted with writing and print cultures. The point here is not simply that verbalization in primary oral cultures and drum language operate in the same sensory field, that of sound. Obviously, they do. The point is, rather, that the structures given to expression and to knowledge itself by the verbalization patterns of oral cultures are strikingly characteristic of drum language as such. The drums are oral or oral-aural not merely in their sensory field of operation but even more basically in their idiom. Talking drums belong to the lifeworld of primary oral cultures, though not all primary oral cultures have used them.

What are the salient features—or, to resort to oral rather than visual or visual-tactile metaphors, the assertive strains, the principal accents— of an oral culture that are advertised or amplified in the use of talking drums? They can be enumerated as follows, under headings which overlap somewhat but which nevertheless appear serviceable in the present state of our knowledge: (1) stereotyped or formulaic expression, (2) standardization of themes, (3) epithetic identification for "disambiguation" of classes or of individuals, (4) generation of "heavy" or ceremonial characters, (5) formulary, ceremonial appropriation of history, (6) cultivation of praise and vituperation, (7) copiousness. These features of oral cultures generally, as contrasted with cultures using writing and print, and particularly the alphabet, have been worked out largely by scholars interested primarily in the transit from orality to literacy in Western classical culture and its consequents. However, grounds for generalization to primary oral cultures as such have appeared in the work of Albert B. Lord and Eric A. Havelock and have been discussed further in my own work, *The Presence of the Word*. The features, as just enumerated, can be taken up in order here with reference to drum language.

Stereotyped or formulaic expression. Carrington has made clear that the use of stereotyped expressions or formulas lies at the heart of drum language. It should be noted that a similar point has been made also by Lord and Havelock and others[7] concerning oral epic performances and indeed concerning careful expression generally throughout oral cultures. The Homeric poems as well as more recent oral or residually oral epics consist largely, if not entirely, of fixed expressions—the "clichés" which oral cultures live on and which literate cultures teach their members to scorn. Havelock has pointed out, moreover, that the use of formulaic phrases in an oral culture is not restricted to poets,[8] but is also necessary for many prosaic purposes. Stereotyped expressions enable primary oral cultures to preserve their knowledge and to recall it when needed. Formulas are necessary for history: the formulary genealogy, set up for the repetition on demand, preserves knowledge of ancestors which would otherwise vanish. Formulas are also necessary for administrative purposes: to get a lengthy message from Sardis to Athens a public official in early, oral Greek society had to cast the message in mnemonic formulas of some sort or it would not be preserved in the messenger's mind for delivery (or in the sender's mind for recall).

One can go further: oral cultures not only express themselves in formulas but also think in formulas. We know what we can recall. If one thinks of something once and never again, one does not say that one knows it. Without writing, if one does not think formulary, mnemonically structured thoughts, how can one really know them, that is, be able to retrieve them, if the thoughts are of even moderate complexity? In a culture without writing one cannot first work out in verbal form an elaborate pattern of thought and then memorize it afterwards: once said, it is gone, is no longer there to be memorized. Thoughts must be elaborated mnemonically in the first instance to be recoverable. Oral cultures thus think by means of memorable thoughts, thoughts processed for retrieval in various ways, or, in other words, fixed, formulaic, stereotyped. The formulaic expressions so common in oral cultures—proverbs, epithets, balances of various sorts, and other heavy patterning—are not added to thought or expression but are the substance of thought, and by the same token of expression as well. Oral cultures think *in* formulas, and communicate *in* them. When drums do the same, persons in a primary oral culture do not find the mode of expression at all so different from the normal as do literate folk.

In a sense, of course, every word is a mnemonic device, a formula, something more or less fixed and retrievable, bringing back to mind an element in consciousness otherwise elusive. Writing and print thus involve themselves in memory simply by the use of words, and they even occasionally make use of set phrases. But oral cultures need set phrases in quantity, for nothing can be "looked up." Primary oral cultures use formulas as units somewhat as writing cultures use words as units. This is one reason why such oral cultures are less "analytic": their thought has to be kept in larger chunks to survive and to flourish.

The same forces in an oral culture that tend to make speech formulaic also tend to make speech redundant. Redundancy is repetition. In a noetic economy dependent on large-scale repetition for its life, efforts to avoid repetition are not only difficult but also often inadvisable. Better too much repetition than too little. Too little repetition is fatal: knowledge not repeated enough vanishes. Too much repetition at worst is only annoying, and in a noetic economy obligated to value repetition, it takes a great deal of repetition indeed to annoy anyone. Not only purely oral cultures but also residually oral cultures, such as the European Middle Ages and Renaissance, are much addicted to "amplification" of a subject—verbal inflation which strikes more chirographic and typographic personality structures as at best flatulent.

For these reasons, and for other reasons to be treated later here in discussing copiousness, verbalization—and particularly highly formal or eventful verbalization—in oral cultures tends to be elaborately verbose. Set expressions themselves tend to be inflated or to be used at times when modern information theory would consider them useless. Why keep saying "wily Odysseus" over and over again when "Odysseus" is a perfectly clear reference?

But perhaps nowhere else in primary oral cultures is set expression so inveterately elaborate as it is on the drums. To translate from the French one of Carrington's examples (p. 46), the spoken expression, "Don't be afraid" becomes in drum language "Bring your heart back down out of your mouth, your heart out of your mouth, get it back from up there." Or again, "Come back" is rendered on the drum "Make your feet come back the way they went, make your legs come back the way they went, plant your feet and your legs below, in the village which belongs to us."

Of course, the reason for this somewhat fantastic lengthening is that to the ordinary oral delight in amplification there is added a special need to "disambiguate" because of the binary nature of the drum signal. The need can be expressed in a formula familiar to telephone engineers and cited by Carrington (p. 47) from an article by R. V. L. Hartley, in the *Bell System Technical Journal*:

$$H=N \log_2 S$$

where H is the amount of information to be conveyed in a given message, N is the number of signs in the same message, and S the total possible *different* signs in the sign system. The fewer the number of possible different signs, the longer the message has to be. Spoken Lokele is said (p. 47) to have 266 possible different signs (each a combination of one of nineteen consonants, one of seven vowels, and one of two tones); drummed Lokele has only two possible different signs, the two tones, so that the number of signs in a given message increases enormously on the drums. Or, to use another example, a binary system of notation results in the use of many more digits to express a given number than a decimal system does. Amplification of phrases, endemic to oral cultures, is thus exaggerated in drum talk almost to the point of caricature.

Use of stereotyped phrases, and of the specialized themes next to be treated here, make oral cultures highly conservative. Drum language, Carrington points out (p. 44), is still more conservative than the spoken word in cultures which know both.

Standardization of themes. Oral noetics, as manifested in poetry and narration of primary oral cultures, organizes thought largely around a controlled set of themes, more or less central to the human lifeworld: birth, marriage, death, celebration, struggle (ceremonial or ludic, and polemic or martial), initiation rites, dance and other ceremonies, arrivals and departures, descriptions or manipulations of implements (shields, swords, plows, boats, looms), and so on. It is true, of course, that all knowledge is organized in some way around themes in the large sense of subject matters—there is no other way to organize it. But the themes that govern oral discourse tend to be relatively limited and bound to the human lifeworld, if only because, as Havelock has explained,[9] elaboration of scientific categories or of quasi-scientific categories (such as are used, for example, in the modern writing of history) depends on the development of writing. There would be no reason to believe that drum talk would not follow similar thematic patterns, and Carrington's report, especially his Chapter 8 (pp. 81-90), leads one to believe that it indeed does (although he himself does not advert to this subject explicitly).

Drum language in fact appears to reinforce the thematic standardization or simplification normal in oral cultures because of the binary signaling system of the drums. Since expressions have to be made very long in a binary signal in order to be relatively unambiguous, multiplication of categories or areas of discourse will make for more and more involved expression, which would soon become so labyrinthine that new depths of ambiguity would appear. Disambiguation by the lengthening of expressions has certain limits. Hence drum talk is encouraged to exploit the standard themes. These will vary to some extent, of course, from culture to culture. What the oil palm is to the West African, the seal is to the Eskimo.

Standardization of themes does not mean that expression is moribund. It does not preclude reference, for example, to new events in individuals' lives. It is quite possible to drum a message that Boyoko is on his way to Kisangani to buy a motorcycle for his brother. But even in such a drum message, the thematic framework asserts itself, assimilating to itself the individuals involved. Boyoko's ordinary name is not a theme, so Boyoko becomes, for drumming purposes (to translate into English Carrington's French translation from Lokele, p. 54), "The-palm-tree-full-of-stinging-ants-where-one-climbs-and-then-has-to-get-rid-of-the-insects." Palm trees and stinging ants, means of sustenance and sources of annoyance in the human lifeworld, thematically absorb and define the individual.

Neither does standardization of themes mean that the drum culture cannot truly appropriate or interiorize new ideas. In fact, appropriation and interiorization are often expertly achieved on the drums. Carrington gives a remarkable instance (p. 93) of appropriation through formulaic expression. Early Christians at Yakusu had problems in finding a suitable word in Lokele to convey the Christian way of conceiving of God. Because the Lokele had thought of God as far off and indifferent to man (as Aristotle had thought of him) except at the time of birth or death or when invoked by sorcerers to curse someone, a common animist word for God was *itoko*, which also meant "smallpox" (imminent death, more or less). When they understood how Christians conceived of God, the drummers, uncoached by European missionaries, worked out on their own a new drum formula to express their new understanding: God as conceived by Christians is *liuwe lisango likasekweleke likolo kondause*, "Living Father who has come down from above." They had got the message and made it their own. But again, standard themes from the human lifeworld are the denominators: life, father, descent (the high, the low).

Epithetic identification for "disambiguation" of classes or of individuals. One of the forms of "disambiguation" is the epithet or standard qualifier. Some of the instances already given consist in such epithets. Other epithets would be these: for "banana" (*likondo*) the drums say (p. 40) "pole-supported banana" (*likondo lobotumbela*), for "forest" (*lokonda*), "dry-wood forest" (*lokonda teketeke*). Similarly, an individual may be designated with the help of an epithetic word or phrase, these often derived from an event in the individual's life. Epithets are a specific manifestation of formulaic tendencies but common and distinctive enough to warrant separate mention. They are particularly in evidence in establishing the "heavy" characters next discussed here.

Generation of "heavy" or ceremonial characters. Havelock has shown how, in the absence of the elaborate categorizations with which writing makes it possible to rack up knowledge more "abstractly," oral cultures commonly organize their knowledge in thematic narrative, peopled with impressive or "heavy" figures, often type characters (wise Nestor, clever Odysseus, faithful Penelope). Around such heavily accoutered figures (and themes associated with them) the lore of the culture is focused. The use of drum language carries ceremonialization to new heights. Again, because of the ambiguities in a sign system with only two variants (low and high tones), to be identifiable on the drum an individual needs epithetic and other ceremonial accouterments which will set his name in extremely high relief. Thus, assigned a drum name made up of his own given drum name plus those of his father and mother, as is customary, a Lokele known to his acquaintances in ordinary oral communication simply as Boyele (p. 52) finds himself exalted on the drums into "The Always Poisonous Cobra, Son of the Evil Spirit with the Lance, Nephew of the Men of Yagonde." "The Always Poisonous Cobra" was his grandfather's drum name, "Evil Spirit with the Lance," his father's.

Any name, even in ordinary parlance, is to some degree ceremonial: it fixes a person ritually or conventionally in a relationship to his fellows, though in patterns which of course vary from culture to culture. When the name is massive, as it has to be on the drums, and is used in its entirety every time the individual is mentioned, as it usually is on the drums, the ceremonial weight of discourse becomes exceedingly heavy. Primary oral culture commonly encourages very formal discourse, but the drums once again here exaggerate oral emphases. (The quasi-confidential public address customary today on radio and television is seemingly unknown in primary oral cultures or even in the residually oral writing and print cultures: it is a late development within the secondary oral culture produced by the electronic media, which for their existence and operation depend upon writing and print.)

Formulary, ceremonial appropriation of history. The history which a society knows is a selection of matter out of the continuum of the society's existence. "History" does not exist on its own but comes into being when human consciousness focuses on certain points in its temporal existence, isolates certain connections, and thereby frames certain elements into what consciousness can register as "events." What in a given society constitutes history—true, well-founded history, for we are not concerned here with unfounded or false history—will depend on a society's ways of constituting and selecting events from the continuum around it, its ways of appropriating its past.

Whereas highly developed writing and print cultures tend to appropriate the past analytically when they verbalize it, oral cultures tend to appropriate the past ceremonially, which is to say in stylized, formulary fashion. How this is so can be seen in part from their handling of names. In an oral culture, as we have seen, knowledge in its entirety tends to be organized around the action of individuals. Hence names, which distinguish individuals from one another, can serve as especially important foci for noetic organization in oral cultures, and in particular for the organization of history. They can become quite complicated because of the load of history they bear. Drum names can become even more complicated.

In all cultures names come from history in one way or another. They refer the individual to his own history, and in doing so help constitute that history in a formulary fashion that confers on it a certain ceremonial weight. An individual may be named "after" an ancestor or another person older than himself, being assigned a "given" name which is or was that of the other person. In addition, he may at the same time automatically bear his father and grandfather's or mother's name as well, thus acquiring further anchorages in history. In another pattern, names may derive directly from an historical event in the individual's own life or that of another or of a group. Drum names appear to work in both these patterns. The drum name for Boyele, just mentioned, incorporates ancestral drum names and thus fixes Boyele in history at the same time that it records history by fixing it in his own given drum name. The drum name given Carrington in a village he once visited records an historical fact in his life (p. 65): "The White Man Who Travels with the Man with Heavy Eyebrows." On a Camerounian village's drums, European colonial power (p. 66) is named in terms of some of its historical effects: "It reduces the country to slavery; those who survive it makes slaves." Or again, a certain medical assistant was named in drum language in accord with his behavior, "The Proud Man Who Listens to No Advice from Another" (p. 54). Another drum name given to Carrington (p. 55) is both patronymic and event-recording. Knowing that his father, who did not have a drum name of his own, had been a member of a group of folk dancers in England, the drummers designated Carrington as "The European, Son of the European Whom the Villagers Laughed at When he Leaped in the Air." Despite the historical rooting of many if not most names through the many cultures around the globe, few other names carry the load of explicit information often borne by drum names as recorded by Carrington.

The fixing of the past achieved in the nomenclature of human beings is affected also by other weighty, ceremonial formulas in the drum tradition. Villages have their own special drum names, at times, Carrington notes (p. 55), reflecting the history of the region. At other times, villagers change their names in accord with their fortunes: the village whose gong name had been "They had medicine to overcome curses," when defeated in war, changed its name to "The evil spirit has no friend nor kin."[10] Often the formulas register cultural institutions, the product of a longstanding experience, as when manioc or cassava is called "manioc which remains in the ground that lies fallow" (manioc roots can be left in the ground for more than a year before being harvested)—a whole agricultural tradition is caught here (p. 40).

It is tempting to regard the elaboration of drum names solely as a disambiguating process which does no more than add specificity by adding more and more separate units or "bits" of information. In fact, drum names do far more than this. The need to add separate units is an inducement to appropriate history. For drummers are historians, who study the flux around them to select the items worth recording. Carrington reports (p. 61) how, when a stranger arrives, before assigning him a drum name, the drummer will want to wait to see what happens to and around the stranger. "Let us watch a little to see how he dances," one drummer said of a new arrival. But the nature of the discourse into which knowledge—historical or other—is to be inserted helps determine the kind of knowledge generated. Havelock has explained how "the psychology of oral memorization and oral record required the content of what is memorized to be a set of doings" and that "this in turn presupposes actors or agents."[11] Because their names necessarily become so protracted, agents (individual human beings) figuring in drum communication would appear to constitute exaggerated and thus highly informative paradigms of actors or agents in oral culture generally and would thus appear to illustrate spectacularly the role of such agents in determining the cast of knowledge in such cultures.

Cultivation of praise and vituperation. An oral noetic economy, as has been seen, necessarily stores knowledge largely in narrative concerned with interacting human or quasi-human figures, involved normally in quite conspicuous struggle with one another. Such a noetic economy is sure to carry a heavy load of praise and vituperation. Indeed, the preoccupation with praise and vituperation, characteristic of primary oral culture generally, remains long after writing in the West, so long as orality is actively fostered by the concerted study of rhetoric (that is, basically, public speaking). Such study continues until the romantic movement finally matures.[12] European Renaissance literature still carried a heavy oral residue and thus was preoccupied with praise and vituperation, often highly ceremonial, to a degree which strikes technological man today as utterly bizarre but which in its persistence suggests the depths at which earlier sets of mind were structured into consciousness.

The drum language shows the characteristic praise-blame polarity of oral cultures generally but, again, in intensified or exaggerated form. Drum soubriquets are often simply praise formulas, common in oral cultures, but elaborated by the paraphrasis which drum language enforces. Indeed, Herskovits reports how drum language can actually come to be largely restricted in a given region to praise of kings and chiefs and to their messages.[13] And Carrington explains how small children use whistles they have fashioned "to broadcast praise names outside the house of some important villager, expecting a reward for doing so."[14] Soubriquets can be vituperative as well as laudatory. Thus the Batomba (p. 66) have two typically polarized paraphrastic names for white foreigners: "The white man, honored by all, companion of our chiefs" or, as occasion may demand, the pointed expression, "You do not touch a poisonous caterpillar."

The drums or slit-gongs themselves become a focus of the personalized praise-blame noetic economy, as they themselves are given names, which are beaten out at the start or end of a message. The Yamongbanga clan of Bokondo names its gong with a praise name, "The bolongo tree is not beaten with the hand for fear of its thorns." But discouraged—as many African villages are—by the exodus of their young people to the city, the Bakama of Bandio call their two gongs "We eat the last bits of food" and "Ears of mine, do not listen to what other people say" (in mockery).[15]

The agonistic ethos of oral cultures commonly mixes praise and vituperation (oral agonistic) with physical struggle. This conjuncture is evident in the *liango*, a special kind of wrestling contest reported by Carrington and involving drums (pp. 84-86). For the *liango*, representatives of two opposing clans or villages encircle their contestants as the drums beat. One contestant steps forward and defies the other side with a scornful gesture (the equivalent of "fliting" or ceremonial exchange of insults, as in the story of David and Goliath or in the *Iliad* or *Beowulf*). The drum thereupon calls out the praise of the defiant contestant, "The hero, full of pride." The wrestling begins to the enthusiastic accompaniment of the drum, and when one of the contestants is downed, the drum begins to praise the winner. Up and down the river villagers at work can listen to the broadcast praises.

On other occasions drum contest is simply verbal, or at least begins as verbal: insults are exchanged on the drums in typical fliting fashion (p. 96). But this verbal polemic can readily modulate into physical attack and thence to enduring feuds between families and entire clans. In oral cultures, speech is a conspicuously aggressive weapon and on the drum, which carries for miles, a particularly forceful one. There are many other uses of the drum for laudatory or vituperative purposes. Among the Tiv, Paul Bohannan has reported the drummed insults which can lead to physical violence and even death.[16] Perhaps the most compelling or efficacious drumming reported by Carrington (p. 95) was in a village wanting to get rid of a loose-living woman who had dropped in on them: the gong beaters drummed her out of town in the fullest sense of the word, insulting her, for everyone to hear for miles around, with "very frank anatomical precision."

Related to its use for praise and blame is the use of the drum for humorous effects, which will at times get a whole village laughing (pp. 95-96).

Copiousness. Oral performance demands flow: though pauses may be used effectively in public speaking, hesitancy is always a vice. Writing has no such strictures. Quite the contrary, good writing is often the product of halts for reflection, of revisions, of all sorts of false starts and stammerings. The smoothest flowing text is likely to be the product of great hesitancy. The economy of oral verbalization is quite different. An orator must have at his immediate command an abundance of things to say and of ways to say them, *copia* in Latin rhetoric, "flow," "abundance," such as Erasmus sought to provide for his residually oral literary milieu in his textbook *De duplici copia verborum ac rerum.* Because of concern for flow, an orator in the old, formally oratorical tradition (pre-television) commonly strikes a chirographically and typographically conditioned denizen of the technological world as gushingly verbose, flatulent, often boring, and conspicuously in love with his own voice. An oral culture would not so readily regard such a speaker this way.

Oral cultures need repetition, redundancy, verboseness for several reasons. First, as has already been noted in other connections, *verba volant*: spoken words fly away. A reader can pause over a point he wants to reflect on, or go back a few pages to return to it. The inscribed word is still there. The spoken word is gone. So the orator repeats himself, to help his hearers think it over. Second, spoken words do not infallibly carry equally well to everyone in an audience: synonyms, parallelisms, repetitions, neat oppositions, give the individual hearer a second chance if he did not hear well the first time. If he missed the "not only," he can probably reconstruct it from the "but also." Finally, the orator's thoughts do not always come as fast as he would wish, and even the best orator is at times inclined to repeat what he has just said in order to "mark time" while he is undertaking to find what move to make next.

All of these reasons for verbosity obtain in the case of drum talk and often with great force. First, the peculiar ambiguities of a language restricted phonemically to tones, without any vowels or consonants at all in the ordinary sense of these terms, make drummed words even more evanescent than spoken words and thus, as has been seen, encourage manifold repetition, even to such an extent that the formula may become a compounding of itself. Examples already cited for other purposes illustrate this point: "Make your feet come back the way they went, make your legs come back the way they went . . ." (p. 46), or "Bring your heart back down out of your mouth, your heart out of your mouth . . ." (p. 46).

Second, parallelisms, synonyms, and the like are common in drum language, as many of the examples already cited show. These are not mere ornamental devices but practical strategies.

The way in which such devices, or formulary devices generally, can implement reconstruction of a part of a drum message the hearer has missed was strikingly illustrated in discussion at a round table in Yaounde with Camerounian poets, novelists, and other writers over which I recently presided. There as here, I had been calling attention to the evanescent character of sound: a sound exists only when it is going out of existence, so that for example when I pronounce the last syllable "-tence" of the word "existence," the first two syllables are gone. One of the Camerounians in the round table intervened: "I am not so sure about the sound's disappearance. I recall many years ago when my great-grandfather caught the sound of a drum in our village, he picked up his fly whisk and waved it imperiously as though he were clearing the air. This also quieted us children. And he could tell what the drum had said even before the point at which he had begun to pay attention to it after he had quieted us." In discussion, the Camerounian speaker agreed that what had happened was that his great-grandfather had caught enough of the stereotyped phrase or the repetition or the parallelism to be able to reconstruct the anterior portion he had not heard or not heard clearly.

Despite this apparent capitulation of my interlocutor, however, his objection in its original bearing was valid in a way. Although sound is ineluctably time-bound, existing only when it is going out of existence, in a certain way the formula, in oral speech or on the drum, gives sound some independence of time. It spreads out the perception of sound, not only beyond the present physical instant, but also beyond the lengthier psychological "present," *la durée* of Henri Bergson. The formula, in this peculiar function, appears as a precocious equivalent of writing—a fact which I have never seen (or heard) commented on before.

Third, there is a good deal of marking time in much drum talk, where it is even more obvious than its equivalent in oral performance. Stereotyped phrases allow an oral poet or an old-style orator to organize his not yet formed thought: once a stereotyped phrase or a repetition is started, it can move to its conclusion more or less automatically so that the speaker's attention can be turned to working out what is coming next. The same advantage attaches to the stereotyped phrases and repetitions which are common, as has been seen, in drum talk: these gain time for thinking.

But the drummers go further, it appears, and develop special "words" serving precisely for marking time. Lokele drummers, Carrington explains (p. 69), have a way of "punctuating" messages by striking simultaneously on both the male and female lip of the drum to produce a sound which they vocalize as "kpei, kpei" (the vowels in this transcription again have French values). Carrington goes on to remark that one has the impression that the drummer who beats out "kpei, kpei" several times in succession is doing so really to gain time for lining up his next phrases. In this connection, it is worth recalling that written punctuation itself was originally thought of as working something like "kpei, kpei," that is, as marking pauses or delays as such. Today technological societies commonly represent punctuation as registering the "structure" or quasi-architectural organization which we impute to discourse: a word or phrase in *apposition* is *set off* by commas; adjectives in a *series* not *connected* by a *conjunction* are *separated* by commas; and so on. Such a structuralist understanding of punctuation and of language is of recent provenience. As late as 1640, the posthumously published *English Grammar* by Ben Jonson (1573?-1637) explains punctuation marks not in such fashion, but as marking the pauses useful for "breathing." Jonson was still thinking of writing and print in basically oral terms.[17] The "kpei, kpei" patterns are thus indeed quite like "punctuation" marks as these were conceived in cultures closer to primary orality.

V

From the evidence adduced here, it appears that African drum talk is an important variant of specifically oral communication not merely in the obvious sense that it operates in a world of sound but more particularly in the deeper sense that it manifests and even exaggerates many features which are distinctive of primary orality (orality untouched by writing or print) as compared with written and printed communication. Drum talk makes extraordinarily conspicuous use of typical oral strategies for gathering, storing, retrieving, and communicating knowledge, such as formulaic expression, standardization of themes, epithetic conceptualization, "heavy" or ceremonial human figures, formulary appropriation of history, polarization of existence in terms of praise and blame, and calculated "copiousness" (verbosity).

Since these strategies are constantly resorted to in normal speech in oral cultures and even more in designedly artistic speech in such cultures, it is hardly surprising that the drummers, too, would employ them. But these strategies are not immutable. They admit of diminution, intensification, and alteration. Certain media of communication work against them. Writing gradually reduces and finally more or less eliminates them—this is why they now stand out as phenomena distinctive of orality as compared to literacy. The drums or slit-gongs appear to move thought and communication in the opposite direction from writing, since, instead of reducing the use of typical oral noetic and expressive strategies, they intensify their use. The drums belong, in a particularly intense way, to the oral world.

This fact has several implications. First, it should warn against too facile assimilation of the drum messages to messages with which the electronic technological world typically deals. For example, the binary signal used by the drums of the Lokele and of other Africans suggests the binary signal of computers, but computers are post-typographic knowledge-storing devices, whereas drums do not store knowledge themselves but rather deal with knowledge stored in the mind of the drummer—which is to say with knowledge conceived in the way demanded by primary orality. Secondly, it appears that African drum language is not simply one among many alternative means of communication, any more than writing or print or radio or television are simply alternative means, each doing no more than what any other mode or medium of communication does, circulating "bits" of information. Each of the various media—oral, chirographic, typographic, electronic—determines differently the constitution of the thought it communicates. Communication in an oral culture, of which drum talk is a part, commonly is less purely concerned with "information," in the sense of knowledge new to the recipient, than communication typically is in writing and print cultures (once these have eliminated their oral residue, which they retain for a long while) or in modern electronic culture. Primary oral communication necessarily deals to a great extent with what the audience already knows: the typical oral narrative, for example, poetic or prose, normally recounts in familiar formulas what the audience has heard before, so that communication here is in fact an invitation to participation, not simply a transfer of knowledge from a place where it was to a place where it was not. Other messages in primary oral culture share, more or less, this involvement with the familiar. Drum language certainly conveys new knowledge or "information," but it likewise imbeds this in an extensive network of the already known. The familiar is not mere superfluity or "noise," as it might be in communication for a technological world: it is part of the message, and the need for it determines the quality of thought: an oral culture necessarily thinks conservatively.

The rooting of drum language in oral modes of thought needs to be taken into account in questions about the future of drum language, questions which are sure to arise—and indeed do arise in Carrington's book itself. Drum talk is already on the wane (pp. 107-110), so much so that it is now being taught in some schools which teach principally reading and writing, in an understandable effort to keep this important part of the African heritage alive in a literate age. Carrington asks (p. 92) whether drum talk is restricted to matters of the past, or at least to matters long traditional, whether it can adapt to change. Drum language can certainly coin new terms for new things, as he shows, such as river steamers or cigarettes. And until electronic communication better penetrates the interior of Africa, the drums will continue to serve very practical, and indeed changing, daily needs for rapid communication over distances. But in the fuller perspectives suggested here, the question of the relationship of drum language to the future involves more than new lexical adjustments, as Carrington himself is well aware.

One cannot be very specific about implications of drum languages for the future. Indeed, some would consider the question of such implications already moot, given the evident progressive decline in skill with the drums. Drums will be of only antiquarian interest in the future, some have contended. Drums will certainly be of antiquarian interest and, what is more important and not the same thing, of historical interest. But there is more than that to the question of their implications for the future. The widespread use of talking drums in

Africa suggests an extraordinarily strong current of orality in African cultures, and this suggestion is further reinforced by the way in which the use of slit-gongs and drums for talking merges with their use for other, nonverbalizing purposes throughout African cultures in civil and religious ceremonies of all sorts, in the dance, in sports, in celebrations, in war, in work, and many other areas of existence.

Cultures bring their past to their present and their future. It appears gratuitous to hold, though some do, that because of some supposedly superhuman technology all cultures everywhere are destined soon to be entirely the same. Marks left by history are permanent. The African entry into the technological world is being made not only from a signally oral base but also in a state of consciousness different from that which governed the entry of the West. The movement from orality in the West to the modern technological world took some six thousand years (calculating the departure from orality as dating from the beginning of script around 3500 B. C.), and it was quite unconscious in the sense that only in the past few decades has the Western world effectively taken note even of the existence of oral cultures as radically distinct from writing and print cultures. In Africa the transit from orality through writing and print to electronic communication is taking place, not over six thousand years, but in two or three generations, and for many in even less time. Moreover, it is taking place consciously, and often with exquisite self-consciousness. Being more conscious, the transit in Africa is thereby more human than it was in the West. Perhaps the present study can contribute to developing ways of assessing this rapid transit.

NOTES

[1] In "Drum and Whistle 'Languages': An Analysis of Speech Surrogates," *American Anthropologist*, 59 (1957), 487-506, Theodore Stern has provided a permanently helpful generalized analysis of various ways in which human speech has been converted into surrogate sounds for transmission by means other than normal vocal articulation of speech itself. The article provides an extensive bibliography on drum languages. For an example of a recent technical linguistic study of drum language, see Pierre Alexandre, "Langages tambourines," *Semiotica*, 1 (1969), 273-281. See also Thomas A. Sebeok and Donna Jean Umiker-Sebeok, eds.,

Speech Surrogates, Vol. I (The Hague: Mouton, 1976), Vol. II in preparation.

2*La Voix des tambours: Comment comprendre le langage tambouriné d'Afrique* (Kinshasa: Centre Protestant d'Editions et de Diffusion, 1974). References in parentheses in the text of the present article are to this book and the translations are my own. The earlier volume in English is *The Talking Drums of Africa* (London: Carey Kingsgate Press, 1949).

3"The Talking Drums of Africa," *Scientific American*, December 1971, pp. 90-94.

4New Haven: Yale University Press, 1967.

5Rafael Karsten, *The Head-Hunters of Western Amazonas: The Life and Culture of the Jibaro Indians of Eastern Ecuador and Peru*, Commentationes Humanarum Litterarum, 7 (Helsingfors: Societas Scientarum Fennica, 1935), pp. 109-113.

6See C. P. Fitzgerald, *The Birth of Communist China* (Baltimore, Md.: Penguin Books, 1964), p. 154: "In colloquial [Chinese] speech one does not say 'chin' for gold, because many other words sounded 'chin' exist; 'huang chin'—yellow gold—is the colloquial term, which identifies the 'chin' in this phrase. But in writing [classical Chinese] it was not necessary to use two words [because Chinese written characters for the various words pronounced 'chin' differ from one another]; only the word of primary meaning was employed and thus a page of the classical style read aloud became a wholly unintelligible string of phonemes."

7Albert B. Lord, *The Singer of Tales*, Harvard Studies in Comparative Literature, 24 (Cambridge, Mass.: Harvard University Press, 1960), pp. 30-67, and *passim*; Eric A. Havelock, *Preface to Plato* (Cambridge, Mass.: Belknap Press of Harvard University Press, 1963), pp. 134-142; Robert P. Creed, "A New Approach to the Rhythm of *Beowulf*," *PMLA*, 81 (1966), 23-33; Michael N. Nagler, *Spontaneity and Tradition: A Study in the Oral Art of Homer* (Berkeley: University of California Press, 1974); John Miles Foley, "Formula and Theme in Old English Poetry," in B. A. Stolz and R. S. Shannon, eds., *Oral Literature and the Formula* (Ann Arbor, Mich.: Center for Coordination of Ancient and Modern Studies, 1976), pp. 207-238—see also the other papers in this volume and the comprehensive annotated bibliography in James P. Holoka, "Homeric Originality: A Survey," *Classical World*, 66 (1973), 257-293.

8Havelock, *Preface to Plato*, p. 140.

9Ibid., pp. 166-190.

10Carrington, "The Talking Drums of Africa," p. 93.

11Havelock, *Preface to Plato*, p. 171.

12See Walter J. Ong, *Rhetoric, Romance, and Technology* (Ithaca, N.Y.: Cornell University Press, 1971), pp. 12-20, 254-283; Ong, *The Presence of the Word*, pp. 252-255.

[13]Melville J. Herskovits, *Dahomey: An Ancient West African Kingdom* (New York: J. J. Augustin, 1938), II, pp. 318-319.

[14]Carrington, "The Talking Drums of Africa," p. 94.

[15]*Ibid.*

[16]*Justice and Judgment among the Tiv* (London: Oxford University Press for the International African Institute, 1957), pp. 142-144.

[17]Walter J. Ong, "Historical Backgrounds of Elizabethan and Jacobean Punctuation Theory," *PMLA*, 59 (1944), 349-360.

The Message of the American Folk Sermon

Bruce A. Rosenberg

This article by Bruce A. Rosenberg serves as a supplement to his major study, The Art of the American Folk Preacher *(1970), relating the techniques used by these preachers, chiefly from the south and southwestern United States, to those employed by the Yugoslav oral poets recorded by Parry and Lord. He characterizes the sermons as belonging to a folk tradition, relying as they do on the assimilation of popular culture (such as blues songs) as well as biblical texts, and on an audience familiar with the genre through long experience. In his analysis of various sermons, Rosenberg explains how the basic text-context-application structure is modified according to the particular audience and situation of each performance, and how the skillful preacher uses the oral techniques of memorization and recreation. Although the sermons do not share all of the characteristics of oral-formulaic poetry, Rosenberg examines classic elements such as thematic construction, patterned phraseology, and regular rhythm. He concludes by showing how these sermon techniques helped to structure the political speeches of Revs. Martin Luther King, Jr., and Jesse Jackson.*

Reprinted from *Oral Tradition*, 1 (1986), 695-727.

The author of *The Art of the American Folk Preacher* (Rosenberg, 1970) had intended, in part, to disprove much of the theory of oral composition developed by Milman Parry and Albert Lord. Nearly all of their work had been done in Yugoslavia, the rest in neighboring Balkan states. The resultant research was based upon a language that few interested scholars could read and fewer could analyze. *Folk Preacher* was going to correct that problem by decomposing materials that were immediately available to English-speaking scholars. If the *guslari* used compositional techniques like those of Homer, thus making him accessible in ways that had not been possible before, then the preachers, whose techniques were also analogous, could be analyzed to comment on both. In the event, however, most folklorists found that the "discovery" of the folk preacher (of a certain kind) only reinforced the Parry-Lord thesis, that it was an extension of the Yugoslavian experience in the United States.

Thus, the original intention of the author had been to address oral-formulaic theory, indirectly, through a detailed examination of American folk sermons that were spontaneously composed and orally delivered; but during the course of recording and interviewing—1966 until 1971—the compelling power of American folk preachers commanded attention in its own right. In the final measure, the research of this scholar and others has concentrated as much upon the folk preachers for their own sake (and intrinsic merits) as upon principles of composition in Homer and several medieval narrators. Rev. Rubin Lacy, Rev. Elihu Brown, and Rev. C. L. Franklin eventually crowded off the page of this research the names of Homer, Turoldus, and the *Beowulf* poet. The historical comparisons have been undertaken, and contemporary American folk preachers have proven to be of interest for what they can reveal not only about the compositional process of the making of *Beowulf* but about themselves and an American oral tradition as well.

These performances were described at length in *Folk Preacher*; nevertheless, the most graphic and effective contextual images are from observers of early nineteenth-century church services. Henry Fearon's 1818 account of a Methodist service, despite its exaggerations and inclination to portray Americans as uncivilized and undisciplined, captures the spirit of the event compellingly. Having heard that American Methodist services displayed "an extreme degree of fanatical violence," he visited an "African" church in which all of the celebrants were black. They numbered more than four hundred. Fearon wrote that the preacher "indulged in long pauses, and occasional loud elevations of voice, which were always answered by the audience with deep groans." After the minister had finished preaching and had departed, an impromptu prayer session followed in which one of the members sang a hymn and, following, another was called on to pray. Fearon felt that "he roared and ranted like a maniac" while "the male part of the audience groaned" and "the female shrieked." One man shouted and another continued for half an hour bawling. A young girl—Fearon thought that she was about eleven years old—was in convulsions while her mother held her up in arms so that the entire congregation might see her ecstasy. A Brother Macfaddin began preaching "with a voice which might almost rival a peal of thunder, the whole congregation occasionally joining in, responsive to his notes. The madness now became threefold increased . . . had the inhabitants of Bedlam been let loose, they could not have exceeded it. From forty to fifty were praying aloud and extemporaneously at the same moment of time: some were kicking, many jumping, all clapping their hands and crying out in chorus. . ." (Fearon, 1818, pp. 162-167).

This is not dispassionate reporting by our contemporary standards; nevertheless, Fearon's descriptions sufficiently demonstrate that the style of the oral preacher has not changed noticeably since 1818 nor has the response of his congregation. For our immediate purposes one important element is missing from this description, that of the preacher's sermon. We assume that it was, as it is today, spontaneously composed and orally performed, without the assistance of a manuscript. By the time a black Methodist or other Fundamentalist has reached the pulpit, he has heard quite a bit of preaching—probably for more than two decades—and has likely done some sermonizing himself. His sermons are not strictly speaking spontaneous, but are derived in large measure from his several years' experience; in that respect they are spontaneous in the way that the heroic songs composed by Parry-Lord singers of tales were spontaneous, in the way that an experienced jazz musician improvises during what used to be called a jam session.

I have partly characterized such sermons as "oral" in that the exclusive mode of delivery is from the preacher's mouth to the congregation's ears. A manuscript is rarely used, and, although a few preachers have been observed relying on small note cards to jog their memories, these sermons were never meant for silent reading. For that reason they have never been printed, though a few of the more famous and accomplished men have had their sermons recorded and then produced on phonograph discs. This is an authentic and exclusively oral form of communication.

These are also properly considered as folk sermons. The source of inspiration for Fundamentalist ministers is exclusively the New Testament; yet that book is thoroughly absorbed by the ministers who then preach from it from memory. But the preacher has also been exposed to a great deal of non-Scriptural lore during his life, and while he consciously recognizes that only the Bible holds the true Word, he nevertheless has usually deeply assimilated the unofficial traditions of his own culture. For instance, when the Rev. Rubin Lacy, while preaching a sermon on "Dry Bones in the Valley" (16 July 1967) said, "The Word of God/Come to the dry bones/Rise and live," what was primarily in his mind was the song, "Dem Bones, Dem Bones, Dem Dry Bones," which was more influential at that moment than was Ezekiel xxxvii, 5. The song has it: "Now hear the Word of the Lord." Ezekiel said, "Thus saith the Lord God unto these bones." Also in the back of Lacy's mind was the well-known spiritual line, "Dese bones gwine rise again"; *rise* is not used by Ezekiel in the King James translation. At another time, while preaching on the appearance of Christ at the end of the world, Lacy described Him "Dressed in raiment/White as driven as the snow" with a "Rainbow 'round his shoulder." Now, Revelation x, 1 reads, in part, "and a rainbow was upon his head. . . ." Lacy's primary inspiration was, again, a popular song: "There's a rainbow 'round his shoulder, and a sky of blue above," etc.—not even a spiritual. So, even in this most Scripturally influenced of traditions, the popular song and the secularized spiritual have made their impact. Ostensibly officially deriving exclusively from the written, learned Word, the preaching studied here is in fact heavily influenced and colored by folklore, by oral traditions.

Rev. Lacy had been a blues singer before he ascended to the ministry in 1930 (as he estimated the date), and so the lyrics of many songs should be expected to be racing around his memory and to find their way out in spontaneous sermons. His colleague, Rev. Elihu Brown (like Lacy from Bakersfield, Calif.), also incorporated folklore in his preaching, as in this sermon of 11 June 1967, "God is Mindful of Man"; here the non-Scriptural tradition employs a cosmic railroad:

> Jesus was so concerned about man
> Until he left richness and glad glory
> Came down here in this old sin-cussed world
> Stepped on the train of nature with a virgin
>   woman
> And brought Himself out an infant baby
> On the train of nature nine months
> Stepped off the train at a little old station called
>   Bethlehem
> Wrapped over there in swaddlin' clothes
> Stayed right there. . . .

A common enough metaphor in several spirituals, the glory train had in this sermon been elevated in stature. Brown was never a professional singer, but he had spent many years in church choirs and had heard the songs which described the glory train many times. And even if he had never been in a choir, Brown would have had to be willfully closed to the music around him not to have heard these songs.

Oral sermons, like most performances of oral narratives, are difficult to define structurally. These edifying pieces are the products of preachers who may not have had much formal training and are recited for the benefit of peer group members. Usually no manuscript is used, enabling the preacher to draw upon Divine inspiration to a great extent. In those few cases in which a preacher has prepared a manuscript, the text is written as though in prose, but, once behind the pulpit during a holy service, folk preachers of the kind we have been describing here will break away from the prepared text into their own rhythm and chanting. The following is a partial transcript of a sermon, "Three Strong Men from Jerusalem," written (for his own use) by Rev. Jerry H. Lockett of Charlottesville, Va.:

> Shadrach, Meshach, and Abednego were three fellows from Jerusalem. They were three Hebrew boys whitch [sic] had been caught in a crisis away from home. The men of the text can justly be styled as fellows, because they were pardners [sic], and comrades, in every secse [sic] of the word.
>
> They were from the same country, held the same religious convictions, and had been appointed to the same position there in Babylon, by the same King for the same purpose. These three men had reached the same conclusion as to what to do about their religious conclusion.

Lockett's sermon began with these two paragraphs; by the time he had reached the last sentence he had begun chanting. The division of his utterances into sentences and of those units into paragraphs broke down. The basic unit of Lockett's performance became the phrase, its length determined by the length of time required for its utterance. However, the structure that Rev. Lockett intended when he wrote out the sermon remained, in large part, because he always had his notes to remind him of the sequence of ideas that he wished to express. (In this sermon, the sequence of events to be related was simplified because they followed the chronology of the Old Testament account.) After the narrative had been rendered, Lockett interpreted the moral values to be derived from this story.

Few oral folk sermons are even this well organized. The preachers interviewed recalled only the "text-context-application" format, which requires that they begin each sermon with an announcement of the Biblical text for the day, its context within the Bible, and its application to contemporary life and morals. That leaves a great deal of latitude for individual expression, both on the level of the single line and the organization of nearly the entire performance. The length of the sermon varies from fifteen minutes to over an hour, though most last for about thirty minutes. However, since so much of each sermon is improvised, and is thus flexible, the preacher can spontaneously lengthen or abridge the performance as the immediate situation dictates. That is, if the congregation is listless, bored, or otherwise distracted, he can use any of several dramatic techniques to liven up his preaching (altering vocal volume and pitch, gesturing, changing expression, and so forth) or he can cut the service short. When this is the mode of the composition, generic definition based on structure is difficult—beyond the "text-context-application" formula.

After text and context, then, the sermon's form is fluid, and is in large measure open to negotiation between preacher and congregation, that negotiation taking place during the performance itself. The sermon's length, and consequently its form, will probably vary among performances. Nor is it accurate to speak of—or to think of—an ideal sermon in the preacher's mind. He does not have such an ideal fixed form before he starts each service, but rather a general outline of what needs to be said. The "text" opening, taken verbatim from the Bible, will be the only inflexible utterance in the performance. Fixity is in fact a notion contrary to these preachers' theology; since they believe that their sermons come from God and they are only His conduits, that He uses their organs of speech when they are preaching, they can hardly be expected to prepare the content and structure of their message when during their performance the Lord will assume command.

A different notion of structural units, and consequently of structure, was posited by Rosenberg and Smith (1975). This research took as the basic elements of structure the semantic groupings of the sermon. For instance, examples taken from four of Lacy's sermons indicated that the preacher used Biblical names and referred to animals, the Scriptures, life and death, faith, units of time, and colors, among many other semantic categories. State diagrams were then constructed which recapitulated the order in which these semantic components were spoken. Since two of the sermons had been enthusiastically received and in two others the congregation's response forced an evaluation of "unsuccessful," the four sermons were then compared to see what, if any, structural differences the state diagrams revealed.

The sermons' semantic clusters were developed in one of three ways. The most complex, and the oldest, mode of arrangement is a parallel organization in which themes are introduced one at a time, developed individually, and then combined with other clusters either to be developed further or to be included in a conclusion. This structural type encourages subtle and extended development of the individual elements of an argument; however, to be effective, the audience must have recall of these developments prior to the conclusion when all components are joined into an organic and logical entity. With this type of structure, major themes will have similar distribution patterns: that is, parallel structure should be reflected in themes that have important concentrations in non-overlapping portions of a sermon before coinciding at the very end.

A second type develops by free association. When the preacher begins with a fixed theme, he then moves from idea to idea in a seemingly random manner. Transitions may occur because of events in the preacher's life which impinge on his consciousness at such performative moments—an event taking place outside the church window that momentarily attracts his attention, a face in the congregation, or whatever stimulus influences the flow of thoughts through an undirected consciousness. Developmental structures of this kind produce truly unique sermons. Because the psychological, social, and physical environments of the churches studied were changing, it would be virtually impossible for a preacher to duplicate the arrangement of themes in an earlier performance.

A third possibility is a clustered structure. Such sermons consist of several major thematic sections that are independent of each other. Within each local development, or cluster, free movement or transition among a subset of ideas is likely to occur. Between ideas, however, there would be few, if any links. The specific order in which clusters are presented could be the result either of free association or of predetermination. The latter possibility would greatly facilitate the memorization process which is so important for spontaneous composition in oral performances. The preacher could memorize the three or four major clustural developments and, once within a particular cluster, could "shift down" to a memorial partition (a commonly used mnemonic aid) or else freely associate. By using this predetermined mode of development, the preacher would most likely deliver sermons on widely separate occasions that, while not identical, would certainly be strikingly similar. Albert Lord (e.g., 1960, pp. 99-123) has made much of similar principles among the Yugoslavian *guslari*.

Thus, the state diagrams revealed to Rosenberg and Smith that these seemingly rambling sermons contained definite, well-defined ideational structures. This research also demonstrated, by analyzing lexical selection, that a sermon's success is closely related to its specificity. The characteristic mode of development, at least in the case of the preacher whose sermons were analyzed (Rev. Lacy), is through relatively unrelated clustered sequences of themes. Nevertheless, the researchers concluded that development by thematic or ideational clusters may be the most reasonable mode, given both the desire of the preacher to repeat favorite sermons and the demands placed upon his memory by the stresses inherent in performance. By remembering the sequence of a few broad conceptual categories, he may rely for his development on contextual recall or on associative improvisation during actual performance. Finally, the ideational patterns of the successful sermons manifest a simple symmetry which is absent in the unsuccessful, and that seems to be a significant compositional factor in this highly organic art form.

Although the original idea of studying the folk sermon was to learn about the compositional techniques of the *guslari*—and by further extension of all oral singers everywhere, if that were possible—the folk sermon is not exactly like those other narrative traditions. And sermon formulas are somewhat different from those of Homer, of the *guslari*, or of the Central Asian *akyn*. The Homeric unit, for instance, is relatively rigid metrically and does not allow variation. Anglo-Saxon verse alliterates, and its metrics are more yielding. The Yugoslav meter is bound neither to the formal metrical patterns typical of Homeric verse nor to alliteration. Nevertheless, the methods of composition are similar enough to allow meaningful comparisons; in some ways what may be said about the folk sermon may be tentatively extended to the oral narratives of other singers of tales.

Lord sought to explain the process by which narratives were composed in the following manner (1960, pp. 65-66):

> From the point of view of usefulness in composition, the formula means the essential idea. . . . But this is only from the point of view of the singer composing, of the craftsman in lines.
>
> And I am sure that the essential idea of the formula is what is in the mind of the singer, almost as a reflex action in rapid composition, as he makes his song. Hence it could, I believe, be truly stated that the formula not only is stripped to its essential idea in the mind of the composing singer, but also is denied some of the possibilities of aesthetic reference in context.

Psycholinguists differ from Lord, assuming that the existence of ideas precedes and is discrete from their expression in utterances. The formula, that special group of words, does not "mean" its essential idea but is rather an expression of it. And the essential idea of the formula does not have priority in the singer's mind but rather the idea itself which must then be encoded into an acceptable language. Many linguists hold that the function of language is to convert ideas into sentences: we first have an idea, so this theory goes, and then we formulate the syntactic structure and lexicon with which to express it. After the syntactic structure has been generated, many of the "blanks can be filled in, which process materializes the actual sentence itself out of its deep structure. In many instances, however, key words form the basis of the generation of syntax, so that prior to forming a sentence the speaker has one or more words already in mind" (Deese, 1970, pp. 50-51). The encoding process then would not necessarily follow the patterning of a generation of the syntax-supplying of lexicon but could

actually begin with the lexical choice. This seems to be what happens
when the oral preacher carries over the same important word from line
to line, as does Rev. C. L. Franklin in "Moses at the Red Sea"
(Rosenberg, 1970, p. 108).

> What do ya think that ya want
> Why the *rod* of your deliverance is in your own
>   hands
> Stretch out the *rod* that's in your hands
> I don't have a new *rod* to give ya
> 5   I don't have a new instrument to give ya
> I don't have a new suggestion for ya
> I do not have a new plan
> Your course has already been charted by destiny
> Stretch out the *rod* that's in your own hand

Each line has been created either by syntactic analogy with the one
preceding, or through similarity of idea, or by the repetition of seminal
words which are bridges to following lines and which are the
cornerstones for the syntactic constructions of them. "Rod" is in the
preacher's mind when he chants this sequence, not the least because he
is addressing "Moses," who is about to stretch out his rod to dry the
Red Sea. When "the rod of your deliverance" has been uttered, the
syntax of the next several lines is being preformulated around the
seminal word, "rod." After a triplet using "rod," it is dropped, but the
syntax of the fourth line and most of its lexical inventory is retained.
"Rod" has already served its purpose.

    Much has been made of the role of memory in oral performance.
Lord (1960, p. 36) thought that the singer

> does not memorize formulas any more than we as children
> memorize language. He learns them by hearing them in other
> singers' songs, and by habitual usage they become part of his
> singing as well. . . . The singer has not had to learn a large
> number of separate formulas. The commonest ones which he
> first uses set a basic pattern, and once he has the basic pattern
> firmly in his grasp, he needs only to substitute another word for
> the key one. . . . The particular formula itself is important to
> the singer only up to the time when it has planted in his mind
> its basic mold. When this point is reached, the singer depends

less and less on learning formulas and more and more on the process of substituting other words in the formula pattern.

Lord's description of the compositional process is much like metaphors of the generative theory, the whole description sounding mechanical: new formulas are created by analogy with old ones, and the compositional process is primarily one of substituting words and phrases in unoccupied slots. There is no doubt that this process does often occur. But generative theory argues that given a certain deep structure, an infinite number of surface structures can be generated. Lord ties the creation of new formulas (metrically governed utterances) to the singer's recollection of "the commonest ones." Actually, the singer is freed from such "memory" and such hydraulic reliance. He has at his command not several score or even several hundred formulas which can be altered by word or phrase substitution but rather a metrical deep structure enabling the generation of an infinite number of sentences or utterances in the meter of his native language.

Memory is certainly involved in traditional conglomerations of formulas rather than in the creation of a single unit. For instance, in 1967 and again in 1968, Rev. Rubin Lacy was recorded preaching two sermons on the same topic, "The Deck of Cards," a pious version of Aarne-Thompson Tale Type 1613, "The Deck of Cards." This is a type of counting song (see Wilgus and Rosenberg, 1971, p. 291) which assigns a religious meaning to each card in the standard deck; the two corresponds to heaven and hell, the three to the trinity, the four to the gospel writers, the five to the five virgins, and so on. A small part of the 1968 sermon included the following passage (Rosenberg, 1970, p. 130):

> And, God
> Said there's two ways to go
> Heaven
> Or either hell
> Mister Hoyle
> Made a two-spot
> He called it a deuce
> God from Zion
> And put it in the deck
> And God
> Made the Father

> Son and the Holy Ghost
> Ain't God all right?
> And Mister Hoyle
> Made a three-spot
> And called it a trey

Several features of these sixteen lines illustrate how Lacy was able to recall this passage with great accuracy even after more than a year had gone by. The lines are closely related associationally. The "counting song" follows the very elementary sequence of the numbers, from one to ten. The identification of each card and its real religious meaning is alternated: God says or does something and Mister Hoyle (His minister on earth?) responds by encoding the Scriptural message in playing card form. Lastly, the syntax of each card-cluster is similar—

> So God
> Made a earth
> * * *
> And God
> Made a year
> * * *
> And God
> Made the Father

—while the responses to God's acts of creation are syntactically identical, and lexically similar:

> Mister Hoyle
> Made a deck of cards
> * * *
> Mister Hoyle
> Made a two-spot
> * * *
> And Mister Hoyle
> Made a three-spot

Lacy had good recall of this passage because of the simple arithmetic progression which corresponded to, in negatives, what "God" had done. The entire sequence was decomposed into a dozen or so sub-sections, each concerned with a different denomination card, each related with similar syntax; stitching them together produced the whole.

Rev. Lacy's friend and colleague, Rev. Elihu Brown, liked to describe the birth of Jesus metaphorized as the Glory Train (Rosenberg, 1970, p. 169), using similar techniques: "God on the train of nature/Stayed there nine months/Stepped off at the station one mornin'/Stayed right there/Until God wanted Him to come on out/God was so concerned brotheren/Till He came all the way to this sinful world/Came in the shape of a baby/Wrapped Himself in human blood." Logical progression, of a train on the track and of pregnancy and birth, orders Brown's passage and assists in his retention of it. Length does not limit these mannered passages—Lacy often used a forty-seven–"line" favorite on the Four Horsemen—but the addition of new and thematically disparate information does. If the content of new material is kept within the associational scope of the remembered material, as Lacy and Brown have done in the above excerpts, the string could be substantially lengthened. Psycholinguists have long ago demonstrated that people can retain only about seven items of information in a random string but several dozen in a sentence. We, like the preachers, are not limited as much by the amount of information we can process as by the number of symbols we may try to assimilate (Miller, 1967, pp. 12, 25).

One trick, then, to effect a successful oral performance is for the performer to find ways of organizing his material. Repetition of his narrative, specifically of certain stories or exempla within the frame of the sermon, greatly helps. In repetition, the smaller units, whether sentences or formulas, tend to be grouped in the performer's mind into larger groups: this enables the performance of such strings as "The Deck of Cards" or "The Glory Train." Some literary scholars now call such sequences "themes" and "type-scenes," the former concentrating on the formulaic structure, the latter on the subject described (Fry, 1968, pp. 48-53). If the oral performer can retain a few themes with reasonable accuracy (enough to make sense in a different performance), his job has been made far easier than if he had tried to manipulate and create anew several hundred formulas. The process of memorization is probably linked to the formation of such large chunks of information, the performer mentally enlarging the blocks until they include nearly all of the material appropriate for the moment (Bousfield and Cohen, 1955, pp. 83-95).

A new narrative, or a new idea expressed as an exemplum and inserted into a sermon, is put into the idiosyncratic syntax and lexicon of the preacher. His own first interpretation is what the preacher remembers, even when the source is Scriptural; in this context memory is a recollection of the initial verbalization (Carmichael et al., 1932, pp. 73-86). This phenomenon provides the basis for the form of orally transmitted narrative. Thus sermons tend to change less the more they are performed, as the preacher recalls not the initial stimuli but his own mental organization of them.

One has only to read (or hear!) several analogous lines from separate sermons that have been repeatedly performed—or to listen to repeated *guslar* songs, for that matter—to appreciate that "by heart" memorization is seldom attained. Many of the sermon lines are non-grammatical jumbles which repeated listening exposure will not decipher. These are the other, salient features of oral communication: when Parry and Lord shifted the focus of their research, and consequently ours, from the audience to the singer and his difficulties, they left the dynamics of the audience little understood. They changed our understanding of the performer's relationship with his audience but mainly from the performer's point of view.

Again, the congregation responding to oral performances is in a position analogous to the audiences of other traditional transmissions. Like the *guslari* and possibly somewhat like the audiences of medieval epic and romance, the congregations are tradition-oriented. They expect to hear the old tales, from the Bible as well as from secular traditions, tales they themselves know well. New stories might well be suspect. Even stories used from the Bible are limited in number, there being fewer than fifty favorites.

The tradition-oriented audience brings to each performance a knowledge of narrative tradition, of language (lexicon and formal considerations such as ritualized openings, closings, means of advancing the story, and so on), and of aural style. The congregation enjoys the sermon because they know what is coming next and how it will be expressed. Too much has been made of the comfort the audience allegedly derives from hearing familiar material; being able to anticipate the performer enables members of the congregation (or of any oral audience) to participate in the performance, to contribute to it (in the case of religious services to call out, rhythmically, to the preacher), to help make what is at that moment being created. Careful listening to audience participation showed that members of the congregation anticipated their preacher not only in the language that was still a few seconds away from his delivery but occasionally in the melody he would use to express it. Some preachers seem to take their cues from exclamations in the congregation. The services are thus much more than antiphonal; they are mutually communicative and creative.

Many times during these "communicative events" the preacher's words were unintelligible. I could not distinguish the parameters of phonemes even after repeated tape reruns, and it does not seem likely that many members of the congregation could either. Yet during the original performance they responded alertly and vigorously. In this art form the message is pretty close to being the medium (Rosenberg, 1970, p. 40) because that message elicits a visceral response to rhythm and melody that is understood by the congregational listener as having informational content. All of the preachers interviewed for *Folk Preacher* felt that they were imparting ideas.

Recorded sentences have been transmitted with background noise in experiments conducted by D. J. Bruce (1974, pp. 245-252), so that the sentences could not be intelligibly heard. The researcher told his subjects the topic of the sentences they were going to hear and then replayed more sentences, again after first introducing the stated subject. Actually, the sentences used for each topic were the same; interpretation by the subjects differed, however, because each was predisposed toward certain information once given a topic introduction. Everyone heard not so much what he wanted to hear but what he expected was going to be said. The interpreting apparatus in the brain, in other words, is able to generate sentences which will match input, even if that input is not real but merely expected.

In another experiment (Mehler and Carey, 1967, pp. 335-338), sentences with different deep structures but identical surface structures, both beginning with the words "they are," were played to subjects, again with disruptively noisy backgrounds. The subjects had the most difficulty in identifying the sentences with the altered deep structure, suggesting that the inability to identify the deep structure distorts the accuracy of perception. To return to the noisy church services, it is clear that something is being understood. That something may not be precisely what the preacher is trying to communicate, but it is meaningful to the congregant, possibly something that he could not paraphrase individually.

The acceptability of sentences is a subjective judgment (Deese, 1970, p. 30). Poor grammar is common in oral sermons, not only because of the relatively low level of formal education of the ministers, but because rapid delivery often leads to mistakes. The following utterances were all spoken during moments of relative calm and were clearly enunciated and heard, yet none drew quizzical looks: "But he's a profession in his field," "He saw the dream, meaning seven years of poordom of no prosperity," and "You know, we as a whole, if we are told to do something that we don't see any sense in doing that we don't think it oughta be did." Communication of some sort was being transacted.

Communication also occurs in the rhythm of language: in one more way, the message has been influenced by the medium. The meter of the chanted sermon line differs slightly from that of the same line spoken in conversation; attention to the musicality of the language forces this change. Yet usually the pause in an utterance, punctuated by an audible gasp, falls at the end of a major component, for example a noun phrase, or between the noun phrase and verb in a verb phrase:

> I heard a fellow—Oh Lord
> Is the strength of my life
> Then whom shall I fear?
> And the Lord is my Shepherd.

Phrases are usually broken at the end of a clause:

> If He hadn't 'a been my shepherd
> I'd 'a been gone a long time ago
> * * *
> The Lord is the strength of my life
> Then whom shall I fear?

In those cases when the break between components is not so clearly junctured, as in conversation, the auditor tends to interpret the break himself (Fodor and Bever, 1965, pp. 414-420). In one experiment, tape-recorded sentences upon which clicks had been superimposed were played to subjects. When later asked to reconstruct the sentences, the subjects showed a marked tendency to place the clicks in the direction of or at the component junctures. The researchers concluded that, even when such delineating factors as hesitation pauses or inflections are not present, listeners interpolate component boundaries on their own. Congregations will, accordingly, punctuate in their own minds what the preacher fails to do behind the pulpit. If the congregation's rhythm is not that of the preacher, during the service they will actually help him regularize it.

Most preachers' performance utterances are grammatically acceptable, and the sermon style may be accurately characterized by a very high proportion of simple, active, declarative sentences. This style does not develop because of poor education or even a low intelligence. We know that nearly all adults have the competence to generate very complicated sentences embodying several transformations. Only speakers who are severely retarded or who suffer from aphasia may be reduced to generating simple sentences exclusively. Rather, the conditions of performance, particularly the need to generate the next formula rapidly, profoundly influence syntactical structures.

Literary critics used to attribute the simplicity of oral narrative diction to the performer's concern for his audience. This explanation held that if the language was too complex or the metaphors too recondite, the listener would lose the thread of the story. While trying to interpret what a particular line (and its image) meant, dozens of following lines would have been recited. That is why, so the explanation went, the style of the oral epic is as it is. Now, however, we are certain that the simplicity of oral syntax comes about because it is easier for the oral performer—the preacher—to recite that way, to compose simple sentences. While there is no evidence that simple active sentences have linguistic priority, they may have some kind of psychological priority. This ordering would be demonstrated if we interpreted complex sentences by first reducing them to their basic propositions in simple ones. But the evidence for this hierarchy is not at all decisive (Deese, 1970, pp. 42-44).

Similar evidence for the ease of processing simple sentences has been deduced from experiments with self-embedded ones. Subjects who could read sentences which contained two embedded clauses were not likely to speak them, nor did they understand them readily when they were heard. Their syntax made them difficult to understand and induced a resistance in people to speak them. Memory is again the limiting factor: we have difficulty processing self-embedded sentences because it is difficult to remember which of the subjects go with separated clauses (Miller and Isard, 1964, pp. 292-303). Remembering requires that we hold the entire sentence in mind while we sort out the clauses. This is difficult enough for formally educated people who have been coached on interpreting self-embedded sentences, and next to impossible for the oral performers studied.

Memory also exerts pressure on the sequence of clauses within a sentence. Clauses tend to be generated chronologically, matching their sequence to the sequence of the sentences describing them. Memory performs better with temporally arranged sentences, and in an experiment reported in Clark and Clark (1977, pp. 129-138) when the input was reversed—so that events were not arranged syntactically as they occurred in the lifeworld——the interpreted sentence was transformed to correspond to events. Clearly the events have an effect on the way sentences are organized. The simplest sort of plot structure characterizes the stories in the sermons: a straightforward single-strand narrative, each episode of which is introduced by such formulas as "after a while" and "by and by." The semantic component of speech is what allows us to distinguish between a concatenation of formulas or lines and a semantically related string which we know as the sermon. Each line can no doubt be explicated in terms of generative theory (in recent years itself controversial) and can be described by the lexicon of psycholinguistics. But these theories are less helpful in understanding why certain sentences follow others or why certain speakers prefer certain expressions and particular melodies. The desire to be "scientific" has led linguists to view the formula as a discrete entity, almost autonomous, almost independent of the person who uttered it. The tendency, doubtless unintentional, has led to viewing the oral performer as a kind of applications system. However, creativity exceeds these parameters.

In an interview, the Rev. Otis McAllister of Bakersfield, Calif., told me that a preacher must entertain as well as educate, though he did not expand on this statement of poetics. He didn't have to; the aesthetics of chanted sermons are readily apparent. One of the deacons of the Union Baptist Church (Bakersfield) and I once heard a sermon that was unsuccessful. The preacher's language never became metrical: he never broke through oration into chanting. The deacon evaluated him with the laconic phrase that the preacher was "teachin', not preachin'": that is, though the message was theologically and morally sound, it had no aesthetic dimension; its preacher was not "preaching." Similarly, Rev. Rubin Lacy once summed up his own philosophy with two sentences: "You want to make the people glad twice: glad when you get up and glad when you sit down." And, "when you've said enough, sit down."

When the sermon's emotional peak has been reached, the preacher has said "enough," and he will sit down. If he has properly brought along the congregation's emotional and spiritual involvement, they will be "glad." And, on anticipation of his next sermon, they will be glad when he moves behind the pulpit to preach. To a great extent, the reader of this paper who has never heard these orally performed sermons cannot understand what is meant by "enough" and "glad." To that extent we can only rely on the old folklorist's maxim that folklore is what gets left out of the performance when it is transcribed onto paper. The preacher's tone of voice, his delivery speed, and the responses of the congregation cannot be heard in a transcribed performance. The experience must be firsthand, or not at all. The only version in print that has come close to capturing the orally preached sermon's ambience is in the last part of Faulkner's *The Sound and the Fury* (see Rosenberg, 1969, pp. 73-87).

The preacher's skill is not slight. The sermon is developed with care, always with the congregation's emotions and emotional level in mind. But that is only one aspect of this aesthetic sense. Consistent observance of the meter of a single line, together with its rhythmical relationship to the lines of its environment, is perhaps the most important facet of the preacher's musical talent. The line is perpetuated with care in that it must be sustained, it must be consistent with its rhythmic environment, and yet it must be used flexibly throughout if the sermon is to have an impact. The preacher sustains, even develops, his rhythm in order to deepen his congregation's involvement in the performance. But he must have sufficient control of himself to be able to deflect or retard or even suppress the emotional response which he himself has largely created, if that should become expedient. Only a few of the most talented preachers can sustain their own rhythm regardless of the congregation's: an intricate symbiotic relationship is at play during the performance of an oral sermon, and the preacher will have to struggle to bring his audience to his emotional level—whether that is actual or merely desired—rather than descending to theirs. In the chanted sermons, syntax and even diction are greatly influenced by rhythm, and when the latter is irregular, other inextricable problems will inevitably ensue.

In these orally preached and spontaneously composed sermons, found in the American South and Southwest, the congregation and preacher are responding not only to each other (as in antiphonal services) but also to themselves and to God. As the preacher strives to move the congregation—to infuse them with the Spirit of the Lord—so is he moved and infused by them. He may have to struggle to keep above the dulled plateau of a listless audience. But when the congregation is "high" and the Lord's Spirit has entered the preacher, members of the audience withdraw more into their own personal experience. At one point during a successful service, manipulation or stimulation is no longer necessary; this is the point at which the congregation have given themselves to religious ecstasy and are hardly aware of the preacher at all. At such moments the congregation members would say that they are consumed by the Spirit, and this is the intention of the preacher. At such moments the congregation is not responding to the preacher, nor he entirely to them; they are both responding to the Holy Ghost. This is likely to take the form of shouting, clapping, dancing, foot-tapping, even speaking in tongues. A catharsis occurs at the end of the service; then the congregation will rest, often exhausted yet exhilarated, thoroughly purged (their sins washed away), happy.

In traditional art, to re-invoke a truism, there is no surprise and little suspense. The listener is satisfied aesthetically because of a sense of the logic and justness of the procedure, the inherent dignity of it, because of the gratifying fulfillment of traditional expectations. Those expectations can be fulfilled on the level of the narrative, as when the master returns and casts out the lazy servant who has merely buried his talents. In learned art this effect can be accomplished, as did Wagner in *Tristan und Isolde*, by the retardation and diverting of the prime melody until the final scene when the melody is presented fully at the moment of the lovers' death. Such dramatic moments also occur in sermons, for instance in the passage below, once delivered by Rev. C. L. Franklin, "Moses at the Red Sea." The Jews hesitate to try the crossing, but for Franklin their obstacle is not water; their task is to recognize that the power to overcome adversity (a Red Sea by any other name) is within each one. In this sermon the individual is embodied in "Moses":

> And here they were standing on the brinks of the
>   Red Sea
> Here they were, when they looked behind them

They heard the rattling of the chariot wheels
Of Pharaoh who had regretted/his decree of
    deliverance
5   And decided to recapture them/ and lead them back/
    into the oppression of Egypt.
When they looked on either side/ mountains
    prevented their escape
When they looked before them the Red Sea/ and
    its perils loomed large/ before their
    imagination
I don't believe you know what I'm talkin' about
And the very same folk who had praised Moses
10   For his valor and for his bravery
For his courage and for his insight
For his great victory of deliverance
Began to complain
And Moses said to them stand still
15   And see the salvation of the Lord
I don't believe you know what I'm talkin' about
Stand still
Sometime you know we can get in not only our
    own way
And everybody else's way
20   But it seems sometime we can get in God's way
Stand still
My God I heard Him say the thing you need
Is in your hands
I don't believe you know what I'm talkin' about
25   The instrument of deliverance
Is within your hands
It's within your possession
The-the-the way out
The powers that need to be brought into exertion
30   Is within you
Good God
What are ya cryin' about Moses
What are ya lookin' for
What do ya think that ya want
35   Why the rod of your deliverance is in your own
    hands
Stretch out the rod that's in your hand
I don't have a new rod to give ya
I don't have a new instrument to give ya

I don't have a new suggestion for ya
40   I do not have a new plan
Your course has already been charted by destiny
Stretch out the rod that's in your hand

The plot is simple. The Israelites, about to make good their escape, think that they are trapped by the Red Sea, the flanking mountains, and the pursuing Egyptians. They have complained, off stage, to Moses. Rev. Franklin in turn addresses his congregation, the larger community of American blacks, the Jews "caught" at the Red Sea, and Moses. Each individual must seek within himself for the strength to overcome adversity. But more is happening than just that, more than even the text will reveal. Rev. Franklin thwarts our expectations for an easy solution again and again, presenting physical obstacles and emotional ones, delaying the simple truth that will solve the Jews' problems until the aesthetic moment is right, gradually building up our anticipations, our suspense over formal considerations inherent in his presentation—since we know that Moses and the Jews do escape, there is no informational suspense.

The scene is established in the first two lines of this narrative within a narrative. We know who "they" are, their relation to Moses, and the predicament of the Jews at that moment in history. The next lines establish the fact of the approaching Pharaoh and his army now that he has decided not to let the Jews go after all. But their escape is blocked, at the moment of this tableau, by the water in front of them and the mountains on either side. The Jews begin to panic (lines 9-17): those same people who had before praised Moses for his many virtues now complain of their plight. Moses advises them that they need do nothing, that the Lord will be their salvation. Franklin reaches a subordinate climax (line 17), significantly followed by three lines of evaluation (18-20); the first stage of the "action" is over, and Franklin culminates this section in the exemplum's message: stand still, and see the salvation of the Lord. But more than this transcription can show, Franklin indicates the climax of this section through his intonation.

The last twenty-three lines in this episode (18-40) repeat the message content of this sermon (the rod of your deliverance in is your own hands), while the expectation of the congregation for Moses' decisive action is thwarted. They know what that must finally be, of course, but they do not know what Rev. Franklin will say has caused Moses to act, or when he will finally act, or how long the preacher will withhold that information. And while this other suspense is being developed in them they will come to look at retardation not as a hindrance to their aesthetic pleasure but as something pleasurable in itself.

This portion of Rev. Franklin's sermon also contains within it an instance of fulfilled form which provides one of its subordinate consummations, within the frame of the entire performance. That is, Rev. Franklin develops the emotional intensity of the sermon slowly from the opening lines to the last, but along the way he infuses it with lesser peaks and troughs. The movement of the entire performance, as can be measured by the preacher's rate of word delivery, his tone of voice, and the frequency and quality of the congregation's responses, is peristaltic. Momentary peaks within sermons are common, since many experienced preachers work towards fruition through a series of them rather than approach the climax in a "straight line." Line 36, "Stretch out the rod that's in your hand," is the culmination of the preceding fourteen lines. As Franklin preached it, the line also relaxed the tension he had been briefly building, though he immediately resumed it while heading toward another subordinate peak. The transition to line 37, "I don't have a new rod to give ya," is provided by "rod." With this utterance a new anaphoric sequence commences which gradually rises in intensity to line 39, "I don't have a new suggestion for ya." The Parry-Lord explanation that new formulas are created by analogy with extant ones looks convincing in this series.

Although the three lines of this anaphoric set (37-39) do not seem alike in their typographical format, Rev. Franklin's interpretation renders them nearly identical in tone and meter. He thus establishes a metrical pattern which arouses an anticipation in his listeners that is largely fulfilled in the hypometric utterance, "I do not have a new plan." This sentence, as chanted, departs from the established pattern ("I don't have a new. . .") and terminates this set. However, Franklin does not end so abruptly, deciding to add a dénouement to the passage which again relaxes the tension that his own anaphoric lines had developed: "your course has already been charted by destiny." The coda is achieved by returning to the language of line 36, "Stretch out the rod that's in your hand." Once again, any transcription is impotent to express the finality with which this line is spoken, but the semantic fulfillment (the answer to Moses' problem) is communicated.

Rev. Franklin's comment on the panic of the Jews and Moses' momentary hesitation occurs in lines 18-21: sometimes we can even get in our own way, we can get in each other's way, and sometimes we can even get in God's way. The right way is that of faith: to stand still and watch the salvation of the Lord. In the next several lines (22-30), Rev. Franklin addresses his congregation in the words that God uses to advise Moses, explicating the previous lines and then applying them to contemporary life. Finally, in another apostrophe, he again addresses Moses, giving him the ultimate command, further elaborating on the message, retarding the conclusion of the action for just a few seconds more. The last two lines summarize the advice and repeat the call to action. Now, but only now, God's evaluation stops and Moses is allowed to save his people.

In the following eleven lines excerpted from a sermon by the Rev. T. J. Hurley, audience participation and anticipation were present, though to a lesser degree of intensity:

```
              He said Oh Lord
              It's not my will
95            It's not my way
              It's not my thoughts
              It's not my ideas
              It's not my opinion
              It's not my theories
100           It's not what I think
              It's not what I do
              It's not what I say
              No God it's Your will be done
```

The expectations of the congregation for a dénouement are developed in more than one way in this series. "It's not my will" may evoke a slight anticipation for the following line, which effectively retains the same syntax, altering only the most important word—correctly uttered last—by substituting an alliterative partner. Experiments have shown that the rhythm of language is more readily retained than syntax, and so it is not wild speculation that the rhythms of such sets as "It's not my will/ It's not my way" involve the audience as much as does the lexical anticipation. The length of the set may vary without substantially altering the demand that the series end with the assertion that "No God it's Your will be done." Aphoristically, then, rhythm creates belief, further involving the congregation in its own religious experience, an experience which is induced by metrics even more than by semantics. So, too, when the famous preacher Rev. J. Charles Jessup begins his defiant challenge, "take it . . . ," the audience expects the concluding ". . . or leave it." So with "like it . . . ," and ". . . or lump it." Expectations in this instance are based on the frequency with which this sequence and these particular variations of it are used in ordinary conversation.

One of the most important leitmotifs of this essay—most important "litanies" would be a more appropriate metaphor—has been the insistence that the sermons and the services being written about will never be adequately understood on the printed page, that folk preaching, like folklore, is everything in the performance that does not get copied down in writing. "You've got to have been there," we might say. And yet, in one important way, all of my readers have "been there." "Everyone" remembers hearing, or has heard of or seen video tapes of, Rev. Martin Luther King Jr.'s "I Have a Dream" speech. That morning, the 28th of August, 1963, he preached his memorable sermon, and I call it a sermon even though it was received by the more than 200,000 in the audience as a civil rights "speech"—which it also was. Rev. King knew how to give a speech when he wanted to and he knew how to preach. His speech to the Fellowship of the Concerned (delivered on 16 November, 1961), for example, is a model of a well-reasoned, precisely organized statement on behalf of "Love, Law, and Civil Disobedience" (Hill, 1964, pp. 345-356). King began:

> Members of the Fellowship of the Concerned, of the Southern Regional Council, I need not pause to say how very delighted I am to be here today, and to have the opportunity of being a little part of this very significant gathering. . . . I would also like to express just a personal word of thanks and appreciation for your vital witness in this period of transition which we are facing in our Southland, and in the nation, and I am sure that as a result of this genuine concern, and your significant work in communities all across the South, we have a better South today and I am sure will have a better South tomorrow with your continued endeavor and I do want to express my personal gratitude and appreciation to you of the Fellowship of the Concerned for your significant work and for your forthright witness.

This speech outlined the philosophy that controlled the nonviolent civil rights demonstrations in America, detailing its chief features and manifestations. He concluded in the same tone of irresistibly sweet reason:

> That is the basis of this movement, and as I like to say, there is something in this universe that justifies Carlyle in saying no lie can live forever. We shall overcome because there is something in this universe which justifies William Cullen Bryant in saying truth crushed to earth shall rise again. We shall overcome because there is something in this universe that justifies James Russell Lowell in saying, truth forever on the scaffold, wrong forever on the throne. Yet that scaffold sways the future, and behind the dim unknown standeth God within the shadows, keeping watch above His own. With this faith in the future, with this determined struggle, we will be able to emerge from the bleak and desolate midnight of man's inhumanity to man, into the bright and glittering of freedom and justice. Thank you.

He was teachin', not preachin', almost; the repetition of parallel syntax in the clauses beginning with "there is something . . ." has the stamp of the pulpit. At the Washington Monument in late August of 1963, however, the teacher was subordinated to the preacher. "Five score years ago, a great American . . ." he began, ". . . signed the Emancipation Proclamation." The preaching style soon commanded this speech (Hill, 1964, pp. 371-375):

> But one hundred years later, the Negro still is not
> free.
> One hundred years later, the life of the Negro is
> still sadly crippled by the manacles of
> segregation and the chains of
> discrimination.
> One hundred years later, the Negro lives on a
> lonely island of poverty in the midst of a
> vast ocean of material prosperity.
> One hundred years later, the Negro is still
> languishing in the corners of American
> society and finds himself an exile in his
> own land.

> So we have come here today to dramatize a
> shameful condition.

No American who was alive in 1963 will forget this preached oration's peroration:

> So I say to you, my friends, that even though we
> must face the difficulties of today and
> tomorrow, I still have a dream.
> It is a dream deeply rooted in the American dream
> that one day this nation will rise up and
> live out the true meaning of its creed—we
> hold these truths to be self-evident, that all
> men are created equal.
> I have a dream that one day on the red hills of
> Georgia, sons of former slaves and sons of
> former slave-owners will be able to sit
> down together at the table of brotherhood.
> I have a dream that one day, even the state of
> Mississippi, a state sweltering with the
> heat of injustice, sweltering with the heat
> of oppression, will be transformed into an
> oasis of freedom and justice.
> I have a dream that my four little children will one
> day live in a nation where they will not be
> judged by the color of their skin but by the
> content of their character.
> I have a dream today.
> I have a dream that one day, down in Alabama,
> with its vicious racists, with its governor
> having his lips dripping with the words of
> interposition and nullification, that one
> day, right here in Alabama, little black
> boys and black girls will be able to join
> hands with little white boys and white girls
> as sisters and brothers.
> I have a dream. . . .

The conclusion of Rev. King's remarks was pure oral sermon:

> So let freedom ring from the prodigious hilltops
> of New Hampshire.

> Let freedom ring from the mighty mountains of
>   New York.
> Let freedom ring from the heightening
>   Alleghenies of Pennsylvania.
> Let freedom ring from the snow-capped Rockies of
>   Colorado.
> Let freedom ring from the curvaceous slopes of
>   California.
> But not only that.
> Let freedom ring from Stone Mountain of Georgia.
> Let freedom ring from Lookout Mountain of
>   Tennessee.
> Let freedom ring from every hill and molehill of
>   Mississippi, from every mountainside, let
>   freedom ring.
> And when we allow freedom to ring, . . .
> (Sentence and paragraph format added for
>   emphasis)

The Washington Monument speech called for rousing oratory, not for finely reasoned philosophy. The subject was basically a religious one, though heavily freighted with patriotic cargoes. Situation and subject called for just such a sermon: the formulas, the repetitive syntax and phrases were produced by a highly literate and sophisticated man, whose very different speech to the Fellowship of the Concerned was highly appropriate to that other audience; and his message showed that he could adjust his style of address according to the needs of the situation, and do it with great effect. He was a great speaker, but those of us who remember the Washington Monument speech know also what a great preacher he was. And we know, too, which style had by far the greater impact on the emotions, the spirit, of the audience.

Though Rev. King is dead, we have by no means heard the last of the oral sermon style; we have not been deprived of its great emotive power. At the 1984 Democratic presidential convention in San Francisco, (Rev.) Jesse Jackson delivered a preliminary speech which the Knight-Ridder reporter called "an emotional, triumphant valedictory address for the 42-year-old Baptist preacher who brought out both the best and worst in people in his eight-month campaign for self-respect and dignity for himself, blacks and the disadvantaged" (K.-R. Synd. Art.). Describing the speech in more detail, the reporter wrote that

> For 50 spellbound minutes, the noisy Democratic Convention came to a stop last night as Jesse Jackson—a descendant of slaves who became this country's first major black presidential candidate—talked of the dream, passions and frustrations that inspired his historic bid for the White House.
>
> Tears, cheers and chants of "Jesse, Jesse, Jesse," greeted Jackson, who came to symbolize the hopes of millions of black Americans.
>
> Thousands of delegates joined hands and rocked from side to side to a soothing gospel hymn when it was over. (*ibid.*)

When it was over—the next evening—TV reporter David Brinkley was not unduly moved or impressed, pointing out that after all, Jackson was a Baptist minister and had been doing that sort of thing for years. One's inference has to be that Baptist ministers all have the ability to move their congregations (which is obviously not so) and that we ought not to be impressed by a preacher's skill in rousing the Spirit. But no church-goer could agree with this evaluation, which slights a great talent. Such comments are all the more surprising when they come from a professional media commentator who has for decades established a substantial career by his speaking voice.

Rev. Jackson's speech began conventionally enough: "Tonight we come together bound by our faith in a mighty God, with genuine respect and love for our country, and inheriting the legacy of a great party—the Democratic Party—which is the best hope for redirecting our nation on a more humane, just and peaceful course." It began conventionally enough (except for the mention of Party) for a sermon, which it was in part. Not yet well into his performance, Rev. Jackson evoked heightened emotion when he apologized (AP Synd. Art., formatting added throughout):

> If in my high moments, I have done some good
> Offered some service
> Shed some light
> Healed some wounds
> Rekindled some hope
> Stirred someone from apathy and indifference
> Or in any way helped someone along the way
> Then this campaign has not been in vain.

He continued:

> If in my low moments
> In word, deed or attitude
> Through some error of temper, taste or tone
> I have caused anyone discomfort
> Created pain
> Or revived someone's fears
> That was not my truest self.
> * * *
> I am not a perfect servant
> I am a public servant doing my best against the
>   odds
> Be patient
> God is not finished with me

This political sermon invokes the message of Rev. Franklin's: "Stand still, and see the salvation of the Lord." In this parable Rev. Jackson places himself in a position analogous to that of Moses at the Red Sea. Like that other public servant, he, too, is not perfect; his followers should be patient; God is not finished with him (either). These passages are replete not only with parallel syntactical constructions but with internal rhyme and alliteration as well. Probably this sermon/speech was not composed with that poetry as a conscious compositional element in mind; rather they are the stock in trade of the oral performer of this tradition, one of whose most skilled practitioners is Rev. Jackson. "Suffering breeds character," he told the convention at the close of his sermon (AP Synd. Art.):

> Suffering breeds character
> Character breeds faith
> And in the end faith will not disappoint
> Faith hope and dreams will prevail
> We must be bound together by faith
> Sustained by hope
> And driven by a dream
> Troubles won't last always
> Our time has come
> Our time has come
> Our time has come

"Thousands of delegates joined hands and rocked from side to side to a soothing gospel hymn when it was over," the Knight-Ridder reporter wrote. Rev. Jackson's use of the folk sermon style—not, in this case, spontaneously composed—for a political speech demonstrates the form's adaptability. Rev. King's "I Have a Dream" sermon/speech was on behalf of a cause that evoked deep religious feelings; Rev. Jackson's performance was more secularized but not entirely. He asked for forgiveness, pleading that he still had a Divinely inspired mission to fulfill: God was not finished with him yet. While it could be counter-argued that men of such backgrounds might well justify almost any of their actions with Scriptural support, their sermon/speeches demonstrate the close similarities between effective orations and moving sermons. In both instances, the minds of the audience were arrested and their emotions engaged. Revs. King and Jackson prepared manuscripts carefully but realized that people are not always moved by reason alone; logic penetrates deepest in quiet chambers, by and by. The green in front of the Washington Monument, the Democratic conventional hall—like a church full of expectant worshippers—required another approach. The sermons that have moved millions since 1800 are thus shown to stimulate a response more fundamental than mere emotion, with more breadth than Protestant Fundamentalism.

REFERENCES

Associated Press syndicated article, (AP Synd. Art.) 1984. "Excerpts from Jackson's Speech to the Convention." July 18, 1984. [Headline of Providence *Journal*, p. A 1].

Bousfield, W. A., and B. H. Cohen. 1955. "The Occurrence of Clustering in the Recall of Randomly Arranged Words of Different Frequencies of Usage." *Journal of General Psychology*, 52:83-95.

Bruce, D. J. 1958. "The Effect of Listeners' Anticipations of the Intelligibility of Heard Speech." *Language and Speech*, 1:79-97.

———. 1974. *And They All Sang Hallelujah*. Knoxville: University of Tennessee Press.

Carmichael, L., H. P. Hogan, and A. A. Walter. 1932. "An Experimental Study of the Effect of Language on the Reproduction of Visually Perceived Forms." *Journal of Experimental Psychology*, 15:73-86.

Clark, Herbert H., and Eve V. Clark. 1977. *Psychology and Language*. New York: Harcourt Brace Jovanovich.

Deese, James. 1970. *Psycholinguistics*. Boston: Allyn and Bacon.

Fearon, Henry Bradshaw. 1818. *Sketches of America*. London: Longman, Hurst, Rees, Orme, and Brown.

Fodor, J. A., and T. G. Bever. 1965. "The Psychological Reality of Linguistic Segments." *Journal of Verbal Learning and Verbal Behavior*, 4:414-420.

Fry, Donald K. 1968. "Old English Formulaic Themes and Type-Scenes." *Neophilologus*, 52:48-54.

Hill, Roy L. 1964. *Rhetoric of Racial Revolt*. Denver: Golden Bell Press.

Knight-Ridder syndicated article (K.-R. Synd. Art.), "Jackson Asks Forgiveness, Vows Support." July 18, 1984. [Headline of Providence *Journal*, p. A 1].

Lord, Albert B. 1960. *The Singer of Tales*. Cambridge, Mass.: Harvard University Press. Rpt. New York: Atheneum, 1968 et seq.

Mehler, J., and P. Carey. 1967. "Role of Surface and Base Structure in the Perception of Sentences." *Journal of Verbal Learning and Verbal Behavior*, 6:335-338.

Miller, George A. 1967. *The Psychology of Communication*. Baltimore: Penguin.

————, and S. Isard. 1964. "Free Recall of Self-Embedded English Sentences." *Information and Control*, 7:292-303.

Rosenberg, Bruce A. 1969. "The Oral Quality of Reverend Shegog's Sermon in William Faulkner's *The Sound and the Fury*." *Literatur in Wissenschaft und Unterricht*, 2:73-88.

————. 1970. *The Art of the American Folk Preacher*. New York: Oxford University Press.

————. 1971. "The Aesthetics of the Folk Sermon." *Georgia Review*, 25:424-438.

————. 1974. "The Psychology of the Spiritual Sermon." In *Religious Movements in Contemporary America*. Ed. Irving I. Zaretsky and Mark P. Leone. Princeton: Princeton University Press. pp. 135-149.

————, and John Smith. 1975. "Thematic Structure in Four Fundamentalist Sermons." *Western Folklore*, 34:201-214.

Wilgus, D. K., and Bruce A. Rosenberg. 1971. "A Modern Medieval Story: 'The Soldier's Deck of Cards'." In *Medieval Literature and Folklore Studies*. Ed. Jerome Mandel and Bruce A. Rosenberg. New Brunswick: Rutgers University Press. pp. 291-304.

Hispanic Oral Literature:
Accomplishments and Perspectives
[excerpted]

Ruth House Webber

Ruth H. Webber's monograph, Formulistic Diction in the Spanish Ballad *(1951), was the very first study to apply oral-formulaic theory to the Hispanic tradition, and her numerous contributions since that time have extended the investigation to medieval Spanish and French narrative poetry. In the present essay, initially published in 1986, Webber surveys fieldwork and analytical scholarship on the genres of epic, ballad, lyric, folktale, and proverb in Spanish and Portuguese oral traditions from the medieval period to the present. Excerpted here are her remarks on epic, which treat the* Cantar de Mio Cid, *the* Roncesvalles *fragment, and the* Mocedades de Rodrigo, *as well as the reconstructed* Siete Infantes de Lara *and a clerical reworking of an epic text, the* Poema de Fernán González. *In this section Webber also discusses various aspects of verse-making and traditional style, the historicity and provenance of the* Cid *poem, the issue of memorization versus improvisation, and the question of aesthetics. Although she has championed the oral traditional provenance of the medieval Spanish texts in her own scholarship, Webber balances the account fairly by*

Reprinted from *Oral Tradition*, 1 (1986), 344-380.

*citing those who disagree. Her survey thus serves as a fine introduction
to the impact of oral-formulaic theory on the Hispanic world.*

Hispanic oral literature, together with the Portuguese which should
not be separated from it, encompasses a great chronological as well as
geographical span, since it is an integral part of the cultural heritage
that has accompanied the Spanish and Portuguese people over the
centuries wherever they have chanced to establish themselves. Scholarly
interest has focused primarily upon two oral genres, the epic and the
ballad, while the lyric and the folktale have been accorded less attention,
and the proverb almost none at all.

The total amount of material published, particularly on the epic and
ballad, is enormous. The last decade or so has produced a veritable
explosion of critical interest in these traditional forms. After
establishing the critical background, we have tried to include here
studies that either make a significant contribution or are representative
of a certain method or approach. This means that many fine studies are
not mentioned solely because of limitations of space. It will be
observed that not all of this work has been carried out by oralists. In the
belief that good basic research is of value to all, no matter what a
particular scholar's theoretical persuasion may be, a number of items
have been cited that were destined to support other points of view.

Epic

Three surveys of scholarship on the Spanish epic were published in
the mid-seventies, all different in emphasis but each valuable in its own
way and worth consulting. Faulhaber (1976) reviews the history and the
application of traditionalist studies to the Spanish epic together with
the opposing arguments of the individualists. It is an objective, well-
reasoned assessment of the problems besetting critics of epic in both
the Spanish and the French fields. Deyermond's 1977 digest, "*Mio Cid*
Scholarship, 1943-73," is more comprehensive, yet succinct and is
organized on the basis of critical issues. Although the author is an
individualist and feels free to express his own opinions, his evaluations
are dependable and fair, making this survey the most useful of the three.
Magnotta's volume entitled *Historia y bibliografía de la crítica sobre el*

"Poema de Mio Cid" (1750-1971) is a considerably more extensive chronological survey of the field. For that reason it is more cursory and has a less secure grasp of the materials covered. Magnotta concentrates on the problems of date and authorship, origins and influences, together with relations to the chronicles and the ballads, while stylistic, aesthetic, and theoretical questions are given less space.

Spanish epic studies have been extraordinarily handicapped by a dearth of texts. There are but three extant epic texts: the *Cantar de Mio Cid*, also called the *Poema de Mio Cid*; the hundred-verse fragment of the *Roncesvalles*; and a corrupt late epic on the youth of the Cid, the *Mocedades de Rodrigo*, variously named the *Mocedades del Cid, Rodrigo y el rey Fernando*, and the *Crónica rimada*. In addition to the foregoing, a large section of the *Siete Infantes de Lara* (or *Salas*) has been reconstructed from chronicle texts, and the *Poema de Fernán González*, a clerical poem, is the reworking of a *cantar de gesta*, of which it bears many traces.

The existence of several additional epic texts has been hypothesized, with more convincing evidence in some cases than in others. Chronicle accounts that display poetization, a narrative that follows the tenets of the epic canon, and continued traditional life in the ballads offer the most secure basis for inclusion in the list of lost epics. Into this category fall the *Canta de Sancho II* together with the *Partición de los reinos* of the *Cid* cycle (Reig, 1947) and *Bernardo del Carpio*, the counter-Roland (Horrent, 1951a, pp. 462-483). More doubtful among those most frequently mentioned are *Rodrigo, el último godo* (Menéndez Pidal, 1925, pp. 54-88), the *Infante García* (Menéndez Pidal, 1934, pp. 33-98), the *Condesa traidora* (Menéndez Pidal, 1934, pp. 4-27), and the *Abad don Juan de Montemayor* (Menéndez Pidal, 1934, pp. 103-233).

Menéndez Pidal's three-volume edition of the *Cantar de Mio Cid* or *CMC* (4th ed., 1964) was the standard one for many years. It comprises a paleographic edition and a critical edition together, with an initial volume of studies plus another containing a glossary. Since his death several new critical editions have come out which adhere more closely to the manuscript text. The most noteworthy are those of Colin Smith (1972), Ian Michael (1975, 1978) and Garcí-Gómez (1978). Another recent two-volume work put out by the city of Burgos includes a new facsimile edition along with the critical edition, the former of which reveals how much the manuscript has deteriorated during the last several decades (*Poema,* 1982, vol. 1).

Because the *CMC* is the only remaining epic text that comes close to being complete, theoretical studies concerning the Spanish epic have perforce been based upon it. There is hardly an aspect of the poem that does not present problems that still have not been satisfactorily resolved. The hypotheses that have been proffered reflect the particular theoretical orientation of each scholar. Here we have no intention of extending the traditionalist-individualist debate, which has provoked such vigorous interchanges in recent years; rather, without arguing the case, we shall set forth these issues based on the premise that the Spanish epic originated as a product of oral tradition.

The only extant manuscript of the *CMC*, which is of relatively small format and modest appearance, dates from the fourteenth century. It is impossible to determine whether at the beginning it was written down from dictation, although Adams (1976) brings out evidence to show that that could have been possible. The nature of the errors reveals that it was recopied more than once, at which times there may well have been editorial revisions. Nor is the text complete. Therefore the date the text was put into writing for the first time cannot be deduced either by internal or by external evidence. For the individualist these dates are one and the same, but not for the traditionalist, for whom the *Cid* was gradually elaborated in successive versions into a text more or less like the one we have today. Horrent has outlined plausibly the course of such a process (1973, pp. 310-311). The prolonged discussion surrounding the question of the date and the purpose for which the *CMC* was committed to writing has been well summarized by Lomax (1977). Menéndez Pidal settled on the year 1140 for a variety of reasons, among them that it was the date of a politically important royal espousal. Aside from the story's inappropriateness in terms of conjugal felicity, there is much other evidence to advance the date to the end of the century, if not to 1207, the date found on the manuscript itself. Some present-day scholars argue that the *CMC* was composed (not just written down) around the turn of the century for propagandistic purposes: Lacarra (1980), that it was a vehicle for political slander in a feud between the Castro and the Lara families, and Fradejas Lebrero (1982), that it served as a model to persuade Christians to renew the Reconquest.

The possibility of the recovery of epic poems prosified in late chronicles is of importance in regard to the three missing folios of the *CMC*, which have been partially restored based on the *Crónica de once (veinte) reyes* (see Dyer, 1979-1980 and Powell, 1983). Since the chroniclers were intent upon amalgamating their sources stylistically, the legitimacy of reconstructed verses has been questioned. Nor is there agreement as to whether it is possible to distinguish different versions of an epic through the medium of chronicle prosifications as Menéndez Pidal believed (1952, p. xvii). It was Diego Catalán who rejected the theory as far as the *Primera crónica general* is concerned by demonstrating that what appear to be increased discrepancies between the second part of the poetic text and the chronicle are in fact the product of a different period and style of prosification (1963, pp. 205-209, 214-215). A re-examination of this and allied questions is to be found in Deyermond's review (1984) of Powell's book. What is manifest is that the question of chronicle prosifications is far from resolved and that much work remains to be done.

Happily the era of the attempts to regularize the versification of the *CMC* with its two-hemistich line in assonating series is long past. However, Harvey's (1963) hypothesis, based on Lord, that the irregularities in verse length are the result of its being a dictated rather than a sung text has found some strong support. If his theory were true, it would mean that the *CMC* is a badly distorted text, which is not at all the case. Discussion still arises periodically concerning the principle underlying the irregular verse length. The theory of stress-timed verse had been proposed and demonstrated by Navarro Tomas (1956), among others, many years ago. Recently Adams reaffirmed the same principle (1972, pp. 118-119) as did Colin Smith (1983, pp. 113-128), but according to the latter, it was developed as an adaptation of the French epic line. Many scholars continue to accept the target-count theory of Menéndez Pidal, according to which it can be shown that hemistichs tend to have seven syllables and verses fourteen, the frequency of deviations diminishing the further removed they are from the norm (1964, vol. I, pp. 83-101). What has not been realized is that any stress-timed verse would probably show a similar target-count pattern if one set about to count syllables.

Menéndez Pidal described and categorized the assonances used in the *CMC* as frequent, rare, and exceptional and indicated their relative frequency in the three *cantares* into which the *CMC* is divided (*ibid.*, pp. 113-123). Although he listed important assonating words, he did not speculate upon why certain assonances were preferred in certain parts of the poem or the possible relationship between assonance and subject matter. Questions of assonance determination, laws of assonance change, and assonance sequence were taken up many years ago by Staaf (1925) and Lahmann (1934) and more recently by Webber (1975), but the final word still has not been said on these matters. Within the assonating series, Menéndez Pidal rejected as erroneous not only single verses in a different assonance but pairs of verses as well, a phenomenon so frequent that it has now been accepted as part of the system by the *CMC*'s recent editors.

Although Menéndez Pidal had set forth certain basic principles of laisse division (1964, vol. I, pp. 107-110), the topic as a whole did not excite much interest until the publication of Rychner's book on the French epic (1955) with its extensive treatment of the subject. In the introduction to his edition of the *CMC*, Michael studied laisse structure and succinctly summarized laisse-linking techniques (1978, pp. 27-33). The question of the narrative function of the laisse has only been briefly treated (Michael, 1978, pp. 27-30; Webber, 1973, pp. 26-27) except for Johnston (1984).

Other aspects of the verse-making of the *Cid* poet have also been the object of scholarly attention. Among them have been several attempts to analyze the acoustic properties of the poem (Smith, 1976; Adams, 1980; and Webber, 1983). All are in agreement as to its exceptionally pleasing sound-system, the work of a poet who was a superb musician with words, even though Smith is not willing to concede that this artist was an oral poet. Since an oral poetic tradition is totally dependent upon sound, all of these directions should be pursued further.

No question concerning the *CMC* has elicited more scholarly interest that its historicity, combined with that of its geographical precision. The Cid as a hero is unique in that his deeds were sung not long after the events themselves took place, in contrast to the several centuries that separate the activities of other historical heroes like Fernán González, Charlemagne, and Roland from the epics that were composed about them. For Menéndez Pidal the *CMC* was essentially a historical document preserving through oral transmission vestiges of the past otherwise long since forgotten. In his two-volume opus, *La España del Cid* (1929), he reconstructed the events of the critical years of the Cid's life, placing more faith, however, in the veracity of the chronicle accounts than do later scholars. Much fine historical research has appeared of late—for example, that of Chalon (1976), who has worked systematically to distinguish in the Castilian epic what is truly historical, what appears to be historical because it conforms to what is perceived as historical reality, and what is poetic invention. One of the most persistent historical researchers is Colin Smith, who has sought to prove thereby that the *CMC* was a learned product whose author, Per Abbat, had had access to historical, legal, and literary texts (1983, pp. 137-179). There is a certain irony in the fact that the argument of historicity can be made to serve quite different ends. Much the same can be said for geography, of which Michael's two studies (1976, 1977) are recent examples. Although the *CMC* displays a much greater degree of historical and geographical accuracy than the French epic, the *CMC* is replete with the names of historical people and identifiable places whose connection with the real-life hero cannot be established, and that is precisely what would have been brought about by oral transmission.

For the scholars for whom the *CMC* is not a historical document, and that represents a sizable majority, the question remains as to what were the principles upon which the narrative was formed. For the traditionalists it is easy to discern the transformation of the figure of the Cid into the heroic archetype. Despite the incompleteness of the Cidian biography in the poem, there are tell-tale signs of a traditional narrative structure well embellished with folkloric detail. Dunn (1962) finds a mythic base to the story in two fundamental patterns, that of the exile and the triumphant return of the hero interwoven with that of the good king released from evil counselors, while Aubrun (1972) isolates three other myths that operate in a more intricate relationship. For Hart (1962) what informs the poem is the portrait of the Cid as an exemplary Christian as part of an hierarchical order leading up to God.

Obvious traditional narrative devices can be cited: pairs of people who share a single role, predilection for the number three in both figures and structure, polarization of pro- and anti-Cid elements. Deyermond and Chaplin (1972) found some forty folk motifs in the poem but did not list them. Other scholars have dwelt upon the mythic significance of the incident of the escaped lion (Olson, 1962; Bandera Gómez, 1966) as well as the possible religious or folkloric base of the vicious attack upon the Cid's daughters by their husbands (Walsh,

1970-1971; Nepaulsingh, 1983; Gifford 1977). A full-scale appraisal of folkloric motifs and similar devices is still lacking.

Whether or not there is a mythic underlay to the narrative structure of the *CMC*, it is a story of two parts that conforms remarkably well to the canon of the folk tale. For those who espouse the king-vassal structural pattern, the critical role is that of the king. In this case the first part has to do with the hero's losing, then regaining the king's favor, or to state it differently, the testing of the hero and secondly the testing of the king who was responsible for the marriages of the Cid's daughters (de Chasca, 1955, pp. 41-44; Dunn, 1970; Walker, 1976). If one accepts the biographical pattern of the hero as the structural base, the first part is the exile followed, after vicissitudes, by the triumphal return of the hero, and the second is the hero's loss of honor, which is regained twofold with the downfall of the perpetrators of the villainy and the royal marriages of his daughters. Still a third theory, developed by Dorfman (1969) for a comparative study of the French and Spanish epic, finds a common structural base in four narremes: the family quarrel, the insult, the act of treachery, and the punishment. For the *CMC* this means that the whole biographical account through the daughters' wedding is degraded to the status of prologue, and that the story proper, whose central element is the act of treachery, does not begin until the poem is almost two-thirds over.

Whatever the deep structure is conceived to be, the actual telling of the story proceeds by small, measured, remarkably regular steps in linear progression. This adding-on technique, in which each narrative unit or minor theme is complete in itself and yet forms part of a larger thematic unit, both of which, small and large, are developed according to a number of oft-repeated patterns, is a process that deserves a great deal more elucidation not only in the *CMC* but in other traditional epics as well. The study of the themes themselves has scarcely fared better, since the narrative content of the *CMC* has most often been discussed on the basis of selected episodes.

Interest in Spanish epic style was given a much-needed impetus thanks to the impact of the Parry-Lord investigations of Serbo-Croatian song. The publication of Waltman's concordance (1972) provided the necessary tool for statistical approaches. Waltman himself used his concordance for several studies that demonstrate that there are no significant formulaic, lexical, or grammatical differences between one part of the poem and another. Whereas there has been no complete study of the formulas of the *CMC*, there are many of more limited scope. An important article by Michael (1961) illustrates the difference in the use of epithets in the *CMC* and the *Libro de Alexandre*. Hamilton (1962) and Webber (1965), among others, studied the form and function of epithets but with differing conclusions. De Chasca devoted three chapters of his *El arte juglaresco en el "Cantar de Mio Cid"* (1972) to formulas, in which he treated selected groups of formulas together with certain parallelistic procedures. Deyermond's article (1973) is also selective, while Montgomery (1975) focuses on grammatical patterns of expression. Although the monograph by Smith and Morris (1967) on physical phrases is a lexical study, much of their material is formulaic.

Concerning formula counts, de Chasca (1972, pp. 337-382), on the basis of his own register of formulas in the *CMC*, calculated that 17 percent of the hemistichs of the poem are formulas. Given the somewhat arbitrary and incomplete character of his formula list and the fact that he had counted as formulas only expressions that were repeated at least three times, it is not surprising that Duggan's later study (1974) should produce quite different results. Duggan, employing the same criteria that he had developed for his earlier study of the formulicity of the *Chanson de Roland* and nine other Old French epics (1973), found that 31.7 percent of the hemistichs of the *CMC* are formulaic, a figure that places it somewhat above the median of the *chansons de geste* tested, for which he had set the borderline between oral and written composition at 20 percent (1973, pp. 23-30).

In addition to formulas and formula density, de Chasca touched upon various repetitive procedures, in particular parallelism and enumeration (1972, pp. 196-206). Dámaso Alonso (1969) examined direct discourse, as did Hart (1972). A whole series of scholars carried out a prolonged interchange about tense usage in the *CMC*. It was begun by Sandmann (1953) and continued by Gilman (1961), Myers (1966), Montgomery (1967-1968), and then Gilman again (1972), who retracted his original thinking in the face of evidence pointing to oral composition. One of the most thought-provoking studies, which came out far ahead of its time and has not been duly appreciated, is that of Louise Allen, "A Structural Analysis of the Style of the *Cid*" (1959). In undertaking to describe its style, she employs the methods (and vocabulary) of structural linguistics and divides the presentation into three parts: discourse analysis, information analysis, and sound-figure analysis. Even though her aim was rigorous description and not application of the results to Cidian problems, the methodology itself opens up new perspectives on the poem's style that merit further consideration, like the contrast established between chronicle style and poetic style and the topics of redundancy and resonance.

Closely allied and frequently intermingled with discussions of stylistic matters are aesthetic considerations. Paeans of well-deserved praise have been showered upon the *CMC* over the years by the most distinguished literary critics (see Magnotta, 1974, Ch. viii). Surely the most impressive and influential of these essays is Dámaso Alonso's "Estilo y creación en el *Poema del Cid*" (1941). Yet we still have not come to terms with the most fundamental problem of all: how should the aesthetics of oral poetry be defined? What are the criteria that can legitimately be applied to traditional verse in order to pass judgment upon it? Even a professed neo-traditionalist like de Chasca fell into the fallacy of demostrating intentionality on the poet's part in his appreciative analyses of passages of the *CMC*. More often we are left with attractive but non-productive rhetoric. Ironically it is a question of aesthetics, the opposition to what appears to be the mechanistic nature of the oral poet's art, that has been most responsible for the critical stance of the individualists.

To complicate matters still further, there are other questions tied up with aesthetic evaluation that will require extensive investigation on a broader scale than that of the *CMC* by itself before satisfactory answers can be found. The first is the significance of literacy vesus illiteracy in a medieval society that was basically illiterate. What sorts of knowledge could be and were acquired orally as opposed to those that could only be acquired through book-learning? Progress is slowly beginning to be made in these directions as more information becomes available.

Aside from Menéndez Pidal's classic study of Spanish minstrels, *Poesía juglaresca* (1957), little has been written recently about the singer except for a stimulating article by Aguirre (1968) in which he scrutinizes, in terms of what Lord discovered in Yugoslavia, the profession of the epic *juglar* and the character of his product.

Among a host of equally perplexing problems that have preoccupied the critics is the relationship between the Castilian and the French epic (see Magnotta, 1974, pp. 90-106). The theory of the dependency of the *CMC* upon the latter has pervaded the work of many scholars. Among the recent adherents to this point of view is Herslund, who, in an interesting but sometimes controversial study (1974), sought to prove that the Spanish *juglares* were trained by the French whose techniques they mastered, and that for all intents and purposes the *CMC* is a *chanson de geste*. For Colin Smith, the most extreme of the current generation of individualists, the learned author of the *CMC* was well acquainted with a number of *chansons de geste* which he imitated specifically in various instances and whose metrical system, formulas, style, and even lexicon he took over (1983, pp. 186-202, 114-124).

Still another dilemma for scholars who treat the *cantares de gesta*, and one that falls strictly within the province of the oralists, is the question of memorization versus improvisation in the transmission of these songs. Lord demonstrated beyond any doubt the role of improvisation on the part of the *guslar*. Whether this was also true of the Spanish or indeed of any of the medieval European epic traditions is impossible to determine. Menéndez Pidal declared late in his career after he had come to know the Parry-Lord investigations, whose conclusions otherwise coincided strikingly with his own, that improvisation was not a feature of the oral poetry of western Europe, where there was greater textual stability (1965-1966, pp. 195-207). Gilman expressed similar doubts as to whether the kind of oral composition represented by the *CMC* was the same as that found by Parry and Lord in Yugoslavia (1972, pp. 10-11). The question arises again with the *romances* (see Beatie, 1964), with the same dichotomy of opinion among the oralists. Whether oral transmission may differ in character from one tradition to another is one more issue that can only be resolved on the basis of research undertaken throughout the whole realm of oral poetry.

The *Roncesvalles* fragment is an extraordinarily valuable document in that it confirms that there was indeed a Spanish epic tradition. Its hundred verses can be made to reveal a great amount of information about the epic from which it became separated as well as about Romance epic relations. It was initially published by Menéndez Pidal (1917) in both a paleographic and a critical edition together with a study of the language, versification, and legend, followed by a hypothetical reconstruction of the whole poem. Some years later Horrent (1951b), with the thoroughness characteristic of all his work, re-edited the *Roncesvalles* and added a two hundred fifty page study that encompasses every conceivable aspect of the poetic text, its narrative content, and its relationship with the French tradition. Formulaic and thematic studies, which might have seemed impracticable given the brevity of the piece, proved to be possible using other epic texts and the ballads as a frame of reference (Webber 1966, 1981). The results indicate that the formulas are very similar to those of the *CMC* in both form and density, while thematic correspondences are to be found in many other traditional narrative poems.

The *Mocedades de Rodrigo (MR)*, published by Menéndez Pidal in *Reliquias de la poesía épica española* (1951), is a degenerate epic found in a late fourteenth-century manuscript which is both corrupt and incomplete. Deyermond included a much-needed paleographic edition in his *Epic Poetry and the Clergy: Studies on the "Mocedades de Rodrigo"* (1969). This admirable study of the text, its background, and the many problems to which it gives rise reveals how thoroughly it has been permeated by learned additions and emendations. Of particular interest to the traditionalist is what the earlier *cantar de gesta* on the Cid's youth may have been like, a topic upon which Armistead (1963) is the undisputed authority. Armistead documents at least six different traditional versions of the story, which include earlier prosifications of the lost *gesta*, the late epic text, summaries incorporated by a fifteenth- and early sixteenth-century author in their work, and various versions that emerge in the ballads (1978, pp. 324-327).

The account of the prodigious deeds of the rebellious hero of the *MR* is very much in accord with the heroic canon, in the course of which a number of folklore motifs manifest themselves (Deyermond, 1969, pp. 177-182). The degree of non-traditional intervention can be roughly measured by a formula count. Geary (1980) calculated that formulas represent only 14 percent of the poem in contrast to the 31 percent tallied for the *CMC*, but its shorter length (1164 verses) makes the figure less valid for comparative purposes. There is unmistakable evidence, however, that the *MR* once had a language system possessing the features that are characteristic of oral traditional poetry and that it was broken down by later reworkings (Webber, 1980b).

The *Poema de Fernán González* is the recasting of an earlier *cantar de gesta* about a historical hero in the form of a *cuaderna vía* poem, and it is in this guise that it has been most often studied. Avalle-Arce in an important essay (1972) sought to determine how the *Cantar de Fernán González* differed from the *Poema*. Its biographical pattern is a mixture of the canon of the hero and of the saint's life and abounds with folklore motifs and legendary material (see the articles of Keller). It has been re-edited several times, among them by Menéndez Pidal in the *Reliquias* (1951), where it is accompanied by versions extracted from several chronicles. The problem in this case is to determine whether it is the *Poema* or the lost *gesta* that has been prosified. Despite not being in epic meter, by Geary's count of formulas, its almost three thousand verses are 17 percent formulaic.

The *Seite Infantes de Lara* (or *Salas*) survives only through Menéndez Pidal's reconstruction from chronicle prosifications, which produced some five hundred and fifty verses (1951, pp. 181-239). It is a brutal story of a family quarrel that leads to treachery and death followed in due time by an equally bloody vengeance, all of which fits into the epic canon in relation to heroes and their missions within a bipartite structure.

*   *   *

It should be manifest from the foregoing that studies in Hispanic oral literature have tended to be self-contained and to go their own way. The recent emphasis on text-collecting will continue to bring forth new materials. Equally worthy of praise are innovative forms of research, particularly those carried out with the aid of the computer. All too infrequently have scholars taken the comparative approach and sought in other oral literatures confirmation or refutation of conclusions reached on the basis of the Hispanic scene. Yet there is in the Hispanic world, perhaps more than anywhere else, an awareness of and pride in oral traditional forms, which bodes well for maintaining these traditions in the future and for continuing organized scholarly investigation concerning them.

REFERENCES

Adams, Kenneth. 1972. "The Metrical Irregularity of the *Cantar de Mio Cid*: A Restatement Based on the Evidence of Names, Epithets, and Some Other Aspects of Formulaic Diction." *Bulletin of Hispanic Studies*, 49:109-119.

———. 1976. "The Yugoslav Model and the Text of the *Poema de Mio Cid*." In *Medieval Hispanic Studies Presented to Rita Hamilton*. Ed. by Alan D. Deyermond. London: Tamesis, pp. 1-10.

————. 1980. "Further Aspects of Sound-Patterning in the *Poema de Mio Cid.*" *Hispanic Review*, 48:449-467.

Aguirre, J. M. 1968. "Épica oral y épica castellana: tradición creadora y tradición repetitiva." *Romanische Forschungen*, 60:13-43.

Allen, Louise H. 1959. "A Structural Analysis of the Epic Style of the *Cid.*" In *Structural Studies on Spanish Themes*. Ed. by Henry R. Kahane and Angelina Pietrangeli. Urbana: University of Illinois Press, pp. 341-414.

Alonso, Dámaso. 1941. "Estilo y creación en el *Poema del Cid.*" *Escorial*, 3:333-372. Rpt. in *Ensayos sobre poesía española*. Madrid: Revista de Occidente, 1944, pp. 69-111.

————. 1969. "El anuncio del estilo directo en el *Poema del Cid* y en la épica francesa." In *Mélanges offerts à Rita Lejeune*. Gembloux: Duculot. I, pp. 379-393.

————, and José M. Blecua. 1964. *Antología de la poesía española: Lírica de tipo tradicional*. 2nd rev. ed. Madrid: Gredos.

Alvar, Manuel. 1966. *Poesía tradicional de los judíos españoles*. México: Porrúa.

Armistead, Samuel G. 1963. "The Structure of the *Refundición de las Mocedades de Rodrigo.*" *Romance Philology*, 17:338-345.

————. 1978. "The *Mocedades de Rodrigo* and Neo-Individualist Theory." *Hispanic Review*, 46:313-327.

Aubrun, Charles V. 1972. "Le *Poema de Mio Cid*, alors et à jamais." *Philological Quarterly*, 51:12-22.

Avalle-Arce, Juan B. 1972. "*El Poema de Fernán González*: Clerecía y juglaría." *Philological Quarterly*, 51:60-73.

Bandera Gómez, Cesáreo. 1966. "Reflexiones sobre el carácter mítico del *Poema de Mio Cid.*" *Modern Language Notes*, 81:202-205.

Beatie, Bruce A. 1964. "Oral-traditional Composition in the Spanish *Romancero* of the Sixteenth Century." *Journal of the Folklore Institute*, 1:92-113.

————. 1976. "*Romances tradicionales* and Spanish Traditional Ballads: Menéndez Pidal vs. Vladimir Propp." *Journal of the Folklore Institute*, 13:37-55.

Beutler, Gisela. 1977. *Estudios sobre el romancero español de Colombia en su tradición escrita y oral*. Bogotá: Instituto Caro y Cuervo.

Canconiero folklórico de México. 1975-1980. Ed. by Margit Frenk Alatorre. 3 vols. Vol. 1. *Coplas del amor feliz*. México: El Colegio, 1975; Vol. 2. *Coplas del amor desdichado y otras coplas de amor*. México: El Colegio, 1977; Vol. 3. *Coplas que no son de amor*. México: El Colegio, 1980.

Catalán, Diego. 1963. "Crónicas generales y cantares de gesta. El *Mio Cid* de Alfonso X y el pseudo Ben-Alfaraŷ." *Hispanic Review*, 31:195-215, 291-306.

Chalon, Louis. 1976. *L'Histoire et l'épopée castillane du moyen âge*. Paris: Honoré Champion.

de Chasca, Edmund. 1955. *Estructura y forma en el "Poema de Mio Cid*." Iowa City: University of Iowa Press and México: Patria.

———. 1972. *El arte juglaresco en el "Cantar de Mio Cid*." 2nd ed. Madrid: Gredos.

Deyermond, Alan D. 1969. *Epic Poetry and the Clergy: Studies on the "Mocedades de Rodrigo*." London: Tamesis.

———. 1973. "Structural and Stylistic Patterns in the *CMC*." In *Medieval Studies in Honor of Robert White Linker*. Madrid: Castalia, pp. 55-71.

———. 1977. "Tendencies in *Mio Cid* Scholarship, 1943-1973." In *Mio Cid Studies*. Ed. by A. D. Deyermond. London: Tamesis, pp. 13-47.

———. 1984. Review of Brian Powell, *Epic and Chronicle: The "Poema de Mio Cid" and the "Crónica de veinte reyes*." *La Corónica*, 13:71-80.

———, and Margaret Chaplin. 1972. "Folk-Motifs in the Medieval Spanish Epic." *Philological Quarterly*, 51:36-53.

Dorfman, Eugene. 1969. *The Narreme in the Medieval Romance Epic*. Toronto: University of Toronto Press.

Duggan, Joseph J. 1973. *The Song of Roland: Formulaic Style and Poetic Craft*. Berkeley: University of California Press.

———. 1974. "Formulaic Diction in the *Cantar de Mio Cid* and the Old French Epic." *Forum for Modern Language Studies*, 10:260-269. Rpt. in J. J. Duggan, ed. *Oral Literature: Seven Essays*. Edinburgh and New York: Scottish Academic Press and Barnes & Noble, pp. 74-83.

Dunn, Peter N. 1962. "Theme and Myth in the *Poema de Mio Cid*." *Romania*, 83:348-369.

———. 1970. "Levels of Meaning in the *Poema de Mio Cid*." *Modern Language Notes*, 85:109-119.

Dyer, Nancy Joe. 1979-1980. "*Crónica de veinte reyes*' Use of the Cid Epic: Perspectives, Method, and Rationale." *Romance Philology*, 33:534-544.

Faulhaber, Charles B. 1976. "Neo-traditionalism, Formulism, Individualism, and Recent Studies on the Spanish Epic." *Romance Philology*, 30:83-101.

Fradejas Lebrero, José. 1982. "Intento de comprensión del Poema de Mio Cid." In *Poema de Mio Cid*. Burgos: Ayuntamiento. II, pp. 245-287.

Geary, John Steven. 1980. *Formulaic Diction in the "Poema de Fernán González" and the "Mocedades de Rodrigo": A Computer-Aided Analysis.* Madrid: Porrúa Turanzas.

Gerineldo, el paje y la infanta. 1975-1976. Ed. by Diego Catalán and J. A. Cid. 3 vols. *Romancero tradicional de las lenguas hispánicas,* Vols. 6-8. Madrid: Cátedra Seminario Menéndez Pidal.

Gifford, Douglas J. 1977. "European Folk-Tradition and the *Afrenta de Corpes.*" In *Mio Cid Studies.* Ed. by A. D. Deyermond. London: Tamesis, pp. 49-62.

Gilman, Stephen. 1961. *Tiempo y formas temporales en el Poema del Cid.* Madrid: Gredos.

―――. 1972. "The Poetry of the 'Poema' and the Music of the 'Cantar.'" *Philological Quarterly,* 51:1-11.

González, William. 1981. "The Religious Ballads of New Mexico and the Canary Islands: A Comparative Study of Traditional Features." In *Oral Traditional Literature: A Festschrift for Albert Bates Lord.* Ed. by John Miles Foley. Columbus, Ohio: Slavica; rpt. 1983, pp. 294-300.

Hamilton, Rita. 1962. "Epic Epithets in the *Poema de Mio Cid.*" *Revue de littérature comparée,* 36:161-178.

Hart, Thomas R. 1962. "Hierarchical Patterns in the *Cantar de Mio Cid.*" *Romanic Review,* 53:161-173.

―――. 1972. "The Rhetoric of (Epic) Fiction: Narrative Technique in the *Cantar de Mio Cid.*" *Philological Quarterly,* 51:23-55.

Harvey, L.P. 1963. "The Metrical Irregularity of the *Cantar de Mio Cid.*" *Bulletin of Hispanic Studies,* 40:120-126.

Herslund, Michael. 1974. "Le *Cantar de Mio Cid* et la chanson de geste." *Revue romane,* 9:69-121.

Horrent, Jules. 1951a. *La Chanson de Roland dans les littératures française et espagnole au moyen âge.* Paris: Les Belles Lettres.

―――. 1951b. *Roncesvalles. Etude sur le fragment de cantar de gesta conservé à l'Archivo de Navarra (Pampelune).* Paris: Les Belles Lettres.

―――. 1973. *Historia y poesía en torno al "Cantar del Cid."* Barcelona: Ariel.

Johnston, Robert M. 1984. "The Function of *Laisse* Division in the *Poema de mio Cid.*" *Journal of Hispanic Philology,* 8:185-208.

Juan Manuel (Don). 1969. *El Conde Lucanor o libro de los enxiemplos del Conde Lucanor ed de Patronio.* Ed. by José Manuel Blecua. Madrid: Castalia.

Katz, Israel I. 1972-1975. *Judeo-Spanish Traditional Ballads from Jerusalem: An Ethnomusicological Study.* 2 vols. New York: Institute of Medieval Music.

Keller, J. P. 1954. "Inversion of the Prison Episodes in the *Poema de Fernán González*." *Hispanic Review*, 22:253-263.

————. 1955. "The Hunt and the Prophecy Episode of the *Poema de Fernán González*." *Hispanic Review*, 23:251-258.

————. 1956. "El misterioso origen de Fernán González." *Nueva revista de filología hispánica*, 10:41-44.

Lacarra, María Eugenia. 1980. "*El poema de Mio Cid*": realidad histórica e ideología. Madrid: Porrúa Turanzas.

Lahmann, Enrique Macaya. 1934. "Las asonancias del *Poema del Cid*: Posibles significados de los diferentes cambios de asonantes." *Hispanic Review*, 1:63-74.

Lapesa, Rafael. 1967. "La lengua de la poesía épica en los cantares de gesta y en el Romancero viejo." In *De la edad media a nuestros días*. Madrid: Gredos, pp. 9-28.

Lomax, Derek W. 1977. "The Date of the *Poema de Mio Cid*." In *Mio Cid Studies*. London: Tamesis, pp. 73-81.

Lord, Albert B. 1960. *The Singer of Tales*. Cambridge, Mass.: Harvard University Press. Rpt. New York: Atheneum, 1968 et seq.

Magnotta, M. 1974. *Historia y bibliografía de la crítica sobre el "Poema de Mio Cid." (1750-1971)*. Portland, Ore.: International Scholarly Book Service.

Menéndez Pidal, Ramón. 1917. "Roncesvalles. Un nuevo cantar de gesta español del siglo XIII." *Revista de filología española*, 4:105-124. Abridged ed. in *Tres poetas primitivos*. Buenos Aires: Espasa-Calpe, 1948, pp. 47-79.

————. 1925. *Floresta de leyendas heroicas españolas: Rodrigo el último godo*. Madrid: Clásicos Castellanos.

————. 1929. *La España del Cid*. 2 vols. Madrid: Plutarco.

————. 1934. *Historia y epopeya*. Madrid: Hernando.

————. 1951. *Reliquias de la poesía épica española*. Madrid: Espasa-Calpe.

————. 1957. *Poesía juglaresca y orígenes de las literaturas románicas*. 6th ed. Madrid: Instituto de Estudios Políticos.

————. 1959. *La Chanson de Roland y el neotradicionalismo*. Madrid: Espasa-Calpe.

————. 1961. "Dos poetas en el *Cantar de Mio Cid*." *Romania*, 82:145-200. Rpt. in *En torno al Poema del Cid*. Barcelona: Editora y Distribuidora Hispano Americana, 1970, pp. 107-162.

————. 1964. *Cantar de Mio Cid*. 4th ed. 3 vols. Madrid: Espasa-Calpe.

————. 1965-1966. "Los cantores épicos yugoeslavos y los occidentales. El *Mio cid* y dos refundidores primitivos." *Boletín de la Real Academia de Buenas Letras de Barcelona*, 31:195-225.

———. 1971. *La leyenda de los infantes de Lara.* 2nd ed. Madrid: Espasa-Calpe.

———, Diego Catalán, and Alvaro Galmés. 1954. *Cómo vive un romance: Dos ensayós sobre tradicionalidad.* Madrid: C.S.I.C.

Michael, Ian. 1961. "A Comparison of the Use of Epic Epithets in the *Poema de Mio Cid* and the *Libro de Alexandre.*" *Bulletin of Hispanic Studies*, 38:32-41.

———. 1975. *El Cid Campeador: The Poem of the Cid, a New Critical Edition of the Spanish Text,* with trans. by Rita Hamilton and Janet Perry. Manchester and New York: Manchester University Press and Barnes & Noble. 2nd ed. 1978.

———. 1976. "Geographical Problems in the *Poema de Mio Cid*: I. The exile route." In *Medieval Hispanic Studies Presented to Rita Hamilton.* Ed. by A. D. Deyermond. London: Tamesis, pp. 117-28.

———. 1977. "Geographical Problems in the *Poema de Mio Cid*: II. The Corpes route." In *Mio Cid Studies.* Ed. by A. D. Deyermond. London: Tamesis, pp. 83-89.

———, ed. 1978. *Poema de Mio Cid.* 2nd ed. Madrid: Castalia.

Miletich, John S. 1975. "The South Slavic *Bugarštica* and the Spanish *Romance*: A New Approach to Typology." *International Journal of Slavic Linguistics and Poetics*, 21, iv:51-69.

Monroe, James T. 1975. "Formulaic Diction and the Common Origins of Romance Lyric Traditions." *Hispanic Review*, 43:341-50.

Montgomery, Thomas. 1967-1968. "Narrative Tense Preference in the *Cantar de Mio Cid.*" *Romance Philology*, 21:253-274.

———. 1975. "Grammatical Causality and Formulism in the *Poema de Mio Cid.*" In *Studies in Honor of Lloyd A. Kasten.* Madison: Hispanic Seminary of Medieval Studies, pp. 185-98.

———. 1977. "The *Poema de Mio Cid*: Oral Art in Transition." In *Mio Cid Studies.* Ed. by A.D. Deyermond. London: Tamesis, pp. 91-112.

Myers, Oliver T. 1966. "Assonance and Tense in the *Poema del Cid.*" *Publications of the Modern Language Association*, 81:499-511.

Navarro Tomás, Tomás. 1956. *Métrica española: reseña histórica e descriptiva.* Syracuse: University Press.

Nepaulsingh, Colbert I. 1983. "The *Afrenta de Corpes* and the Martyrological Tradition." *Hispanic Review*, 51:205-221.

Ochrymowycz, Orest R. 1975. *Aspects of Oral Style in the "Romances juglarescos" of the Carolingian Cycle.* Iowa City: University of Iowa Press.

Olson, Paul. 1962. "Symbolic Hierarchy in the Lion Episode of the *Cantar de Mio Cid.*" *Modern Language Notes*, 77:499-511.

Paredes, Américo. 1976. *A Texas-Mexican Cancionero: Folksongs of the Lower Border.* Urbana: University of Illinois Press.

Poema de Mio Cid. 1961. Facsimile of the manuscript. Madrid: n.p.

Poema de Mio Cid. 1982. 2 vols. Burgos: Ayuntamiento.

Portuguese and Brazilian Oral Traditions in Verse Form. 1976. Ed. by Joanne Purcell. Los Angeles: n.p.

Powell, Brian. 1983. *Epic and Chronicle: The "Poema de Mio Cid" and the "Crónica de veinte reyes."* MHRA Texts and Dissertations, 18. London: Modern Humanities Research Association.

Reig, Carola. 1947. *El cantar de Sancho II y cerco de Zamora.* Madrid: C.S.I.C.

Romanceros del rey Rodrigo y de Bernardo del Carpio. 1957. Ed. by R. Lapesa et al. *Romancero tradicional de las lenguas hispánicas,* 1. Madrid: Gredos.

Rychner, Jean. 1955. *La Chanson de geste: Essai sur l'art épique des jongleurs.* Geneva: Droz.

Sandmann, Manfred. 1953. "Narrative Tenses of the Past in the *Cantar de Mio Cid.*" In *Studies in Romance Philology and French Literature Presented to John Orr.* Manchester: Manchester University Press, pp. 258-281.

Smith, Colin, ed. 1972. *Poema de Mio Cid.* Oxford: Clarendon Press.

―――. 1976. "On Sound-Patterning in the *Poema de Mio Cid.*" *Hispanic Review,* 44:223-237.

―――. 1983. *The Making of the "Poema de Mio Cid."* Cambridge: Cambridge University Press.

―――, and J. Morris. 1967. "On 'Physical' Phrases in Old Spanish Epic and Other Texts." *Proceedings of the Leeds Philosophical and Literary Society, Literary and Historical Section,* 12:129-190.

Staaff, E. 1925. "Quelques remarques concernant les assonances dans le *Poème du Cid.*" In *Homenaje ofrecido a Menéndez Pidal.* Madrid: Hernando, II, pp. 417-429.

Szertics, Joseph. 1967. *Tiempo y verbo en el romancero viejo.* Madrid: Castalia.

Walker, Roger M. 1976. "The Role of the King and the Poet's Intentions in the *Poema de Mio Cid.*" In *Medieval Hispanic Studies Presented to Rita Hamilton.* Ed. by A. D. Deyermond. London: Tamesis, pp. 257-266.

Walsh, John K. 1970-1971. "Religious Motifs in the Early Spanish Epic." *Revista hispánica moderna,* 36:156-172.

Waltman, Franklin M. 1972. *Concordance to the "Poema de Mio Cid."* University Park: Pennsylvania State University Press.

―――. 1973. "Formulaic Expression and Unity of Authorship in the *Poema de Mio Cid.*" *Hispania,* 56:569-578.

————. 1974. "Synonym Choice in the *Cantar de Mio Cid.*" *Hispania*, 57:452-461.

————. 1975. "Tagmemic Analysis and Unity of Authorship in the *Cantar de Mio Cid.*" *Revista de estudios hispánicos*, 9:451-469.

Webber, Ruth House. 1951. *Formulistic Diction in the Spanish Ballad.* Berkeley: University of California Press.

————. 1965. "Un aspecto estilístico del *Cantar de Mio Cid.*" *Anuario de estudios medievales*, 2:485-496.

————. 1966. "Diction of the *Roncesvalles* Fragment." In *Homenaje al Prof. Rodríguez-Moñino.* Madrid: Castalia, II, pp. 311-321.

————. 1973. "Narrative Organization of the *Cid.*" *Olifant*, 1:21-34.

————. 1975. "Assonance Determination in the *Cid.*" *Olifant*, 3:57-65.

————. 1980a. "Lenguaje tradicional: epopeya y romancero." In *Actas del Sexto Congreso Internacional de Hispanistas.* Toronto: University of Toronto Press, pp. 779-82.

————. 1980b. "Formulaic Language in the *Mocedades de Rodrigo.*" *Hispanic Review*, 48:195-211.

————. 1981. "El *Roncesvalles*: lenguaje y temática tradicionales." In *Actas del VIII Congreso de la Société Rencesvals.* Pamplona: Institución Príncipe de Viana, pp. 547-551.

————, 1983. "The Euphony of the *Cantar de Mio Cid.*" In *Florilegium Hispanicum: Medieval and Golden Age Studies Presented to Dorothy Clotelle Clarke.* Ed. by John Geary et al. Madison: Hispanic Seminary of Medieval Studies, pp. 45-60.

Oral Tradition and Biblical Studies

Robert C. Culley

In this chiefly bibliographical essay, Robert C. Culley, author of Oral Formulaic Language in the Biblical Psalms *(1967) and* Studies in the Structure of Hebrew Narrative *(1976), summarizes and reviews scholarship based on a variety of oral traditional approaches to biblical studies. In his chronological scheme, the first era of such scholarship culminates in the works of Julius Wellhausen and Hermann Gunkel at the turn of the century which recognize orality of genre, style, and structure in Old Testament texts. Culley divides the more recent period into Old and New Testament studies, although most scholarship has continued to focus on the more ancient Hebrew poetry and prose as products of oral culture, with the notable exception of recent work on the Gospels by Werner H. Kelber. For studies since 1963, Culley explains the influence of the Parry-Lord theory of oral composition, which has led to work on formula, theme, and story-types in Old and New Testament texts.*

    The discussion of oral tradition and biblical studies has a rather long history so there would be no point in trying to review everything or to examine all the material with equal thoroughness. This review,

Reprinted from *Oral Tradition*, 1 (1986), 30-65.

then, will attempt to cover the ground in three chronological stages.
The first stage, up to the early decades of this century, will do little
more than consider two remarkable scholars from the end of this period,
Julius Wellhausen (d. 1914) and Hermann Gunkel (d. 1932). The next
stage will note the main features of three streams of research which run
alongside one another from around 1930 to about 1960. The last stage
will review the last twenty-five years, and here the aim will be to cover
all relevant contributions and authors. For the last two stages, the Old
Testament and the New Testament will be treated separately.

The terms "Bible" and "biblical studies" are ambiguous in the sense
that both may refer to overlapping entities. The Christian Bible
contains the Old Testament written in Hebrew with a small amount of
Aramaic and the New Testament written in Greek. The Jewish Bible is,
of course, that Hebrew collection which Christians adopted as the Old
Testament. In what follows, the terms "Bible" and "biblical studies"
will retain some of this basic ambiguity, since both Hebrew Bible, or
Old Testament, and New Testament will be taken into account.
Scholarship has also divided along these lines in that scholars tend to be
identified as specialists in the Hebrew Scriptures or Old Testament on
the one hand or New Testament on the other. While I would be known
as a student of the Old Testament, I will venture gingerly into New
Testament studies in order that biblical studies in both senses of the
term may be included.

There is no single book or article on oral tradition in the Bible
which covers the whole territory and so could serve as a basic reference
work. The most extensive study of oral tradition in biblical studies
covers only the Hebrew Bible and was published in 1973:
Rediscovering the Traditions of Israel by Douglas A. Knight. This
ample volume contains a critical history of the study of tradition in Old
Testament studies. While Knight's interest is mainly in work done
during this century in Germany and Scandinavia, he notes some earlier
discussions.

My own article in *Semeia* (1976a) and my chapter in *The Hebrew
Bible and Its Modern Interpreters* (1984) attempt to cover research in
Old Testament studies over the last twenty-five years. An encyclopedia
article on oral tradition by Robert E. Coote (1976) covers part of the
modern period. For New Testament Studies, there is an article by
Leander E. Keck, "Oral Traditional Literature and the Gospels: The
Seminar" (1978). Werner Kelber's work (1979, 1983) also offers

background and assessment of earlier discussions, as does the book by Güttgemanns (1979, original German 1971).

As this simple chronological scheme is followed, it will be important to keep a basic question in mind: how have biblical scholars formed their opinion about oral tradition and its significance for the Bible? As with most other ancient texts, we lack substantial information as to how it was composed and reached its present form. Little can be said directly about the role of oral tradition. Since no clear picture can be reconstructed on the basis of evidence from the Bible and its historical context, one must resort to other means. Three avenues have been followed. First of all, there is the shape of the biblical text itself and the extent to which it yields clues to modes of composition and transmission. Second, one may turn to other cultures, ancient or modern, which seem to give a clearer picture of oral tradition and use these as analogies to draw conclusions about biblical texts. Third, a general picture may be assumed or a general model may be constructed which contains what appear to be the more or less universal characteristics of an oral culture; or the picture may include the main features of both oral and literate societies placed in contrast. Such a broad schema is then used to discern the presence or absence of features related to oral and written texts.

I. Up to the Time of Gunkel (d. 1932)

Douglas Knight traces discussion of oral tradition among biblical scholars back as far as the time of the Reformation (1973, pp. 39-54), although at this stage oral tradition was enmeshed in debates between Catholics and Protestants about inspiration and the authority of Scripture. Because it was accepted that Moses had written the first five books of the Bible, some assumed that he must have had oral traditions concerning those things recorded in the book of Genesis which had occurred before his lifetime. While this idea persisted for some time, two figures contributed significantly to an important change. Johann Gottfried Herder assumed oral sources not only for early parts of the Old Testament (Knight, 1973, pp. 57-58) but also for the Gospels, as noted by Kelber (1983, pp. 77-78) and Güttgemanns (1979, pp. 178-81). A contemporary of Herder, Johann Christoph Nachtigal (1753-1819), was, in Knight's estimation (pp. 61-63), the first to propose in detail a post-Mosaic oral tradition of historical and prophetic material with his theory that oral and written traditions emerged as literature only in the period of David.

During the late nineteenth and early twentieth centuries, two scholars emerged as leading figures in biblical studies, Julius Wellhausen and Hermann Gunkel, and indeed they have continued to effect a remarkable influence up to the present day. Their views on oral tradition were quite different. For Wellhausen (1844-1918), authors and documents were the critical elements in any study of composition of the Bible. Drawing on the work of many predecessors, Wellhausen fashioned the classic statement for the source analysis of the first five books of the Bible. His version of the literary analysis of the Pentateuch entails four documents: J was the Yahwist document from the ninth century B.C.E., E was the Elohist from the eighth century, D or Deuteronomy came from the seventh century, and P or the Priestly tradition from the fifth century. Wellhausen also analyzed other parts of the Hebrew Bible and produced a literary analysis of the Gospels. In his famous *Prolegomena to the History of Ancient Israel* (1883), oral tradition comes up in only a few, scattered comments. These are discussed, among other things, in an article by Knight in *Semeia* (1982). Wellhausen assumed that oral tradition lay behind the documents but consisted of individual stories only loosely related to each other (p. 296) and bound originally to localities having special features like sacred sites or geographical oddities reflected in the stories (p. 325). Bringing oral stories together into larger, organized structures was the work of authors producing written sources. As a historian, Wellhausen did not credit oral traditions with much reliability (p. 326).

While Hermann Gunkel (1862-1932) accepted the general framework of Wellhausen's documentary theory, he displayed a much greater interest in the role of oral tradition in shaping the material which ultimately emerged as document. Gunkel began from a basic distinction which he made between the literature of ancient peoples and the literature of modern times (1963; reprint of 1925, pp. 1-4). While modern literature is marked by the dominant role of authors who produce *Kunstpoesie*, the literature of Israel is closer to folk literature. The notion of *Gattung*, sometimes translated in English as "form" but more recently as "genre," is a key concept in Gunkel's general approach which he referred to as *Gattungsgeschichte* but which is known in

English as "form criticism." In his view, most of the basic genres of Israel's literature were formed in an oral period when each had a specific setting in the life of the people (*Sitz im Leben*). Even when writing and authors took over, ancient patterns were still employed. Using this perspective, Gunkel made important contributions to the understanding of the narrative and prophetic traditions of the Hebrew Bible, as well as the Psalms.

Gunkel does not indicate how he arrived at this approach to biblical literature or where he came by his perception of oral tradition, although he acknowledges a general debt to Herder. In a major study of Gunkel's life and work, Werner Klatt mentions a number of possible, indirect influences on Gunkel's thought (1969, pp. 104-125), such as the Grimm Brothers, but Klatt is strongly inclined to attribute the large part of Gunkel's approach to his own originality (pp. 110-112; but see the views of Warner, 1979 and Kirkpatrick, 1984).

The fullest discussion of oral tradition by Gunkel may be found in the introduction to his commentary on Genesis. An English translation of the introduction to the second edition has appeared under the title *The Legends of Genesis*, although in what follows reference will be made to the third edition of 1910. A number of references can be found in this edition to the now famous article by Axel Olrik, "Epische Gesetze der Volksdichtung" (1909). However, these are clearly used to substantiate insights Gunkel had already arrived at and stated in earlier editions of his commentary. He was a perceptive reader of the biblical text.

The style of the Genesis stories may be understood, Gunkel argues, only if it is seen that they are legends from oral tradition. As folk tradition, these stories are in some real sense the common creation of the people and thus express their spirit. The setting of these stories in the life of the people is the family. Here Gunkel offers a picture, frequently cited, which describes the family seated around a fire on a winter's evening listening with rapt attention, especially the children, to the familiar, well-loved stories about early times (p. xxxi). Gunkel also envisages a class of storytellers, well-versed in the traditional narratives, who travelled the country and appeared at festivals. While he agreed with Wellhausen that the basic unit in narration was the single legend, he estimated that groups of stories were already brought together into small collections at the oral stage (*Sagenkränze*). Nevertheless, the main blocks of material in Genesis (primeval history, the patriarchs, and the Joseph story) were assumed to have been the result of literary collection, at which point some artistic reformulation may have taken place.

Gunkel imagined that an oral period must have entailed substantial limitations of both an intellectual and literary nature on the part of both listeners and storytellers. For example, he believed that only short works could be produced. Hence the axiom: the shorter the story, the older it must be. He spoke of the poverty of the ancient artistry from an oral period (p. xxxiv). To this he traced the repetition of expressions as well as the simplicity of the description of character and the development of action. Nevertheless, legends of Genesis were for Gunkel a mature and developed art form which appealed to him very much. Oral tradition involved both stability and change. While Gunkel spoke of a remarkable reliability in the transmission of stories, he noted that transmission was characterized by change, for oral tradition exists in the form of variants (p. lxv). Still, in the long term, this multiformity was also a limitation. Inability to retain its purity renders oral tradition an unsuitable vehicle for history, which can arise only in a period of writing.

To be sure, Gunkel's views are open to criticism on a number of points, and indeed apt critiques have been produced by a number of scholars, for example Sean Warner, Alois Wolf (a Germanist), and Patricia Kirkpatrick. But given the fact that he was writing over eighty years ago, one is rather impressed with what he attempted to do and how far he got with it. His perception of oral tradition in the biblical texts appears to be based on a sensitive reading of the texts along with a rather general notion of oral tradition and oral culture, perhaps owing much to Herder. Having sensed distinctions in style, structure, and genre between the stories in Genesis and the literature of his own day, he sought to explain them in terms of his idea of what oral tradition must have been like. He also devoted considerable attention to the presence of folklore genres and motifs in biblical texts.

Gunkel's form-critical approach and the notion of oral tradition that went with it have had a remarkable and persistent influence in both Old and New Testament scholarship up to the present. In what follows these two fields will be treated separately. Broadly speaking, they carried on their research and discussion apart from each other, even though significant overlapping and interplay can be discerned.

II. The Hebrew Scriptures or Old Testament

A. From Gunkel to the Sixties

The period from Hermann Gunkel to the early sixties can be traced by considering the work of scholars in three geographical areas: Germany, Scandinavia, and North America.

1. *Germany.* After Gunkel little was written by the German scholars who followed him and developed his approach on the subject of oral tradition. Knight (1973, pp. 84-142) provides a good survey of the contribution made to the study of tradition by scholars like Gressmann, Alt, and von Rad. Only one scholar will be mentioned by way of example.

Martin Noth (1902-1968) produced major studies of the history of tradition in the historical books and in the Pentateuch, as well as writing an important history of Israel. His broad aim in the study of tradition was stated on the first page of *A History of Pentateuchal Traditions* (1972, original German 1948), namely, to trace the growth of the tradition from its earliest preliterary elements to the final form we now have in the Bible. He assumed a significant role for oral tradition but made no substantial comment on its nature. Discussion and analysis of Noth's work may be found in Knight (1973, pp. 143-171) and especially in Bernard W. Anderson's introduction to his English translation of *Pentateuchal Traditions* (Noth, 1972). Noth is known particularly for his frequent use of aetiological elements to trace the origins of the oral legends he identified in the Bible. He assumed they were frequently bound to specific localities.

As with Gunkel, Noth's conclusions are derived from minute examination of the characteristics of the biblical text in conjunction with some general assumptions of what must have happened in oral tradition. He did not draw a clear line between literary and oral tradition. While he accepted J and E as written sources, he posited a common tradition behind them identified as G (*Grundlage*). It could have been oral or written and Noth did not seem to think it mattered which.

2. *Scandinavia.* Alongside developments in Germany, and to some extent in reaction to them, a debate about oral tradition arose among Scandinavian scholars and continued over two decades or more. Actually, oral tradition was only one of a number of issues under

discussion. For example, one finds a particular interest in the role of the cult in Israel's religion, especially sacral kingship. Knight's *Rediscovering the Traditions of Ancient Israel* provides a very useful guide to this discussion along with a full bibliography (pp. 215-382). Since the debate on the issue of oral tradition moves back and forth among a number of scholars, it would not be helpful to try to describe the whole debate or trace the exact chronology of discussion. Thus, only a broad account of the main figures and central issues in a rough chronological order will be attempted.

Most agree that the debate began with the publication of *Studien zum Hoseabuche* by the Swedish scholar H. S. Nyberg (1935). In a few brief comments Nyberg argued the following. Tradition in the ancient Orient was mainly oral and only on rare occasions purely written. A period of oral tradition lay behind most written texts, and even after inscription the principal means of transmission continued to be oral. No support was offered for these statements beyond cursory mention of two examples: the memorization of Qur'an by Muslims and the case of a Parsee priest who knew the Yasna by heart but had trouble using a written text. Nyberg claimed to have more material which has never been published (1972, p. 9; also Widengren, 1959, pp. 205-206).

Nyberg seems to have envisaged a relatively fixed and stable transmission through memorization even though he spoke of the possibility of changes through a *lebendige Umformung* (1935, p. 8). In large part the traditions of Israel achieved a written form after the Babylonian Exile of the fifth century B.C.E. Nyberg also stressed the contrast between cultures which rely on memory to preserve literature orally and cultures which rely on writing. Texts from ancient times should not be read like the written literature with which we are familiar because such texts are only supports for an oral tradition which remained dominant.

Others were influenced by Nyberg's views. In a monograph on the prophetic books, *Zum Hebräischen Traditionswesen* (1938), Harris Birkeland sought to support Nyberg's proposal further by appealing to descriptions of how early Arabic poetry was transmitted. While he argued for the priority of oral tradition, he accepted an interplay between oral and written.

However, the most lively and controversial supporter of Nyberg's views was Ivan Engnell. His earliest comments appeared in *Gamla Testamentet* (1945), which has never been translated into English. In

1949 he published *The Call of Isaiah*, a volume containing a brief summary of his views in response to some of his critics. A further presentation may be found in *A Rigid Scrutiny* (1969, original Swedish 1962). For Engnell oral tradition was part of a larger approach to biblical texts, called the traditio-historical method, which rejected the theory of literary documents in the Pentateuch (Wellhausen's J, E, D, and P) as well as similar documentary analysis for other parts of the Bible.

Engnell followed Nyberg in maintaining that the Old Testament was essentially oral literature which only gained written form at a later period. Oral tradition could be reliable and resistant to corruption, although he too spoke of change in terms of a "living remodelling" (likely Nyberg's term). Analysis of texts was not a matter of sorting out documents which had been put together with scissors and paste but of attempting to determine the units and blocks joined in the process of oral transmission to make larger elements of tradition (Engnell, 1969, p. 6). Cultic texts like the Psalms may have been treated differently and written down well before the Exile, so that oral and written should not be set in absolute opposition (1949, p. 56). As evidence for the oral composition and transmission of the biblical text, he pointed to features like the use of word association, doublets and variants, epic laws, and various kinds of patterning in poetry and prose (1969, p. 8).

Engnell did not in the end accept Arabic traditions as useful comparative material on the question of oral tradition. They were too far removed in time and space and existed in a context with very different religious and cultic perspectives. He stressed the special character of the traditions of Israel as sacred text.

Perhaps the best known book in the English-speaking world that summarized the exposition of Nyberg and Engnell is *Oral Tradition* (1954) by Eduard Nielsen. The author reviews comparative material from the ancient world for learning by heart, such as the Qur'an and the Rigveda, and adds some arguments in support of oral tradition in Mesopotamia. He also covers topics like the creators and bearers of the tradition, and the interplay of oral and written and the reduction to writing. His list of the formal characteristics of oral tradition include: monotonous style, recurring expressions, paratactic style, conformity to Olrik's laws, and emphasis on memory words and representative themes (p. 36). Nielsen tries to show that similar conditions applied for Israel.

Other Scandinavian scholars took a critical stance. One of these was the Norwegian, Sigmund Mowinckel, whose views were noted in his *Prophecy and Tradition* (1946) as well as in an encyclopedia article (1962). He held that both traditio-historical (Nyberg, Engnell) and literary-critical (Wellhausen, Gunkel) methods are important and must be allowed to interact (1962, p. 685). He agreed that a substantial amount of the biblical traditions must be oral. But popular traditions were not, according to Mowinckel, passed on in a fixed form. Unchangeable traditions came only with the notion of a sacred text. For him oral transmission is a living process in which the traditions constantly gained new forms and entered new combinations (p. 27). Another critic, J. van der Ploeg, expressed his doubts about any major role for oral tradition (1947).

The most vehement critic of Nyberg and Engnell was G. Widengren. In a book on the prophets, *Literary and Psychological Aspects of the Hebrew Prophets* (1948), he questioned the analogy of early Arabic poetry, claiming that it had been written down much earlier than usually assumed. He proposed rather a scribal culture in which oral tradition was not nearly as reliable as written texts (p. 29). In Arabic tradition he distinguished two kinds of historical literature: one which was largely oral tradition and one which had mixed oral and written from the start. There was also a more developed historical literature in which the hand of an author could be discerned (p. 56). On the basis of this analogy, Widengren concluded that the role of oral tradition in Israel should not be exaggerated, especially with reference to its reliability. He would only assume a long oral tradition in Israel where the literature reflects nomadic or semi-nomadic conditions (p. 122). This might be so for Joshua and Judges but not for Samuel and Kings, which must have involved a mixture of oral and written materials. In a later article, "Oral Tradition and Written Literature among the Hebrews in the Light of Arabic Evidence with Special Regard to Prose Narratives" (1959), Widengren reasserted his earlier position with further discussion of Arabic and other traditions. In addition he suggested a distinction between Indo-European cultures, which emphasize oral, and the Ancient Near East, which had developed written traditions (pp. 218-225).

Finally, one might note a study by Helmer Ringgren (1949). Aware of the difficulty of using analogies, he attempts a study of parallel texts (e.g., Psalms 40:14-17 and 70) in the Hebrew Bible in an effort to determine whether the small differences that exist between the texts can be traced to written or oral transmission. Since some of the differences appear to be errors in hearing, he urges that one should allow for oral as well as written transmission.

In this debate the characteristics of the biblical texts retained a central place, although Engnell read the evidence differently from Wellhausen or even Gunkel. It is significant also that the Scandinavian discussion produced attempts to find suitable analogies in other cultures, although the appeals made on both sides were usually to examples from antiquity. Beyond this, some attempt was made to distinguish appropriate analogies from those that were not.

3. *North America.* Oral tradition was also discussed on the other side of the Atlantic, although not as extensively. This was very much the work of William Foxwell Albright (1891-1971), a brilliant and inquisitive scholar whose interests ranged far and wide through many disciplines and whose influence has been quite remarkable in biblical scholarship in North America.

It is astonishing that as early as 1950, in an article on "Some Oriental Glosses on the Homeric Problem," Albright referred to Parry's view that Homeric style with its repeated language and patterns was the product of many generations of singers. Albright suggested that the Canaanite texts from Ugarit may have been the result of a similar mode of composition in which poets employed traditional diction while remaining creative artists. On the basis of Parry's suggestion, Albright criticized Gunkel's proposal that oral poetry necessarily must have begun with very short compositions. He also surmised that even in such literate regions as Egypt, Babylonia, Iran, India, and China, composition and transmission of literary works were largely oral and frequently without use of writing.

Later comments by Albright on the subject of oral tradition take no further account of Parry or even Lord. In *From the Stone Age to Christianity* (1957), there is a brief section on the characteristics of oral tradition. Here he discerns no clear line between oral and written transmission of the sort one finds in connection with texts like the Qur'an, the Rig-Veda, and the Talmud in which oral transmission exists both before and after the written texts. Still, he finds prose less suited than verse for reliable oral transmission and so prefers poetry to prose as historical sources. On the grounds that prose was frequently a secondary form behind which lay a poetic version, Albright agreed with the suggestions of some preceding scholars that early Hebrew prose had a poetic background. The first chapter of his *Yahweh and the Gods of Canaan* (1969) bears the heading "Verse and Prose in Early Israelite Tradition" and is devoted to presenting "some of the evidence for early oral transmission of historical information through archaic verse" (p. 52). It is urged that orally transmitted poetic saga lay behind the sources of the Pentateuch (p. 35).

Albright's comments are frequently directed toward the problem of assessing the historical reliability of biblical texts. In contrast to Wellhausen and Noth, who put little trust in the early traditions of Israel, Albright urged historians to take these early stories much more seriously as sources for historical reconstruction and to be cautious in their use of aetiology in explaining origins of narratives. While conceding that oral tradition was liable to refraction and selection through adding folkloristic elements or dramatizing for pedagogical reasons, he continues to insist on the general accuracy of oral tradition and the substantial historicity of the biblical traditions (1964, p. 56). This appears to mean the essential outline of events (1966, p. 11).

Former students and colleagues of Albright have also spoken of an original poetic epic. In an article on the Pentateuch in *The Interpreter's Dictionary of the Bible* (1962), D. N. Freedman leans toward the notion that G (*Grundlage*), the common source which Noth assumed lay behind the Pentateuchal sources, was "a poetic composition, orally transmitted" and had its setting in the sacred festivals of Israel (p. 714). In a later article, he doubts the notion of an epic, however attractive, and thinks rather of several poems of considerable length (1977, p. 17). In *Canaanite Myth and Hebrew Epic* (1973), Frank M. Cross argues that the sources J and E are prose variants of a cycle in poetry from the time of the Judges. In his opinion, this cycle was "originally composed orally and was utilized in the cult of covenant-renewal festivals" (p. 294).

Neither Albright nor his successors resorted to specific analogies from other cultures to support their conception of oral tradition, although as we shall see Cross is fully aware of the work of Lord. Nor do they present any substantial argument for the existence of a poetic epic. Albright supports his theory of the priority of verse with a study of Canaanite and early Israelite poetic style (1969, pp. 1-52).

B. From 1963 to the Present

In 1963 a new dimension was introduced into the discussion of oral tradition in Old Testament studies. Attempts were now undertaken to employ field studies describing modern oral transmission in order to define the nature of oral tradition and the characteristics of oral texts. The intention was to examine the Hebrew Bible in the light of whatever information might be gained. This strategy resulted in large part from the work done by Milman Parry and Albert Bates Lord in collecting Serbo-Croatian oral narrative. Added to this original focus was the interest their work generated in disciplines like classics as well as Old and Middle English. Texts from an oral narrative tradition of Serbo-Croatian bards, along with some commentary, became available in the first volume of *Serbocroatian Heroic Songs* (1954), edited by Lord, and in his book *The Singer of Tales* which appeared in 1960.

In my own article, "An Approach to the Problem of Oral Tradition" (1963), I tried to describe oral tradition in broad outline by surveying the comments of a number of scholars who had observed oral tradition at first hand. The aim was to sample descriptions from as broad a range of different oral traditions as possible, involving a wide variety of literary types in poetry and prose in both long and short texts. From the limited studies available, it was clear that alongside the fixed form of transmission assumed by many earlier biblical scholars there was also an unfixed form. In fact, this latter form appeared to be the more common variety. Transmission of traditional songs, poems, and stories was accomplished by improvisation during performance involving the use of traditional language. The work of Parry and Lord, the most detailed study of this kind of transmission, suggested that ready-made language—*formulas* and formulaic phrases as well as stock scenes and descriptions called *themes*—enabled the poet to compose rapidly in performance.

My conclusion was that one would need to hold open a number of possibilities regarding composition and transmission of Old Testament texts. Some may have been written by authors. Some might have been dictations taken from an oral performer. Complexes of relatively stable material may have been joined in oral tradition. There may have been so-called "transitional" texts composed in writing but in an oral style. Finally, one would have to allow for oral texts produced in a fixed form and passed on through memorization until written down.

In what follows the studies relating to Hebrew poetry will be examined first, then studies on prose, and finally other kinds of studies.

1. Biblical Hebrew Poetry

Also in 1963, two scholars attempted to relate the work of Parry and Lord to biblical poetry. William Whallon, not a biblical scholar, published an article with the title "Formulaic Poetry in the Old Testament." He argued that parallelism was a prosodic requirement analogous to meter in Homer and alliteration in Anglo-Saxon. Thus, the equivalent of the formula in Hebrew poetry was the pair of synonymous words in parallel sections of the line. Numerous examples were supplied. In a later book (1969), Whallon accepted both word pairs and repeated phrases as formulaic.

In the same year, and independently, Stanley Gevirtz commented briefly on "fixed pairs" (synonymous, parallel words) in the introduction to a book on Hebrew poetry. This phenomenon had already been recognized by some biblical scholars as an important feature of Canaanite and biblical poetry, but Gevirtz made the suggestion that these fixed pairs were part of a traditional language used by Syro-Palestinian poets in oral composition (1963, p. 10). Having come across the writings of Parry on Homer, he proposed that Hebrew poets (unlike Greek) constructed their verse primarily with the aid of these fixed pairs rather than with formulaic phrases, although he did not exclude the presence and use of such phrases as well (p. 12).

My dissertation on formulaic language in the biblical psalms (1963) appeared as *Oral Formulaic Language in the Biblical Psalms* in 1967. This study collected phrases, usually of a line or a half-line in length, repeated either exactly or with some modification. Recent descriptions of oral poetry from three distinct areas and traditions were used as analogies: Serbo-Croatian narrative, Toda songs from South India, and Russian narrative and ceremonial poetry. It appeared that the mode of composition and transmission was similar in each case. Stock phrases were present in all these traditions. The descriptions of Toda and Russian poetry suggested that improvised composition was used for different kinds of poetry, even for short non-narrative poems. Since the fullest and most detailed account of oral composition and transmission came from Parry and Lord, their description was relied upon extensively and their terminology was adopted in a modified form. Analyses of other ancient documents like Homer and Anglo-Saxon texts were used to amplify and illustrate the field studies.

Repeated phrases were identified as formulas and formulaic phrases on the basis of close similarity in syntactical pattern and lexical items as well as conformity to line or half-line length. Since Hebrew meter was, and remains, a much-disputed question, it was left out of consideration. One hundred and seventy-seven examples of formulas and formulaic phrases were listed. Almost half of these occurred at least three times (some more than this), the rest twice. There were fifteen examples of small blocks of lines being repeated. A small number of psalms showed a clustering of repeated phrases, but only a handful of psalms contained over 40 percent of this language. While it was argued that the phrases were traditional, oral-formulaic language, it was left open as to whether or not any of the present psalms are oral compositions.

A brief reply was made to Gevirtz and Whallon. While conceding the force of their suggestion, I argued then that the presence of a body of repeated phrases similar to formulas and formulaic phrases found in other traditions suggested that the major formula in Hebrew was related to lines and cola rather than parallelism and was thus the fixed phrase rather than fixed pair. It was proposed that, while parallelism was almost always present, there was something more basic to the structure of Hebrew poetry, perhaps meter, which had to do with building lines and cola within certain limitations (1963, p. 119). I left open the question of precisely how fixed pairs might be related to oral composition.

In a 1970 dissertation followed by an article, "A-B Pairs and Oral Composition" (1971), Perry B. Yoder made a strong case for fixed pairs as the Hebrew formula. With no demonstrable metrical limitations, he urged, formulas and formulaic phrases would not be needed. On the other hand, fixed pairs could be explained in terms of the need to produce parallel lines. Thus, Yoder contended that parallelism and not meter was the formal requirement which had to be met by the poet (1970, p. 102). He appealed to the examples of Ob-Ugric and Toda poetry, where paired words appear to be found. Fixed pairs are then formulas, and formulaic systems involve substitution of another word in one of the positions. In psalms where I found clustering of phrases, he finds clustering of fixed pairs (1970, pp. 205-206).

The views of Culley, Gevirtz, and Whallon are specifically criticized in another study of word pairs by William R. Watters (1976). In his view, what repeated phrases exist are not sufficient to be marks of traditional oral diction, and this goes for word pairs as well. Thus he does not relate his study of fixed pairs to oral language.

About this time an interest in oral-formulaic studies became evident among some students of Frank M. Cross at Harvard University. The first sign of this interest came through a thesis on Ugaritic poetry, which is usually taken to be very closely related to biblical poetry if not part of the same Syro-Palestinian tradition (as Gevirtz [1963] has said). Richard E. Whitaker's unpublished dissertation, "A Formulaic Analysis of Ugaritic Poetry" (1969), began with a study of epithets and how they were paired to build parallel cola. From there he studied the patterns of lines which yielded traditional features like fixed line positions for elements, conventional phrases, traditional verse patterns, and groups of cola which cluster (p. 154). One text showed a level of 82 percent formulaic language. He concluded that the poetry was created in oral tradition (p. 157).

Further comments on the oral nature of the Ugaritic poems may be found in an article by Cross (1974). He offers a few examples where, in his view, irregularities have occurred in the process of dictation to a scribe, and in this interpretation he is relying on Lord's discussion of dictation. A number of restorations are proposed which "reconstruct the original text" (p. 8).

Another Harvard thesis, "Evidences of Oral-Formulaic Composition in the Poetry of Job" (1975), came from William J. Urbrock. It remains unpublished, but some of his material has appeared in a paper on Job (1972) and a later article (1976). Urbrock contends that significant evidence of formulaic language in Job suggests oral antecedents. This evidence includes traditional word pairs, which are deemed the basic building blocks for composing parallel cola. Over a hundred examples of colon-length formulas and formulaic systems are proposed. In selecting formulaic phrases, Urbrock was less restrictive than I was, not demanding as great a measure of semantic identity. A particular contribution of Urbrock's study is his attempt to deal with traditional *themes* in Joban poetry. Fifteen examples of repeated groups of ideas are presented which occur more than once in Job or elsewhere in the Hebrew Bible. Smaller units or motifs are also identified.

Two articles by another Harvard graduate, Robert B. Coote, appeared in the same year (1976a and b) with a general assessment of the application of the oral theory of Parry and Lord to biblical studies. Limitations are noted. Features like conformity to meter, formulaic density, and thrift, which made the theory convincing for Homer and Yugoslav poetry, are lacking in Hebrew poetry. Since Hebrew meter has never been described and the length of line, while apparently subject to limitation, is rather flexible, Coote wonders why Hebrew oral poets might need stock language. In addition, formulaic density is difficult to establish in any substantial way due to the paucity of comparative material. Nor can thrift be measured. The result is that, while one can make a good case for conventional language in the Psalms and Job, it cannot be demonstrated positively that this language was functional in oral composition (1976b, pp. 56-57). It is, then, hardly possible to establish whether or not a given poem was orally composed. What studies on oral language have shown, however, is that Hebrew poetry at least derived from an oral tradition. Coote defines the formulas in terms of the line or colon rather than the fixed pair, which he nevertheless accepts as a device which facilitates the composition of parallel lines. As far as the present biblical text is concerned, he is inclined to think of oral language as traces of an oral heritage in a written tradition. The question then becomes: "how is written convention shaped by the oral tradition from which it derives its constituent elements?" (p. 57). He relates this question to those posed by form criticism and tradition history.

Coote identifies two areas where discussion of the oral nature of biblical texts may prove helpful. First, he argues that the constraints of oral Hebrew poetry have been clarified, and that they are two: "the line is of a certain length, and its meaning is self-contained" (p. 58), although the metrical characteristics of written poetry in the Bible are still an open question. The other area is textual criticism. Since oral tradition exists in multiforms at all levels, the notion of a single original text may have to be modified at the very least. It may be useful to consider retaining variants rather than reducing and harmonizing them (1976a, pp. 915).

Three further discussions of oral poetry may be noted. A 1978 monograph by a Scandinavian scholar, Inger Ljung, applies the results of formulaic analysis to a biblical problem. Ljung tries to test the theory that there was a specific genre known as Servant of Yahweh psalms, which were rituals or reflected rituals depicting the suffering of the sacral king in an annual festival. Using the phrases collected in my work on the Psalms, she finds no clustering of this language. On the assumption that there would be a close link between oral-formulaic language and genre, she concludes that lack of this clustering rules out a special genre of Servant of Yahweh psalms.

Yehoshua Gitay turns to the question of oral tradition and a prophetic book, Isaiah 40-45, in a 1980 article, "Deutero-Isaiah: Oral or Written?" He contends that any phenomenon which might be identified as oral style can also be found in written texts. He goes on to assert that it is not appropriate to ask about oral or written, since all early texts were produced to be heard and not read.

Finally, one should note some brief comments made on the subject of oral poetry by M. O'Connor in a massive study on Hebrew meter entitled *Hebrew Verse Structure* (1980). Since this author's main interest lies in the problem of Hebrew meter, his comments on oral poetry are presented rather cryptically in a few paragraphs. He does not discuss any of the analyses carried out on Hebrew texts but limits himself to a few general assertions about formulas. O'Connor accepts the notion that Canaanite poetry, which in his terminology includes Hebrew, was essentially oral (p. 103). A principal reference in his discussion of oral poetry is the collection of articles in *Oral Literature and the Formula* (Stolz and Shannon, 1976), and he shows a great deal of sympathy for the views expressed in Paul Kiparsky's essay in particular. As a result, O'Connor prefers to separate the formula from the definition of meter, feeling that meter does not create the formula (pp. 104-106). He does not believe that Parry's definition of the formula, because of its metrical component, can be made to fit Hebrew or Ugaritic, which in O'Connor's view are not metrical, although they have constraints. In his opinion fixed pairs, which he calls dyads, appear to belong to the same phenomenon as do formulas in other poetic traditions, but he does not wish to tie formulas to oral composition. For example, he suggests that Homer is orally based but does not assume that it is orally composed (p. 106).

2. Biblical Hebrew Prose

David M. Gunn has produced four articles (1974a and b, 1976a and b) on aspects of oral prose style and biblical texts. His views are summed up conveniently in chapter three of a subsequent book, *The Story of King David* (1978). Gunn is well-acquainted with the work of Parry and Lord but also with a wide range of descriptions of oral prose. In his approach to the biblical text he makes a distinction between what he calls *traditional material*, conventional for the author and his audience, and *oral traditional material*, where the mode of composition of the conventional material can be specified as oral.

Examples of traditional material given by Gunn entail some specimens of repeated patterns which he calls traditional motifs. He identifies these with labels like "the two messengers" and "the woman who brings death." Examples of a given motif share a general similarity in form and content but not in wording.

Examples of oral traditional material offered by Gunn consist of short patterns which show some close verbal correspondences along with a significant measure of dissimilarity. That is to say, they seem to reflect both fixity and fluidity (1978, pp. 49-50). These, he argues, correspond to the stock description or incident identified by students of oral tradition as *theme* or *type-scene*, and so provide evidence of some kind of a connection with oral tradition. Since he has only a limited number of examples, Gunn is cautious about what conclusions can be drawn, but he is prepared to say that "somewhere behind the story of King David (or parts of it) lies a tradition of oral narrative composition" (p. 59). As to how biblical texts may be related to oral tradition, Gunn holds open a range of possibilities which include: transcription of a dictation of an oral story, a text written by a literate author but in an oral style, or a text in a written style with some traces of oral style. On the basis of the relatively small amount of evidence usually available, he concedes that it would be difficult to choose among these options. What keeps the possibility of some oral influence open for Gunn is the general likelihood that the stories of Israel had their formative stage in an oral tradition.

My own monograph, *Studies in the Structure of Hebrew Narrative* (1976), deals in part with the question of oral prose. The first chapter sought on the basis of four field studies from such different geographical areas as Africa, the Bahamas, and Europe to determine what it is possible to say about the creation and transmission of oral prose. Only some general observations could be made. It seemed evident that traditional stories were passed on in such a way that both the loyalty to tradition (stability) and the creativity of the narrator (variation) were blended. Among the traditional elements commonly used in one way or other was the stock incident or episode, similar to the theme, or at least one kind of theme, discussed by Lord. It was concluded that, while the identification of such a device provided interesting clues to the nature of orally composed texts, it did not offer a definitive test for distinguishing oral texts from written. In the second chapter of the monograph, some of the famous cases of variants in the Hebrew Bible were examined in the light of the discussion of oral prose. As I had anticipated, clear judgments were not possible on the basis of such a small number of variants. Evidence for both stability and variation was compatible with what one would expect in oral variants, but it was difficult to rule out the possibility that the same sort of thing might occur in a scribal tradition which stood somewhere between a distinct oral tradition and a fully developed literary tradition. It was urged that more needs to be known about the possibility of such a "transitional" phase.

A very different approach to the oral nature of a text is found in Heda Jason's "The Story of David and Goliath: A Folk Epic?" (1979). A whole range of criteria is applied to the biblical story. This analysis is based on a model developed by Jason for the study of folklore. It is organized under two main headings: narrative syntax (texture and plot) and narrative semantics (terms of content and dimensions of time and space). Jason presumes that a written text would not respond to measurement by folkloristic models. Since this one does, Jason takes the story to be "an original work of oral literature or a successful imitation" (p. 61).

A few other studies that touch on the oral question in connection with prose texts from the Bible may be noted briefly. Alexander Rofé in his "Classification of Prophetical Stories" (1970) identifies some tales which may have had their origin in oral tradition. Because they are so short in their present form, he assumes that a skillful narrator must have condensed them drastically to produce the purest form of the written *legenda*. Using a statistical approach, R. E. Bee (1973) offers a method for distinguishing oral from written texts, although he makes no reference to any studies of oral style in ancient texts. A lengthy study of the Jacob story by Albert de Pury (1975) includes several references to the work of folklorists and students of oral literature in the discussion of the nature of the cycle (pp. 463-502). In a study comparing Ancient Near Eastern and biblical tales (1978), Dorothy Irvin identifies and gives some examples of a "traditional episode" used to build stories in oral narration, although she derives this notion from Parry's description of epithets in oral narrative poetry. Finally, a study by Hans-Winfried Jüngling (1981) examines the role of formulas (repeated phrases) in Judges 19 as marks of oral prose. He concludes that the text was a written composition based on folk models.

A much more restricted view of oral tradition in biblical prose comes from John Van Seters and is summed up in comments found in his two books: *Abraham in Tradition and History* (1975) and *In Search of History* (1983). Van Seters is unable to accept the notion of scholars like Gunkel and Noth that there was a long period of oral tradition in which significant collection and formation of tradition took place. He is even less enthusiastic about Albright's idea of an oral epic poem behind the prose sources. Gunn's approach is not acceptable either, as can be seen from Van Seters' 1976 article and Gunn's response (1976). Like Wellhausen, Van Seters stresses authors and documents, arguing that we must think primarily of scribal traditions in a literate society (1975, pp. 158-159, 164). As far as he is concerned, much of the writing took place rather late in the history of Israel and was the activity of distinct authors working in a scribal tradition.

To support this contention Van Seters appeals to Herodotus as an analogy (1983). A clear parallel is proposed between Herodotus and the Deuteronomist, the presumed historian of Joshua to 2 Kings. The same would be true, he suggests, of the Yahwist (J) in the Pentateuch. Like Herodotus, such historians would have both oral and written sources at their disposal. Oral tradition is envisaged as a major source not only for material but also for genres. That is to say, the historian might well have employed imitations of oral forms to invent stories for his own purposes. A historian in "a literate society as small and closely knit as the Jerusalem religious community" (1983, p. 48) would have the writing of previous historians available to him. Consequently, while variants may be due to oral tradition, it is more likely that they can be explained as instances of literary dependence on other texts. In his book on Abraham, Van Seters was prepared to identify a few oral sources using certain criteria which he had established. Such stories must have "a clear narrative structure, movement, and unity and have features that correspond to Olrik's epic laws" (1975, p. 243). Questions about the usefulness of Olrik's laws as criteria for distinguishing oral texts from written have been raised by myself (1972, pp. 28-30) and by Kirkpatrick (1984, pp. 85-88).

A recent Oxford thesis, "Folklore Studies and the Old Testament" (1984) by Patricia G. Kirkpatrick, examines some basic issues of oral tradition raised by scholars in connection with the patriarchal traditions and then investigates the Jacob stories in the light of this discussion. While Kirkpatrick agrees that oral and written literature are different, she concludes that no sure test exists which can distinguish between oral and written in the stories of the Patriarchs. Lord's work is discussed, but it is held (following Finnegan, 1977) that repetition cannot be used to distinguish oral from written texts (pp. 83-84). Nor can appeal to the presence of originally oral genres like legend help, since potential oral contexts cannot be deduced on the basis of genre (p. 162). It is further concluded from studies on oral history that oral tradition does not preserve accurate descriptions of events for long periods of time. The work of a number of biblical scholars like Gunkel, Noth, Engnell, and Van Seters is discussed, although the contribution of Gunn is not. When the Jacob tradition is analyzed in the light of this discussion, Kirkpatrick argues that there is no reason to posit oral units behind it. The absence of clear evidence for oral background leads her to conclude that the original Jacob story may well have begun as a continuous written narrative sometime during the reigns of David and Solomon, with some elements being added after the fall of the Northern Kingdom (722/721 B.C.E.).

3. Other Issues

Two scholars treating oral tradition in biblical texts have emphasized an anthropological point of view. In an article (1975) and a subsequent book, *Genealogy and History in the Biblical World* (1977), Robert R. Wilson makes a contribution to the problem of the historiographic value of biblical genealogies. Wilson is sensitive to the difficulty of applying modern studies from one discipline to ancient texts in another, and so he suggests four guidelines for biblical scholars to follow when using anthropological data (p. 16). First, comparative material must be systematically collected by trained observers. Second, the anthropological material must be seen in its own context. Third, a wide range of societies must be considered to avoid the pitfall of atypical material. Fourth, one should concentrate on the data and seek to avoid the interpretive schema placed on the data.

On the basis of an extensive examination of the relevant anthropological literature on genealogies, Wilson establishes the formal characteristics of oral genealogies in terms of segmentation, depth, fluidity, and internal structure. He concludes that genealogies are used not so much for historical purposes but rather for domestic, politico-jural, and religious goals. Oral and written genealogies are similar, except that written ones tend to become frozen while oral ones remain open to continual change. Since biblical genealogies appear to reflect the same characteristics and functions seen in the anthropological studies, historians must use them with care (pp. 199-202).

Burke O. Long also develops an anthropological slant in two articles from the year 1976. The first article (1976b) is a survey of recent field studies, especially those available since my survey of 1963. These come largely from Africa and are mostly by anthropologists. Long stresses the social and cultural dimensions of oral tradition and is primarily interested in the social context and the dynamics of performer-audience-occasion. Nevertheless, he does touch on some of the issues involved in applying information on oral performance to texts in the Hebrew Bible: the presence of doublets and variants as common features of oral tradition, a critique of analysis of the Ugaritic texts by Cross, and the appearance of formulas in texts (contending that their presence as such proves nothing). In his other article (1976a) Long focuses on the concept of *Sitz im Leben*, or setting in life, a basic element in Form Criticism from Gunkel onward. Long argues that information from some field studies indicates that the connection between genre and setting is not nearly so close as had been suggested by Gunkel.

Two further studies relating to prose may also be noted. An article by Everett Fox (1978) attempts to deal with the oral nature of the Samson story. First, he provides an English translation which seeks to reflect this oral nature and then, pointing to various kinds of repetitions in the text, he attempts to indicate their significance for interpretation. In this he harks back to Martin Buber's notion that the bible arose from recitation. The other article by Yair Zakovitch (1981) offers a number of suggestions as to the changes both in content and form which took place when oral traditions became written text.

With regard to oral tradition and historicity, three brief studies can be mentioned. There is my own article on the subject (1972), a chapter in a book by Beat Zuber (1976, pp. 73-98), and a section of Kirkpatrick's dissertation (1983, pp. 163-190). All three studies urge varying degrees of caution about the usefulness of oral tradition for historical reconstruction.

III. The New Testament

While less has been written about oral tradition in the field of New Testament studies, the course followed has been somewhat parallel to what happened in the Old Testament field, at least up until the most recent contributions. There is no complete survey of the New Testament discussions, although an article by Leander E. Keck gives a brief review of research in the sixties and seventies (1978, pp. 106-113).

One of the leading figures in New Testament studies in the twentieth century was Rudolph Bultmann (1884-1976). He had studied with Gunkel and was a leader in the application of Form Criticism to the New Testament. Nevertheless, Bultmann's comments on oral tradition are limited. An analysis of his position may be found in Kelber's works (1979, pp. 8-20 and 1983, p. 208). Broadly speaking, Bultmann assumes a mixture of oral and written in the gospels. However, in his *History of the Synoptic Tradition* (1963, third German edition 1958), he makes the claim that one cannot distinguish in the end between oral and written traditions since the written material displays no specifically literary character (p. 6). As a consequence, whether the gospels were oral or written is not an issue. Thus Bultmann speaks in general terms of tradition and even mentions some laws of tradition, which may go back to Gunkel and Olrik. He argues that the person who produced the Gospel of Mark was the first to connect existent tradition complexes into a continuous story, and in this he functioned largely as a redactor.

The first major study of oral and written transmission in the New Testament period came in 1961 from a Scandinavian New Testament scholar, Birger Gerhardsson, and it owes something to the significance attached to memorization and oral tradition by Nyberg and Engnell in Old Testament studies. This book, *Memory and Manuscript* (1961), sought to establish from a technical point of view how the early gospel tradition was passed on. He argues that the preservation and transmission of the gospels followed the practices employed for sacred materials in Judaism of the New Testament period, although these methods are projected back from and reconstructed on the basis of Jewish writings from later periods. His analysis is long and impressive but has received sharp critique, some of which is summarized briefly in Kelber (1983, pp. 8-14). According to Gerhardsson, Jewish transmission had two features: text and interpretation; this involves an interplay between a fixed tradition which is memorized and a more flexible commentary which is less fixed. In the last few pages of the book, Gerhardsson indicates how he would apply his proposals to the gospels. Jesus taught, he claims, using the same scheme of text and interpretation. He had his disciples memorize teachings, but he also gave interpretation in a more flexible form. Differences between the gospels can be explained by assuming different redactional procedures on the part of the evangelists who worked from a Jesus tradition which was partly memorized and partly written down (pp. 334-335).

A few years later Thorlief Boman published *Die Jesus-Überlieferung im Lichte der neueren Volkskunde* (1967). The first two chapters of this book attempt to apply the results of folklore studies to the Jesus tradition. Drawing on a small selection of folklorists from the preceding half-century or so, Boman discusses a number of issues, among them topics like the narrator, the sociological setting, and the difference between *Märchen* and *Sagen*, including their historical reliability. When he examines the gospels on the basis of this discussion, he favors, in general agreement with Gerhardsson, a period of relatively stable oral transmission of fairly large blocks of material by a series of gifted narrators extending back to Jesus.

Four other articles touch on oral tradition in various ways. A 1961 study by C.H. Lohr showed some slight awareness of new directions initiated by Parry and Lord; these are also noted in Klemm (1972). Elements of a different strategy were proposed by Ernest L. Abel (1971) and John G. Gager (1974), who have appealed to studies on the transmission of rumor as potential sources of information about what may have happened to the traditions lying behind the gospels.

At the beginning of the seventies a book by Erhardt Güttgemanns, *Candid Questions Concerning Gospel Form Criticism* (1979, from the second German edition 1971), engaged form criticism in an extensive critique. At the same time, considerable space was devoted to various aspects of the question of oral tradition and New Testament studies, and this examination included the roots of Form Criticism in Herder and Gunkel. On the basis of a brief treatment of the work of Lord, Güttgemanns concluded that one should anticipate a sharp cleavage between oral and written tradition. Thus he calls into question the notion that there was an unbroken continuity from early traditions to final gospel (pp. 204-211). The views of Gerhardsson and Boman are explicitly rejected.

In 1977 a colloquy on the relationships among the gospels was held at Trinity University in San Antonio, Texas. The papers were edited by William O. Walker and published in the following year. One of the four seminars in the colloquy bore the title "Oral Traditional Literature and the Gospels" and featured an invited paper by Albert B. Lord with a response by Charles H. Talbert. As Leander Keck noted in his paper summing up the seminar, Lord and Talbert delineate two clear and mutually exclusive alternatives.

In his contribution to the discussion, Lord considers two kinds of evidence. First, he examines the presence of an oral traditional mythic pattern based on the life of the hero which he calls the "life story" pattern. In the case of the gospels this covers birth, precocious childhood, investiture, death of a substitute, and death and resurrection. The way the pattern appears in each of the gospels suggests to Lord that they are independent traditions. Second, he investigates sequences of episodes and how they vary among the gospels as well as the nature of verbal correspondence. The picture of stability and flexibility which he discovers is compatible with what he would expect in oral traditional versions of the text. On the basis of such a brief study and conscious of his restricted familiarity with New Testament studies, Lord does not wish to offer firm conclusions. However, he notes four ways in which the gospels appear to show oral characteristics which would relate them very closely to oral traditional literature: (1) texts vary in such a way as to rule out copying, (2) sequences of episodes betray chiastic ordering, (3) there is a tendency toward elaboration, and (4) duplications are like oral multiforms.

In his response, Charles Talbert seeks to turn each of these points around so that it supports the notion of a literary text. Supplying examples from authors around the New Testament period, he claims that (1) authors varied the sources they copied, (2) agreement of some episodes is so close that a literary explanation is necessary, (3) authors expanded their sources, and finally (4) authors would often draw on more than one source. Thus, while the oral traditional model might well be relevant to pre-gospel materials, it is not in his opinion appropriate for the present gospels, which do not fit the pattern of oral traditional literature and which emerged in a Mediterannean culture in which books were common for a large reading public.

Finally, there is the approach of Werner H. Kelber. His article on oral tradition in Mark appeared in 1979, and there was a response from T. Wheeden in the same year. This exchange was followed by Kelber's book, *The Oral and the Written Gospel* (1983), which also concentrates on the Gospel of Mark but extends the discussion into the other synoptic gospels and the writings of Paul. Kelber is concerned with both the oral and the written, described broadly as the world of orality and textuality, as well as interaction between the two (p. xv). He seeks thereby to broaden the scope of biblical hermeneutics.

For Kelber oral and written are significantly distinct and there is no smooth transition from one to the other. He explains that he wants to move beyond the work of Bultmann and Gerhardsson to a reconsideration of a synoptic model along the lines of Güttgemanns using the categories proposed by scholars like Parry, Lord, Havelock, Ong, Peabody, Finnegan, and Goody. In addition, he wants to go further than "a formal analysis of speech patterns," since "literary purism" cannot "penetrate to the soul of oral life" (p. 45). From oral forms one should learn the way in which "information is organized and conceptualization transacted" (p. 45). In other words, while he accepts the results of particular models of oral tradition in specific cultural settings and is prepared to use them, he gives a prominent place to a more general, universal model of oral culture of the type suggested especially in the work of Havelock and Ong.

In Mark, the feature of storytelling is chosen as an appropriate element through which to study pre-Markan oral tradition. While Kelber explores things like story types, language, and the arrangement of episodes, he also introduces as tools of analysis a number of general principles for defining orality. It is assumed, for example, that an oral culture grasps life in its opposites (p. 55), values confrontation over harmony (p. 71), and is homeostatic and self-regulated (p. 92). It is argued that the present Gospel could not have emerged from oral composition and so must be a literary work. Thus a tension exists in Mark between the oral and the written, orality and textuality, and this tension can be seen in the way Mark seeks to "disown the voices of his oral precursors" (p. 104) and to transform the oral traditions into a new kind of unity (p. 130). Kelber follows this tension in the writings of Paul and concludes as a result of his whole study that the written gospel is a counterform to oral hermeneutics (p. 185).

IV. Final Comments

After many decades of discussion, much remains unresolved. Almost all agree that the Bible probably has oral antecedents, but there is little agreement on the extent to which oral composition and transmission have actually left their mark on the text or the degree to which one might be able to establish this lineage. The difficulties may be summed up under the headings mentioned at the beginning: the use of the biblical text, the use of analogies, and the use of broader theories.

a. *The Biblical text.* As one might expect, most scholars have sought to base their discussions on evidence derived from the Bible. Clearly, any case must finally rest on the kind of support found in the biblical text. Unfortunately, the evidence which has been used to argue for the oral nature of the biblical text is ambiguous. This is in no small measure due to the rather limited amount of evidence produced so far, a limitation which in turn is inherent in the relatively small amount of prose and poetry in the Bible. Thus, close verbal repetition of phrases, pairs of words, or blocks of material suggestive of formulaic language do not lead to definitive conclusions.

Larger repeated patterns with little or no verbal correspondence may also be compatible with what one might expect in oral variants. Nevertheless, some of the same evidence has been used to support a notion of copying and imitation in a scribal or literary tradition. This was seen in the debates between Gunn and Van Seters for Old Testament and between Lord and Talbert for New Testament. What complicates matters further is the fact, inevitable though it may be, that evidence from the biblical text is always selected consciously or unconsciously in conjunction with some general description or theory about the nature of oral or written texts. As often happens, the more ambiguous the evidence, the more decisive the outside theory becomes.

It may well be time to review again the question of repeated language of various kinds in the light of recent discussions among students of oral literature. As far as Hebrew poetry is concerned, renewed discussion of parallelism and metrical structure has taken place over the past few years. Some issues are emerging also in the study of prose. Even if there are at the moment no substantial grounds for optimism with regard to a solution of the oral/written problem, there may be room for some clarification.

Another matter worth noting is that biblical scholars have taken up the issue of oral tradition with different interests in mind. An historical interest may be prominent. In order to reconstruct the political, social, or cultural history of the people of Ancient Israel, one must assess the nature of the sources—oral or written—and their reliability. Even a history of the literature requires that one be able to identify early sources from later ones. On the other hand, the focus may be more on the nature of text. In this case, one would seek to discover whether different modes of composition have a decisive influence on the shape of the text and what response may be required in defining critical approaches most appropriate to its interpretation.

b. *Analogies.* Discussions of oral tradition and biblical texts have frequently made use of descriptions of oral traditions in other cultural settings as analogies. The Scandinavians were the first to exploit this method to any great extent in their appeal to other ancient cultures. Some pointed to the role of oral tradition in cultures like Mesopotamia, India, or in early Arabic literature. As analogies these cultures had the advantage of being relatively close in time and space to Ancient Israel and of bearing some social, cultural, and political similarities to that people. Still the descriptions were challenged or the evidence was interpreted differently by others, all of which variety of opinion illustrates the problem of studying oral tradition in ancient societies. These situations can be no less difficult to interpret than that of the Bible.

As far as the use of field studies is concerned, the disadvantages lie not so much in the gap in time and geography, although this is a factor to consider, but in the unlikelihood of finding societies in the modern world with social, political, and cultural features closely similar to those of the biblical period. At the same time, field studies permit descriptions of what actually happens in oral situations in a wide range of different societies and cultures. On the basis of several specific descriptions of composition and transmission, one should be able with care to develop a thorough general model of what is possible and likely in oral tradition when seen as a whole.

There remains the problem of how one moves from these analogies to the biblical text. Wilson's concern about guidelines with regard to drawing on the results of descriptions of oral tradition by anthropologists, folklorists, and comparatists has some pertinence. It is necessary to seek the broadest spectrum of descriptions possible, and in so doing priority needs to be given to thorough studies by careful observers. Studies of other ancient literature like Homer or *Beowulf* are important but remain secondary to field studies in that the latter are applications of fieldwork. It is also important to take account of the different interpretative schemata being used by investigators.

When biblical scholars have discussed oral tradition, they have almost always made reference to written tradition also. It seems difficult to avoid dealing with the one without the other. While some progress has been made toward a more accurate perception of what oral tradition is, the concepts of "scribal," "written," and "literate" have been left more or less vague. Perhaps it is taken for granted that we know what these terms mean, since scholars go about their business by reading and writing. To be sure, Van Seters has proposed Herodotus as a model to explain how some sections of the biblical text may have been produced. In his response to Lord, Talbert has also offered a number of analogies to show how authors used written documents. It would be very useful to pursue this whole matter further to see what can be said about scribal practice in the biblical era, a period of some several hundred years. Some Old Testament scholars (Culley, Gunn, and Coote) have alluded to the difficult concept of a "transitional" text or period which presumably involves a mixture of oral and written styles or perceptions. New Testament scholars like Güttgemanns and Kelber argue for a sharp tension between the two.

c. *Broader theories.* Oral tradition may be discussed principally in terms of the nature of texts and the value of specific analogies. Yet even in Gunkel one catches a glimpse of a broader, more general view of oral culture distinct from a literary one. Nyberg also appeared to hold a similar general distinction when he claimed that we cannot read texts produced in oral tradition as we do modern literature. Kelber quite consciously and explicitly employs features of a general model of orality and textuality, here understood in terms of different media which handle information differently, an oral medium linking mouth to ear and a written one linking eye to text (p. xv).

The difficulty in adopting such a broad theory as a tool for text analysis lies in assessing the validity of the rather broad and general principles laid down to define orality and textuality. Old Testament scholarship has encountered similar models in the past, developed variously in terms of pre-logical or primitive mentality, corporate personality, mythopoeic thought, as well as Hebrew mentality. These models are usually based on a sharp contrast, such as pre-logical versus logical, worked out in terms of opposites. It is somewhat disconcerting to find features used in these theories now taken up and explained in terms of orality.

On the other hand, these general models have been produced because scholars have sensed distinctions and have struggled to articulate and explain them. Such general models have been challenging in the past and continue to be suggestive. Perhaps this is their primary value. They serve as probes, in McLuhan's sense, to stimulate thought and provoke reaction which may lead to new ways of looking at problems. Kelber is certainly aware of this when he treats orality and textuality as a hermeneutical problem related to how we perceive texts. It remains to be seen how matters proceed in this area, although discussion is under way. At the 1984 annual meetings of the Society of Biblical Literature, for example, one of the sections on the program was a consultation on "The Bible in Ancient and Modern Media."

REFERENCES

Abel, Ernest L. 1971. "The Psychology of Memory and Rumour Transmission and Their Bearing on Theories of Oral Transmission in Early Christianity." *Journal of Religion*, 51:270-281.

Albright, W.F. 1950. "Some Oriental Glosses on the Homeric Problem." *American Journal of Archaeology*, 54:162-176.

———. 1957. *From the Stone Age to Christianity*. 2nd ed. New York: Doubleday.

————. 1964. *History, Archaeology and Christian Humanism.* New York: McGraw-Hill.

————. 1966. *New Horizons in Biblical Research.* London: Oxford University Press.

————. 1969. *Yahweh and the Gods of Canaan.* New York: Doubleday.

Bee, Ronald E. 1973. "The Use of Statistical Methods in Old Testament Studies." *Vetus Testamentum*, 23:257-272.

Birkeland, H. 1938. *Zum Hebräischen Traditionswesen: Die Komposition der prophetischen Bücher des Alten Testaments.* Oslo: Jacob Dybwad.

Boman, Thorleif. 1967. *Die Jesus-Überlieferung im Lichte der neueren Volkskunde.* Göttingen: Vandenhoeck & Ruprecht.

Bultmann, Rudolph. 1963. *The History of the Synoptic Tradition.* Trans. by John Marsh. New York: Harper and Row. From the German 3rd ed.

Coote, Robert E. 1976a. "Tradition, Oral, OT." *The Interpreter's Dictionary of the Bible, Supplementary Volume.* Ed. by Keith Crim. Nashville: Abingdon Press, pp. 914-16.

————. 1976b. "The Application of the Oral Theory to Biblical Hebrew Literature." *Semeia*, 5:51-64.

Cross, Frank Moore. 1973. *Canaanite Myth and Hebrew Epic: Essays in the History of the Religion of Israel.* Cambridge, Mass.: Harvard University Press.

————. 1974. "Prose and Poetry in the Mythic and Epic Texts from Ugarit." *Harvard Theological Review*, 67:1-15.

Culley, Robert C. 1963. "An Approach to the Problem of Oral Tradition." *Vetus Testamentum*, 13:113-125.

————. 1967. *Oral Formulaic Language in the Biblical Psalms.* Near and Middle East Series, 4. Toronto: University of Toronto Press.

————. 1972. "Oral Tradition and Historicity." In *Studies on the Ancient Palestinian World.* Ed. by J.W. Wevers and D.B. Redford. Toronto: University of Toronto Press, pp. 102-116.

————. 1976a. *Studies in the Structure of Hebrew Narrative.* Semeia Supplements, 3. Missoula: Scholars Press.

————. 1976b. "Oral Tradition and the OT: Some Recent Discussion." *Semeia*, 5:1-33.

————. 1984. "Exploring New Directions." In *The Hebrew Bible and Its Modern Interpreters.* Ed. by Gene M. Tucker and Douglas A. Knight. Chico: Scholars Press and Philadelphia: Fortress Press, pp. 160-200.

de Pury, Albert. 1975. *Promesse divine et légende culturelle dans le cycle de Jacob.* 2 vols. Paris: J. Gabalda.

Engnell, Ivan. 1949. *The Call of Isaiah.* Uppsala Universitets Årsskrift, 4. Uppsala: Lundequistska.

――――. 1969. *A Rigid Scrutiny: Critical Essays on the Old Testament.* Trans. by John T. Willis. Nashville: Vanderbilt University Press.

Finnegan, Ruth. 1977. *Oral Poetry: Its Nature, Significance, and Social Context.* Cambridge: Cambridge University Press.

Fox, Everett. 1978. "The Samson Cycle in an Oral Setting." *Alcheringa: Ethnopoetics,* 4:51-68.

Freedman, David Noel. 1962. "Pentateuch." *The Interpreter's Dictionary of the Bible.* Vol. 3. Ed. by George A. Buttrick. Nashville: Abingdon Press, pp. 711-727.

――――. 1977. "Pottery, Poetry and Prophecy: An Essay on Biblical Poetry." *Journal of Biblical Literature,* 96:5-26.

Gager, John G. 1974. "The Gospels and Jesus: Some Doubts about Method." *Journal of Religion,* 54:244-272.

Gerhardsson, Birger. 1961. *Memory and Manuscript.* Acta Seminarii Neotestamentici Upsaliensis, 22. Trans. by Eric J. Sharpe. Lund: C. W. K. Gleerup.

Gevirtz, Stanley. 1963. *Patterns in the Early Poetry of Israel.* Studies in Ancient Oriental Civilization, 32. Chicago: University of Chicago Press.

Gitay, Yehoshua. 1980. "Deutero-Isaiah: Oral or Written?" *Journal of Biblical Literature,* 99:185-197.

Gunkel, Hermann. 1910. *Genesis.* Göttinger Handkommentar zum Alten Testament I, 1. 3rd ed. Göttingen: Vandenhoeck & Ruprecht.

――――. 1963. *Die Israelitische Literatur.* Darmstadt: Wissenschaftliche Buchgesellschaft, rpt. from 1925.

――――. 1964. *The Legends of Genesis.* Trans. by W. H. Carruth. New York: Schocken.

Gunn, David M. 1974a. "Narrative Patterns and Oral Tradition in Judges and Samuel." *Vetus Testamentum,* 24:286-317.

――――. 1974b. The 'Battle Report': Oral or Scribal Convention?" *Journal of Biblical Literature,* 93:513-518.

――――. 1976a. "Traditional Composition in the 'Succession Narrative'." *Vetus Testamentum,* 26:214-229.

――――. 1976b. "On Oral Tradition: A Response to John Van Seters." *Semeia,* 5:155-161.

――――. 1978. *The Story of King David: Genre and Interpretation.* Journal for the Study of the Old Testament, Supplement Series, 6. Sheffield: JSOT Press.

Güttgemanns, Erhardt. 1979. *Candid Questions Concerning Gospel Form Criticism.* The Pittsburgh Theological Monograph Series, 26.

Trans. by William G. Doty. Pittsburgh: The Pickwick Press. Original German 1971.

Havelock, Eric A. 1963. *A Preface to Plato.* Cambridge, Mass.: Harvard University Press, rpt. 1982.

Irvin, Dorothy. 1978. *Mytharion: The Comparison of Tales from the Old Testament and the Ancient Near East.* Alter Orient und Altes Testament, 32. Kevalaer: Butzon & Berker.

Jason, Heda. 1979. "The Story of David and Goliath: A Folk Epic?" *Biblica,* 60:36-70.

Jüngling, Hans-Winfried. 1981. *Richter 19—Ein Plädoyer für das Königtum.* Analecta Biblica, 84. Rome: Biblical Institute Press.

Keck, Leander E. 1978. "Oral Traditional Literature and the Gospels: The Seminar." In *The Relationships Among the Gospels: An Interdisciplinary Dialogue.* Ed. by William O. Walker, Jr. San Antonio: Trinity University Press, pp. 103-122.

Kelber, Werner. 1979. "Mark and Oral Tradition." *Semeia,* 16:7-55.

"Markus und die mündliche Tradition." *Linguistica Biblica,* 45:5-58.

———. 1983. *The Oral and the Written Gospel.* Philadelphia: Fortress Press.

Kiparsky, Paul. 1976. "Oral Poetry: Some Linguistic and Typological Considerations." In *Oral Literature and the Formula.* Ed. by Benjamin A. Stolz and Richard S. Shannon. Ann Arbor: Center for the Coordination of Ancient and Modern Studies, pp. 73-106.

Kirkpatrick, Patricia G. 1984. "Folklore Studies and the Old Testament." Unpub. Ph.D. Dissertation, Oxford University.

Klatt, Werner. 1969. *Hermann Gunkel.* Göttingen: Vandenhoeck & Ruprecht.

Klemm, Hans G. 1972. "Heiliges Epos und evangelische Rhapsoden." *Zeitschrift für Theologie und Kirche,* 69:1-33.

Knight, Douglas A. 1973. *Rediscovering the Traditions of Israel.* Society of Biblical Literature Dissertation Series, 9. Missoula: Scholars Press.

———. 1982. "Wellhausen and the Interpretation of Israel's Literature." *Semeia,* 25:21-36.

Ljung, Inger. 1978. *Tradition and Interpretation: A Study of the Use and Application of Formulaic Language in the So-Called Ebed YHWH-psalms.* Coniectanea Biblica: Old Testament Series, 12. Lund: C. W. K. Gleerup.

Lohr, C.H. 1961. "Oral Techniques in the Gospel of Matthew." *Catholic Biblical Quarterly,* 23:403-435.

Long, Burke O. 1976a. "Recent Field Studies in Oral Literature and the Question of *Sitz im Leben.*" *Semeia,* 5:35-49.

———. 1976b. "Recent Field Studies in Oral Literature." *Vetus Testamentum*, 26:187-98.

Lord, Albert B., ed. 1954. *Serbocroatian Heroic Songs. Vol. 1: Novi Pazar: English Translations*. Collected by Milman Parry and ed. and trans. by A. B. Lord. Cambridge, Mass.: Harvard University Press.

———. 1960. *The Singer of Tales*. Harvard Studies in Comparative Literature, 24. Cambridge, Mass.: Harvard University Press; rpt. New York: Atheneum, 1968 et seq.

———. 1978. "The Gospels as Oral Traditional Literature." In *The Relationships Among the Gospels: An Interdisciplinary Dialogue*. Ed. by William O. Walker, Jr. San Antonio: Trinity University Press, pp. 33-91.

Mowinckel, Sigmund. 1946. *Prophecy and Tradition*. Oslo: J. Dybwad.

———. 1962. "Tradition, Oral." *The Interpreter's Dictionary of the Bible*. Vol. 4. Ed. by George A. Buttrick. Nashville: Abingdon Press, pp.683-685.

Nielsen, Eduard. 1954. *Oral Tradition: A Modern Problem in Old Testament Introduction*. Trans. by Asta Lange. Studies in Biblical Theology, 11. London: SCM Press.

Noth, Martin. 1972. *A History of Pentateuchal Traditions.*. Trans. by Bernhard W. Anderson. Englewood Cliffs, NJ: Prentice-Hall. Original German 1948.

Nyberg, H.S. 1935. *Studien zum Hoseabuche*. Uppsala: Lundequistska Bokhandeln.

———. 1972. "Die Schwedischen Beiträge zur alttestamentlichen Forschung in diesen Jahrhundert." *Vetus Testamentum Supplements*, 22:1-10.

O'Connor, M. 1980. *Hebrew Verse Structure*. Winona Lake: Eisenbrauns.

Olrik, Axel. 1909. "Epische Gesetze der Volksdichtung." *Zeitschrift für deutsches Altertum und deutsche Literatur*, 51:1-12.

Ong, Walter J. 1982. *Orality and Literacy*. London: Methuen.

Ploeg, J. van der. 1947. "Le rôle de la tradition orale dans la transmission du texte de l'Ancien Testament." *Revue Biblique*, 54:5-41.

Ringgren, Helmer. 1949. "Oral and Written Transmission in the O.T.: Some Observations." *Studia Theologica*, 3:34-59.

Rofé, Alexander. 1970. "The Classification of the Prophetical Stories." *Journal of Biblical Literature*, 89:427-440.

Stolz, Benjamin A. and Richard S. Shannon, eds. 1976. *Oral Literature and the Formula*. Ann Arbor: Center for the Coordination of Ancient and Modern Studies.

Talbert, Charles H. 1978. "Oral and Independent or Literary and Interdependent? A Response to Albert B. Lord." In *The Relationships Among the Gospels: An Interdisciplinary Dialogue*. Ed. by William O. Walker, Jr. San Antonio: Trinity University Press, pp. 93-102.

Urbrock, William J. 1972. "Formula and Theme in the Song-Cycle of Job." In *SBL 1972 Proceedings*. Vol. 2. Ed. by Lane C. McGaughy. Missoula: Scholars Press, pp. 459-487.

————. 1975. "Evidences of Oral-Formulaic Composition in the Poetry of Job." Unpub. Ph.D. Dissertation, Harvard University.

————. 1976. "Oral Antecedents to Job: A Survey of Formulas and Formulaic Systems." *Semeia*, 5:111-37.

Van Seters, John. 1975. *Abraham in Tradition and History*. New Haven: Yale University Press.

————. 1976. "Oral Patterns or Literary Conventions in Biblical Narrative." *Semeia*, 5:139-154.

————. 1983. *In Search of History*. New Haven: Yale University Press.

Warner, Sean M. 1979. "Primitive Saga Men." *Vetus Testamentum*, 29:325-335.

Watters, William R. 1976. *Formula Criticism and the Poetry of the Old Testament*. Beihefte zur Zeitschrift für die alttestamentliche Wissenschaft, 138. Berlin: Walter de Gruyter.

Wellhausen, Julius. 1883. *Prolegomena to the History of Ancient Israel*. New York: Meridian Books. German ed. 1883.

Whallon, William. 1963. "Formulaic Poetry in the Old Testament." *Comparative Literature*, 15:1-14.

————. 1969. *Formula, Character, and Context*. Publications of the Center for Hellenic Studies. Cambridge, Mass.: Harvard University Press.

Wheeden, Theodore J. 1979. "Metaphysical Implications of Kelber's Approach to Orality and Textuality." In *Society of Biblical Literature 1979 Seminar Papers*. Vol. 2. Ed. by Paul J. Achtemier. Missoula: Scholars Press, pp. 153-166.

Whitaker, Richard E. 1969. "A Formulaic Analysis of Ugaritic Poetry." Unpub. Ph.D. Dissertation, Harvard University.

Widengren, Geo. 1948. *Literary and Psychological Aspects of the Hebrew Prophets*. Uppsala Universitets Årsskrift, 10. Uppsala: Lundequist.

————. 1959. "Oral Tradition and Written Literature among the Hebrews in the Light of Arabic Evidence, with Special Regard to Prose Narratives." *Acta Orientalia*, 23:201-262.

Wilson, Robert R. 1975. "The Old Testament Genealogies in Recent Research." *Journal of Biblical Literature*, 94:169-189.

————. 1977. *Genealogy and History in the Biblical World.* Yale Near Eastern Researches, 7. New Haven: Yale University Press.

Wolf, Alois. 1980. "H. Gunkels Auffassung von der Verschriftlichung der Genesis im Licht mittelalterlicher Literarisierungsprobleme." *Ugarit-Forschungen,* 12:361-374.

Yoder, P. B. 1970. "Fixed Word Pairs and the Composition of Hebrew Poetry." Unpub. Ph.D. Dissertation, University of Pennsylvania.

————. 1971. "A-B Pairs and Oral Composition in Hebrew Poetry." *Vetus Testamentum,* 21:470-489.

Zakovitch, Yair. 1981. "From Oral to Written Tale in the Bible." *Jerusalem Studies in Jewish Folklore,* 1:9-43 (in Hebrew).

Zuber, Beat. 1976. *Vier Studien zu den Ursprüngen Israels.* Orbis Biblicus et Orientalis, 9. Freiburg: Universitätsverlag.

The Literary Character of Anglo-Saxon Formulaic Poetry*

Larry D. Benson

Some thirteen years after Magoun's seminal essay introducing oral-formulaic theory to Old English studies, Larry D. Benson, well known for such works as Art and Tradition in Sir Gawain and the Green Knight *(1965) and the recent new edition of* The Riverside Chaucer *(1987), reacted with the cleverly titled paper, "The Literary Character of Anglo-Saxon Formulaic Poetry." Benson's major concern was to break the necessary linkage made by Magoun between a high density of formulaic phraseology and oral provenance, and he proceeded by showing that four Old English verse texts likely to have been composed in writing—the metrical preface to Alfred's* Pastoral Care, *Riddle 35, the* Phoenix, *and the* Meters of Boethius—*have about the same formulaic density as* Beowulf *and the Cynewulf poems, which Magoun and others had claimed were orally composed. This argument was to prove important in the years to come, not only because it struck at the foundation of oral-formulaic theory but also because it provided a locus classicus for those who wished to dismiss oral tradition and return to a strictly literary study of Old English poetry.*

Reprinted from *Publications of the Modern Language Association,* 81 (1966), 334-341.

Perhaps the most fruitful and exciting development in Old English studies in recent years has followed from F. P. Magoun's discovery that the Parry-Lord theory of oral verse-making can be applied to Old English poetry.[1] This theory has caught the imagination of critics and has produced a "kind of revolution in scholarly opinion" not simply because it shows us that the style of this poetry is traditional—that has been known for many years—but because it offers a new and useful way of approaching the problems raised by this style, because it provides a new way of considering some of the relations between these poems, and because it casts light on an area that we thought was forever darkened, the pre-literary history of Germanic and Old English verse.[2]

So useful has the theory proved and so widely has it been accepted that it is not surprising to find it already hardening into a doctrine that threatens to narrow rather than broaden our approach to Old English poetry. It is this doctrine, this object of faith rather than the good works based upon it, that I wish to consider in this short paper, for despite the caution of Magoun in his original work and of the perceptive critics who followed him, there are many for whom the demonstration that the techniques of analyzing oral verse can be applied to Old English poetry is proof that this poetry was itself orally composed. It has consequently become fashionable to speak of "oral singers" rather than "Old English poets" and to warn the readers of Old English verse that they must reject their idea of a poet writing in his cell and regard the surviving poems as something closer to records of performances than to fixed literary texts. Assuming that Old English poems are oral compositions and also that the oral tradition has been fully defined, the unwary critic is apt to believe that his job is finished once he has fitted the poem to the doctrine and that he can reject whatever is left over, deciding, as one does, that transverse alliteration must be accidental because "it is out of harmony with both formulaic theory and practice," or holding, as does Magoun himself, that *Beowulf* must be a number of lays "soldered" together because "seldom, if ever, does an oral singer, composing extemporaneously without benefit of writing materials, compose a cyclic poem."[3]

Few of us would want to follow the theory this far. And yet we seem to have no choice. We know that there was a lettered as well as an oral tradition in Old English times, and we know too that the difficulties of collecting even modern oral poetry would argue for the fact that our surviving texts come from this lettered tradition.[4] Perhaps we even, as Professor Lord writes, "cannot tolerate the unwashed illiterate," but we "cannot disprove the evidence of his style."[5] That evidence does seem to be overwhelming, for the formulaic character of Old English poetry has been amply demonstrated, and the only explanation for this fact seems to be the oral theory, which holds that "oral poetry is composed entirely of formulas . . . while lettered poetry is never formulaic."[6] Thus, though we have Cynewulf's own word for the fact that he was literate and used written sources, and even though the visual punning of the runic signatures shows that he wrote for readers, the theory holds that "If the narrative parts of his poem prove on testing to be formulaic, one must assume that those parts at least were composed in the traditional way."[7]

One must, that is, if it is indeed true that the presence or absence of formulas is a test of oral composition, for the whole doctrine of the oral composition of Old English poetry rests on its use of formulas. But the fact is that poems which we can be sure were not orally composed use formulas as frequently and sometimes more frequently than supposedly oral compositions such as *Beowulf* or the poems of Cynewulf. Alfred's *Pastoral Care*, for example, contains a preface that was undoubtedly intended for readers and almost certainly composed in writing, since the poem itself is made to say, in the style of the Riddles, "Siðða n min on englisc Ælfred kyning [heht]/ awende worda gehwelc, and me his writerum/ sende suð and norð" (vv. 11-13a). Yet the poem contains about the same percentage of formulaic verses as the poems of Cynewulf.[8] Likewise, Riddle 35 of the Exeter Book is a very close translation of Aldhelm's *De Lorica*, with exactly two lines of English text for each line of the Latin; despite the closeness of the translation and the untraditional nature of its materials, at least half of its verses are demonstrably formulaic.[9] Robert Diamond's study of the Old English translation of the Psalms shows that it too is a close, word for word translation and yet is written in a style that is heavily formulaic.[10] Or, to take a more artful and even more heavily formulaic example, there is the lovely Old English *Phoenix*. It is almost unique in subject matter, and it employs the allegorical technique in a way that links it as closely to Latin learning as to Germanic song. Moreover, it is also a translation, a freer translation than the riddle mentioned above but nevertheless so close to its Latin source that it is almost impossible to assume that its poet worked in the traditional way of hearing a tale, meditating on it, and then simultaneously singing and composing his

own version.[11] Yet its style is as heavily formulaic as can be found in
any Old English poem:[12]

85   Ðone wudu weardaþ wundrum fæger
            fugel feþrum strong, se is fenix haten.
            þær se anhaga eard bihealdeþ,
            deormod drohtað; næfre him deaþ sceþeð
            on þam willwonge, þenden woruld stondeþ.
90   Se sceal þære sunnan sið behealdan
            ond ongean cuman godes condelle,
            glædum gimme, georne bewitigan,
            hwonne up cyme æþelast tungla

            ofer yðmere eastan lixan
95   fæder fyrngeweorc frætwum blican,
            torht tacen godes. Tungol beoþ ahyded,
            gewiten under waþeman westdælas on,
            bideglad on dægred, ond seo deorce niht
            won gewiteð; þonne waþum strong
100   fugel feþrum wlonc on firgenstream
            under lyft, ofer lagu locað georne,
            hwonne up cyme eastan glidan
            ofer sidne sæ swegles leoma.
            Swa se æþela fugel æt þam æspringe
105   wlitigfæst wunað wyllestreamas.

    Other passages drawn at random from the poem are as heavily
formulaic as the passage printed above, and so traditional is the poet's
style that he uses formulas even in the macaronic conclusion to his
poem, as in these final lines:

675   geseon sigora frean sine fine,
            ond him lof singan laude perenne,
            eadge mid englum. Alleluia.

When a poet can write in Latin and English simultaneously and yet use
formulas—and the author of the *Phoenix* is not the only one to do
so[13]—then I think we must accept the fact that literate poets could quite
easily write in a formulaic style, and when such a poet writes so
heavily a formulaic style as we find in the *Phoenix* I think we can reject
any lingering suspicion that the relative percentages of formulas might

be used to distinguish between oral and lettered productions. To prove that an Old English poem is formulaic is only to prove that it is an Old English poem, and to show that such a work has a high or low percentage of formulas reveals nothing about whether or not it is a literate composition, though it may tell us something about the skill with which a particular poet uses the tradition.

By "literate composition" I mean a work composed to the accompaniment of the pen rather than the harp, and I mean further a work composed with the leisure and forethought that literary composition allows. Here, in the manner of composition, is the central problem raised by the oral theory, and that in turn raises the even more pressing question of the kinds of criticism we are justified in bringing to this poetry, for the poet who composes extemporaneously, whose work satisfies Lord's criterion for oral poetry—"the composition *during* performance"[14]—cannot be held to the same aesthetic demands that we make of a poet who composes in the literary way on parchment in his cell, even though he, like most medieval poets, might compose in writing for later oral delivery.[15] The oral delivery of the work, the literacy of the poet, and even the use of writing do not affect the central issue, for, difficult theoretically as they may be, we must admit the possibility of "transitional texts."[16] But we must admit them not because of the assumption that poets composed in their heads before committing their words to writing; one assumes that before the invention of cheap scrap paper and New Criticism most poets composed in that way. We must admit them only if it is indeed true that a formulaic writer inevitably composed in the traditional way, with his lines and his poems shaped by the demands of oral composition despite the use of the pen, and with the singer himself still composing as he performs, though now singing for an audience of one. That is, we must admit them if it was impossible for Old English formulaic writers to compose in the literary way, selecting their expressions and shaping their poems with all the care that their own skill and the leisure of writing allowed and with goals greater than those imposed by the mechanics of their medium and by the pressures of simultaneous composition and performance.

I believe that translations such as the *Phoenix* allow us to infer that poets could and did write in this literary manner, but we need not remain content with mere inference, for we do have some texts that allow us to watch the very process of composition. From them we can

see that not only can literate poets write formulaic verse, they can write
it pen in hand in the same way any writer observes a literary tradition.[17]
The best and most extended example is provided by the *Meters of
Boethius*. They are rich in formulas, so rich that if their source were not
known they would easily fit the tests that have been used to establish
the supposedly oral composition of poems such as *Beowulf*.[18] But we
do know their source, which is not Boethius' own Latin but Alfred's
prose translation of the Boethian meters. As Sedgefield wrote of these
poems, "They reproduce in metrical dress the prose version, omitting
little and adding few thoughts of any importance, and they seem to have
been composed by rearranging the words of the prose . . . and inserting
poetical commonplaces or 'tags' to bring the lines into alliterating
form."[19]

From the passages printed below one can see that Sedgefield is
generally correct. That is why these poems have attracted so little
attention. But that is also why they are so valuable to Old English
studies at present; by comparing the prose translation with the verse,
we can watch an Anglo-Saxon poet at work. {The second passage below
is the complete prose translation of Bk. II, met. 3, of Boethius' *De
Consolatione Philosophiae*; the first passage is the metrical version of
that prose:}[20]

1   Ða se wisdom eft wordhord onleac
        sang soðcwidas, and þus selfa cwæð:
        Ðonne sio sunne sweotolost scineð,
        hadrost of hefone, hræðe bioð aðistrod
5   ealle ofir eorðan oðre steorran,
        forðæm hiora birhtu ne bið auht
        to gesettane wið þære sunnan leoht.
        Ðonne smolte blæwð suðan and westan
        wind under wolcnum. þonne weaxeð hraðe
10   feldes blostman, fægen þæt hi moten.
        Ac se stearca storm, þonne he strong cymð
        norðan and eastan, he genimeð hraðe
        þære rosan wlite, and eac þa ruman sæ
        norðerne yst nede gebædeð,

15 þæt hio strange geondstyred on staðu beateð.
   Eala, þæt on eorðan auht fæstlices
   weorces on worulde ne wunað æfre!

   Dja ongan se Wisdom
   singan 7 giddode þus:
   þon seo sunne on hadrū heofone
   beorhtost scineð, þon aþeostriað
   ealle steorran
   forþāþe heora beorhtnes ne beoð nan
   beorhtnes for hire.
   þon smylte blaweð suþanwestan
   wind, þon weaxað swiðe hraðe
   feldes blosman;
   ac þon se stearca wind cymð
   norþaneastan, þon toweorpð he swiðe hraþe
   þære rosan wlite; swa oft þone to smylton sæ
   þæs norðawindes yst
   onstyreð.
   Eala þæt nanwuht nis fæste stondendes
   weorces a wuniende on worulde.

We can see the poet transferring whole phrases from the prose to the
verse, keeping as much of the prose phrasing as his form allows and
even using the prose to establish the alliterating sound in almost every
line he writes. We can see, too, that even with so uninspired a poet as
this, it is not the formula that dominates the poet but he who
dominates his medium. When the prose supplies a phrase whose syntax
fits both his syntax and his meter, he accepts it as it stands, as in line
8—"ðonne smolte blæwð." Yet a phrase such as "beorhtost scineð,"
which has the syntactic structure of a formula even as it stands in the
prose, he feels free to alter, because, though its form is right, it does
not fit his purpose; he wants the line to alliterate on /s/, and he is
saving "on hadrū heofone" for use in the next line. Though such
changes alter the prose only slightly, we can also see where the bare
mention of "norðawindes yst" provides the poet with an opportunity to
depart slightly from the prose and add one of his favorite themes, the
storm at sea.[21]

The poet's use of such themes even within the limitations imposed by his source shows that he belongs to the main Old English tradition. This is also apparent in his use of kennings, for he often departs slightly from his text to add a traditional kenning, and apparently he is even capable of creating new ones, unrestrained by his literary techniques of composition.[22] Furthermore, he could compose narrative with all the traditional touches his source allowed, and he does this in his treatment of Alfred's historical preface, which he evidently knew was not part of Boethius' text and which he could therefore treat more freely. He thereby turns the unadorned prose narrative into what suggests a small epic, complete with litotes—"Næs þæt hærlic dæd" (l. 43)—with the customary summarizing half-lines—"Wæs gehwæðeres waa" (l. 25)—and even with the traditional introduction of *wyrd*:

> þeod waes gewunnen   (l. 28)
> wintra mænigo, oðþæt wyrd gescraf
> þæt þe Ðjeodrice þegnas and eorlas
> heran sceoldan.

The hero of this narrative is described in this manner:

> þæt wæs rihtwis rinc, næs mid Romwarum   (l. 49)
> sincgeofa sella siððan longe.
> He wæs for weorulde wis, weorðmynða georn,
> beorn boca gleaw; boitius
> se hæle hatte.

The discovery that this "hæle," this "giver of treasure," "eager for honor," is Boethius, the celebrated philosopher rather than a Germanic chieftain, brings us abruptly back from the mead-hall to the study.

But we should not have been in the mead-hall in the first place; only our assumptions about formulaic poetry lead us to believe that such a style is necessarily connected with oral composition, and those assumptions, drawn from other literatures and other times, do not fit the facts of the Old English period; in that age literate poets could and did write heavily formulaic verse and, as the *Meters of Boethius* shows, they could do so pen in hand, referring to Boethius as "sincgeofa sella" or "weorðmynða georn" not because the demands of the meter or the pressures of oral composition prevent the poet from pausing to select some more suitable phrase but because this phrase *is* suitable, is part of a poetic diction that is clearly oral in origin but that is now just as clearly a literary convention.[23]

The same is true of the other stylistic features that may have originally been devices of oral verse and that in other literatures are tests of oral composition—the use of end-stopped lines, the themes, and the poets' own conventional references to oral tradition. As Kemp Malone has shown, in Old English the presence or absence of enjambement is a matter of date rather than mode of composition; the riddle that I mentioned previously is in the sharply end-stopped style, though it seems clear that its author was literate, and there is no significant difference in this respect between poems such as *Beowulf* and *Christ and Satan* on the one hand and the *Phoenix* and the *Meters of Boethius* on the other.[24] So, too, with themes; we have seen how easily the author of the *Meters* slips into the "storm at sea," and the author of the *Phoenix* draws on what appears to have been a widespread theme for his description of Paradise.[25] As for the poets' references to the oral tradition, the *Phoenix* opens with the traditional assertion of hearsay— "Hæbbe ic gefrugnen . . . firum gefræge"—and the author of the *Meters* scatters the same conventional claim throughout his text.[26]

Consequently, the stylistic evidence by no means forces the unwashed illiterate upon us. That Old English oral singers used a heavily formulaic style is only an attractive theory—probably true but necessarily unproven; that lettered poets, such as the author of the Boethian *Meters*, did use such a style is a demonstrable fact. Therefore, we must use the greatest caution in assuming the oral composition of any surviving Old English poem. Some of the poems that survive may indeed be oral compositions, but we can never be sure which ones they are. When we know that a poet was literate, used written sources, and intended at least part of his poems for readers, as is the case with the signed poems of Cynewulf, we should assume written composition.[27] Likewise, we should assume literate production of those poems, such as *Beowulf*, with qualities contrary to what oral composition might lead us to expect, and I refer here not to its cyclic character but to the sophistication of its diction and structure. And in no case must we assume oral composition as an explanation for the style.

But this does not mean that we should reject the discoveries of Magoun or the many illuminating works based upon them, for this poetry is obviously formulaic even when lettered, and the study of its formulas and themes need not be based on an assumption of oral

composition. Because Old English poetry is formulaic, our study of it
must begin with the exciting and useful techniques developed by
students of oral verse, but because this poetry is also literature, our
study need not end there. Indeed, I believe that a recognition that Old
English poetry is both formulaic and lettered would lead to an even
more exciting and fruitful development in our discipline, for the most
significant contribution of the formulaic and thematic studies made thus
far has been the demonstration that the Old English poetic language
carried with it a richness of reference that allows us to approach these
poems with an aesthetic sympathy unknown to critics in the days of
Sedgefield.[28] Perhaps more such studies combined with a more
widespread recognition that the poems we study are indeed poems will
bring us closer than ever to an understanding of those distant poets,
each of whom deserved the praise that an unknown Old English writer
paid to Aldhelm, who was both the first English secular poet whom we
know by name and the first Englishman to write Latin verse:[29]

> Beorn boca gleaw, bonus auctor,
> Ealdhelm, æþele scop etiam fuit.

NOTES

*This paper was read to the English 1 Discussion Group (Old
English) at the MLA meeting in New York on 27 December 1964. I owe
thanks to the chairman of that group, Professor Rowland L. Collins of
Indiana University, to Professor Kemp Malone of The Johns Hopkins
University, and to Professor William Alfred of Harvard for encouragement
and suggestions. Though he does not agree with my argument, Professor
Robert P. Creed of the State University of New York, Stony Brook,
kindly offered suggestions that saved me from a number of blunders.

[1] F. P. Magoun, Jr., "The Oral-Formulaic Character of Anglo-Saxon
Narrative Poetry," *Speculum*, XXVIII (1953), 446-467; rpt. in Lewis E.
Nicholson, ed., *An Anthology of Beowulf Criticism* (Notre Dame, Ind.,
1963), pp. 189-221, from which the quotations in the text below are
taken. Since Magoun's article appeared, Albert B. Lord's *The Singer of
Tales* (Cambridge, Mass., 1960) has been published, so perhaps now, as
William Whallon suggested to me, we should speak simply of the "Lord
theory"; certainly I have depended heavily on Lord's work for a definition
of oral verse.

[2] Robert E. Diamond, *The Diction of the Anglo-Saxon Metrical Psalms* (The Hague, 1963), pp. 5-6, provides a convenient bibliographical study of formulaic and thematic studies.

[3] William Whallon, "The Diction of *Beowulf*," *Publications of the Modern Language Association*, LXXVI (1961), 317; F. P. Magoun, Jr., "*Beowulf* B: A Folk Poem on Beowulf's Death," in Arthur Brown and Peter Foote, eds., *Early English and Norse Studies Presented to Hugh Smith* (London, 1963), p. 128.

[4] By "lettered tradition" I mean a tradition consisting of poems written by scribes for an audience of readers, poems which thereby have a fixed text that is transmitted to an audience by reading (probably aloud). Leaving aside for the moment the problem of their composition, it is clear that all surviving Old English poems had this mode of existence once they were committed to writing. Such written poetry may have existed alongside oral verse, since Asser tells us that King Alfred delighted in hearing poems as a boy and when an adult set his children to studying Saxon books, "especially Saxon poems." Asser's authority may be doubted, but even if he be a "pseudo-Asser" writing in the late tenth century he provides testimony on attitudes toward Anglo-Saxon poetry at the time most of our surviving manuscripts were written. He tells us (*De Rebus Gesti Ælfredi*, ed. W. H. Stevenson, Oxford, 1904, c. xxiii) that young Alfred once earned a book of Old English poetry by memorizing it when he read it over to his teacher (in the previous paragraph Asser remarked that Alfred remained "illiteratus" throughout his youth, but evidently he meant that the boy was ignorant of Latin letters). The poems to which Alfred listened in his father's court may have been oral, and that experience may have helped to develop his memory, but this episode shows him operating on the same assumptions about poetry as would be held by a schoolboy of today: the poem has a single text, fixed and recorded in a book; one learns the text by reading it aloud to his teacher, and then one recites what he has learned—"quo lecto, matri retulit et recitavit." By "lettered tradition" I also mean poems composed in writing, the sort of poems that Alfred himself may have written if he was the author of the metrical preface to the *Pastoral Care*, discussed in the text below; as will appear later in my essay, I hold that most of our surviving poems were composed in writing. On the difficulty of recording oral texts, see Lord, *The Singer of Tales*, pp. 125-127.

[5] *The Singer of Tales*, p. 129.

[6] Magoun, "The Oral-Formulaic Character," p. 190. This position has gained currency because of the widespread assumption that there are only two kinds of composition, the traditional, oral way on the one hand, and the modern way with its emphasis on "originality" on the other. But a poet can be traditional even in diction and phrasing without being oral,

and some literary periods prefer tradition to "originality." The Anglo-Saxon period seems to have been such an age. This is apparent not only in the English verse but in the Latin poetry of the time. Aldhelm, for example, begins his *Carmen de Virginitate* with "Omnipotens genitor mundum dicione gubernans,/ Lucida stelligeri qui condis culmina caeli" (*Aldhelmi Opera*, ed. Rudolphus Ehwald, *Monumenta Germaniae Historica, Auctorum Antiquissimorum Tomus XV*, Berlin, Editio Nova, 1961, p. 352). As Ehwald's notes show, the first line has parallels in the poems of Virgil, Sedulius Aethilwulf, Angilbertus, and Alcuin, as well as in Aldhelm's other works, and the second line has parallels in the works of Sedulius Scottus, of Æthilwald, and in later parts of the *de Virginitate* itself.

⁷Magoun, "The Oral-Formulaic Character," p. 212. Kenneth Sisam, *Studies in the History of Old English Literature* (Oxford, 1962), p. 25, suggests how listeners could have understood Cynewulf's "signatures."

⁸Robert Diamond, "The Diction of the Signed Poems of Cynewulf," *Philological Quarterly*, XXXVIII (1959), 234, finds that Cynewulf's work is 62.7 percent formulaic. Of the 32 half-lines in the *Metrical Preface*, at least nineteen (about 59 percent) are demonstrably formulaic. . . . The text itself is the *Anglo-Saxon Poetic Records*, ed. G. P. Krapp and E. V. K. Dobbie (New York, 1931-1942), VI, p. 110. [The lengthy citations have been deleted to save space—Ed.]

⁹The text is to be found in the *ASPR*, III, 198. [The lengthy citations have been deleted—Ed.]

¹⁰Diamond found that the Psalms are about 50 percent formulaic; *The Diction of the Anglo-Saxon Metrical Psalms*, p. 6.

¹¹Lord, *The Singer of Tales*, pp. 13-29, describes the process of oral composition and discusses, pp. 129-130, the lettered text and the oral singer. For an example of how Old English singers might have handled translation, see F. P. Magoun, Jr., "Bede's Story of Cædmon: The Case History of an Anglo-Saxon Oral Singer," *Speculum*, XXX (1955), 49-63.

¹²The Latin from which the following passage is translated is printed in A. S. Cook's edition: *The Old English Elene, Phoenix, and Physiologus* (New Haven, 1919). The passage was chosen at random and my analysis of other samples shows that it is typical of the poem. [The lengthy citations have been deleted—Ed.]

¹³Other examples are the *Summons to Prayer* (*ASPR*, VI, p. 69) and *Aldhelm* (*ASPR*, vi, p. 97), quoted at the end of this essay. In *Aldhelm* a few Greek words are also used.

¹⁴*The Singer of Tales*, p. 129. This is the sense in which oral verse is "extemporaneous." R. P. Creed, "On the Possibility of Criticizing Old English Poetry," *Texas Studies in Lang. and Lit.*, III (1961), 97-106, notes some of the implications of this sort of composition; he observes

that "the hypothesis of oral art must involve the hypothesizing of a special kind of audience. This audience must respond, and *respond immediately* to what it hears. . . . The singer can expand his story in the warmth of a delighted audience and contract it when the audience grows cold" (p. 100). The immediate reaction of the audience and the function of that reaction in shaping the narrative is what sets oral verse apart from other medieval poetry, most of which was written for oral delivery in a style that was partially shaped by this method of publication. See Ruth Crosby, "Oral Delivery in the Middle Ages," *Speculum* XI (1936), 88-110, and "Chaucer and the Custom of Oral Delivery," *Speculum*, XIII (1938), 413-432, and B. H. Bronson, "Chaucer's Art in Relation to His Audience," in *Five Studies in Literature*, Univ. of Calif. Publ. in English, VIII, No. 1 (1940).

[15]This is not to say that the standards a critic might apply to an orally composed text are necessarily lower than those he brings to a written work, but it is to say that the standards are different in such matters as structure, for example. As Creed says of oral verse ("On the Possibility of Criticizing Old English Poetry," p. 98), "We should *not* look for *certain* excellences in such a poem," where the apparently singular phrase or the use of a certain theme may be due to the tradition rather than the poet. This is true of any highly traditional work, whether a Latin poem of Aldhelm's, a Middle English romance, or an Old English narrative, but for oral verse it is more nearly a rule than for written verse, in which, after cautiously observing such warnings, we should discover whatever excellences are there. Especially should we do so in Old English poetry, whose excellences are still but imperfectly known.

[16]Lord, *The Singer of Tales*, p. 129, rejects the tendency of medievalists "to seek a solution to the problems raised by the discovery of oral characteristics in some of the poems in their fields by recourse to the term 'transitional.'" R. D. Stevick, "The Oral-Formulaic Analyses of Old English Verse," *Speculum*, XXXVII (1962), 382-389, discusses the difficulties raised by the "transitional" hypothesis.

[17]Claes Schaar, "On a New Theory of Old English Poetic Diction," *Neophilologus*, LX (1956), 301-305, has argued for this position. A small but neat example to support it is offered by Riddle 35 in the Exeter Book. It evidently shared an exemplar with the Leiden Riddle, since the two versions are practically identical up to the last two lines, which translate Aldhelm's final verse: "Spicula non vereor longis exempta pharetris." The Leiden Riddle has the translation: "ni anoegun ic me aerigfaerae egsan brogum,/ðeh ði n[. . .]n siae niudlicae ob cocrum" (*ASPR*, VI, p. 109). These lines were either missing or corrupt in the Exeter scribe's copy, and so he added two formulaic lines to provide a conclusion (see n. 9 above). The scribe who translated the Old Saxon

Genesis also wrote formulas, even though he tried to be very faithful to his source. The first line in the surviving Old Saxon fragment is "'Uuela that thu nu, Eua, habas,' quað Aðam, 'ubilo gimarkot'"; the English scribe changes this to the more formulaic, "Hwæt, þu Eue, hæfst yfele gemearcod" (Gen. 791; for the Old Saxon fragment see *ASPR*, I, p. 171).

[18]Magoun's sample passages show that *Beowulf* is around 75 percent formulaic and *Christ and Satan* about 65 percent ("The Oral-Formulaic Character," in Nicholson, pp. 216-221); Diamond (see n. 8 above) finds that Cynewulf's work is about 63 percent formulaic. If the search for evidence is restricted only to the works of Cynewulf, his poems are about 43 percent formulaic ("The Diction of the Signed Poems of Cynewulf," p. 234); Creed found that within *Beowulf* about 4200 of the 6364 verses— about 66 percent—are formulaic ("On the Possibility of Criticizing Old English Poetry," p. 97). Depending only on the *Meters* themselves for evidence, the passage below is around 60 percent formulaic, and an analysis of a number of other passages yields about the same percentage. A full analysis of the 3500 verses (1750 lines) of the *Meters* shows that they contain about 250 whole-verse formulas used around 700 times; one such formula, "ealla gesceafta," is used at least twenty-two times. Diamond (p. 234) found that this sort of "whole-verse" formula accounts for 19.9 percent of Cynewulf's verses, 1037 out of 5194 (2598 lines). Creed (p. 97) reports, "I have counted and classified over 400 *different* whole-verse formulas in *Beowulf* repeated at least once—some as many as twelve times and therefore constituting over 1200 of the 6364 verses of the poem." In the passage from *Phoenix* analyzed above, the 42 half-lines contain nine whole-verse formulas repeated elsewhere in the poem, again around one in five. It is curious that the proportion should remain roughly the same despite the size of the sample.

[19]W. J. Sedgefield, *King Alfred's Old English Version of Boethius'* De Consolatione Philosophiae (Oxford, 1899), p. xxxviii.

[20]The prose is from Sedgefield's edition, p. 21. [The lengthy citations have been deleted—Ed.]

[21]I am using "theme" in the way it has been used in Old English studies, as in Magoun's "The Theme of the Beasts of Battle in Anglo-Saxon Poetry," *Neuphilologische Mitteilungen*, LVI (1955), 85-90, in which a "theme" seems to be a conventional situation combining formulaic elements in a number of ways. For examples of the storm see *MBo* 3.3-8a, 5.4-11, 12.11-17, and see *Rdl* 2.5-10a, 3.17-21a, *Gen* 1324b-26. The ingredients are wind, sea, cliff or shore, and sometimes darkness and noise, and it appears to be related to the theme of "cold weather" discussed by Robert E. Diamond, "Theme as Ornament in Anglo-Saxon Poetry," *Publications of the Modern Language Association*, LXXVI (1961), 468.

[22]"Runcofa," 22.59 is apparently unique to the *Meters*; 20.171-175 is a most effective use of metaphor, with the sun as "se scire scell."

[23]The situation was apparently rather similar to that which obtained in Middle English times; the poems of the Alliterative Revival were also indebted to an oral tradition, as shown by Ronald A. Waldron, "Oral-Formulaic Technique and Middle English Alliterative Poetry," *Speculum*, XXXII (1957), 792-804, but these poems were clearly literate productions.

[24]For the "end-stopped" versus the "run-on" styles see Kemp Malone's discussion in *A Literary History of England*, ed. A. C. Baugh (New York, 1948), pp. 26-28. Though editors' punctuations are surely no absolute test, the punctuation of the *Anglo-Saxon Poetic Records* is useful at least for comparing the relative degrees of enjambement in different poems, since presumably the editors' practice was uniform from one poem to another. Here are the numbers of full stops (periods, colons, semicolons) at the ends of the first half-lines and at the ends of the second half-lines in the first 100 typographical lines in each of the following poems: *Beowulf* 17 and 20; *Christ and Satan* 20 and 23; *Meters of Boethius* 28 and 19; *Phoenix* 15 and 16; *Elene* 31 and 12. Counting every mark of punctuation, the figures are: *Beowulf* 47 and 64; *Christ and Satan* 47 and 67; *Meters of Boethius* 56 and 46; *Phoenix* 61 and 61; *Elene* 65 and 59.

[25]Probably such a theme accounts for the resemblances between *Phx* 393-423 and *Glc* 819-70, 980-96, *Chr* 1379-1413, *XSt* 408-19, 471-78, *Jln* 494-505. The similarities led Cook (see his note to *Phx* 393 in his *The Old English Elene, Phoenix, and Physiologus*, New Haven, 1909) to accept the theory of C. Abbetmeyer, *Old English Poetical Motives Derived from the Doctrine of Sin* (Baltimore, 1903), p. 28, that these passages have a common source.

[26]E.g., 20.82, 20.248; in *The Coronation of Edgar* (*ASPR*, VI, p. 21) the formula "mine gefræge" appears in l. 9, and in l. 14 a written source is claimed—"þæs ðe gewritu secgað."

[27]There is the possibility, as Alain Renoir has pointed out to me, that the runic signatures originated with some scribe rather than Cynewulf himself; it seems to me easier to regard them as Cynewulf's.

[28]See especially Stanley B. Greenfield, "The Formulaic Expression of the Theme of 'Exile' in Anglo-Saxon Poetry," *Speculum*, XXX (1955), 200-206, and Robert P. Creed, "On the Possibility of Criticizing Old English Poetry."

[29]If William of Malmesbury can be trusted, then it is possible that Aldhelm was an oral singer (*De gestis pontificum Anglorum*, ed. N. E. S. A. Hamilton, London, 1870), p. 336. If so, literacy and oral verse-making co-existed from very early times in England. It is equally

possible that Aldhelm wrote his poems, since, again on William's authority, they survived in manuscript until at least the time of Alfred, who regarded Aldhelm as the best poet of his age.

What Is Oral Literature Anyway? Comments in the Light of Some African and Other Comparative Material

Ruth H. Finnegan

Anthropologist Ruth Finnegan has been one of the most frequent and most influential critics of oral-formulaic theory. In her Oral Poetry: Its Nature, Significance, and Social Context *(1977), and in earlier works such as her magisterial* Oral Literature in Africa *(1970), she has insisted on broadening the model for oral tradition from what she sees as an overdependence on Serbo-Croatian oral epic to a worldwide arena, with special emphasis on the complexities of African traditions. In the present essay she concentrates on three interrelated and major points, all of which have crucial implications for oral-formulaic theory; she denies (1) that there is a single, definable phenomenon we can call "oral literature," (2) that a clear boundary can always and everywhere be drawn between oral and written forms of verbal art, and (3) that oral composition is a single, universal process. Thus the* formula *is for Finnegan too restrictive a concept to apply across the international spectrum of oral forms and genres, and this lack of an archetypal*

Reprinted from *Oral Literature and the Formula*, ed. by Benjamin A. Stolz and Richard S. Shannon (Ann Arbor: Center for Coordination of Ancient and Modern Studies, University of Michigan, 1976), pp. 127-166.

structure urges her all the more strongly to advocate a pluralistic view of and approach to oral traditions. Although Finnegan's work has been used narrowly to undermine the conclusions of oral-formulaic theorists and positivistically to restore texts of ambiguous provenance to the more comfortable confines of the literary canon, it has also contributed to a necessary complication of our ideas about traditions as inherently various as ancient Greek and modern African narratives—and to that extent has helped oral-formulaic studies move forward.

What I want to do in this paper is to offer some comments on the general subject of the conference ["Oral Literature and the Formula"] in the light of findings from empirical research on oral literature in Africa (and to a lesser extent elsewhere).

The great strength of the whole oral-formulaic theory of course comes largely from field research—the first-hand experience of Parry and Lord with Yugoslav oral poets. It was the comparative insights from this field experience that have given the theory such a solid base in empirical evidence as well as its theoretical illumination. But since its formulation, the main interest for many scholars in this area has understandably been its application to existing texts, supported by study of detailed stylistic points and formulaic systems leading to statistical conclusions. Such study can indubitably provide many insights into the stylistic properties of the text and *perhaps* point to some interesting speculations about the probable processes of composition. But I would suggest that it is now timely to look again at the findings of field research and that the comparative evidence should not be drawn only (or even mainly) from the situation in Yugoslavia at a certain period but should be extended more widely to include empirical data about recent studies of oral poetry elsewhere too.

Recent field research from elsewhere cannot of course replace detailed analysis of specific texts, nor can it prove or disprove the "oral-formulaic theory" as such. But it can perhaps throw further light on some of the basic concepts in the theory—including those often invoked in its application to other texts—and also suggest that some misleading conclusions may have been drawn by relying too heavily on the Yugoslav analogy.

In other words, this is *not* a scholarly paper about the detailed analysis of specific texts, statistical conclusions about formulae, or even—very much—about the exact definition of a "formula." Even if I was competent to deal with these aspects, this is not my brief; and in any case they are not central to the main points I want to make. I am not, either, going to invoke "modern linguistic theory" or "the new anthropology." All I am attempting is to make some points that have occurred to me in the light of empirical evidence accumulated in the course of some comparative study of oral poetry. This has led me to query certain somewhat misleading assumptions—as they appear to me—in some oral-formulaic studies, and to wonder whether certain preconceptions in the initial formulation of the theory have not got us onto the wrong tack.

It is clear that some aspects of the general approach in the Parry-Lord research have proved extremely illuminating for the interpretation of empirical research on recent oral literature in Africa, as in non-literate contexts elsewhere, and their explicit formulation marked a great step forward in the comparative study of oral literature. *The Singer of Tales*—to take just that book—is a classic and must deeply affect any student of oral literature who reads it. Though—as is appropriate with any classic—I will go on to query certain implicit assumptions in, and from, the book, I want first to comment on some of its strengths in the light of the African material: these are pertinent for a full understanding of the further queries that need to be raised.

From the standpoint of analysing African oral literature, the two really salient points about oral literature that are made in *The Singer of Tales* are, first its variability: the absence of *the* single correct version; and second, the unique nature of *each* performance by the composer/performer: the poem or story as delivered, as a unique creation, on that particular occasion. There is, further, the elucidation of how conventional themes are used and re-used in differing combinations and contexts by poets as a basis for their own original compositions: the blend of tradition and creativity.

None of these points were, admittedly, totally new discoveries. All had been stated in one form or another before, as those acquainted with, say, Russian studies or the great opus of the Chadwicks, *The Growth of Literature*, will know well. But their explicit formulation and detailed demonstration through rich empirical evidence to a wide circle of readers was something new. It was the more valuable because of the great influence in the field of oral literature of the romantic folklore school which stressed the significance, for non-literate and "folk" forms, of "age-old tradition," "transmission from far-back ages" and, in some cases, exact reproduction and memorisation over the generations.

This rejection of memorisation and emphasis, instead, on variability, unique performance and balance of creativity/tradition, is directly applicable to much African oral literature, prose as well as poetry. Only too many would-be experts on Africa had (apparently) leapt to the conclusion that stories and songs were memorised word-perfectly, and had made dogmatic pronouncements to this effect in their publications. (Behind such assertions lay not only the romantic folklore model, but also the concept of *the* text, on the model of a manuscript tradition.) Other commentators, however—perhaps often those with longer first-hand experience—had with equal certainty stressed the changeability of local oral forms. I think that anyone who has read *The Singer of Tales* and grasped the influence of earlier theories on the interpretation of the "facts" would have no hesitation in finding the latter group of observers the more convincing.

Take, for instance, this description of story-telling among the Thonga people published by H. A. Junod in 1913—long before Parry and Lord incidentally—from information gathered during his many years as missionary in the area.

> This antiquity is only relative: that is to say they are constantly transformed by the narrators and their transformations go much further than is generally supposed, further even that the Natives themselves are aware of. After having heard the same stories told by different story-tellers, I must confess that I never met with exactly the same version. First of all *words* differ. Each narrator has his own style, speaks freely and does not feel in any way bound by the expressions used by the person who taught him the tale. It would be a greater error to think that, writing a story at the dictation of a Native, we possess the recognized standard form of the tale. There is no standard at all! . . .
>
> The same can be said with regard to *the sequence of the episodes*: although these often form definite cycles, it is rare to hear two narrators follow exactly the same order. They arrange their material as they like, sometimes in a very awkward way. . . .

I go further: *New elements* are also introduced, owing to the tendency of Native story-tellers always to apply circumstances of their environment to the narration. This is one of the charms of Native tales. They are living, viz., they are not told as if they were past and remote events, in an abstract pattern, but considered as happening amongst the hearers themselves. . . . So all the new objects brought by civilisation are, without the slightest difficulty, made use of by the narrator. . . .

Lastly, my experience leads me to think that, in certain cases, the *contents of the stories* themselves are changed by oral transmission, this giving birth to numerous versions of a tale, often very different from each other and sometimes hardly recognisable. (Junod, 1913, II, pp. 198-200)

This description certainly rings true to anyone familiar with the Lord-Parry work—and, indeed with more recent first-hand field experience in many areas of Africa. I found much the same processes at work when I did field research on oral narratives among the Limba rice-farmers of northern Sierra Leone in the early 1960s. A brief comment on my findings may be relevant.

It was common for a Limba story-teller to assert that he was telling "exactly the same story" as one previously told by another narrator (or even by himself on another occasion). If I had left the matter there—and on the face of it there seemed no reason to disbelieve such a definite statement—I might have accepted and passed on this clear assertion on the grounds that the local people must surely know the facts of their own literary activities best. Probing further I discovered, of course, precisely the same thing as with the Yugoslav singers: despite the verbal description by narrators, their versions in practice *did* differ. The "same" basic episodes appeared in different stories with different protagonists (sometimes a human, sometimes an animal or supernatural being, for instance) and in varying combinations and orders. There was also a series of stock endings which were selected or not according to the wishes of the narrator and nature of the audience. Thus the "same" story might end in one telling with a moral, on another with a joke or dilemma, on another again with an aetiological explanation. A close comparison of the "same" story (in terms of plot) told by two different narrators showed extensive differences; these extended far beyond mere wording to affect the course of the action, detailed episodes, names of characters, general atmosphere, characterisation and conclusion. Even when the same narrator told the story, his versions differed in different performances. The same balance as that described by Parry and Lord between "tradition" (the stock in trade on which the Limba narrator could draw) and "originality" (the creative contribution of the individual narrator) can be detected in the corpus of Limba stories and the observed activities of story-tellers. It was, in fact, excellently summed up by one thoughtful Limba narrator when he explained that in telling he was "taught by the dead [the ancestors] and my own heart" (for further details see Finnegan, 1967).

This assessment of Limba story-telling obviously draws much from the insights of Lord and Parry (supplemented by the earlier work by Propp [trans., 1958] on "functions" in Russian fairy tales). One can see the same points so well stated in *The Singer of Tales* coming up again and again; variability, the uniqueness of separate performances, and the interplay of known themes. The theoretical backing given by the research of Lord and others has been of the greatest assistance to students of African oral narratives in helping them rid themselves of many earlier mistaken notions about exact memorisation and reproduction.

More has, overall, been published about African oral prose than poetry, so that I have drawn my initial examples from prose narratives. But similar points have been made about oral poetry too. Some of these instances will be treated further later, but here it is worth noting that there is plenty of evidence that songs and poems are often not memorised, *not* handed down by inert tradition, nor delivered in accordance with the concept of a "correct" version—all of which used to be the conventional wisdom in many circles about African poetry.

In a number of cases, too, there is clear evidence of the kind of simultaneous composition/ performance described by Lord for Yugoslav poets. One instance—the *nyatiti* "lyre" song of the Luo of East Africa—is described by Anyumba (1964). Here the composer/performer builds on common and known themes to create a new and unique composition of his own. The most common context for his performance is a funeral when he is expected to deliver laments. He appears on the occasion and sits there, singing at the top of his voice, sweating profusely and drinking plenty of beer: a good performance pays dividends for before him is the plate into which his admirers drop their pennies. There are set conventions within which he must compose. These are partly musical but also include stock themes and word-groups like "sealed in dust," "asleep on its arm," "sleep seated," and a series of praise names which can be introduced into the verse: the stock referents of these names are those of the maternal and paternal uncles of the deceased, his family, clan, country and loves. His song is elaborated further by the introduction of particular circumstances and incidents, popular ones being the adventures and conversations of the deceased which are conventionally used to epitomise the sorrow and shock of the bereaved. Building on these various conventions, the poet puts together his song, aided by a great deal of repetition. It is based in one sense on the traditional conventions and on his own ready-made repertoire, but he makes sure that it is suitable to the given occasion by adding in "an uncle here and a grandfather there, together with any knowledge he may have of the attributes of the deceased" (Anyumba, 1964, p. 189). The Luo poet thus produces a unique and appropriate lament on a specific occasion, one in which his powers of composition and performance are greatly admired: "The skill and beauty with which the musician is able to improvise at such moments is a measure of his musical and poetic stature" judged both by his skill on the instrument and by "his ability to weave a story or meditate on human experience" (Ibid., pp. 190, 188).

Even in the case of group singing—on the face of it the least likely place for anything but memorisation (see Chadwick, 1940, III, p. 868)—there can be adaptation and innovation in a way not unlike the Yugoslav model presented by Lord. This is because of the common pattern of leader/chorus singing found in African oral literature. The chorus either follows the soloist's lead in merely repeating his lines, or sings a known and repeated refrain—or a series of different combinations of these principles.

This process is described, for instance, by Hugh Tracey (1929). Writing of Shona lyrics in Southern Rhodesia, he explains how in many Shona songs—those sung while harvesting for instance—the chorus part remains the same but the soloist (*mushairi*) is allowed scope for originality of phrasing. He has stock ways of coping with this. If he is unable to compose the next verse quickly enough, he repeats the last one several times or yodels the tune to give himself time to think. If he is completely stuck he ends up by signing to a neighbour to replace him in the lead.

Oral epic poetry on the model of the Yugoslav, Turkic or Homeric poems is not—perhaps surprisingly—a typical African form. There are a few somewhat controversial cases (one of which I will return to later) but by and large most of the African forms that have claimed the title of epic are either closely related to written forms in the Arabic script (some of the Swahili *utenzi*, for instance, being apparently direct translations from Arabic originals) or in practice probably mainly in prose with merely a few verse insets, as with their famous Lianja "epic" from the Congo (for further comment see Finnegan, 1970, p. 108 ff). In the absence of a strong epic tradition, however, the great African form seems to be the panegyric. Praise poetry is a developed and specialist genre in most of the traditional states of Africa and one that is logically often regarded as the most highly valued and specialized of their poetic genres. In this poetry incidents in the hero's life are depicted, but in general the chronological element is relatively undeveloped, and the style is laudatory rather than narrative. It thus differs from epic poetry in its tone and intention, as well as in length: the number of lines in African panegyric poetry is generally to be reckoned in—at most—hundreds rather than the thousands of much epic poetry.

Despite the differences, however, this panegyric poetry is lengthy and specialized enough as a genre to provide an illuminating parallel to heroic poetry. In a number of cases, it is clear that certain aspects of Lord's general analysis would certainly apply.

This is brought out in a vivid account by M. G. Smith (1957, see also Scharfe and Aliyu, 1967) of the context and composition/performance of one type of praise-singing among the Hausa of Northern Nigeria. Smith describes the solo praise-singers who operate on a free-lance basis, roving round the various villages of the countryside. What happens is that the poet arrives in a village and, first of all, makes a point of finding out from the local praise poets who the wealthy and important individuals in the area are. Having obtained this vital information, he then takes up his stand in some public spot and calls out the name of the man he is intending to eulogise: his "praisee." He proceeds to his praise poem proper, building in the conventional themes of references to the praisee's ancestry, nobility, prosperity and influence, the numbers of his dependants and his political connections. He intersperses this with frequent demands for gifts from the praisee. If sufficient or nearly sufficient recompense is paid over, he then sings his thanks and announces the amount. But if an adequate gift is not forthcoming, his tone changes. The song continues using the same

themes, but this time all put in an unfavourable light: it recounts the
praisee's meanness, poor reputation, menial occupation, poor treatment
of his dependants, and disloyalty to his political allies. If there is still
nothing paid over, the innuendo gradually becomes sharper, the delivery
more staccato, until at last the final insult is reached: imputation of
servile ancestry. Since an experienced singer knows how to choose a
time when all the local people are likely to hear—in the evening or the
early morning when people are still at home from the farm, or on a
market day—the unhappy victim is usually only too thankful to
surrender and pay up.

In this case, it is clear that there are a number of ways in which
Smith's findings fit with those of Parry and Lord in Yugoslavia. There
is fluidity of the detailed wording, dependent on the circumstances and
personnel involved; the inevitable lack of any concept of the correct
version of a given praise song; and the combination and recombination
of conventional themes by the poet, manipulated in this case to his
material advantage. The older model of exact memorisation and a single
authentic text would clearly have been useless for the understanding of
this Hausa example.

The sort of points I have been illustrating here will be to many
people very obvious ones by now and might perhaps seem too general
to be worth lingering over. But there was a period not so long ago (and
it is not finally past everywhere) when, with a few magnificent
exceptions, this sort of appproach would not have seemed so obvious at
all. The earlier concentration tended to be either—on the one hand—on
the concept of inert tradition from the far-distant past or—on the
other—on the spontaneous improvisation to be expected from the
"primitive" as the unself-conscious "child of nature," unfettered (and
unhelped) by recognised artistic conventions. Both emphases were, in
their different ways, inheritances from the romantic movement and its
attitude to "folklore." Added to this was the stress by many earlier
functional anthropologists on stability, lack of change and the
institutions of "the tribe" and "the society" as a whole—with therefore
little interest in the processes of creativity, far less the personalities of
individual poets or the balance between originality and tradition.

There is much, then, in the interpretations of the oral-formulaic
school that turns out to be of great significance when applied in general
terms to oral literature in Africa. Others, of course, besides Parry and
Lord had made some of these points earlier—Junod for instance—but

their explicit and convincing exposition in *The Singer of Tales* was able to provide a very important stimulus and standard to which workers in the field could respond and appeal.

But—and this is the main point I have been working up to—this approach is perhaps *too* good. Because the *general* insights of *The Singer of Tales* are, as I have suggested briefly, so applicable and so useful in the study of oral literature in recent Africa, as well as elsewhere in the "Third World," it is tempting to swallow the theory whole and to go overboard for all the detailed analysis and implicit assumptions in the Lord-Parry thesis (and the pronouncements of its adherents). This, I want to argue in the rest of the paper, would be a mistake, and one the more important to recognise because of the unquestionable attraction and applicability of many aspects of the theory.

The main points I want to tackle are first, the basic concept and differentiation of "oral literature" and then, arising from that, of "oral composition." This will eventually bring me round to the topic of the "formula."

Reading through many of the oral-formulaic analyses, one gains certain impressions (not always stated explicitly) which I will initially lay out in schematic form:

1. That there is a single and identifiable phenomenon called "oral literature" (or more specifically "oral poetry") about which it is possible to generalise.

2. That this "oral literature" (or "oral poetry") is radically different from and opposed to written literature (or poetry).

3. That the term "oral composition" likewise refers to some clear-cut and identifiable process, so that when/if one has deduced "oral composition" from the evidence (e.g. from a study of the formulae), one has deduced something definite and meaningful.

These three assumptions are the ones I suggest we need to take a hard look at, as I will explain in the rest of my paper.

Take, first, the differentiation of "oral" from "written" literature, and the idea that this is a single phenomenon about which one can generalise. This idea comes out both in the writings of Parry and Lord and among many of the followers (whatever their detailed positions) of the oral-formulaic school. It is stated quite explicitly in Parry's own description of his aim in turning to Slav poetry. His purpose was to

> obtain evidence on the basis of which could be drawn a series of
> generalities applicable to all oral poetries: which would allow
> me, in the case of a poetry for which there was not enough
> evidence outside the poems themselves of the way in which
> they were made, to say whether that poetry was oral or not, and
> *how* it should be understood if it was oral. . . . A method is here
> involved, that which consists in *defining the characteristics of
> oral style*. (Parry and Lord, 1954, p. 4)

This interest in generalising about "oral literature," "oral poetry," "the
oral style" and so on has been very much part, too, of work inspired by
Parry and Lord. One meets the constant use of terms like "the oral
method," "the oral technique" (Buchan, 1972, pp. 55, 58), "the oral
poet," "the oral technique of verse making," "oral texture" (Notopoulos,
1964, pp. 21, 24, 52 etc.), "the clearly oral characteristics" of the *Song
of Roland* (Nichols, 1961, 9n), "the irrefutable statistical facts that
distinguish the texts of Homer from those of poets known to have
composed by writing" (Nagler, 1967, p. 274), or "the method of oral
poetry" (Curschmann, 1967, p. 42). Following on Lord's claim that
"With oral poetry we are dealing with a particular and distinctive
process in which oral learning, oral composition, and oral transmission
almost merge" (1968, p. 5) are many equally confident generalisations.
I need only mention Magoun's much-quoted "oral poetry, it may safely
be said, is composed entirely of formulas, large and small, while
lettered poetry is never formulaic" (1953, p. 447), Notopoulos'
discussion of the "facts of life about oral poetry" which includes the
generalisation that "the society which gives birth to oral poetry is
characterized by traditional fixed ways in all aspects of its life" (1964,
pp. 50, 51), or Nichols' comment that "the existence and propagation of
an oral tradition, as the now classic studies of Milman Parry and Albert
B. Lord have shown, depend on conditions of composition and
recitation which are quite distinct from those found in a literary
tradition" (1961, p. 9).

Parry and Lord seem to make a rigid distinction between written
and oral poetry. In *The Singer of Tales* we read that "the two techniques
[oral and written] are . . . contradictory and mutually exclusive. Once
the oral technique is lost, it is never regained. The written technique . . . is not compatible with the oral technique, and the two
could not possibly combine to form another, a third, a 'transitional'
technique" (Lord, 1968, p. 129). Similarly, "as literacy spreads

throughout the world at a now rapid pace, oral poetry seems destined in time to disappear" (Lord, 1965, p. 591). This has been echoed by later writers. "One important lesson of the field experience of Parry and Lord," writes Kirk, "is that literacy destroys the virtue of an oral singer . . . we have seen in Yugoslavia at least that the acquisition of writing invariably destroys the powers of an oral poet" (Kirk, 1965, pp. 22, 29-30). Again, "the literary and oral techniques of composition do not mix in a true oral poet" (Notopoulos, 1964, p. 19).

These two assumptions about the identity of "oral literature" and its differentiation from written literature need to be examined carefully.

There are, of course, ways in which oral literature clearly does differ from written literature—chiefly, I consider, in the matter of its being *performed*—but to speak as if there is a definite break between them is an exaggeration and a misleading one. The two terms are, I would argue, relative ones, and to assign any given piece unequivocally to either one category or the other—as if they were self-contained and mutually exclusive boxes—can distort the nature of the evidence.

It is very evident in Africa that oral and written literature often in practice comprise relative and overlapping rather than mutually exclusive categories. In Africa, the influence of literacy through Christian missionary activity has deeper roots than is sometimes recognised by the romanticised "primitive state of nature" model. In addition there has been the enormously important effect of Islam and Islamic literacy, which dates back many centuries, and in the great Sudanic and East coast areas has become a truly African rather than superficial and intrusive phenomenon from outside. In West Africa, for instance, the long Hausa "Song of Bagauda" appears in both written and unwritten form (Hiskett, 1964-1965). In Swahili verse there is a constant interchange and influence as between orally-composed and written verse (Werner, 1918, pp. 113-27; Harries, 1962, pp. 3-5; Whiteley 1958), while in modern Somali oral literature poets not only make use of the radio in addition to face to face delivery, but in the case of the oral poetry in traditional alliterative verse designed for dramatic performance, some poets "have used writing . . . as a visual aid to their oral memory" (Mumin, 1974, p. 3). In fact, what some might consider as "mixed forms" have had a long history in the continent of Africa— forms which are at some point written but reach their fullest actualisation and circulation by being performed orally. This includes, for instance, modern political songs and hymns in many areas (see

Finnegan, 1970, pp. 284 ff, 185 ff); Swahili religious poems publicly intoned for the enlightenment of the masses; Fulani poems declaimed aloud; or Hausa compositions memorised as oral poems and sung by beggars, chanted on the streets at night or (nowadays) performed over the radio.

What about the oral composers/performers themselves? A highly relevant question to ask is whether they themselves have to be basically non-literate to practise as oral singers?

I do not know of any detailed study in Africa specifically directed to comparing the productions of non-literate with literate individuals as a test of Lord's claim that literacy inevitably destroys the capacity of the oral composer and hence oral poetry generally (it might not be a very easy hypothesis to operationalise and test experimentally anyway). But on the face of it there is plenty of evidence that literacy and an acquaintance with written literature does not necessarily interfere with oral composition and performance. I will give just a few instances of what I consider is in practice a widespread phenomenon in Africa.

Let me take my own fieldwork among the Limba. There, it is true, one of the best story-tellers I encountered was totally illiterate— Karanke Dema, a smith, one in touch with the secret mysteries of the men's society: a truly creative artist, musically, poetically and dramatically. In his blend of creativity and tradition as well as his brilliant and personal use of the local conventions, he was a beautiful example of the typical oral artist—albeit in prose not verse—depicted in *The Singer of Tales.* But I have to admit that he was run very close indeed—and possibly, in local eyes, excelled—by another Limba story-teller, Kelfa Koneth, a young man in the middle of his teacher's training course: in other words, pretty highly educated in the uses of the written word. He relied on the same kind of interplay of recognised themes and structure (adding in some episodes pretty clearly drawn from his school background) as well as all the accepted tricks of delivery, with perhaps even more dramatic effect. He was far from the only literate narrator, too. I would find it hard to differentiate in terms of performance and composition between those oral narrators who were non-literate, on the one hand, and those with varying degrees of literacy on the other. I based my analysis of style and composition among Limba oral narrators on the production of both categories.

This situation is far from unparalleled. I have heard a magnificent oral narrative performed by a highly-educated Yoruba pastor in Western

Nigeria, for instance—reminding one how widely the sermon has been practised as an oral art form by highly literate preachers (as Rosenberg too has shown from American Negro preachers [1970, 18 ff]). Many accounts too of contemporary oral poetry in Africa include references to school songs among the other categories of oral art. These are not necessarily just crude rhymes or derivative aping of foreign teachers. Note for instance the Dinka "school songs" from the southern Sudan, in which the position of schoolboys is seen as parallel to that of the traditional age sets:

> The moon of December has appeared
> Our age-set in white [lit. "the White Bull"] sees it
>   from all flanks
> The age-set which obeys orders. . . .

ending the 45-line poem with

> I am building my home
> The home of the children of learning
> The home where words of children flow even at
>   night.
> To the age-set in white, jealousy is unknown.
>   (Deng, 1973, pp. 250-251)

Such poems by clearly literate composers are considered by Deng as in principle no different from other more "traditional" types of poetry in terms of their structure and composition.

It is, after all, hardly surprising to find this kind of interplay between oral and literate modes, for the two have interacted and overlapped for centuries in extensive areas of the world. It is not only in Africa that such instances are documented. Take, for instance, the mediaeval Chinese ballad singers, whose art was clearly an oral one with their compositions in "mixed musical modes" designed for the ear rather than the eye. Yet these singers sometimes relied on brief written notes "to jog their memory before and during the performance" or even on written compositions by "a professionally skilled author" who wrote ballads specifically for performance; similar ballads also appeared in printed versions designed for literate readers (Doleželová-Velingerová and Crump, 1971, p. 2). Again, with the great epic cycle of Gesar in Tibet and Mongolia, the many oral and written versions are said to have been interdependent over at least three centuries (Stein, 1959, esp. Chap. 3). The well-known case of English and American ballads too has clearly involved much interplay between oral and written forms. Particular ballads go in and out of the oral tradition, perhaps beginning in printed broadsheet form (some of these, in turn, apparently based on earlier oral forms), sung around by those peddling the songs, then circulating—more, or less—by oral means (Laws, 1957; Rollins, 1919). And even singers who would be classed as oral by most observers, in the sense of depending very much on performance and introducing variations of their own on "traditional texts," may also like to have written versions which they can consult if necessary—Almeda Riddle, for instance, the American ballad singer, whose mother sang ballads by ear and father insisted on going by the book (Abrahams, 1970). The productions of oral singers of this kind cannot be unequivocally assigned to a clear-cut and separate category "oral" as opposed to "written," for elements of both "oral" and "written" forms enter in.

A similar point about the *relativity* of the concepts of "oral" and "written" can be made about many other kinds of literature too. It applies well to many of the modern so-called "songs of protest," to work songs (those for instance of miners, lumberers, roadworkers, or prisoners [see, e.g., Greenway, 1953; Jackson, 1972]) and to Irish "rebel songs"—in some senses composed and performed orally, and yet produced in a context of widespread literacy which it is impossible to believe has not affected the poets. One can also mention forms like the recent development of "jazz poetry"—poetry specifically intended for oral performance—or the so-called "underground" English poets with their insistence on public performance as their preferred mode of publication, including the preparedness of a leading poet like Adrian Mitchell to improvise when delivering his own poetry: "I change poems when I read them aloud" (quoted in Horovitz, 1969, p. 358). This recalls the same kind of overlap between partially oral and partially written media in classical antiquity where oral performance coexisted with a literate tradition: "Among the Greeks the regular method of publication was by public recitation . . . [which] continued to be the regular method of publication even after books and the art of reading had become common" (Hadas, 1954, p. 50). In medieval Europe too the main means of circulation of much literature has been claimed to be "oral delivery" and many literary pieces were composed specifically for public recitation and oral performance (Crosby, 1936). A number of cases have been suggested, too, in mediaeval literature where there seems to be the kind of blend of oral and written elements that the rigid distinctions envisaged by Lord and Parry simply cannot account for (see, e.g., Curschmann, 1967, p. 50 ff), and for Old English much evidence has been cited that, in some sense, there really were what Lord might have called "transitional" texts and that—as Shippey sums it up—"though literacy and the fixed text may have killed 'oracy' in the long run, the change need not have happened . . . quickly . . . [there was] an overlap of the oral and the written" (1972, pp. 97-98).

This hasty list may seem to be either labouring the obvious or else setting up so wide a definition of "oral literature" that the term ceases to have any meaning. But this latter point is really the main thing I am driving at. When one looks hard at the detailed circumstances and nature of literary phenomena in a wide comparative context, historically as well as geographically, the concept of "oral literature" *does* cease to be a very clear one, because of the varying ways in which a literary piece can be oral (or written): "orality" is a relative thing.

It is, of course, possible to set up a narrower definition of "oral"— in the way Lord in effect does—confining it, say, *solely* to pieces composed during oral delivery on the model of Yugoslav singers. There is nothing *in principle* impossible about such a definition. But this kind of restrictive definition seems to me to do no justice at all to the practical realities of the many different and overlapping forms which literary formulations have taken throughout space and time.

A convinced disciple of Parry and Lord might claim that much of this is beside the point, for what is involved in their approach is not the medium itself or the outward circumstances of composition or (still less) performance, but the oral "mentality" of the poet. After all, when one comes down to it, a number of Parry and Lord's "oral poets" were in fact literate, and Lord himself admits that literate poets are possible. But what he *is* concerned about is whether they have an "oral" or a "written" "mentality" (Lord, 1968, p. 138). This line has been followed by many other writers, focussing on the "psychology" of oral composition, "the mental processes" in oral poetry (Notopoulos, 1964, p. 59), the "mental template" involved (Nagler, 1967, p. 269) or even "the oral mind" (Buchan, 1972, p. 57).

This, however, I find equally unconvincing and unhelpful for two reasons. First, the general impression is given in *The Singer of Tales* that there is solid evidence for the claimed "incompatibility" between "oral" and "written" methods—yet all this ultimately comes down to is what must be, in effect, a psychological speculation which is never proved and which anyway comes very close to being a tautology.

Second, the tone in which this argument is put forward smacks very much of older ideas about "primitive mentality" which were once current in anthropology. This approach connected up the supposed special mentality of non-literate (and "primitive") peoples with their so-called reliance on "tradition" and unchanging norms, and their involvement with magic and religion, in a way I am reminded of by some writings in the oral-formulaic school (e.g., Lord, 1968, pp. 66-67, 155; Notopoulos, 1964, p. 51 [quoted earlier]). Since some of the speculation about "the oral mind" may perhaps appear to derive some support from the earlier notion about "primitive mentality," it is worth stressing that this idea has been under heavy fire for some time in modern anthropology and is at best a highly controversial notion (see, e.g., Horton and Finnegan, 1973).

The idea of a basic divide between oral and written may also seem to have additional appeal because of another current manifestation of romanticism—as I would classify it. I am thinking of the enthusiasm for the writings of Marshall McLuhan with his stress on the "auditory and magical domain . . . of primeval man" (1969, p. 79) and concern with man's movement from an oral to a visual mode of knowing with the development of writing and print. (His work has clear links with *The Singer of Tales* as he himself makes explicit in the Prologue to his *Gutenberg Galaxy*). Similar notions, perhaps stemming from the same romantic background, are found in the image put forward in many modern African novels: of an individual torn between "two cultures"— often presented as incompatible with each other—the world of "tradition" and that of literate and industrial "modernity."

This is not the place for a dissection of McLuhan's ideas, so I will merely state my conclusion that not only are his interpretations elusive and emotive in the extreme, but he also takes little account of the complexity of the actual facts. He thus exaggerates both the "orality" of earlier and non-industrial cultures (and individuals) and the "literacy" of more recent Western civilisation. To ignore the complicated and mixed way in which human beings, now and in the past, have made use of a whole range of different media may result in an elegant model but does scant justice to the complexity of the real world. A similar point could be made of the "torn between two worlds" image in African novels. It makes for effective literature: but it is by no means so self-evident that it presents an accurate reflection of the real world. As Ajayi put it recently, "These dramatic presentations of culture conflict may be good literature, but are seldom good history or psychology" (1974, p. 15).

There are therefore pressures in our intellectual background which make the separation of "oral" and "written" seem initially plausible—until one looks hard at the facts. So it is worth repeating once again one of the basic contentions of this paper: "orality" and "literacy" (and similar terms) are complex and relative notions, and ones which manifest themselves in the real world in a number of overlapping ways. "Oral literature" (or "oral poetry") is similarly not a strictly separable and clearly defined category.

This point—obvious though it must seem in many ways—is significant for many of the findings of the oral-formulaic school. For one frequently senses the implication in these writings that a conclusion from detailed and scholarly study of "formulae," that a given piece is an instance of "oral literature" or "oral poetry," has provided solid new information about the piece: that by assigning it to the category of "oral literature" one has said something specific and meaningful that fits in with a whole accepted background of assumptions about the "oral mind" or the "natural" context for oral poetry. I would suggest, on the contrary, that saying something is "oral" could only be the beginning. One also wants to know "oral" in what sense? how far? in what circumstances? for whom and when? and so on. Since "oral literature" turns out to be so *relative* a phenomenon, taking so many differing forms and relating in varying ways to writing, it seems sensible to regard it as setting the parameters within which further questions can be asked rather than accepting it, as such, as the end result of a piece of research. I suggest that we can no longer be as certain as Lord and his followers when they assume that we now know exactly what "oral poetry" and its characteristics must be like. The reality, alas, is usually more complex and unpredictable.

A further point that emerges is the need for a greater awareness of the temptation I think we have all felt: to exaggerate the "orality" of non-literate cultures and individuals. There are traces of this in the Lord-Parry research,[1] and it certainly seems to be an implication in some later oral-formulaic studies which treat the literary piece under consideration in a kind of vacuum, divorced from the written media that in almost all cases certainly lurked, nearer or further, in the poet's background.

This leads on to my next topic: the whole question of "oral composition." Here again one receives the impression in some writing that this is something clear-cut and definite, discoverable through a series of perhaps controversial analyses—but in principle identifiable; and, furthermore, that it is a single and specific thing. Thus, if one can conclude from an analysis of the evidence ("formulaic" or whatever) that what was involved in, say, The *Odyssey* or *The Song of Roland* (see Duggan, 1973; Nichols, 1961) was "oral composition," the implication is that one has discovered something definite and precise.

This impression is given in many of the statements in *The Singer of Tales.* "For the oral poet," writes Lord, "the moment of composition is the performance . . . singing, performing, composing are facets of the same act," and "we know exactly what is meant by these terms [oral poet and oral poems], at least insofar as manner of composition is concerned" (Lord, 1968, pp. 13, 141). A similar generalization is made in Lord's encyclopaedia article on "oral poetry" which opens "Oral poetry is poetry composed *in* oral performance by people who cannot read or write" (Lord, 1965, p. 591). This claim has been accepted with alacrity by many adherents of the oral-formulaic school. Lord is credited in general terms with "demonstrating how a traditional poetry is composed," and thus clarifying "our understanding of oral poetry's characteristics of style" and the "principles" of "oral composition [which] are basic and hold good for all oral traditions" (Buchan, 1972, pp. 55, 58). There are frequent references to the process of "oral composition" as if this is one single and identifiable process: "the manner in which oral poetry is composed" (Curschmann, 1967, p. 40), "the technique of oral composition" (Alexander, 1966, p. 21), "the oral method of composition" (Kirk, 1965, p. 17) and so on. A theory which perhaps began as primarily applicable just to epic soon became extended—sometimes even by the original theorists themselves—to encompass every kind of "oral poetry," the crucial thing apparently being its characteristic of "oral composition."

I want to query this impression on two main grounds.

The first is really no more than an extension of what I have argued already. If there is no one simple category called "oral literature" (or "oral poetry") but only a complex and relative series of possibilities, the same is likely to be true for "oral composition." It cannot be assumed without a detailed investigation of comparative evidence beyond just the Yugoslav case that "oral poetry" and, correspondingly, "oral composition" is of one predictable kind. There may be a number of different ways of composing orally, corresponding to the different social circumstances of the literary piece involved or the vaying ways in which literary production and distribution is organized in different cultures and periods. The impression, therefore, that one often receives from oral-formulaic work that there is something clear-cut and definite called "oral composition" is misleading.

The second reason for querying certain assumptions about "oral composition" is perhaps a more interesting and specific one. This is that, contrary to the impression in *The Singer of Tales* and elsewhere that oral poetry is *always* composed-in-performance, this is just not true empirically. There are a number of known cases where the emphasis is on composition *before* performance and of instances where, contrary to all the expectations so many of us had built up from our reading of Parry and Lord, etc., memorisation rather than improvisation is in fact involved. In these cases, the aspects of composition and performance, conjoined so inseparably in the Parry-Lord analysis, can be split apart.

I will give some instances to illustrate this assertion.

The first is the case of Somali poetry. In Somalia, in the Horn of Africa, oral poetry is a highly developed art. It has been extensively studied, both in its modern phase where radio and tapes as well as face-to-face delivery are employed, and in its earlier development. It includes many different genres, from lengthy *gabay* poems, sometimes of several hundred lines, to the short one- or two-line compressed *balwo* lyrics (described in Andrzejewski and Lewis, 1964). Poetic composition is a highly prized and much-discussed art among the Somali—who have been described by observers as "a nation of bards"—and an admired and successful poet can become widely acclaimed throughout the country. A Somali poem is always the subject of interest and discussion—and merits criticism if it is considered mediocre—and because they are aware of this "Somali poets rarely perform their work until composition is completely finished in private" (Johnson, 1971, p. 28) and "spend many hours, sometimes even days, composing their works" before they perform them (Andrzejewski and Lewis, 1964, p. 45). A poet's compositions, furthermore, become his own property, under his own name, and any other poet reciting them has to acknowledge from whom he has learnt them. A good poet has an entourage of admirers some of whom learn his poems by heart and recite them. Then others too hear these recitations and they in turn memorise them if they consider them sufficiently beautiful and important. As is made clear in the analysis by Andrzejewski and Lewis, it is indeed memorisation rather than simultaneous composition/performance that is involved here.

While we may admire Somali poets for achieving worthwhile results in the very difficult medium of Somali prosody, we are no less impressed by feats of memory on the part of the poetry reciters, some of whom are poets themselves. Unaided by writing they learn long poems by heart and some have repertoires which are too great to be exhausted even by several evenings of continuous recitation. Moreover, some of them are endowed with such powers of memory that they can learn a poem by heart after hearing it only once, which is quite astonishing, even allowing for the fact that poems are chanted very slowly, and important lines are sometimes repeated. The reciters are not only capable of acquiring a wide repertoire but can store it in their memories for many years, sometimes for a lifetime. We have met poets who at a ripe age could still remember many poems which they learnt in their youth.

In the nomadic interior whole villages move from place to place and there is constant traffic between villages, grazing camps, and towns. Poems spread very quickly over wide areas and in recent times motor transport and the radio have further accelerated the speed with which they are disseminated.

A poem passes from mouth to mouth. Between a young Somali who listens today to a poem composed fifty years ago, five hundred miles away, and its first audience there is a long chain of reciters who passed it one to another. It is only natural that in this process of transmission some distortion occurs, but comparison of different versions of the same poem usually shows a surprisingly high degree of fidelity to the original. This is due to a large extent to the formal rigidity of Somali poetry: if one word is substituted for another, for instance, it must still keep to the rules of alliteration, thus limiting very considerably the number of possible changes. The general trend of the poem, on the other hand, inhibits the omission or transposition of lines.

Another factor also plays an important role: the audience who listen to the poem would soon detect any gross departure from the style of the particular poet; moreover among the audience there are often people who already know by heart the particular poem, having learnt it from another source. Heated disputes sometimes arise between a reciter and his audience concerning the purity of his version. It may even happen that the authorship of a poem is questioned by the audience, who carefully listen to the introductory phrases in which the reciter gives the name of the poet, and, if he is dead, says a prayer formula for his soul. (Andrzejewski and Lewis, 1964, pp. 45-46)

It is clear from an instance like this that there are cases in oral poetry where memorisation is indeed involved and when the concept of a "correct" version is locally recognised. All this is not what one should expect if one relied mainly on the analogy of Yugoslav singers or of the various analyses of the oral-formulaic school. The practice of Somali poetic composition helps to bring home the point that there are other possible modes of composition in oral poetry.

Another instructive instance is that discovered by Gordon Innes' research into Mandinka griots' narrations. Here he found a fascinating blend of stability and change, with both memorisation and fluidity involved.

At first sight the various versions of the "Sunjata epic" throughout the Manding area of West Africa seem to offer an exact instance of the kind of composition/performance blend familiar from Lord's writings. It concerns the exploits of the great hero Sunjata who established himself as King of Manding and Susu in the thirteenth century, and many versions of the story are extant even in the restricted area of just the Gambia. As Innes writes

From these and from published versions from elsewhere in the Manding area one almost has the impression that the Sunjata legend consists of a repertoire of various motifs, incidents, themes (call them what you will), and that each griot makes a selection which he strings together into a coherent narrative. (Innes, 1973, p. 105)

He goes on however to show that this initial impression is in fact wrong, for it suggests greater fluidity than is actually the case.

Innes made a detailed comparison of a number of versions. One set were those recorded by two brothers, Banna and Dembo Kanute, both widely regarded as outstanding performers. They had basically learnt their craft from their father, assisted (in the case of Banna) by the elder of the two brothers. The point Innes notes in this case is the differences in their versions. Starting presumably from the same repertoire, their performances differ in the ground covered in two major incidents and in a number of details. So far then, there is the sort of fluidity one would expect from the comparative Yugoslav material. Furthermore, there are indications that each brother adapted his version to the situation in which he performed—what leading persons were present in the audience, for instance, who could trace their descent from figures in the Sunjata story.

But when Innes came to a detailed comparison between two versions by one and the same griot—Bamba Suso—a different aspect emerged. Bamba was widely regarded as one of the leading griots in the Gambia with extensive historical knowledge. In his seventies, two recordings were made of his version of the Sunjata story, one for Radio Gambia, another at Brikama to an audience which included Innes himself. The most striking point to emerge from a comparison of the two is their close similarity, in places extending to word-for-word repetition. Here are two passages quoted by Innes to illustrate the point

(1)

Sunjata had been a cripple from birth and when the time came for him and the other boys of his own age to undergo circumcision and training, he was still unable to walk, so the smiths made stout iron crutches for him. This passage opens at the point when Sunjata tried to lift himself up by means of these crutches.

Brikama Version

Biring a ye wolu muta, wolu bee katita.
When he had taken hold of them, they all broke.
I ko, 'Sunjata dung si wuli nyaadi?'
People asked, 'How will Sunjata get up?'
A fango ko i ye, 'Ali n naa kili;
He said to them, 'Call my mother;
Ning dingo boita, a naa le kara a wulindi.'
When a child has fallen, it is his mother who picks him up.'
Biring a baama naata,
When his mother came,
A ye a bulo laa a baama sanyo kang,

He laid his hand upon his mother's shoulder,
A wulita a loota.
He arose and stood up.
Jalolu kara a fo wo le la, i ko,
It is from that that the griots say,
'Jata wulita,' i ko, 'Manding Jata wulita,
'The Lion has arisen,' they say, 'The Lion of Manding has
                              arisen,
Feng baa wulita.'
The mighty one has arisen.'

Radio Gambia Version

A ye wolu muta, i bee katita.
He took hold of them, they all broke.
Sunjata fango ko i ye ko,
Sunjata said to them,
'Ning dingo boita, a naa le kara a wulindi;
'When a child has fallen, it is his mother who picks him up;
Ali n naa kili.'
Call my mother.'
Sukulung Konte naata,
Sukulung Konte came,
A ye a bulo laa a sanyo to,
He laid his hand on her shoulder,
A wulita a loota.
He arose and stood up.
Jalolu kara a fo wo le la ko,
It is from that that the griots say,
'Jata wulita,' i ko, 'Manding Jata wulita,
'The Lion has arisen,' they say, 'The Lion of Manding has
                              arisen,
Feng baa wulita.'
The mighty one has arisen.' (Innes, 1973, pp.111-112)

(2)

Brikama Version

A loota a baama kunto a ko a ye,
He stood by his mother's head and said to her,

Ni a ye a tara m be Manding mansaya la,
If I am to be king of Manding,

Janning fano be ke la bii ye faa.
Before dawn breaks today, may you be dead.
Ni a ye a tara n te Manding mansaya la,
If I am not to be king of Manding,
Ye tu kuuranding,
May you remain ill,
Kaatu n te i kuurang to tu la jang.
Because I will not leave you here in sickness.
Janning fano be ke la,
Before dawn broke,
Sukulung Konte faata.
Sukulung Konte died.
A ko a be Sukulung Konte baade la.
Sunjata said that he would bury Sukulung Konte.
Faring Burema Tunkara ko a ye,
Faring Burema Tunkara told him,
'I te a baade la
'You will not bury her
Fo ye a baade dula sang.'
Unless you buy her burial plot.'
A ko a ye, 'M be a sang na nyaadi?'
Sunjata asked, 'How shall I buy it?'
A ko, 'I si minkallolu bula nyo la,
He said, 'You must put earrings together,
Ye doo laa a fongo to,
And lay one on her forehead,
Ye doo laa sing-kono-nding kumba to,
And lay another on her big toe,
Ye a sumang banko to;
And measure it on the ground;
A kanyanta dameng i si jee sing,
And you must dig the corresponding length,
I si i baama baade jee.'
And you must bury your mother there.'

Radio Gambia Version

A naata loo a baama kunto,
He came and stood by his mother's head,
A ko a ye. 'N naa, ye n kili Manding mansaya la.
He said to her, 'Mother, they have called me to the kingship
                              of Manding.

Bari ni a ye a tara n te mansaya la,
But if I am not to be king,
Ye tu kuuranding,
May you remain ill,
Kaatu n te i kuurang to tu la jang.
Because I will not leave you here in sickness.
Bari ni a ye a tara m be Manding mansaya la,
But if I am to be king of Manding,
Ye faa janning fano be ke la.'
May you die before dawn breaks.'
Janning fano be ke la,
Before dawn broke,
Sukulung Konte faata.
Sukulung Konte died.
I taata fo Faring Burema Tunkara ye,
They went and told Faring Burema Tunkara,
I ko a ye, 'Sukulung Konte faata de.'
They told him, 'Sukulung Konte is dead.'
A ko, 'Ali a fo Sunjata ye,
He said, 'Tell Sunjata
A te a baama baade la
He will not bury his mother
Fo a ye a baade dula sang.'
Unless he buys her burial plot.'
A ko, 'M be a sang na nyaadi?'
Sunjata asked, 'How shall I buy it?'
A ko, 'I si sano dung nyo daa la,
He said, 'You must put gold together,
Ye doo laa a fongo to,
And lay one on her forehead,
Ye doo laa a singo to;
And lay another on her leg;
Wo kanyanta banko dameng fee,
The corresponding length of ground
I si jee sing i si i naa baade jee.'
You must dig, and you must bury your mother there.' (Innes,
                        1973, pp. 115-116)

In these extracts, there is certainly not word-for-word *identity*
throughout. Nevertheless there is perhaps a greater degree of verbal
repetition that one might expect from pressing the Yugoslav analogy. It
is also clear that to some extent memorisation *is* involved here; at the

very least it would be misleading to insist that "original composition" played a very large part in the actual performance. The model of simultaneous composition/performance must in this case be modified to include the point that much of the "composing" must in some sense have preceded the performance—to a much greater extent than, say, in the composition/performance of the Yugoslav Avdo Medjedović or the Kirghiz bards described by Radlov. One cannot, then, assume that the composition/performance process so well illustrated in the case of certain Eastern European singers by Lord and others is *always* characteristic of oral poetry (even of all oral narrative poetry). Much (though not necessarily all) of the composing may well take place *before* the moment of performance.

What emerges from this is the need for more careful and detailed research on the respective parts played by composition, memorisation and performance not only in particular situations but also by different individual singers and even perhaps by the same singers at differing ages. On the Mandinka evidence, Innes sums up his findings as follows:

> At first sight the two pieces of evidence presented here seem to contradict each other. The evidence from the Kanute brothers shows that in the course of his professional career a griot's version of the Sunjata legend may undergo considerable change. The evidence from Bamba, on the other hand, shows that a griot's version may remain remarkably stable, both in content and language, over a period of time. Different interpretations of this evidence are no doubt possible, but, taken along with other evidence, it suggests to me a pattern of life in which a griot in his younger days travels extensively, listens to other griots and borrows selectively from them, repeatedly modifying his own version until eventually he arrives at a version which seems to him the most satisfying. With repetition, this version will become more or less fixed, and even the words will tend to become fixed to some extent. But even this version will of course vary from performance to performance, depending upon such factors as who happens to be present and in whose honour the performance is being given. (Innes, 1973, p. 118)

In other words, a single model of the relation of composition to performance will not necessarily cover all cases. To accept too uncritically Lord's dictum that what is important in oral poetry is "the composition *during* oral performance" or claim that "oral narrative is not, *cannot* be, memorized" (Lord, 1965, p. 592) is liable to blind one to the many interesting ways in which the elements of composition, memorisation, and performance may be in play in or before the delivery of a specific oral poem.

Similar points about the division between composition and performance come out in a number of other African examples. The long panegyric poems in Ruanda and South Africa, for instance, are often quoted as outstanding examples of specialist oral art. Yet in Ruanda there was often memorisation of received versions of the praise poems, with minimal variation in performance, and the original composers were remembered by name (Kagame, 1951). And for the Zulu a recent study states quite categorically that the specialist praise singers attached to the courts were concerned more with "performance" than "composition": the singer "has to memorize [the praises of the chief and the ancestors] so perfectly that on occasions of tribal importance they pour forth in a continuous stream or torrent. Although he may vary the order of the sections or stanzas of the praise-poem, he may not vary the praises themselves. He commits them to memory as he hears them, even if they are meaningless to him" (Cope, 1968, pp. 27-28).

Again, the practice of prior composition followed by careful rehearsal before public performance is apparently widespread. Among the Dinka, for instance, people sometimes call on an expert to compose a song to their requirements.

> While an expert composes for others, people must be near him to memorize the song as it develops. The composer mumbles to himself, constructs a few lines, tells the people to "hold this" and sings the lines. As he proceeds, they follow him. When a song is completed, the expert is likely to have forgotten it, while they remember it in full. (Deng, 1973, p. 85)

Another case is that of women's songs among the Zambian Ila and Tonga. The special song called *impango* is composed prior to performance. The woman whose special song it is to be first thinks out the rather lengthy words, then calls in some of her friends to help her. Together they go to a well-known maker of *impango* songs, who listens to the "owner's" ideas and then works on the song over several days. The women are all called together for a rehearsal for several evenings until they have thoroughly mastered the song. Then the owner continues to "sing the song in her heart" and practise it on her own so that if she forgets at all she can ask one of her practice party for help. By now she can feel fully mistress of her *impango* and when she is invited to a festival is prepared to stand up and sing it in public (Jones, 1943, pp. 11-12).

Similar cases of prior composition and rehearsal for later performance are mentioned not infrequently in descriptions of African oral literature.

The examples quoted so far to illustrate the possibility of a greater split between composition and performance than in the Yugoslav case have all been drawn from Africa. But similar cases are also recorded from elsewhere. A few illustrations from other continents may help to fill out this account of the way deliberate composition can take place prior to performance.

Eskimo poetry provides one excellent instance of this. Not only is long and careful consideration given to the composition of the words of many Eskimo poems before their performance, but the poets themselves are articulate about the problems and delights of composition; indeed this is a constant preoccupation in many of the poems themselves. In this extract for instance, the poet compares the difficulties of fishing with those of poetic composition:

> . . . Why, I wonder
> My song-to-be that I wish to use
> My song-to-be that I wish to put together
> I wonder why it will not come to me?
> At Sioraq it was, at a fishing hole in the ice,
> A little trout I could feel on the line
> And then it was gone,
> I stood jigging
> But why is that so difficult, I wonder?. . .
> (Rasmussen, 1931, pp. 517-518)

The Eskimo combine their awareness of the deliberate and conscious struggle involved in "putting together words into a song" with the concept of poetic inspiration. One of the outstanding Eskimo poets was Orpingalik, who used to call his songs his "comrades in solitude" and "his breath." He described some of the processes of composition to Rasmussen in these terms.

"How many songs I have I cannot tell you. I keep no count of
such things. There are so many occasions in one's life where a
joy or sorrow is felt in such a way that the desire comes to
sing. . . . All my being is song, and I sing as I draw
breath. . . . Songs are thoughts, sung out with the breath
when people are moved by great forces and ordinary speech no
longer suffices. . . .

"Man is moved just like the ice floe sailing here and there
out in the current. His thoughts are driven by a flowing force
when he feels joy, when he feels fear, when he feels sorrow.
Thoughts can wash over him like a flood, making his breath
come in gasps and his heart throb. Something like an
abatement in the weather will keep him thawed up. And then it
will happen that we, who always think we are small, will feel
still smaller. And we will fear to use words. When the words we
want to use shoot up of themselves—we get a new song."
(Rasmussen, 1932, pp. 16 and 321)

The same kind of emphasis on inspiration and waiting for the right
words to be born is given by the description of an Alaskan Eskimo of
how one must wait in silence and "stillness" for the poems to come—
then "they take shape in the minds of men and rise up like bubbles
from the depths of the sea, bubbles that seek the air to burst in the
light" (quoted in Freuchen, 1962, pp. 280-281). This process is far
from the kind of composition in the heat of the performance which we
associate with Yugoslav epic singers; for this waiting for inspiration is
expected to take place, not at the moment of public performance, but in
the dark, in deep silence as an act of artistic concentration. Walking
about outside in solitude is another common occasion for Eskimo
poetic composition. Rasmussen describes how great pains are taken to
put the words together skillfully so that "there is melody in them,
while at the same time they are pertinent in expression," and how "a
man who wants to compose a song may long walk to and fro in some
solitary place, arranging his words while humming a melody which he
has also made up himself" (Rasmussen, 1931, p. 321).

Perhaps the most vivid expression of the combination of hard work
and of heightened emotive perceptiveness inherent in Eskimo poetic
composition is to be found in the Eskimo poet Sadlaqé's account of
trying to compose a song:

Once when I was quite young, I wished to sing a song about my village, and one winter evening when the moon was shining, I was walking back and forth to put words together that could fit into a tune I was humming. Beautiful words I found, words that I should tell my friends about the greatness of the mountains and everything else that I enjoyed every time I came outside and opened my eyes. I walked, and continued walking over the frozen snow, and I was so busy with my thoughts that I forgot where I was. Suddenly I stood still and lifted my head up, and looked: in front of me was the huge mountain of my settlement, greater and steeper than I had ever seen it. It was almost as if it grew slowly out of the earth and began to lean out over me, deadly dangerous and menacing. And I heard a voice from the air that cried out: "Little human! The echo of your words has reached me! Do you really think that I can be comprehended in your song?" (Freuchen, 1962, pp. 279-80)

Improvisation or adaptation in the moment of performance is certainly not completely unknown in Eskimo poetry—witness for instance, the special song an old woman sang to welcome the visiting Rasmussen. But the emphasis is on deliberate and studied compositions, with recognised personal ownership of particular songs by the individual who composed them.

Another clear instance of deliberate and painstaking composition separated from the act of performance is documented for oral poets in the Gilbert Islands of the southern Pacific. When one reads a Gilbertese love song like the following, one's first impression may well be of apparent spontaneity of expression:

> How deep are my thoughts as I sit on the point of
>   the land
> Thinking of her tonight
> Her feet are luminous over dark ways
> Even as the moon stepping between clouds.
> Her shoulders shine like Kaama in the South[2]
> Her hands, in the sitting dance,
> Trouble my eyes as the flicker of stars;
> And at the lifting of her eyes to mine I am
>   abashed,
> I, who have looked undaunted into the sun.
>   (Grimble, 1957, p. 202)

But in fact such a poem rests on a long process of deliberate composition. Grimble has described how when a Gilbertese poet "feels the divine spark of inspiration once more stirring within him," he leaves the village and goes off to some lonely place where he can do the initial work on his composition completely alone: "This is his 'house of song,' wherein he will sit in travail with the poem that is yet unborn. All the next night he squats there, bolt upright, facing east, while the song quickens within him. The next morning he returns to the village to collect a group of friends to help him." It is their job to criticise and assess the poem—"to interrupt, criticise, interject suggestions, applaud, or howl down according to taste. Very often they do howl him down, too, for they are themselves poets. On the other hand, if the poem, in their opinion, shows beauty they are indefatigable in abetting its perfection" (Grimble, 1957, p. 205). They spend the whole day with the poet, working with him on his "rough draft"— "searching for the right word, the balance, the music that will convert it into a finished work of art." After a day spent in this joint process, the friends leave and the poet is left on his own once more:

> He remains alone again—probably for several days—to reflect upon their advice, accept, reject, accommodate, improve, as his genius dictates. The responsibility for the completed poem will be entirely his. (Grimble, 1957, pp. 204-205)

The result of this deliberate process of oral composition is that the poem that is finally produced has been worked and reworked over many days. This long-drawn-out process results in Arthur Grimble's words in "clear-cut gems of diction, polished and repolished with loving care, according to the canons of a technique as exacting as it is beautiful." The Gilbertese, he continues, are "consummate poets" who,

> Sincerely convinced of beauty, enlisted every artifice of balance, form and rhythm to express it worthily. The island poet thrills as subtly as our own to the exquisite values of words, labouring as patiently after the perfect epithet. (Grimble, 1957, p. 200)

There are many other examples of deliberate and protracted composition, divorced from the act of performance. There is not space to illustrate them here, but a brief mention could at least be made, to take just a few, of the protracted period of composition of the Chopi *ngodi* songs (see Finnegan, 1970, p. 268 f), the hours or days spent by Somali poets constructing their poems (Andrzejewski and Lewis, 1964, p. 45) or the preparatory work put by a Pueblo poet into composing a new song for an approaching festival:

> Yellow butterflies
> Over the blossoming virgin corn
> With pollen-painted faces
> Chase one another in brilliant throng. . . .
> (Curtis, 1907, p. 484)

Mediaeval Gaelic court poets composed their poems orally in a darkened room. When the poem was complete it was recited or chanted to the chief not by the poet himself but by a bard who, according to a near-contemporary source "got it well by heart, and now pronounc'd it orderly" (as quoted in Knott and Murphy, 1967, pp. 63-64). This clear distinction between poets (responsible for composition) and reciters (responsible for performance) is clearly unlike the Yugoslav model when "singing, performing, composing are facets of the same act" (Lord, 1968, p. 13). It is a distinction not unknown in a number of other poetic traditions too; compare the distinction between the mediaeval European *trobador* (composer) and *joglar* (performer), for instance, the Somali poet and reciter (Johnson, p. 29) or the composers as opposed to the performing bards of Ruanda.

When one allows the facet of writing to enter in—and as argued earlier it is hard to know just where one can draw a strict line regarding this—then there are many cases of prior composition with some reliance (at times) on writing which is then used, in varying degrees, as an aid to memory for later oral performance. There are, for instance, written narratives used as a basis for mediaeval Chinese ballad singers, versifiers attached to native operatic troupes in Malaya who "write words to well-known tunes" for later performance, or the texts of Irish street ballads (Doleželová-Velingerová and Crump, 1971, pp. 2, 8; Wilkinson, 1924, p. 40). All these have some part to play in the process of composing "oral poetry."

In short, when one starts looking hard at the concept of "oral composition" it becomes clear that it is not a single unique process at all—as is sometimes implied in the oral-formulaic school—but takes different forms in different cultures and circumstances. Even if one leaves out of the account any contexts in which writing plays a part—unrealistic though this omission might be—it emerges that even in the narrow sense of totally unwritten composition and performance, the relationship between these two processes varies; sometimes they are closely fused into one single activity (as with Yugoslav or Kirghiz epic), sometimes the performance is preceded by composition as a separate and distinct activity (as with Eskimo), with varying degrees of separation and fusion between these two extremes.

What emerges from this, is that the relationship between composition and performance in oral poetry is a more open one that the rather definite sounding term "oral composition" might seem to imply. Anyone who has read Parry and Lord will suspect that there may often *also* be some individual impact in actual performance—but the claim that oral composition and performance are always fused and that there is basically just one kind of "oral composition" turns out not to be true in the light of the comparative evidence.

This brings me finally to a brief mention of the "formula." The concept has already been queried fully enough for it to be inappropriate for me to add further comment on its detailed application (one need only cite the discussions in, e.g., Watts, 1969; Benson, 1966, or Rogers' damning comments, 1966, p. 102). But I would like to suggest that one reason for the continuing popularity of the concept of "formula" as a would-be precise tool in face of such searching attack has been the faith that here at last was some *real* characteristic of that special and perhaps mysterious mode called "oral poetry." This special category could, after all, be supposed to have its own peculiar characteristic, and in the concept of the "formula" we had finally found it—even if at the same time having to admit that its detailed definition presented a bit of difficulty. "The formula," I would venture to suggest, is a matter of faith rather than a precise term that corresponds to something definite and specific to be found in all oral poetry (or even in all oral epic poetry).

Once one removes the idea of a special and separate category of "oral poetry," as I have suggested we must do, then some of the hidden justification for identifying "formulae" and "formulaic phrases" disappears with it. There is no need to look for some special stylistic feature of the single category of "oral poetry"—for there is no such specific and identifiable category for it to apply to.

In any case, what really is "formulaic" about the kind of poetry that has been analysed by "oral-formulaic" scholarship? Is it really something precise and separate? If one takes a narrow definition—in terms say of identically repeated word patterns—then, as has often been pointed out, this does not always easily apply to literatures other than those in which it was first "discovered" by Lord and Parry. While if one takes a wider definition—one in effect implied not only in later extensions of the theory but also in earlier statements like Lord's "every line and every part of a line in oral poetry is 'formulaic'" (1965, p. 592)—then the specificity of the concept seems to evaporate and one is left with nothing very precise, despite the statistics. Are we not then beginning to talk about something much vaguer and harder to pin down that in fact tends to be common to *all* verse (written as well as oral): the patterned repetitiveness of poetry altogether, building on accepted patterns recognised within the particular poetic culture involved? As has been pointed out by Nagler (1967, p. 291) this is in a sense no different from the structured repetitiveness of language itself—the combination and recombination of known elements in new but old patterns. In this sense poetic language *whether "oral" or written* is merely one kind of language, and the occurrence of repeated patterns in oral poetry need not in principle any longer be regarded as some special and puzzling case to be explained in quasi-mystical terms like "dependence on formulae" which seem to set it apart from other poetry.

Thus to spend too long trying to pick out some satisfying definition of "formula" on the assumption that here at last is something specific to oral art—its necessary or its sufficient condition—seems to erect oral art into a special mysterious domain characterized by an apparently precise but in practice wholly elusive type of unit: "the formula." But any poet—whether Anglo-Saxon *scop* or modern jazz poet—has to "work within the retstrictions of his medium" (Cassidy, 1965, p. 83) and within his social and cultural context; and this surely applies to both "oral" and "literary" poets. Why therefore look primarily to repeated word patterns (as in the narrower definition) which form only part of the poet's conventional art, and not to all the other accepted patterns like music, parallelism, figurative language, use of soliloquy or address, themes known to be specially evocative for specific audiences, and so on? These often equally shape (and aid) the poet's diction, written or oral, and form part of accepted convention and yet are often not included in discussions of "formulaic style." The only reason for this relative neglect, I can only conclude, is that such more complex points, so obviously shared with much written poetry, could only cloud the apparently simple yardstick, achievable in essence by word counts, which seemed to have emerged as the next differentiating element between the accepted category of "oral literature" on the one hand and "written literature" on the other.

This paper has perforce been a somewhat negative one. "Oral literature," I have argued, is not after all a single clear-cut category, nor is it opposed in any absolute way to written literature. "Oral composition" similarly is not just one kind of process, predictable from some detectable kind of style called "formulaic" but on the contrary—and despite the assertions of Lord and others—can take a number of different forms. From this point of view I fear this has been a critical rather than a constructive paper.

However I would also claim that something positive has emerged too. The main point to emphasise is our growing awareness of how very varied oral literature/oral poetry can be. It is found in many more manifestations than *just* the form of the Yugoslav heroic poetry on which so much analysis has been founded. Thus, even if one knows that a piece is in some sense "oral," it is still an open—and a fascinating—question just what form that "orality" actually takes. There are many other aspects worth exploring in order to try to answer that question like: how was the piece delivered and performed? how widely known? how circulated and why? performed for whom (a very significant point often)? and in what circumstances? Questions like these can sometimes no longer be answered—hence the great attraction perhaps of the oral-formulaic approach in Homeric studies where answers could apparently be deduced from the text itself, possibly all we now have to go on. But in other cases, I suspect, more information could be found on these aspects than has perhaps come to the fore because of the concentration on discovering the special characteristic of "oral composition by means of formulae."

Since, then, there is a great variety of oral literary forms and a number of differing ways in which "oral composition" can take place, there is no short cut to discovering the exact process of composition and performance involved: in each case one has to ask further detailed questions about the circumstances and conventions of the particular piece itself and of its social and poetic background, as well as the personality (and in some cases age) of the individual poet. It is entirely appropriate too, I suggest, to ask about its relation to the written word. To rule out a possible relationship with writing on the grounds of some supposed absolute quality called "orality" seems totally unjustified, and I would certainly go along with considering the kinds of questions raised by, say, Kirk or Adam Parry (1966) about the possible relation of the Homeric epics to writing, even at the same time as saying they are in some senses "oral."

In an early planning paper for this conference it was asked, "Do we need a looser definition of 'oral'?" To this, in the light of the arguments in this paper, I would answer most definitely "yes." And if we answer "yes" to this then, as the paper goes on, "hope for scientific precision must be left behind." Here again I would agree if by this phrase is implied the attempt to establish scientifically precise generalisations that can be applied to some single category (whether "oral literature," "oral poetry" or even the more specific "oral narrative poetry") *as a whole* or to "oral composition" as a single identifiable process across space and time irrespective of cultural and personal differences. The variations are too wide and too important for such generalisations to be either true or useful.

NOTES

[1] Despite all the emphasis on orality, it emerges that several of the singers recorded were in fact literate (Parry and Lord 1954, p. 54 ff), even though the recordings themselves were selective already, for Parry refused singers he considered not to be "the inheritors of a genuine tradition" on the grounds that he was only concerned with "the poetry as it exists naturally" (p. 13). The underlying unwillingness to accept the literate background of some of these singers comes out in such comments as the grudging "Murat is a good singer despite his book background" (p. 55).

[2] Southern Cross.

REFERENCES

Abrahams, R. D., ed. 1970. *A Singer and Her Songs. Almeda Riddle's Book of Ballads.* Baton Rouge: Louisana State University Press.

Ajayi, J. F. A. 1974. "The Impact of Europe on African Cultures and Values." Unpub. paper at African Studies Association of United Kingdom conference. Liverpool, Sept.

Alexander, M. 1966. *The Earliest English Poems*. Harmondsworth: Penguin.

Andrzejewski, B. W. and I. M. Lewis. 1964. *Somali Poetry*. Oxford: Clarendon Press.

Anyumba, H. O. 1964. "The Nyatiti Lament Songs." *East Africa Past and Present (Présence africaine)*. Paris.

Benson, L. D. 1966. "The Literary Character of Anglo-Saxon Formulaic Poetry." *PMLA*, 81.

Buchan, D. 1972. *The Ballad and the Folk*. London: Routledge and Kegan Paul.

Cassidy, F. G. 1965. "How Free Was the Anglo-Saxon Scop?" in J. B. Bessinger and R. P. Creed, eds. *Medieval and Linguistic Studies*. London: Allen and Unwin.

Chadwick, H. M. and N. K. Chadwick. 1932-1940. *The Growth of Literature*. 3 vols. Cambridge University Press.

Cope, T. 1968. *Izibongo. Zulu Praise Poems*. Oxford: Clarendon Press.

Crosby, R. 1936. "Oral Delivery in the Middle Ages." *Speculum*, 11.

Curschmann, M. 1967. "Oral Poetry in Mediaeval English, French and German Literature: Some Notes on Recent Research." *Speculum*, 42.

Curtis, N. 1907. *The Indians' Book*. New York and London: Harper and Bros.

Deng, F. M. 1973. *The Dinka and Their Songs*. Oxford: Clarendon Press.

Doleželová-Velingerová, M. and J. I. Crump, tr. 1971. *Ballad of the Hidden Dragon (Liu Chih-yüan chu-kung-tiao)*. Oxford: Clarendon Press.

Duggan, J. J. 1973. *The Song of Roland. Formulaic Style and Poetic Craft*. University of California Press.

Finnegan, R. 1967. *Limba Stories and Story-telling*. Oxford: Clarendon Press.

————. 1970. *Oral Literature in Africa*. Oxford: Clarendon Press.

Freuchen, D. 1962. *Peter Freuchen's Book of the Eskimos*. London: Barker.

Greenaway, J. 1953. *American Folk Songs of Protest*. Philadelphia: University of Pennsylvania Press.

Grimble, A. 1957. *Return to the Islands*. London: Murray.

Hadas, M. 1954. *Ancilla to Classical Learning*. New York: Columbia Univ. Press.

Harries, L. 1962. *Swahili Poetry*. Oxford: Clarendon Press.

Hiskett, M. 1964-1965. "The 'Song of Bagauda': A Hausa King List and Homily in Verse." *Bull. School of Oriental and African Studies*, 27-28.

Horovitz, M., ed. 1969. *Children of Albion: Poetry of the "Underground" in Britain*. Harmondsworth: Penguin.

Horton, R. and R. Finnegan, eds. 1973. *Modes of Thought. Essays on Thinking in Western and non-Western Societies*. London: Faber.

Innes, G. 1973. "Stability and Change in Griots' Narration." *African Language Studies*, 14.

Jackson, B. 1972. *Wake Up Dead Man: Afro-American Worksongs from Texas Prisons*. Cambridge: Harvard Univ. Press.

Johnson, J. W. 1971. "The Development of the Genre *heello* in Modern Somali Poetry." Unpub. M.Phil. thesis, University of London.

Jones, A. M. 1943. *African Music*. Rhodes-Livingstone Museum Occasional Paper, 2.

Junod, H. A. 1912-1913. *The Life of a South African Tribe*. 2 vols. Neuchâtel.

Kagame, A. 1951. *La poésie dynastique au Rwanda*. Inst. Royal Colonial Belge, Mémoires, 22. Brussels.

Kirk, G. S. 1965. *Homer and the Epic*. Cambridge Univ. Press.

———. 1966. "Formular Language and Oral Quality." *Yale Classical Studies*, 20.

Knott, E. and G. Murphy. 1967. *Early Irish Literature*. London: Routledge and Kegan Paul.

Laws, G. M. 1957. *American Ballads from British Broadsides*. Philadelphia: American Folklore Society.

Lord, A. B. 1965. "Oral Poetry." In A. Preminger, ed. *Encyclopedia of Poetry and Poetics*. Princeton: Princeton Univ. Press.

———. 1968. *The Singer of Tales*. New York: Atheneum. 1st pub. 1960.

McLuhan, M. 1962. *The Gutenberg Galaxy*. London: Routledge and Kegan Paul.

———. 1969. *Counterblast*. London: Rapp and Whiting.

Magoun, F. P. 1953. "Oral-formulaic Character of Anglo-Saxon Poetry." *Speculum*, 28.

Mumin, Hassan Sheikh. 1974. *Leopard Among Women. Shabeelnaagood. A Somali Play*. London: Oxford University Press.

Nagler, M. N. 1967. "Towards a Generative View of the Oral Formula." *Trans. Am. Philological Assoc.*, 98.

Nichols, S. G. 1961. *Formulaic Diction and Thematic Composition in the Chanson de Roland*. Univ. of North Carolina Press, Studies in the Romance Languages and Literatures, 36.

Notopoulos, J. A. 1964. "Studies in early Greek Oral Poetry." *HSCP*, 68.

Parry, A. 1966. "Have We Homer's Iliad?" *Yale Classical Studies*, 20.

Parry, M. and A. B. Lord. 1954. *Serbocroatian Heroic Songs. I. Novi Pazar: English Translations*. Cambridge and Belgrade: Harvard University Press and Serbian Academy of Science.

Propp, V. 1958. *Morphology of the Folktale*. Eng. trans. Bloomington.

Rasmussen, K. 1931. *The Netsilik Eskimos. Social Life and Spiritual Culture*. Copenhagen: Gyldendalske Boghandel, Nordisk Forlag.

Rogers, H. L. 1966. "The Crypto-Psychological Character of Anglo-Saxon Poetry." *English Studies*, 47.

Rollins, H. 1919. "The Black-letter Broadside Ballad." *PMLA*, 34.

Rosenberg, B. A. 1970. "The Formulaic Quality of Spontaneous Sermons." *J. Am. Folklore*, 83.

Shippey, T. A. 1972. *Old English Verse*. London: Hutchinson.

Scharfe, D. and Y. Aliyu. 1967. "Hausa poetry." In U. Beier, ed. *Introduction to African Literature*. London: Longmans.

Smith, M. G. 1957. "The Social Function and Meaning of Hausa Praise-singing." *Africa*, 27.

Stein, R. A. 1959. *Recherches sur l'épopée et le barde au Tibet*. Paris: Presses universitaires de France.

Tracey, H. T. 1929. "Some Observations on Native Music in Southern Rhodesia." *NADA*, 7.

Watts, A. C. 1969. *The Lyre and the Harp. A Comparative Reconsideration of Oral Tradition in Homer and Old English Epic Poetry*. New Haven and London: Yale Univ. Press.

Werner, A. 1918. "Swahili Poetry." *Bull. School of Oriental Studies*, 1.

Whiteley, W. H. 1958. *The Dialects and Verse of Pemba*. Kampala: East African Swahili Committee.

Wilkinson, R. J. 1924. *Malay Literature*. Kuala Lumpur: FMS Government Press.

The Traditional Phrase:
Theory of Production

Michael N. Nagler

One of the thorniest issues raised by oral-formulaic theory is the matter of aesthetics, for from Milman Parry's first writings onward the question of whether Homer's art was in some way limited or qualified by his formulaic style has arisen again and again. Instead of making an impossible choice between the oral-mechanistic and literary-creative models offered by a highly polemical criticism, Michael Nagler argues for understanding Homer's texts as the individual, spontaneous realization of inherited traditional ideas and impulses. In the section of Spontaneity and Tradition: A Study in the Oral Art of Homer *(1974) reprinted below, he examines the associative pathways of sound and idea that yield "families" of phrases, adducing a generative model that locates traditional meaning in a network of preverbal Gestalts and viewing the actual text and its phraseology as one instance of traditional potential. Nagler's analysis and explanation have been very influential on later work, for his shift of primary emphasis from the repeated lines themselves to their traditional ambience has freed Homeric (and other) specialists from the impasse described above. In later chapters of* Spontaneity and Tradition *he extends the gestalt theory to various kinds*

Reprinted from *Spontaneity and Tradition: A Study in the Oral Art of Homer* (University of California Press, 1974), pp. 1-26.

of narrative patterns, finding as in this section on phraseology that "all is traditional on the generative level, all original on the level of performance."

We may begin our study by reinvestigating a type of resemblance among phrases which afforded Parry some important insights into the production of "new" formulas. He called this resemblance *calembour* and illustrated it with a pair of phrases,

ἀμφήλυθεν ἡδὺς ἀϋτμή   [*Od.* 12.369]
ἀμφήλυθε θῆλυς ἀϋτή   [*Od.* 6.122],

about which he remarked: "ἀμφήλυθε, used to describe the odor of sacrifice as it spreads through the air, is also suitable for the description of a sound that *seems* to fill the air" (Milman Parry, *The Making of Homeric Verse*, ed. Adam Parry (Oxford, 1971) [hereafter *MHV*] p. 72).[1] I have italicized the word "seems" in Parry's sentence because it brings home right at the outset a problem he often spoke of (e.g., *MHV*, pp. 72, 206, 307; cf. Emeneau, *Style and Meaning*, 342), that the phrases produced by the oral poet are designed to convey the ideas of his world view, not of ours: the striking similarity of these two expressions arises from a very similar view of the suffusion of odor and of sound through their respective media. A close study of oral formulas is bound to shed light on Homer's metaphysics, ethics, and morality and provide a valuable complement to the large number of illuminating studies that have dealt with individual words from these points of view. A converse, which will also be encountered continually in this book, is that Homer's world view must always be kept in mind in any attempt to understand his formulaic language.

But Parry's main point, and mine, is that the impression of sameness felt in the juxtaposition of these two phrases rests on combined and possibly interrelated factors of sound and sense. It is difficult to be more specific; and it becomes increasingly difficult the further one looks into the evidence. Parry would surely have felt that the phrases περὶ φρένας ἦλυθ' ἰωή and θείη δέ μιν ἀμφέχυτ' ὀμφή which describe the effects of the "hallo" of Nestor which awakens Odysseus (*Il.* 10.138ff) and the "heard presence" (?) of the divine utterance which awakens Agamemnon (2.41—a much less tangible concept), are related to the pair that first attracted his attention—but how? A simple replacement system, with ἀϋτμή/ἀϋτή/ἰωή/ὀμφή as one item, would not begin to describe the other resemblances one sees in the diction, sense, and phonemic pattern of the four expressions; and the further juxtaposition could be added to confirm the feeling that the whole phrase is involved in the phonemic and other resemblances:[2]

θείη δέ μιν ἀμφέχυτ' ὀμφή   [*Il.* 2.41]
δεινὴ δὲ θεείου γίγνεται ὀδμή   [*Il.* 14.415]

Ought one to go still further and include . . . θῆλυς ἐέρση and βοῶν δ' ὥς γίγνετο φωνή, each of which is connected by contiguity with one of the original pair (respectively, *Od.* 5.467 and 12.396)? If so, one would have a series of seven like-sounding expressions, six of which describe the state of consciousness of a man being literally or figuratively awakened to an important fact by a sensory message arising from that fact in some manner: In *Odyssey* 12 the fatal transgression of Odysseus's men is conveyed by the aroma of the roasting cattle of Helios Hyperion (v. 369), while divine recognition of that grotesque sacrifice is quite explicitly relayed to the men, in turn, by a series of omens which include the bizarre "bellowing" at 396. In Book 6, after the θῆλυς ἐέρση phrase which I shall consider shortly, Odysseus is literally and figuratively awakened to the presence of life on Scheria by the voices of Nausicaa and her maidens. In the above-mentioned passage from the second book of the *Iliad*, a divine message is also personified as "baneful dream" and hypostasized as Nestor (see chapter 4, below), the same person who literally awakens Odysseus in the phrase from Book 10. Finally, the "terrible odor of sulphur" four books later arises from Zeus's thunderbolt in a simile that compares Ajax's felling of Hector to Zeus's headlong destruction of an oak—a sight that strikes men with dread of Zeus's power (14.414ff; cf. 8.135 and *Theog.* 696).

By these criteria one could certainly add two phrases from the battle scenes, juxtaposing each with the expression already gathered, to which it is phonetically most similar:[3]

ἀκούετο λαὸς ἀϋτῆς   [*Il.* 4.331]
ἀμφήλυθε θῆλυς ἀϋτή   [*Od.* 6.122]

ἔκαθεν δέ τε γίγνετ' ἀκουή   [Il. 16.634]
... θεείου γίγνεται ὀδμή   [Il. 14.415]

Of the seven examples I have thus added to Parry's original pair two
have the same commonly found noun-epithet combination after the
bucolic diaresis, while the remaining five share another, but not
unrelated, syntactic pattern.

Curiously enough, Parry (following Ellendt) listed two more like-
sounding final phrases in the context of the same discussion without
attempting to connect them with his original pair. Would he have done
so if he had looked at the whole verses involved, and if he had foreseen
that the "separation" of formulaic components was to become a
recognized mode of generating new phrases by analogy in oral
composition (see Hainsworth, *Flexibility* 80ff; and note 2, above)?:

ἀμφί μ' 'Οδυσσῆος ταλασίφρονος ἵκετ' ἀϋτή
                        [Il. 11.466]
ἔμπης ἐς γαῖάν τε καὶ οὐρανὸν ἵκετ' ἀϋτμή
                        [Il. 14.174]

Thus, if one does not accept all of the criteria which have now been
accumulated for formulaic resemblance, one is faced with the dilemma
of which to accept and reject, a point on which hardly two scholars
today would be in complete agreement; while if one does accept them
all impartially, the resultant formula hunting must quickly lead to
embarrassingly rich and diverse ramifications.

One of the most intriguing of these pathways is suggested by the
last-quoted example above, a description of the rather miraculous
diffusion of the perfume that Hera will soon be using for the
Beguilement of Zeus: All of the persons reached in one way or another
by the "messages" in the above examples are male, while the sense
datum in question sometimes emanates from a female figure and is
always expressed in a grammatically feminine noun. Hardly
enlightening in itself, this fact does pique a certain curiosity in view of
the mild anomaly in the diction that was noticed long ago, that both of
the ἀμφήλυθεν phrases, like Aristonicus's variant reading for the
former (ἀ. θερμὸς ἀϋτμή, and like the Homeric phrases associated in his
mind with his reading (ὀλοώτατος ὀδμή, the stench of the seals at *Od.*
4.442) have a simplex, morphologically masculine adjective modifying
the feminine noun.[4] Perhaps the odd expression θῆλυς ἐέρση at *Od.*

5.467 will become more understandable against this background, for it also has a grammatically masculine adjective modifying a feminine noun (indeed, the adjective means "feminine," and see Onians 177, note 4). Θῆλυς ἐέρση by itself would have the etymological meaning "nourishing moisture," but in the context, Odysseus is expressing his fears that this "feminine dew" may be dangerous, and, as I have mentioned, the phrase seems to be linked with the θῆλυς ἀϋτή of Nausicaa and her followers a hundred or so lines later.[5]

One does not know what to make of this, if anything, but the fact that two of the contexts (*Od.* 5-6 and *Il.* 14) explicitly involve the overcoming of a male figure by a temptress suggests that one might at least suspend judgment as to the role of grammar in what appears to be a highly suggestive associational pattern of sound and sense, having some connection with a mythic tale type.[6] Although the same narrative situation does not obtain in all nine like-sounding phrases, neither does any other specific resemblance I have been able to cite on any level; its lack of regularity is only a matter of degree.

A small group of phrases like this one raises a host of questions, not all of which need apply to oral poetry alone; the diction of premeditated and written works sometimes shows similar associations of sense and even of sound. It is probably the use that he makes of these associative pathways that will distinguish the oral poet—and that perhaps only quantitatively—from the writer.

Let me take a more extensive group of phrases, part of which could be considered a formula system by Parry's definition (*MHV*, p. 275, but see also pp. 17 and 227). This group involves, among other things, an interplay of δῆμος and δημός in the dative case combined with the adjective πίων to realize that portion of the verse falling after the bucolic diaeresis, which Porter would call the C^1 form of the final colon and which I shall refer to, for descriptive purposes, as the adonean clausula.[7] These combinations give end-line phrases such as πίονι δημῷ "(hidden in) rich fat" (*Od.* 17.241) and πίονι δήμῳ "(amid the) flourishing populace" (9 times). Whatever difference the pitch accent may have made in actual pronunciation during an epic performance, few would deny that the overwhelming similarity of rhythm and phonetic sound among these phrases is "formulaic." Yet it is obvious that they do not express one "given essential idea." One may wish to rescue Parry's definition by considering them subsets of formulas in the same system, rather than ten examples of the same formula (and the doubt is itself instructive), but no very positive purpose would be served by such a manoeuver. It has already been demonstrated by a number of writers that the criterion of the same essential idea does not always apply to those phrases, even to those noun-epithet combinations, which are sufficiently similar to be regarded as allomorphs of a single template, whatever one may choose to call it.[8]

While the phrases cited thus far are true noun-epithet combinations, there are other examples with δημός where the adjective is not in the dative case but in the accusative (singular or plural), modifying a noun that occurs earlier in the verse. In these cases, the final δημῷ necessarily stands in quite different syntactic relation to the adjective and to the line as a whole from that seen in *Od.* 17.241:

> ὔμμ' ἐπὶ μηρία κῆε, καλύψας πίονι δημῷ
> [*Od.* 17.241]
> καρπαλίμως δὲ τὰ μῆλα, ταναύποδα, πίονα δημῷ
> [*Od.* 9.464]
> ἔργῳ δ' ἔργον ὄπαζε ταμὼν κρέα πίονα δημῷ
> [*h.Merc.* 120]
> δευτέρῳ αὖ βοῦν θῆκε μέγαν καὶ πίονα δημῷ
> [*Il.* 23.750]

This is a more serious matter than the so-called conjugation of a ready-made formula to fit a different grammatical slot (Hoekstra, *passim*), for it indicates that the oral poet who "knew," consciously or otherwise, that he could produce πίονα δημῷ (δήμῳ) as an adonean clausula, knew in the same way that he could do so with . . . πίονα δημῷ to end a verse with an entirely different periodicity of thought, one in which the adonean portion might not be a self-contained syntactic unit.[9]

Furthermore, there is a strong similarity between the δῆμος phrases and the common θεὸς δ' ὥς τίετο δήμῳ (cf. *MHV* 226ff and Meister 31), especially since the adonean portion of the group is often preceded by ἐν (or ἐνί).[10] Τίετο certainly sounds enough like πίονι for the resemblance to be called formulaic on subjective grounds, but the former is a different part of speech and stands again in a different syntactic relationship to the final word of the verse from the adjective, epithet or not. Πίονι δήμῳ and τίετο δήμῳ, therefore, confront one with a strong resemblance not accounted for by even the broad (or "soft-Parryan") concept of the structural formula. Only the most fundamental criterion for formulaic resemblance remains common to all the present examples—that of the metrical pattern itself; that is, the repeated metrical unit (colon?) in the same position and with the same internal distribution of word end (cf. Russo p. 239, and Hainsworth, *Flexibility*, p. 59f).

But there is no lack of phrases connected in some way with the present group whose resemblances to it pass the boundaries set by even this criterion, in much the same way that ideational boundaries are passed by βοῦν ... πίονα δημῷ (or ἀμφί ... ἵκετ᾽ ἀϋτή, see note 2, above). This can be shown by arranging the following endline phrases as a series, with πίονι δήμῳ as an arbitrary starting point and progressively greater variation in phonological and then in various metrical features:

1. πίονι δήμῳ   [9 times]
2. τίετο δήμῳ   [6 times]
3. ἵκετο δῆμον δήμῳ   [*Od.* 15.238]
4. παντί τε δήμῳ   [twice, cf. *Od.* 8.157)
5. τῷδ᾽ ἐνὶ δήμῳ   [*Od.* 2.317]
6. φαῖν᾽ ἐνὶ δήμῳ   [*Il.* 18.295]
7. Τρώων ἐνὶ δήμῳ   [*Od.* 1.237]
8. ἀλλοδαπῷ ἐνὶ δήμῳ   [*Il.* 19.324]
9. ἀλλογνώτῳ ἐνὶ δήμῳ   [*Od.* 2.366]
10. ἄλλων ἐξίκετο δῆμον δήμῳ [*Il.* 24.481]

Note that by the time one reaches example 4 the disposition of word boundaries has begun to alter; by itself — υ plus enclitic τε is not very different from a single word of the shape — υ υ, but in the series it appears as a transition to examples 5 and 6 in which the inner word end of the pattern is one step more recessive (although ἐνί is like τε in being a semantically "light" or functional word). The crucial step is to example 7, where the phrase itself has outgrown the adonean clausula by two *morae*, for from there it quickly spreads right to the midline caesura, or rather first to within one *mora* and then to the caesura itself:

8. χήτεϊ τοιοῦδ᾽ υἷος· ὁ δ᾽ ἀλλοδαπῷ ἐνὶ δήμῳ [*Il.* 19.324]
9. διογενὴς Ὀδυσεὺς ἀλλογνώτῳ ἐνὶ δήμῳ [*Od.* 2.366]
10. φῶτα κατακτείνας ἄλλων ἐξίκετο δῆμον [*Il.* 24.481]

If any additional caesura is to be sought between the midline and the end of the verse on a basis of word end in examples 8 and 9 it would have to be placed after position 9 (note the absence of correption) which would metrically separate ἐνὶ δήμῳ from the preceding adjective. This was not yet clearly so with the "transitional" examples 4-7 (note elision in 5 and 6).

On the other hand, there are almost uncanny phonemic "corresponsions" between the adonean parts of each of these last three verses and one of the first three phrases:[11]

πίονι δήμῳ	τίετο δήμῳ	ἵκετο δῆμον
-πῷ ἐνὶ δήμῷ	-τῳ ἐνὶ δήμῷ	-ίκετο δῆμον

This fact raises as a rather startling possibility the notion that there may be formulas that are not made up of word groups at all, and, more generally, that considerations other than the present concept of word end may contribute to feelings of rhythmical subdivision within the epic hexameter. At the very least, these corresponsions should suggest the operation of psychological cola or rhythmical groups of some sort bearing a hitherto undetermined relation to formulas and based upon factors that are not always statistically quantifiable, indeed, not readily apparent to those who read the poem as a text.

Whatever may be the larger implications of these observations for metrical theory, it is clear that objective metrical criteria, as now known, will not provide an indispensable *differentia* for every member of the above-mentioned series of phrases. Nor would it be difficult to extend the series by allowing for positional variation ("mobility"— Hainsworth); especially since the "adonic" metrical sequence itself is about evenly distributed between inner parts of the hexameter and verse end (see Kirk, *YCS*, pp. 20, 100):

> πίονα δῆμον ἔχοντες versus example 1
> > [*Il.* 5.710, cf. 15.738, 17.330]
> ἐς δῆμον ἵκηται versus example 3, 10
> > [*Od.* 14.126]
> δήμῳ ἐν ἀλλοδαπῷ versus example 8
> > [*Od.* 8.211, cf. 8.220, 13.266, 24.31]

or for further substitution of one word:

πίονι νηῷ	[*Il.* 2.549]
πίονα ἔργα	[twice]
πίονα μῆλα	[6 times]
πίονες ἀγροί	[*Il.* 23.832]
πίονος αἰγός	[*Il.* 9.207]

or of both:

μήκαδες αἶγες	[twice, 3 times in Acc.]
ἴφια μῆλα	[9 times]

But these points, too, have already been adequately established by Hainsworth and others with regard to these and comparable "formulasystems."[12]

The aggregate of related phrases in the ἀμφήλυθεν group could not be explained by a simple replacement system. There are now many phrases whose mutual variations in length, position, and "separation" further undermine the descriptive adequacy of such a system, and with it the general approach to formulaic composition whereby word is added to prefabricated word, phrase to phrase, and so on, to build up completed verses.[13] The whole issue of meaning aside, some of the phonological and rhythmical patterns encountered in oral verse show that any theory of their production must take into prior consideration some basic linguistic concepts, such as the word boundary, if not, indeed the word.

Before I do this, however, let me consider one further group, to demonstrate that the fluidity of the compositional units one would have to postulate as templates for the first two groups of phrases investigated above is not an exception, but the norm. Here is a series of whole lines giving all the appearances of κρήδεμνον as simplex or adjectival compound in the Homeric corpus:

κρήδεμνον = "veil" [18 times]

ἄντα παρειάων σχομένη λιπαρὰ κρήδεμνα	[4 times]
ἄϊεν ἐξ ἄντρου Ἑκάτη λιπαροκρήδεμνος	[*h.Cer.* 25]
τῇσιν δ' ἐγγύθεν ἦλθ' Ἑκάτη λιπαροκρήδεμνος	[*h.Cer.* 438]
τὴν δ' ὧδε προσέειπε Ῥέη λιπαροκρήδεμνος	[*h.Cer.* 459]
τὴν δὲ ἴδε προμολοῦσα Χάρις λιπαροκρήδεμνος	[*Il.* 18.382]

ἄν κεφαλαῖσιν ἔθεντο θεαὶ λιπαροκρήδεμνοι   [Cypria v. 3]
σῖτον δὲ σφ' ἄλοχοι καλλικρήδεμνοι ἔπεμπον   [Od. 4.623]
σφαίρῃ ταί γ' ἄρα παῖζον, ἀπὸ κρήδεμνα βαλοῦσαι [Od. 6.100]
Ὡς ἄρα φωνήσασα θεὰ κρήδεμνον ἔδωκεν   [Od. 5.351]
τῇ δέ, τόδε κρήδεμνον ὑπὸ στέρνοιο τάνυσσαι   [Od. 5.346]
αὐτίκα δὲ κρήδεμνον ὑπὸ στέρνοιο τάνυσσεν   [Od. 5.373]
καὶ τότε δὴ κρήδεμνον ἀπὸ ἕο λῦσε θεοῖο   [Od. 5.459]
ἀμβροσίαις κρήδεμνα δαίζετο χερσὶ φίλῃσι   [h.Cer. 41]
κρηδέμνῳ δ' ἐφύπερθε καλύψατο δῖα θεάων   [Il. 14.184]
κρήδεμνόν θ', ὅ ῥά οἱ δῶκε χρυσέη 'Αφροδίτη   [Il. 22.470]

κρήδεμνον = "battlement crenelation" [4 times]

ὄφρ' οἷοι Τροίης ἱερὰ κρήδεμνα λύωμεν   [Il. 16.100]
οἷον ὅτε Τροίης λύομεν λιπαρὰ κρήδεμνα   [Od. 13.388]
ᾄσομαι, ἥ πάσης Κύπρου κρήδεμνα λέλογχεν   [h.Ven. 2]
δήμου τε προύχουσιν, ἰδὲ κρήδεμνα πόληος   [h.Cer. 151]

κρήδεμνον = "stopper, seal" [once]

ὤϊξεν ταμίη καὶ ἀπὸ κρήδεμνον ἔλυσε   [Od. 3.392]

This series exhibits striking correspondences of various kinds here
and there among all the examples, despite the fact that the word I have
chosen as an arbitrary control has at least three different denotations.
Again, the resemblances in the series as a whole are accounted for only
partially by the objective criteria thus far advanced for the oral formula.
Metrical criteria are baffled straightaway by the variations in word order
(Il. 6.100, Od. 5.459 vs. Od. 13.388), syntactic and positional criteria
for the "structural formula" by λιπαρὰ κρήδεμνα versus
λιπαροκρήδεμνος, κρήδεμνον . . . τάνυσσαι (imperative) versus
κρήδεμνα βαλοῦσαι (participle), and so forth.[14]
     However, one is justified in feeling that the resemblances among
these expressions, like those of the preceding groups, are more than
coincidental; in other words, that they are groups of something, and the
fact that some of the resemblances answer to the criteria that have
actually been put forward for the formula, while others do not, begins
to look like an accident of present methodology.

Can one account for this subjective feeling of coherence in another way? I believe so, but one must be prepared to sacrifice some of the boundaries and apparent objectivity of the various definitions of the terms "formula," "formulaic," "formula system," etc. in current usage. In fact, it may prove expedient, at least provisionally, to abandon the word "formula," which means different things to different people, in favor of an entirely new concept. A conceptual framework promising to suit the facts with less procrustean anguish than that which has been the basis of study until now is available in the general area of linguistics, in disciplines that have recently been drawn closer to classical philology after an unfortunate period of estrangement. In this framework, a group such as the πίονι δήμῳ (δημῷ) phrases would be considered not a closed "system" classifiable as a subset of a larger system and susceptible of sub-classifications within its own boundaries, but an open-ended "family," and each phrase in the group would be considered an "allomorph"; a derivative not of any other phrase but of some preverbal, mental, but quite real entity underlying all such phrases at a more abstract level.

The open-endedness of the family can be looked at from two points of view. Descriptively, it is open-ended because one may link phrase with phrase until—there being no good reason to stop—one has joined under one head phrases that have no features in common.[15] This is easily illustrated by any number of associative pathways that could lead away from the phrases in the πίονι δήμῳ family:

καλύψας πίονι δημῷ   [*Od.* 17.241]
Ἰθάκης ἐς πίονα δῆμον   [*Od.* 14.329, 19.399]
θεὸς (δ') ὣς τίετο δήμῳ   [6 times]
θεὸν ὣς τιμήσουσι   [3 times]
θεὸν ὣς εἰσορόωσιν   [*Od.* 8.173; cf. *Il.*12.312]

Sometimes these pathways can be made to reconverge, almost at the fancy of the investigator (the following phrases are in final position unless otherwise indicated):[16]

πίονι δήμῳ   ἀλλοδαπῷ ἐνὶ δήμῳ
ἐν πόλει ἄκρῃ   δήμῳ ἐν ἀλλοδαπῷ
[four times]   [*Od.* 8.211]
πῖαρ ὑπ' οὖδας   χώρῳ ἐν οἰοπόλῳ
[*Spontaneity and Tradition*, p. 41]   [twice]

αὐτὰρ ἐν ἄκρῳ   ὄζῳ ἐπ' ἀκροτάτῳ
[*Il.* 5.729]   [*Il.* 2.312]
ὀξὺν ἐπ' ἄκρῳ   ὀξὺ κατ' ἀκροτάτης
[*Od.* 9.382]   [*Il.* 20.52]
                                      ὀξὺν ἐπ' ἄκρῳ
                                        [*Od.* 9.382]

Now, wherever the corpus is not overly large, including that of Homer, it is easy to see how the slightest preconception of the individual investigator could curtail these ramifications and give a controllable, but illusory finitude to the description. One aspect of this illusory neatness has been the inevitable but seldom acknowledged tendency to see a given phrase from the vantage point of only those related phrases which one has already noticed: ὀξὺν ἐπ' ἄκρῳ for example, when stumbled upon by three Homerists working independently has been seen in the context of their respective preoccupations and duly enlisted as an example of three respectively different and in some ways mutually exclusive phenomena.[17] In the description of "formula systems," to say nothing of the attempt to trace their origins, objectivity is easier to call for than to provide.

But I would propose that this open-endedness is not merely a descriptive device, that the family is in fact open-ended because the abstract template that generates its members is not limited in its production of particular phrases but can be realized in more or less similar forms in an endless variety of contexts.

This brings me to the nature of that preverbal template. In the West, where no scholar feels particularly comfortable dealing with the intangible, there does not seem to be a more accurate term for such an entity than "Gestalt." Among certain early Sanskrit grammarians (better called philosophers of language), there was a highly developed theory of meaning, language, and language acquisition built around a similar term of somewhat wider metaphysical implications.[18] The term, *sphoṭa*, is derived from an onomatopoeic root *sphuṭ* "to burst," its application to language being the intuitive perception of meaning which in our idiom also "bursts" upon the mind in some unknown way either spontaneously or when triggered by a linguistic symbol: word, phrase, or sentence. The concept of *sphoṭa* was defined from two points of view, both of which are useful for my purposes: (a) "that from which the meaning bursts forth," "the linguistic sign in its aspect of meaning-bearer" and (b) as an entity which itself is (at least partially) manifested by speech (Raja, p. 98). But any one Gestalt or *sphoṭa* beggars definition, for it is itself undifferentiated with respect to any describable phonological feature. The given word, phrase, or sentence is only a kind of hypostasis of this entity—an allomorph, as I have been using the term—as a particular geometrical shape is a hypostasis of its Platonic Form.

The apparent imprecision and frankly mystical tone of this concept can hardly be welcome in a field where other kinds of imprecision have caused unnecessary diversities of opinion and in a general cultural environment where "mystical" has often a pejorative sense. Yet it is more "mystical," it seems to me, to maintain that an *Iliad* was created with a number of predictable transformations. It is important to realize that one is committed to the existence of unknowns even if one assumes that the poet memorizes and reproduces a fixed formula. What form does the formula take when not being consciously remembered? What is the "organic unity" that some scholars detect in certain fixed combinations of words themselves (cited by Hainsworth, *Flexibility*, p. 90)? And as for the softer Parryists, by the time one has "conjugated," "expanded," "separated," and "displaced" the hapless formula, economy of description alone would seem to indicate that one may just as well "put it out of its misery" (as A. Parry has said in another connection) and frankly accept the concept of an undetermined sphoṭa on a higher ontological or psychological plane than any given phrase. M. Parry and Lord both realized that the creation of oral epic verses is the production of language, like any other "speech act" (as the Behaviorists say), and it is unreasonable to expect a description of such a process without admitting so much as a Lucretian swerve to allow for an indeterminate element, an element of creativity.[19]

An analogous imprecision—that is to say, unwillingness to impose unwarranted precision on a mass of evidence—has by now made its appearance in a number of modern disciplines. It was part of the psychological concept of the archetype propounded by Jung (though often lost sight of by his epigoni), and there is a particularly useful formulation by Wittgenstein in his metaphorical presentation of the concept of "family" resemblance which I have already borrowed:[20]

> And the result of this examination [or activities included under the label "game"] is: we see a complicated network of similarities overlapping and crisscrossing: sometimes overall similarities, sometimes similarities of detail.

67. I can think of no better expression to characterize
these similarities than "family resemblances"; for the various
resemblances between members of a family: build, features,
color of eyes, gait, temperament, etc. etc. overlap and criss-
cross in the same way. . . . And I shall say: "games" form a
family.
     And for instance the kinds of number form a family in the
same way. . . . And we extend our concept of number as in
spinning a thread we twist fibre on fibre. And the strength of
the thread does not reside in the fact that some one fibre runs
through its whole length, but in the overlapping of many
fibres.

The individual fibres of the metaphorical thread would answer to
our objective criteria for formulaic resemblance, which seldom seem to
stretch from one end to the other of a series like πίονι δήμῳ. . .
ἄλλων ἐξίκετο δῆμον or τεῦχε κύνεσσιν. . . δῶκεν ἑταίρῳ. . .
δῶκε φορῆναι (Russo, with additions). From a generative standpoint,
they would correspond to the several features (metrical, lexical,
phonetic, etc.) in which the singer realizes the preverbal Gestalt in the
form appropriate to each moment of utterance; it may be valid
psychology to look upon them also as the "parameters" or particular
features that—separately or in various combinations—make the Gestalt
present to his mind as he performs.

These questions are still highly controversial among modern
linguists; but my main concern, fortunately, is not to probe the
mysteries of speech but only to find a more adequate model with which
to improve our understanding of oral poetics, and particularly Homer.
The grammarian Bhartṛhari devised a fundamentally simple, three-stage
model which will serve that purpose: between the timeless, indefinable
sphoṭa and its actual utterance as a unique series of sounds, differentiated into tone of voice, etc. (the "surface structures" of modern
linguistics) lies an intermediate stage consisting of patterns of
phonological and syntactic norms. These patterns are imperfectly
revealed by individual speech acts, which Bhartṛhari calls vaikṛta dhvani
"altered sound," or "secondary signal," and they could theoretically
reveal in turn the underlying sphoṭa.[21] It is to some such intermediate
stage, which he calls prākṛta dhvani, "natural, primary resonance," that
formula systems, however arbitrary and inadequate, have reference.
Though useful as a guide to the poet's creative processes, these systems

cannot themselves represent his ultimate "mental furniture" (Hainsworth); for if spontaneous-traditional poetry resembles living speech in the dynamics of its creativity, it must share in the indeterminacy and mysteries of speech. But one is not prevented from improving one's understanding of oral poetry; this may be done precisely by examining what lies beneath its surface.

In a field more obviously germane to oral poetry than that of Indian linguistic theory, a great deal of progress has been made with analogous notions of deep and surface structures, namely in the structuralist school of folklore and anthropology. The best known exponents of this view are still Vladimir Propp and Claude Lévi-Strauss, who have described the fluidity of the living mythopoeic process as fresh realizations of a basic structural idea along similar but ever-varying lines, rather than as repeated presentations of finished products, which are copies of earlier finished products accidentally or otherwise altered by their successive recipients.[22] The structural approach has won wide acceptance in its overall outline, but in one respect it seems not suitable to my purposes. Lévi-Strauss himself has referred to the "singularity of myth among other linguistic phenomena. Myth is the part of language where the formula *traduttore, traditore* reaches its lowest truth value" (*Structural Study of Myth*, § 2.5). Unlike our preverbal entity, the structural model of a myth or folktale can, it seems, be completely recovered from a given array of allomorphs. Thus, Cadmus's slaying of the water dragon and Oedipus's defeat of the sphinx are equally allomorphs of the ancient Near Eastern combat myth, twice reused within the Theban cycle to express a pattern that Lévi-Strauss interprets to mean "denial of the autochthonous origin of man" (§ 4.8).

It may be doubted, however, whether the structure and meaning of the myth can be quite this simple. Fontenrose would interpret the same stories as late reflexes of creation myth, with a subpattern something like "culture hero overcomes chaos demon," and other investigators would no doubt prefer other formulas. Here again it seems safest to place the patterns and paraphrasable meanings discovered by shrewd investigators like Propp, Lévi-Strauss, and Fontenrose at a level between the individual tale (*vaikṛta-dhvani*, surface structure) and a more inchoate generative impulse (*sphoṭa, Gestalt ab initio*) of less constrained potentiality.[23]

In part, the difference cited by Lévi-Strauss between the workability of simple schemata for myth texts (to the extent that they really are workable) and the inadequacy of the formula-system model for oral-formulaic phrases may be a function of size—a small pattern can be deduced from a large story more easily than from a phrase, but is such a pattern the more real for that? Indeed, it was among folklorists working with smaller units that some imaginative scholars first saw the need to abandon ironclad definitions where such definitions seemed inappropriate or were simply not attainable. B. H. Bronson, after exhaustive compilations of certain ballad tunes and their variants, expressed this situation with particular clarity in 1954:[24]

> It is moreover to be kept in mind that the folk-memory does not recall by a note-for-note accuracy, as a solo performer memorizes a Beethoven sonata. Rather, it preserves a melodic idea in a state of fluid suspension, as it were, and precipitates that idea into a fresh condensation with each rendition, *even with each new stanza sung*. There is no correct form of the tune from which to depart, or to sustain, but only an infinite series of *positive* realizations of the melodic idea.

All of these precedents from other areas of inquiry do not show that a preverbal Gestalt generating a family of allomorphs must be the best conceptual framework for the Homeric formula, but they do show that the prevailing concept of the fixed and determinable structure, be it superficial (the completed phrase) or relatively deep (e.g., a localized metrical sequence) is not *a priori* the only working model to explain the production of phrases in spontaneous verse composition.

If one would pursue further the generative approach, it would be well to keep in mind that it is necessarily ahistorical, at least in part. While not for a moment denying the process of diachronic change or the power of tradition—quite the contrary—it draws attention to the hitherto neglected aspects of the creative process which are not determined by these factors. I will, however, correlate the theory I have briefly outlined thus far with the three stages in the training of an oral poet which Lord describes in *ST*, chapter 2. As he rightly insists, the aspiring bard does not memorize phrases that he hears from the lips of mature singers. More than this, he does not, properly speaking, memorize prototypes or templates. It is not a question of hearing, e.g., πίονι δήμῳ as verse end, committing the phrase to memory and then simply uttering πίονι δήμῳ whenever it suits the economy of his own systems, nor of deducing adj. υ υ / N –// from such phrases as πίονι δημῷ, ἀργέτι δημῷ etc., and then inventing or substituting to produce, say, πίονι νηῷ; as we have seen, it may not be simple question of phrases at all.[25] Rather, in a more complicated and subtle, because more intuitive way, he takes in many hundreds of lines containing units like βοῦς ἐνὶ νηῷ, . . .πίονι δήμῳ, θεὸς δ' ὣς τίετο δήμῳ, ἀλλοδαπῷ ἐνὶ δήμῳ, δήμῳ ἐν' ἀλλοδαπῷ etc., from all of which he develops an intuitive feel for an underlying Gestalt which is retained in his unconscious mind probably in the same unknown way that the phrasal impulses of any natural language are retained in the mind between their realizations. He then tries to realize that Gestalt at appropriate times and in appropriate ways—i.e., in the appropriate forms of its potential features—in his fledgling attempts at verse-making (Lord's second stage), further securing in his mind his favorite patterns of realization, and in some sense, the Gestalt itself, by actual practice. Eventually (the third stage) he is ready for interaction with a highly critical and highly appreciative audience.

In this process and in whatever developments accrue as his career unfolds, he does not learn any concrete thing so much as he acquires an intuitive habit or method; that is why his own uses of a traditional Gestalt will inevitably differ from those of his teachers and his contemporaries.[26] The singer's acquisition of his professional skill may not be as intuitive as his acquisition of his native language, which psychologists now think can normally occur only once and only in our youth, but it is interesting to observe that the two processes are usually not far removed in time (*ST*, p. 32). To all indications, it is time to experiment with a synchronic view of oral composition, on the rough analogy of a generative grammar of a natural language.

A series of phrases like that which I have arranged from πίονι δήμῳ to ἀλλοδαπῷ ἐνὶ δήμῳ should therefore not be taken to indicate historical development. It is not safe to guess which phrase is "the original form of the formula" even if there is one that shows relatively archaic linguistic features (see below), for the simple reason that no recorded example as such is actually the origin of any other, not even in the analogical sense intended by Parry. Still, a generative viewpoint is not necessarily a non-Parryan one. Parry himself stated, "That moment which criticism must seek to create [is] that instant when the thought of the poet expressed itself in song," and more recently Hainsworth has affirmed the desirability of taking this view, "so far as it can be imagined."[27] Let me try to imagine it then, with the help of the theoretical work on language that has recently become available.

One must begin with the poet's desire to speak.[28] External factors such as the social setting and even monetary rewards may, of course, enter the picture, but motivations like these could never have brought a poem like the *Iliad* into existence by themselves. There is profound meaning to the career of Achilles, a meaning which must have been at least latent in the poet's mind when he began to sing. For this reason an analysis of Homer's language, in the broad sense of the term, should not merely prepare the way for an account of the overall meaning of the poem; it must have such an account, what H. Fränkel called, "*die simple Frage: Was meint der Verfasser?*" (*Wege und Formen*, p. 314), in view at all times. The higher criticism to be attempted in the latter chapters of the present study is thus not an application but a necessary component of my approach to Homer's art.

The first step toward fulfilling the poet's desire to express himself—and here I shall be speaking of these steps as though they follow in chronological succession (cf. Chafe [note 28, below] p. 6) is a search for form. There must be a story of recognizable shape and appropriately meaningful pattern; in the case of the *Iliad*, a pattern which I shall describe in Chapter 5. When a basic story is chosen or devised, closely identified with the *persona* of a particular hero, the poet's next move is to contrive an episode which will get that story under way. All this may be taking place while he is doing his proem and thereby alerting his audience to his selection of a protagonist and a particular aspect of that protagonist's career (see Van Groningen, *Proems*). It makes no essential difference whether or not the poet has done the same story in any number of earlier performances; his reselection and reinterpretation will in a very real sense be equally spontaneous and creative each time.[29]

With the formulation of a fitting dramatic episode in the poet's mind begins the actual composition of verses. Here associations crowd in upon him from all sides: meanings, the senses of particular words, syntactic and phonological echoes, all in the form of the rhythmical impulses that make up the "language" in which he has learned to "think" through his narrative as an epic singer. Every type of association one notices among given phrases in the text may have been, for all we know, a viable mechanism for the formation of parts of the hexameter at the mysterious moment when thought was condensing into art language. It is at this stage that the phrasal Gestalts come into play, as preverbal focal points that help the poet organize his condensation of particular metrical shapes with appropriate semasiological associations. These Gestalts are not generative in the ultimate sense of that word (compare Hainsworth, *Flexibility*, pp. 110, 123, etc.), in fact they are partly limiting: although they can suggest new phrases to the poet, their main usefulness as devices, or speech habits which he has acquired in his early training, must be to guide him through the *embarras de richesse* that the potential infinitude of metrically possible phrases would otherwise present to his mind at every moment of the performance.

Once the story is under way, secondary associations are touched off by the completed phrases that are now being uttered, and these associations summon certain Gestalts back into play and thus lead to the fresh creation of new phrases in resonance with some of the focal centers that have already been used. This process (Ruijgh's "agglomeration") does not differ in kind from that which brought about the very first utterances of the performance, but it does add a dimension of great artistic usefulness.

At the same time, various kinds of local ordering begin to develop within the larger structural pattern that the poet has selected. These structures and substructures of traditional stories apparently exist in the poet's mind as thematic ideas, which bear the same relationship to particular scenes and episodes as do the phrasal templates to completed phrases; indeed, a theme is often realized in the form of a single phrase. Narrative themes, however, usually unfold in such a way as to generate expectations or produce certain tensions in the mind of the singer and his audience. The fulfillment of these expectations becomes another guiding factor during successive moments in the singing of the tale, operating with particular importance at certain structural climaxes and especially as the whole performance nears its end.

This reconstruction is theoretical and highly speculative, but so is any conceptual framework yet in use (acknowledged or not) to account for the observable features of Homer's craft; and this particular reconstruction will leave room for a creative element when compositional units of any size come into discussion. It is not a special theory of oral poetry, but oral poetry might be expected to embody it more clearly than those forms of artistic or ordinary communication that require the interposition of the medium of writing between poet and audience. In its application to oral poetry, this view does more than reveal a basic similarity in the creation of phrase, scene, whole plot, etc.: it gives a comprehensive insight into a still unresolved problem of Homeric unity, by putting a number of smaller Homeric problems in perspective.

For example, noun-epithet combinations are sometimes thought to be inherited by the poet as fixed expressions, differing in this respect from the major part of his diction, and much debate has therefore arisen as to whether he can or cannot use them to express meanings that are apposite to the particular context, either literal denotations or poetically suggestive nuances.[30] To begin with, the fixity of these expressions has been somewhat exaggerated, as is shown by πίονα δημόν alongside βοῦν . . . πίονα δημῷ, λιπαρὰ κρήδεμνα with λιπαροκρήδεμνος, etc. More importantly, however, the problem has gotten out of proportion because sufficient attention has not been paid to the generative side of the picture. The relatively greater regularity of form and metrical location of the noun-epithet combinations is strictly a secondary matter, controlled by considerations that enter the picture prior to the realization of a given instance but after the phrasal impulse is, so to speak, set in motion: these phrases are meant to convey a generic effect, to add a gnomic dimension which counterpoints the exposition of the particular narrative at each moment, and this generic function is realized in their denotative meaning, as it is in their phonetic, syntactic, and metrical features.[31] Noun-epithet combinations are basically, as are all other expressions, produced anew from some inchoate generative impulse each time they appear.

A fortiori, absence of variation among more complex phrases, whole lines, or groups of lines need by no means imply a fixity in the tradition which hampered the poet's creative powers or, for that matter, rendered them unnecessary. The real "variation" is what some contemporary linguists refer to as "transformation"—the obscure process that transmutes preverbal Gestalt into spoken phrase, line, or scene. If I may propose an answer to Hainsworth's searching question, "What exigencies of composition induce modifications?" it is the exigency of composition itself.

Similarly with early and late linguistic features. An archaism like the crusty πολέμοιο γεφύρας (4 times) was in a sense handed down unchanged through generations of singers, but in another sense it was also produced anew each time it was uttered. Its relatively inflexible appearance is again due to a variety of factors, including meter—cf. πολέμου ἀκορήτω (*Il.* 12.335), and similarly ἀνὰ πτολέμοιο γεφύρας (3 times) alongside ὀπιπεύεις πολέμοιο γεφύρας (*Il.* 4.371).[32] In giving the moment of creation its due, one can understand how even an atavism like πολέμοιο γεφύρας was under the poet's artistic control, as has recently been shown to be true of such linguistic features as metrical lengthening.[33] One should exercise caution, then, in suspecting earlier poetry even where one finds a large accumulation of linguistically earlier expressions. To say that a form is early or late by the perfectly valid criteria of Meister, Chantraine, and others means only that it is a form such as would have been produced in a speech context that was early or late. By itself such evidence says nothing further about the poet's mode of composition or his originality, as he was capable of reproducing the forms of other linguistic strata, other dialects, or indeed of no natural stratum or dialect with the same instinctive artistic control that he exercised over every other aspect of his singing.[34]

Most modern attempts to analyze Homer are conceptually akin to the ancient ones and are undertaken because the unity of an oral poem (as well as the unity of the style and the tradition as a whole) is not what readers have been, since Aristotle, conditioned to expect.[35] A generative view will facilitate our reconditioning by placing in a new perspective the dichotomy upon which neo-analysis is based—"traditional versus original." Even when couched in the seemingly scientific terms, "norm versus variant" (often as rather arbitrary designations of statistically frequent and infrequent or unique occurrences),[36] these polarities inevitably strike the modern sensibility as freighted with positive and negative values, which in fact are quite irrelevant.[37]

Most recently these polarities, in the form, "tradition versus innovation," have been applied to some neglected aspects of Homer's use of myth.[38] This work has great value, particularly in revealing the points of articulation of mythic stories with the needs of particular epic narrative situations (cf. *Singer and Tradition*, pp. 123, 158, etc., for the analogous work with traditional themes), but without the generative side of the coin to remind one that the poet was equally in control of all the details of the myth, that they were in fact equally recreated at the moment of singing with the same amount of mythic background and the same element of spontaneity, the distinction between "tradition" and "innovation" can appear disproportionately great. There was no fixed form of the myth from which the oral bards (or, for that matter, the fifth century tragedians) departed, any more than there were fixed phrases or fixed themes. All these existed in the minds of the bearers of the tradition in the abstract form of general ideas, which the poets realized when and in the particular ways in which they needed them, thereby enriching the tradition by making available to it their own associative pathways, their own experiments in usage and meaning. It was Parry's cardinal principle that, "The fame of a [good] singer comes not from quitting the tradition but from putting it to the best use" (*MHV*, 335).

I shall be trying to verify this principle throughout the present study, but it should be clear at the outset that once the oral poet is seen as realizing his own reflexes of the tradition behind him at the moment of his singing, the distinction between traditional and original cannot be simplistically applied at the same level, e.g. to various particular phrases produced in the same performance.

The terms "traditional" and "original" do have a legitimate application in a theory of oral poetics but not as mutually exclusive alternatives. Rather, they describe two poles, perhaps two stages of the same creative process, variously designated as base structure, or Gestalt, and (*vaikṛta*) *dhvani*, surface structure, or realization.[39] Since the former is always traditional and the latter always original in the linguistic process, these terms merely indicate necessary attributes of the successive stages; they are not in the least controversial and need not enter into any discussion of artistic quality. A modern linguist would no doubt put it this way: "All is traditional on the generative level, all original on the level of performance."

NOTES

[1] Parry implied no humorous or other word play behind such resemblances, nor even that one passage was meant to recall the other; rather, the "pun" meant to him an "analogy" of sound which caused the (apparent) imitation when the desire arose to express the same "essential idea." A similar case of phrases related by sense and *calembour* is discussed by Gunn, *Singer and Tradition*, p. 112, and cf. the discussion by Edwards, *Homeric Craftsmanship*, p. 177; to which may now be added G. P. Edwards, *Language of Hesiod*, pp. 74-84.

[2] Cf. in particular θῆλυς and (-)ηλθ(-), the latter linking these phrases with the common end-line phrase with the simplex verb, ἤλυθ'

ἀκωκή, as γίγνεται ὀδμή can be linked with γίγνετ' ἐρωή (twice). "Ἄμπνυτο δὲ θερμὸς ἀϋτμή (*h.Merc.* 110) could be considered an "efferent" version of these phrases with a like-sounding preposition. On the importance of sound patterns in oral poetry generally, cf. Lord, *The Singer of Tales* (Cambridge, Mass., 1960) [hereafter *ST*], pp. 50-57; "Homer as Oral Poet," *HSCP*, 72 (1968), 37, 41; Emeneau, *Style and Meaning*, p. 340; and for progressive "separation" (Hainsworth) of various parts of the phrase, Hes., *Theog.* 696, *Od.* 12.369 (etc.), *Il.* 11.466, and *Od.* 9.210f, 4.442, *h.Merc.* 131f, *h.Cer.* 277 (similarly, *Od.* 9.210 alongside 5.59f). This phenomenon too has been seen in other oral traditions; cf. Robert Creed, in *Old English Poetry* (Providence, 1967), p. 81ff.

[3]Note the noun-epithet phrase at the end of *Il.* 4.328, associated with 4.331 by contiguity ("agglomeration," see below). Both phrases concern the din of battle, the former as a generic idea, the latter as a concrete instance in the narrative. For another group possibly connected with this one (and thus with all our examples) see Hoekstra, p. 122.

[4]So also Aristarchus's reading δεινὸς ἀήτη, *Il.* 15.626, in many ways comparable to the present group. Cf. Ameis-Hentze, *Anhang* on *Od.* 12.369; West on *Theog.* 406 and 696. Whatever the true reading is for *Od.* 12.369, Ameis-Hentze's judgment that θερμός is more apposite than ἡδύς is not cogent: only in the latter adjective is there a suggestion of the temptation of Odysseus, so much a part of these scenes. There is positive temptation here, in both instances from the Scheria episode, and the Dios Apate (*Il.* 14.174), along with negative temptation (to flee an unpleasant odor) at *Od.* 4.442; but the decisive parallels are *h.Merc.* 110, 131f, 137.

[5]'Εέρση, like its Sanskrit cognate *varsa* is not just material "dew" but an aspect of the life force, or principle of fertility (cf. *Od.* 14.245, and *Il.* 23.598, 24.419 with Onians 254). It (or she) later became Διὸς θυγάτηρ, see Usener, 138, and compare Aesch., *Ag.* 141. The scholia connect θῆλος ἐέρση with πολὺς ὑγρά and πουλὺν ἐφ' ὑγρὴν (ostensibly only for the grammatical reason; cf. Eustathius on *Od.* 4.709, 5.467, 6.122). On the meaning of θῆλυς see Chantraine, *Dictionnaire étymologique* s.v. θηλή.

[6]This connection is now made more likely by William F. Hansen, *The Conference Sequence: Patterned Narration and Narrative Inconsistency in the* Odyssey, *UCPCS*, 8 (1972), 22f.

[7]I mean to imply nothing here about the "ethical" value of the terms "adonean," or even "clausula"; cf. H. N. Porter, "The Greek Hexameter," *YCS*, 12 (1951), 13. (In Fränkel's original scheme this is the C_2 break, cf. *Wege und Formen*, p. 104). The phrases in question are sometimes preceded by enclitic ἐνι or ἐν, sometimes by metrically and semantically

"heavier" words, so that the adonean portion as such can vary in its
syntactical independence from the rest of the verse. The question of a
greater metrical fixity at the end of the verse is of some relevance here
(see below, n. 12) but most of the phrases in this group can also occur
in other positions. As this goes to press, a discussion of the original
form in which these arguments were published has appeared: W.
Ingalls, "Another Dimension of the Homeric Formula," *Phoenix*, 26 (1972), 111-
122.

[8]See W. Whallon. "The Homeric Epithets," *YCS*, 17 (1961), 95-142,
Hoekstra, 13, discussed by W. B. Stanford in *Hermathena*, 103 (1966),
89-90. On puns, and on sound without sense as a formulaic element, see
Style and Meaning, pp. 335-340.

[9]Note that there is punctuation before the adonean clausula in only
the second of these examples. Hainsworth (*Flexibility*, pp. 79, 81, 94f)
treats *Od.* 9.464 in the context of a different discussion and considers it a
"separation" and "expansion" of μῆλα πίονα (cf. *Od.* 24.66 cited on his
p. 95). There is no *a priori* reason not to go on to word groups like . . .
βοῦν . . ./πίονα πενταέτηρον . . .(*Il.* 2.420f). Another striking set
would be *Il.* 1.40, 15.373, *Od.* 4.764, against *Od.* 9.217 (note
anastrophe of the preposition). *Od.* 23.311 and *Il.* 18.541 vs. *h.Apol.*
250=290 is also helpful, and a juxtaposition of *Od.* 14.419 and *Il.* 5.710
with the above will raise doubts as to what is the "atomic" unit of these
formulaic "molecules," μάλα πίονα or πίονα δῆμον (note further the
assonance of μάλα with μῆλα). Obviously, as Hainsworth says
(*Flexibility*, 50) we need to explore further the patterning of Homeric
syntax generally, in the directions initiated by Parry, Kirk, and Edwards,
before answering these questions; cf. respectively, *MHV*, pp. 251-265;
YCS, 20 (1966), 76-152; and *Homeric Craftsmanship*.

[10]Ὥς and ἐν(ί) may both be considered semantically "light," which
would lead us to the metrically longer ἀπόπροθι πίονα οἶκον, which
makes the phrase the same length as the θεὸς δ' ὥς group (*Od.* 9.35; and
see the beginning of n. 36 for the list below). G. P. Edwards has
evidence confirming this association (*Language of Hesiod*, p. 78f). The
traditional (Alexandrian) classification of the parts of speech is not very
apposite for Homeric usage in general or formulaic patterns in particular:
cf. Joseph A. Russo, "The Structural Formula in Homeric Verse," *YCS*, 20
(1966), 230, n. 25, and *Language of Hesiod*, p. 128. Modern linguistics
has developed simpler systems which would probably prove more
workable for investigating the "structural formula."

[11]The term was used by Mezger and Bury for Pindar. This particular
kind of corresponsion of vocalic and consonantal patterns is in fact
present to some degree among all our examples and in the δημός group
as well; ἀργέτι δημῷ, δίπλακι δημῷ (*Il.* 11.818, 23.243), etc. Cf. also

ταναύποδα πίονα δήμῳ with ταμὼν κρέα πίονα δημῷ. Κρατερῷ ἐνὶ δεσμῷ also applies (*Il.* 5.386 and *Theog*. 618); much of this corresponsion is morphemic and a natural outcome of syntactic patterning, but that does not mean it should be excluded from an account of formulaic resemblances; cf. ἀμειλίκτων ὑπὸ δεσμῶν (*Theog.* 659). Further examples are in Gunn, *Singer and Tradition*, p. 112; Meister, p. 30 (with *Il.* 18.20, 208, 9.12, *Od*. 18.52, etc.), and Hainsworth, *Flexibility*, p. 51; many of the patterns cited ignore word boundaries.

[12]See Hainsworth, "Structure and Content in Epic Formulae: the Question of the Unique Expression," *CQ,* 14 (1964), esp. 160; see also Hoekstra, p. 13, on this series in particular, and Schmidt's introduction to the *Parallel-Homer* (Göttingen, 1885), pp. 5-7, on alternation in word order of binary phrases in general. It has recently been claimed that word order can be a syntactic factor (syntagma) even in adjective-noun combinations; cf. Haiim B. Rosén, *Strukturalgrammatische Beiträge zum Verständnis Homers* (Amsterdam, 1967), p. 31 (reviewed by Ruijgh in *Mnemosyne*, 4 [1968], 113-131).

[13]This theory was current in the early stage of research on oral-formulaic problems; see James A. Notopoulos, "Studies in Early Greek Oral Poetry," *HSCP*, 68 (1964), 50. It is still in evidence probably because the vocabulary still used in Homeric studies implies that every "modification" of a formula or theme is a conscious act (e.g. Gunn, *Narrative Inconsistency*, 203). Against this we have Lord, *ST*, pp. 24, 36, etc.; Anne Amory in *YCS*, 20 (p. 38), and now in *CQ*, new ser. 21 (1971), 10, G. P. Edwards (*loc. cit.* n. 1, above), a growing awareness of the role of associations like Ruijgh's concept of "agglomeration" (cf. Hainsworth, *Flexibility*, pp. 14, 126 *et passim*; *Homer*, p. 31 and n. 3) and the influence of modern linguistics in general. In the present chapter the accepted terms for the various kinds of formulaic "modification" will be kept in quotation marks because they are entirely acceptable as descriptions but questionable as designations of real psychological (or psycholinguistic) transformations.

[14]Further examples: *Il.* 14.214f, 219f, esp. with *Od*. 5.346; θεοείκελ' Ἀχιλλεῦ (twice) vs. θεοῖς ἐπιείκελ' Ἀχιλλεῦ (5 times), λᾶαν ἀείρας vs. τῶν ἐν ἀείρας, etc., and cf. Hainsworth, *Flexibility*, p. 33, n. 1. Modern editors vary in the ascription of word boundaries to the common διι—φιλος.

[15]Provided the extant corpus is large enough, the chain of associations can go on indefinitely, as is implied by Hainsworth's remark that the (binary word) formula is "a system consisting entirely of variables" (see n. 12 above; but I owe this observation to my studies with Professor Bundy).

308   Michael N. Nagler

¹⁶Cf. also ἀγροῦ ἐπ' ἐσχατίην (Od. 4.517) alongside ἄκρον ἐπ'
ἀνθερίκων (Il. 20.227) for the case relations, ἵξετ' ἄχος κραδίην (Il.
23.47) for entirely different syntax. An "agglomerated" series of phrases
from this family seems to be touched off in Iliad 20 by the realization at
line 52 followed by a pair at 225 and 229, describing the supernatural
lightfootedness of the horses of Erichthonius (a "formulaic" idea—cf. Il.
13.beg.): 328, 368, 385, 392, 395. Line 385 shows, by its closely
repeated syntactic pattern, another sort of connection between both
families: Τμώλῳ ὕπο νιφόεντι, Ὕδης ἐν πίονι δήμῳ, and so forth.

¹⁷As cause of "runover" expression by Edwards (Homeric
Craftsmanship, p. 128), as an example of "separation" of a binary
formula by Hainsworth (Flexibility, p. 103 and n. 2), and as a use of the
same phrase templates by epic and lyric poets, in this case Sappho fr.
105 (Lobel and Page), by myself ("Oral Poetry and the Question of Originality in Literature," Proceedings of the Vth Congress of the
International Comparative Literature Association [Belgrade, 1967], p.
453f). For another branch of related phrases, see Il. 17.54, 677 (both
halves of the verse): 18.320, and, for another example of different
accounts of the same phrases, n. 3, above (myself and Hoekstra).

¹⁸The main exposition is Bhartṛhari's Vākyapadīya, tr. by K. A. S.
Iyer (Poona, 1965) and by Madeleine Biardeau (V ākyapadīya Brah-
makāṇḍa, Paris, 1964); see also Maṇḍana Miśra's sphoṭasiddhi, tr.
Biardeau (Pondichery, 1958) and Iyer (Poona, 1966). Very helpful studies
are by Kunjunni Raja (Indian Theories of Meaning) and J. Brough, "Some
Indian Theories of Meaning," TPS (1953), 161-176. Raja confirms my
feeling that the sphoṭa, is very like a "Gestalt ab initio" (Raja, p. 135).
I am grateful to my colleague Professor Barend A. Van Nooten for
guiding me in this difficult study, and to the American Council of Learned
Societies for making it possible for me to pursue them.

¹⁹According to the theory of sphoṭa, "the distinction between
'formulae' and 'free expressions' is not . . . clear-cut" (Brough, op. cit.
supra, p. 168). The linguists of Ancient India (at least, Patañjali and
Bhartṛhari) are if anything more emphatic than modern transformational
grammarians on the question of creativity, as they begin with the
indeterminate factors in the recognition of a single word, let alone of
"syntactic structures" (cf. Chomsky's book of that name [The Hague],
1962), though they probably would not have agreed with Professor
Chomsky that, "One cannot hope to determine either the underlying
abstract forms or the processes that relate them to signals by
introspection"; Language and Mind (New York, 1968), p. 36; compare
Raja, p. 125f.

On the other hand, Emeneau has argued that his Toda corpus is not
open ended; see Style and Meaning, esp. p. 328.

[20]Cf. C. G. Jung, *Four Archetypes*, in Vol. 9, i, of the *Collected Works* (Princeton 1969), p. 13, and L. Wittgenstein, *Philosophical Investigations*, tr. G. E. M. Anscome (New York, 1964), p. 32; Bhartṛhari also uses the analogy of kinds of number to words (Sutra 1: 87). Emeneau refers to "open-ended classes" (*Style and Meaning*, p. 328) rather than "families," which is descriptively more cautious, but I shall venture to stick to the latter term in what follows.

[21]One can deduce what a word must be from hearing it a sufficient number of times (a process which must make up at least a part of normal language acquisition) but one cannot sensuously hear the word itself as *prākṛta dhvani*, much less as *sphoṭa*, for the latter is eternal and partless, manifested in time but not affected by time; see Raja, p. 120, Brough, "Theories of General Linguistics in the Sanskrit Grammarians," *TPS* (1951), 34f.

[22]Vladimir Propp, *Morphology of the Folktale*; Claude Lévi-Strauss, "The Structural Study of Myth," *JAF*, 68 (1955), 428-444, reprinted in *Myth: A Symposium*, ed. Thomas A. Sebeok (Bloomington, 1955). Cf. also Lévi-Strauss's extended review of Propp, "L'Analyse morphologique des contes russes," in *International Journal of Slavic Linguistics,* 3 (1960), 122-147; Alan Dundes, *The Study of Folklore* (Englewood Cliffs, N.J., 1965); and, for some discussion of Parry's contribution to these developments, Richard Dorson, "Current Folklore Theories," *Current Anthropology,* 19 (1963), 109. A recent expression of the point just mentioned will be found in Bremond, p. 76.

[23]Cf. *Python*, pp. 306-320. The list of themes and common allomorphs given in the introduction to *Python* (pp. 9-11) is not meant to represent a historical prototype of the combat myth or a comprehensive, closed list of its potentialities but an abstract representation of its general pattern on this intermediate level. More recent writings by Lévi-Strauss, too, have developed more open-ended interpretations than the extracts given above; cf. *Les mythologiques*, esp. *Le cru et le cuit* (Paris, 1964).

[24]"The Morphology of Ballad Tunes," *JAF*, 67 (1954), 5-6 (italics added); cf. the work mentioned in *Wege und Formen*, p. 153f. It is appropriate that Eric Havelock (*Preface to Plato* [Cambridge, Mass., 1963], p. 147 has cited the improvisatory methods of jazz as a parallel to Greek oral composition, just as Robert Stevick has for Anglo-Saxon, "The Oral-Formulaic Analyses of Old English Verse," *Speculum*, 37 (1962), 382-389. Lest the analogy be discounted on the grounds of artistic quality, as that of the South-Slavic songs often is, I draw attention to the classical music of India, which is still very largely improvisatory.

[25] See above, p. 287f. One is not justified in assuming, from the existence of a repeated word group in these texts, that the oral poet, "naturally thinks of this formulaic word association in its most familiar form, and this form we may call the primary shape of the formula." (Hainsworth, *Flexibility*, p. 61). This assumption inevitably leads to what I consider the fallacy of "norm vs. variant" (see below).

[26] See *ST*, pp. 63-65, and West, p. 78f. "It may truthfully be said that the singer imitates the techniques of composition of his master or masters rather than particular songs." (*ST*, p. 24). This is amply confirmed by Gunn, who finds that, "There seems to be no *necessary* relation in terms of linguistic expression between the themes of singers, one of whom has probably learned his song (or even, possibly, to sing) from the other." (Gunn, *Singer and Tradition*, p. 88). Lord, Amory, and now G. P. Edwards agree that the process of acquisition must be partly unconscious; on the *sphoṭa* theory of acquisition, see Raja, p. 125f.

[27] Respectively, *MHV*, p. 441, and *Flexibility*, p. 123. However, Hainsworth still has reservations about the generative view put forward here (see *Homer*, p. 25), and his own use of the term in *Flexibility* denotes production of one phrase from another.

[28] The technical term for this in Sanskrit was *vivakṣa*, literally "desire to speak." For the same emphasis in a contemporary setting see Wallace L. Chafe, "Directionality and Paraphrase," *Language*, 47 (1971), 1-26. Many a modern discussion of philological problems in Homer has gone astray precisely because the poet's intention was left out of account (for one example, see my review of Dihle in *CW* [1971], 131f, and Chapter 5, below). Note that the usual term for "meaning" among Sanskrit grammarians was *artha*, lit. "purpose."

[29] This is not to say that the poet cannot improve his interpretation of a particular song (i.e., a particular whole plot associated with a particular hero) each time he performs it, until his artistic "purpose" has been realized with that particular piece and boredom induces him to leave it aside. But for the oral poet it is more important that each performance of any song will improve his ability to interpret any other. I hope that these remarks will help to reconcile to the concept of an oral poet those who still feel that this term implies an "illiterate improviser"; cf. Douglas Young, "Never Blotted a Line? Formula and Premeditation in Homer and Hesiod," *Arion*, 6 (1967), 279-324.

[30] For some representative studies, see Whallon, *loc. cit.* (n. 8, above); Alfred C. Schlesinger, "Penelope's Hand," *CPh.*, 64 (1969), 236 f; and Jean Humbert's (Budé) edition of the Homeric Hymns (Paris, 1959), p. 22. Hainsworth makes clear that there are difficulties even in defining a noun-epithet formula (*Flexibility*, p. 43f). For what follows, see Brough, *op. cit.* (n. 21, above), p. 19.

[31]A good example is the use of φιλομμειδὴς 'Αφροδίτη at *Il.* 5.375 to counterpoint the unusual particular situation in which the goddess is very much "out of character," cf. 331-333, 350f, 428-430. Note in the same passage, incidentally, a generic epithet used with the particularly apposite force (as opposed to the literal illogicality of φιλομμειδής) to bring out the same contrast: μελαίνετο δὲ χρόα καλόν (354).

[32]See Chantraine, *Grammaire homèriqúe,* I, pp. 165, 194; Meister, *passim*; and on this expression in particular, D. L. Page, *History and the Homeric Iliad* (Berkeley and Los Angeles, 1959), p. 243. The repeated use of πολέμοιο in the *Batrachomyomachia*, on the other hand, since the poet self-consciously insists that he is writing (1.3), must be more conscious archaism than spontaneous recreation; see lines 123, 134, and 201 for this metrical position. This view of early and late language is taken to some extent by Dihle (see *Homer-Probleme*, p. 7) and is well expressed by Dodds in Platnauer, ed., *Fifty Years of Classical Scholarship* (Oxford, 1954), p. 22: "The present writer was inclined to regard the different linguistic ingredients as so many colors on the palette of the artist; the history of the pigments, it might be argued, has little relevance for the critic concerned with the design and composition of picture." A mixture of old and new is typical of oral and/or heroic poetry; see Lee M. Hollander, *The Skalds* (Ann Arbor, 1968), p. 19f, and, for an interesting theory on the subject, W. F. Jackson Knight, *Many-Minded Homer* (London, 1968), p. 126.

[33]See William F. Wyatt, *Metrical Lengthening in Homer* (Rome, 1969), esp. p. 242f.

[34]See n. 33. On dialectal *Mischwesen* in epic, see Chantraine, *Grammaire homèrique* I, pp. 495-513, and Ruijgh, *Etudes sur la grammaire et le vocabulaire du grec mycénien* (Amsterdam, 1967), pp. 39-41. This is not to deny that archaic forms are sometimes used less flexibly by the poet, as Ruijgh has shown (in *L'Element Achéen*) for αὐτάρ/ἀτάρ. But the statistical importance of assumed "traditional" and "innovating" usages in such cases has often been exaggerated (put *Il.* 7.94, for example, alongside the sparse examples adduced by Hoekstra, pp. 38-41; cf. *Homeric Craftsmanship*, p. 75) and in any case the principle of Dodds and others still holds: less flexible usage may even be part of the poet's desire for an archaic tone.

[35]This problem has been brought out, and somewhat alleviated, during this century by work on linguistic and conceptual parataxis in early Greek; for bibliography, see B. A. Van Groningen, *La Composition littéraire archaïque grecque* (Amsterdam, 1958).

[36]I take this opportunity to thank Professors McLeod and Dihle for bringing to my attention impressive lists of phrases in which only one example varies from the "normal" usage in some feature or other, along

the lines of the 30:1 split shown by Parry with the phrases νεφεληγερέτα Ζεύς vs. στεροπηγερέτα Ζεύς (*MHV*, p. 277, cf. 15 and Gunn, *Singer and Tradition*, p. 92). In interpreting such evidence, however, one must bear in mind the following: (1) fixity of (habitual) usage does not necessarily imply a fixity of the underlying entity and consequent constraint upon the poet, as I have shown above (and cf. Hainsworth, *Flexibility*, p. 111); (2) lists of this type arbitrarily select certain features of the phrase; Hainsworth, for example, correctly lists θηλὺς ἀϋτή and ἡδὺς ἀϋτμή as "unique expressions" with regard to their metrical shape and position (*ibid.*, p. 132), but the poet thought of them, as I have shown in the first part of this chapter, as potentialities within a much larger and more subtle framework; (3) a scientific assessment of such statistics would involve the more abstract operation of comparing such lists with other lists showing a 29:2 split, and so on; cf. *MHV*, p. 234, and the balanced discussion by Hainsworth in *Flexibility*, p. 69. It is hard to know what sized sample is really significant; Rainer Spiecker's 3:1, in "Die Beschreibung des Olympos (Hom. *Od.* 6.41-47)," *Hermes*, 97 (1969), 140, is surely a bit thin.

[37]The subjectivity of these values is seen most clearly in the fact that they can be used to argue in opposite directions: some feel that the "traditional" stuff alone was of high quality, others that the tradition consisted of ossified clichés against which the "original" genius of the (of "our") poet struggled to get free. Davison gives a good account of the former, romantic, persuasion in Wace and Stubbings, p. 250; and cf. *MHV*, p. 237f, where Parry gives a valid example which may have helped keep the fashion alive; the latter is an outgrowth of modern literary attitudes and is hence slightly more common.

[38]See L. L. Willcock, "Mythological Paradeigma in the *Iliad*," *CQ*, N. S. 14 (1964), 141-154; Julia Haig Gaisser, "Adaptation of Traditional Material in the Glaucus-Diomedes Episode," *TAPA*, 100 (1969), 165-176; Bruce Karl Braswell, "Mythological Innovation in the *Iliad*," *CQ*, N. S. 21 (1971), 16-27; and in a somewhat different vein, Seth L. Schein, "Odysseus and Polyphemus in the *Odyssey*," *GRBS*, 11 (1970), 73-83. These scholars are, of course, not analysts, in the original sense of the term.

[39]The concept of *sphota* is located so deep in consciousness by the Indian grammarians that one cannot properly speak of it as pertaining to, or even affected by, a particular cultural tradition.

Oral-Formulaic Context:
Implications for the Comparative Criticism
of Mediaeval Texts

Alain Renoir

In the application of oral-formulaic theory to medieval studies, where almost exclusive attention has been paid to matters of structure and morphology, formula density, provenance, and the like, the contribution of Alain Renoir has been the exception. In a great many of his numerous studies, most recently A Key to Old Poems: The Oral-Formulaic Approach to the Interpretation of West-Germanic Verse *(1988), Renoir seeks to illuminate the aesthetic implications of oral traditional structure, to ask what difference formulaic and thematic patterns make in understanding the art of medieval poetry. In this seminal essay, he explores the issue of context: by identifying and analyzing the "theme of the singer" in the ancient Greek* Odyssey, *the Anglo-Saxon* Beowulf, *and the Old High German* Hildebrandslied, *he shows how to substitute for the lack of the usual historical context by invoking a relationship through oral traditional structure. This kind of process enables aesthetic criticism by providing "a flexible but* specific *context whose integrity is readily ascertainable and against which we*

Reprinted from *Oral Traditional Literature: A Festschrift for Albert Bates Lord,* ed. by John Miles Foley (Columbus, Ohio: Slavica, 1981), pp. 416-439.

*may in turn measure the integrity of a given text." In short, Renoir's
method widens our perspective from the individual text to the
background tradition that is every text's natural context and sheds
important new light on the problematic works of the ancient and
medieval periods.*

If one may paraphrase Jane Austen, it is a truth universally
acknowledged that the professional scholar who wishes to carry on with
his trade in relative comfort had better be thought willfully wrongheaded
than innocently blind. In this light, the most elementary caution urges
me to proclaim here and now my full awareness of the fact that anyone
who includes the terms *oral-formulaic, context, criticism,* and *text* in
the same title is off to a bad start.

Every American teacher of literature today knows that it has been
almost ten years since Stanley E. Fish demonstrated to the apparent
satisfaction of the world that "the objectivity of the text is an
illusion."[1] In the intervening years, the erstwhile function of criticism
as a tool to help a given audience understand and evaluate a given text
has become as uncertain as the objectivity of the text. At any rate, we
may surely be permitted this assumption when we hear one of the very
most respected formulators of our current critical canons praise an
equally respected practitioner for being both incoherent and subjective. I
am referring to Geoffrey H. Hartman's introductory eulogy of Harold
Bloom's work as "this dense, eloquent, and experiential brooding,"[2] and
I am not the only one to suspect that the respective activities of
Hartman and Bloom—as well as those of their colleagues in New
Haven and of the French structuralists whose names constantly crop up
on their pages—are doing yeoman's service to disconnect criticism from
individual works of literature and establish it as a totally independent
literary genre.[3] Nor does Hartman prove much more encouraging about
the integrity of the context within which a work of literature may be
understood, since he assures us that interpretation "implies . . . that a
work has become detached from its original context or that criticism
helps detach (decontextualize) it. . . ."[4] In other words, the models from
whom rapidly multiplying numbers of young teachers of literature are
taking their cue have decided that the text is in the reader's mind,
criticism is an ineffable experience, and the context changes with the
critic's intended audience, location, and time. Indeed, as Robert

DeMaria, Jr., has recently pointed out, current criticism is increasingly practiced "to the exclusion, and even the avowed extinction, of authors and literary objects."[5] Carried to its logical and no longer very remote extreme, this trend must perforce reduce any critical discussion of literature to the informatory level of a conversation with Humpty Dumpty.

Perhaps because my own trade as a student of the early Germanic Middle Ages requires constant attention to both text and context and perhaps also because my training has conditioned me to read literature for its own sake and turn to criticism only when some aspect of literature or its history seems in need of clarification, I find myself somewhat less than thrilled with the prospects of the situation outlined here. I should be both dishonest and unfair, however, if I failed to acknowledge my chagrined realization that the trend to which I object constitutes a logical response to a historical development and that the unquestionably brilliant manifestations which grate most harshly against my sensitivities are perfectly legitimate solutions to a very real problem. At a time when the explosive growth of communication and dissemination has caused such a proliferation of important texts available in any one location that no single human being may hope to read more than an infinitesimal portion of them, the critic attempting to discuss either a general phenomenon or a broad area of literature has only two choices: one is rigorous selectivity based on clearly stated principles (but democracy in its twentieth-century manifestation does not exactly encourage selectivity) and the other is pure theory independent from the chronological and geographic shackles of individual texts (and this method offers the obvious advantage of appealing to a society which agrees with Henry Ford that history is bunk and has convinced itself that theory will always come to the rescue in the nick of time to solve our problems). The rejection of an objective context may be explained on similar grounds, and professional mediaevalists should be especially attuned to the process, since they must often work with texts whose time, place, and original language of composition have thus far defied identification. As for the integrity of the text, anyone who has ever glanced at Fredson Bower's *Textual and Literary Criticism* knows only too well that even the most elementary physical features of a modern printed page are open to question;[6] and the scholar who examines two different editions of the same mediaeval text will not seldom find discrepancies serious enough to warrant mutually exclusive interpretations.

In different respects and from a different point of view, the term *oral-formulaic* is almost as slippery as the other terms in my title. A few decades ago—say, after the pioneering views which Milman Parry had published in 1928, 1930, and 1932 had been substantiated by Albert B. Lord in 1938 and applied to a new context by Francis Peabody Magoun, Jr., in 1953[7]—it referred to the recurrence of certain verbal, syntactic, and metrical patterns whose high density in a poetic text was supposedly indicative of oral composition and whose formal study was almost exclusively the property of scholars concerned with Archaic Greek, South Slavic, and Old English traditional poetry. Today, however, things are no longer so clearcut. Primarily as a result of the formidable impact of Lord's *The Singer of Tales*—whose first hard-cover edition appeared in 1960 and whose seventh paperback reprint was published in 1976—constant and energetic research has both deepened and broadened our understanding of the nature and mechanics of metrical formulas as well as of such larger oral-formulaic units as the song and the theme or type-scene; and Haymes' *Bibliography of the Oral Theory* shows that the study has been extended to materials composed in some twenty different languages whose geography circles the entire globe.

Since 1973, for example, Joseph J. Duggan has drawn upon the theory and facts of oral-formulaic composition in order to solve previously insoluble problems in the *Song of Roland* and has modified our concept of oral-formulaic composition in the process;[8] Ching-Hsien Wang has found in Chinese poetry "clear characteristics and abundant traces of composition by themes, to an extent comparable in technique to classical Greek and Old English poetry";[9] Michael N. Nagler has examined oral-formulaic patterns in Homer as "an expression of the poet's conscious or unconscious purpose, . . . part of his 'semiotic system'";[10] John Miles Foley has used computer analysis to show that "we may have to revise our thinking about 'mistakes' and 'inconsistencies'"[11] in texts of oral-formulaic origin; Gregory Nagy has shown the relative importance of both synchronic and diachronic approaches "for solving the problem of formula and meter in the study of oral poetry";[12] Jeff Opland has drawn upon his field work among Xhosa tribal singers to define the relationship between "general improvising, memorizing, the refined improvising of the *imbongi*, and writing";[13] and the list of brilliant contributions could be extended almost at will. The price of this intense activity and quasi-geometric increase in scope and knowledge is that the meaning of the term *oral-formulaic* and its relationship to oral composition are no longer certain. A few years before the publication of the investigations listed here, Walter J. Ong had already argued the presence of legitimately oral-formulaic elements in Renaissance prose composed in writing for the printing press,[14] and at the opposite end of the spectrum of scholarly convictions Larry D. Benson had argued with equal authority that certain poems with a particularly high density of oral-formulaic elements could not possibly have been the product of oral-formulaic composition.[15] The situation as it now stands has been neatly summed up by Donald K. Fry in respect to Old English: ". . . a consensus seems to be emerging that written Old English poetry used oral forms, but no reliable test can differentiate written from oral poems."[16] In other words, the term *oral-formulaic* may now be used by different scholars to refer to different degrees of orality.[17]

Since I have almost conclusively demonstrated that my proposed subject does not exist, I suppose that I should bring my discussion to an end right here. But then, as I shall try to show in the remainder of my discussion, I see no reason to disagree with Lord's recent statement that "the increase in the last few years in the number of studies of oral literature is very encouraging."[18] Not only, once again in Lord's words, are we "learning about many aspects of this phenomenon in many hitherto either unexplored or inadequately described traditions" ("Perspectives," p. 24), but the very multiplicity of directions taken by this new learning enables us to draw upon the theories of oral-formulaists in order to examine aspects of literature whose formal study would have been assigned to totally different bailiwicks in the days when the concerns of oral-formulaic investigation were limited to inquiries into the mode of composition of certain poems and the description of certain techniques. For mediaevalists reluctant to reject the ideal of possible textual and contextual integrity—especially for those engaged in the critical study of literature from a comparative point of view—I believe that certain aspects of oral-formulaic composition may occasionally prove workable substitutes for, or additions to, the often hypothetical and increasingly discredited geographic and chronological contexts upon which we have been used to rely for the interpretation of literary texts. I shall now try to illustrate my contention and to suggest that, in contradistinction to its geographic and chronological counterparts, the oral-formulaic context can often be stretched in many pragmatically convenient directions without losing anything of its specificity or validity.

My assumption is that, even though the notion of context may well be as arbitrary and controllable as Hartman's argument seems to imply, the recognition of some kind of objective context is nevertheless necessary to intelligible interpretation. The context may, of course, be either extrinsic or intrinsic, but the principle remains the same. In *The Wasps* of Aristophanes, for example, a modern reader opening the book at the point where the choryphaeus has urged Philocleon to seek a way of escaping from his confinement and the latter has answered "You seek it, for I'd do anything; I so long to go about small boards with a little mussel" ("*Zêteith' humeis, hôs pan an egôgepoioiên./houtô kittô dia tôn sanidôn meta choirinês perielthein*"[19]), might well draw upon information gathered from a handbook of tourism to conclude that the intended context of Philocleon's wishful statement is simply one of the famous seafood bars of Madrid. Another reader, however, might construct the extrinsic context from editorial commentary to the effect that in Aristophanes' time a *choirinê* was a small sea-mussel used by the Athenian dicasts in voting.[20] We need not surmise here which of the two contexts may prove more appropriate to our interpretation of the passage, but we must recognize that the tone and in part the action itself will be decidedly affected by our choice of one or the other. The same principle applies to the effect of intrinsic context, as may be illustrated with Chaucer's use of the auditory image of a thunderclap in both *The Miller's Tale* and *Troilus and Criseyde*. In the former, the image describes a massive flatulence delivered pointblank into the face of a ridiculous small-town parish clerk who has been characterized a little earlier as "somdeel squaymous/ Of farting"[21] and has spent nearly an entire day preparing himself for a bout of romantic love with a concupiscible young woman. I do not think that I am offering more than a reminder in pointing out that, within this context, the image of a thunderclap clinches the lustily farcical tone of the whole episode, and I hope to be forgiven for suggesting that one needs only read Chaucer's words to appreciate the full olfactory quality of the action:

> This Nicolas anon leet fle a fart,
> As greet as it had been a *thonder-dent*,
> That with the strook he was almost yblent. (3806-8)

In the latter, the very same image describes a blast coincident with the glorious death of a proud knight on the battlefield before Thebes, and it concludes a descriptive list of the heroes who died there. Within this context, it inescapably brings to mind the detonation of artillery as well as the opaque smoke and acrid smell of the black powder used in the cannons of Chaucer's time; and, in so doing, it emphasizes the noble futility of heroic recklessness:

> She tolde ek how Hemonydes asterte,
> Whan Tideus slough fifty knightes stoute.
> She tolde ek . . . .
> . . . .
> How Tideus was sleyn, lord of Argeyes,
> And how Ypomedoun in litel stounde
> Was dreynt, and ded Parthonope of wownde;
> And also how Capaneus the proude
> With *thonder-dynt* was slayn, that cride loude.(V, 1492-1505)

The image remains the same in both cases, but the action which it evokes and the tone which it governs in *The Miller's Tale* are vastly different from their counterparts in the *Troilus*, so that an interpretation totally unrelated to the factual context of either would probably be unintelligible to anyone but its author.

We must note that in the foregoing instances the alternative contexts have affected the significance of a seashell and a loud noise, respectively, by enabling us to relate these to actually or vicariously familiar situations which are wont to evoke certain predictable responses in us. This function of context happens to correspond precisely to one of the functions which scholars have attributed to oral-formulaic elements in poetry. As early as 1955, for example, Stanley Greenfield wrote that "the association with other contexts using a similar formula will inevitably color a particular instance of a formula so that a whole host of overtones springs into action. . . ."[22] Since that time, Adrien Bonjour has argued that the effective use of an oral-formulaic theme makes the audience see things "in advance, and thereby implies deeper connotations,"[23] and Fry has pointed out that these themes "provide the audience with a supply of associations. . . ."[24] More recently, Foley has shown that the presence of a particular formula is likely to affect our reaction to "speech and character by locating them with relation to archetypal paradigms" ("Formula and

Theme," p. 218). The fact is that—regardless of the ways in which one may wish to define the term *oral-formulaic*—a given narrative element gets to be labeled "formulaic" as a result of some kind of repetition. We know, of course, that the repetition need not be immediately apparent. To draw an obvious example from what is probably the best-known oral-formulaic statement of Old English poetry: "X (nominative) *maðelode, bearn* Y (genitive)," the letters *X* and *Y* may stand for any two of an almost infinite number of alliterating names, and even the structure of the statement may be changed along with the alliterative pattern, as in the case of "X (nominative) *ma ðelode*, Y (genitive) *sunu*." Nevertheless, one need not have been a student of Old English very long to recognize the basic pattern and to come to expect it under certain circumstances; conversely one soon learns to expect the circumstances whenever the formulaic pattern turns up. Unless we wish to assume oral-formulaic poetry to be usually composed for audiences completely unfamiliar with the system of composition, we have to grant the likelihood that the audience of that poetry would be better attuned to both the patterns and circumstances than most academic students are likely to be,[25] and we may even suppose that a gifted oral-formulaic poet thoroughly familiar with his materials and techniques might wish to shape these materials so as to take advantage of the familiarity and expectations of his audience. To put the same thing differently, what I am suggesting is that the particular oral-formulaic elements within a given poem are likely to be apprehended—at least by the intended audience—within the context of familiar occurrences of the same elements and, under these circumstances, may be said to function very much like the extrinsic and intrinsic contexts which I have discussed in respect to Aristophanes and Chaucer.

Since I have already mentioned that scholars are by no means agreed that the presence of oral-formulaic elements should be taken as incontrovertible proof of oral composition, I should point out now that the validity of the views which I have advanced does not depend on the actual mode of composition of whatever texts may happen to fall under the critic's scrutiny. I should admittedly be a happier man if I knew for a fact that the texts with which I must deal were first-hand records of oral performances, but the principles outlined here would apply almost as well to texts composed on a typewriter, as long as these texts were demonstrably composed in accordance with oral-formulaic techniques and addressed to an audience consciously or unconsciously familiar with these techniques either through the ear or through the eye. In a different context, Lord has suggested that the transition from heroic to religious poetry in Anglo-Saxon England may well have resulted in the composition of what he calls "'transitional' or 'mixed'" poems, and he has drawn on Fry's work to surmise that "the audience for the poems must have been still enough of a traditional audience to feel that the working out of these models was right" ("Perspectives," p. 24). I submit that, to a certain extent, the same principle may be considered to apply to the transition from oral performance to written composition, unless we posit a situation in which both poets and audiences forget every aspect of their common tradition the moment someone brings the first pen and ink within the community.

Of course, one need not accept the foregoing argument or any part thereof. To the extent that we accept it, however, we must also accept the concomitant claim that, for the critical study of both oral and written texts composed under the conditions outlined here, the oral-formulaic context can be altogether as specific and relevant as its chronological and geographical counterparts. Furthermore, because oral-formulaic patterns retain their integrity over long periods of time, attestations necessarily accumulate in the records and may provide a rich context for works whose immediate chronological context happens to be poverty-stricken. This fact is precisely what has enabled Fry to produce a particularly masterful study of *Cædmon's Hymn* by, in his own words, "using post-Cædmonian verses to explain Cædmon" ("Cædmon," p. 60). Since the integrity of certain oral-formulaic patterns seems to endure in various branches of the same family, the oral-formulaic context may at times prove, not merely relevant, but indeed indispensable when the literary critic happens to be a comparatist working with texts drawn from several literatures; and whatever truth there may be in my statement becomes even truer when our hypothetical critic-comparatist further happens to be one of the many mediaevalists working with documents whose dates of composition are very much in doubt.

The point which I have been trying to make may be illustrated with a brief examination of the function of the same oral-formulaic theme in the Archaic Greek *Odyssey*, the Old English *Beowulf*, and the Old High German *Song of Hildebrand*. The oral-formulaic quality of both the Greek and the English poems has received so much attention in the past few decades that it needs no further discussion here, and Haymes has convincingly argued that the German poem "does belong to the improvisory oral-formulaic tradition that produced Old-English epics and the *Heliand*."[26] Although I readily confess that I have not the slightest notion regarding the respective dates and places of composition of the poems under consideration, we can safely say that the received texts were probably copied down more than a millenium apart.[27] Since there is no compelling reason to think that the composers or scribes of the English and German texts were directly imitating each other or the *Odyssey*,[28] and I seriously doubt that Homer kept annotated copies of *Beowulf* and the *Song of Hildebrand* by his bedside, I submit that we have here a case where the comparatist may do at least as well by working within the factual oral-formulaic context as he would within the hypothetical chronological context.

The theme which I have in mind was first pointed out by Robert P. Creed in an extremely important essay which he published in 1962[29] and in which he called attention to basic but yet unrecognized similarities between, on the one hand, the performance of the poet Demodocus, in the *Odyssey*, when he composes orally in front of Odysseus himself an account of the exploits of Odysseus and, on the other hand, the performance of an unnamed Danish poet who, in *Beowulf*, composes in front of Beowulf himself an account of the exploits of Beowulf. Creed's essay shows that the resultant type-scene occurs explicitly once in *Beowulf* (871b-74a: after the visit to Grendel's Pond, the morning after Beowulf has wounded Grendel to death) and twice in the *Odyssey* (VIII, 72-82: immediately before the Phaeacian Games; and VIII, 499-520: beyond Demodocus' account of the love affair between Ares and Aphrodite, immediately after the reconciliation between Odysseus and Euryalus).[30] In addition to the obvious parallelism of the initial situation, the principal thematic similarities between the Greek and Old English episodes may be summed up as follows.

1) *In both texts, the narrator within the poem composes a story orally*: we have in effect a smaller oral narrative within a longer narrative, or a mini-epic within an epic.

2) *In both texts, the hero whose exploits are recounted in the mini-epic has travelled far and wide and has only recently reached the location where the recounting is taking place*: most recently, Odysseus has sailed from Calypso's homeland and Beowulf from his own native country.

3) *In both texts, the recounting takes place in the presence of a substantial crowd*: at the court of King Alcinous in the *Odyssey* and among riders returning from Grendel's Pond in *Beowulf.*

4) *In both texts, the hero must face a challenge of physical strength soon after the completion of the story to which he is listening*: after the first recounting, Odysseus is insultingly prodded by Laodamas and Euryalus into competing in the Phaeacian Games, and after the second recounting and a brief sea-crossing to Ithaka he has to face the suitors in his own home; the day after the recounting, Beowulf dives into Grendel's Pond, where he must meet Grendel's Mother in mortal combat.

5) *In both texts, the occasion has the makings of a joyful scene and is celebrated as such*: in the *Odyssey*, the first recounting takes place during the feast which King Alcinous arranges to welcome the stranger Odysseus (e.g., VIII, 40-43), and the second takes place during the feast that follows the Phaeacian Games; in *Beowulf*, the recounting is part of the festivities with which the Danes greet the undoing of Grendel.

6) *In both texts, the story-teller and the hero are totally unrelated strangers, but the former nevertheless succeeds in retelling the latter's adventures as they really happened*: in the *Odyssey*, both recountings are so true to facts that Odysseus weeps upon hearing them (VIII, 92 and 531); and, in *Beowulf*, the hero's adventure is specifically said to be recounted "*on sped*" (873a).

Creed's perceptive analysis reveals additional similarities, but those listed above will do for my immediate purpose. Because his primary concern was the actual act of *singing* rather than the thematic situation regardless of the mode of performance, his essay necessarily kept clear from possible occurrences of the theme in which the story-telling might not explicitly take the form of a song. Because I am primarily concerned with the theme rather than with the explicit mode of performance of the story within the story, I should like to point out that the very same pattern occurs in the fighting between Unferth and Beowulf (499a-529b). In addition to the same initial situation, we find that (1) Unferth explicitly tells (499a) his story orally (2) in front of Beowulf, who has come from far away and has only now entered (402a-403a) Heorot; (3) the recounting takes place in the presence of a large group of Danes and Weders (498a-b); (4) Beowulf answers Unferth's insulting account by reasserting his intention to fight Grendel (601b-6b), whose challenge he will actually meet a few lines later (745b-

823a); (5) the occasion is a joyful feast (497b) filled with the laughter of warriors (611b); and (6) Unferth and Beowulf are totally unrelated strangers, but the former nevertheless succeeds in telling a belittling story that has just enough of an air of truth to send the latter flying into a rage and prompt him to offer his own interpretation of nearly the same facts (530a-583a).

Since the *Song of Hildebrand* is not such a familiar part of the common repertory as the *Odyssey* and *Beowulf*, I am outlining its contents here for the sake of communication: *Two warriors named Hildebrand and Hadubrand meet alone between two armies. When asked to identify himself, Hadubrand answers that his father, who was named Hildebrand and thirty years ago left a woman and a young child behind to follow Dietrich von Bern in exile, was the best of warriors and is probably long dead. Realizing that he is facing his own son, Hildebrand tries to conciliate him, but the other answers with insults and reasserts his own conviction that the real Hildebrand died in battle. Hildebrand then notes the bitter irony in the fact that he, whom no warrior could ever kill in battle, must now be killed by his own son unless he kills him first; and the poem comes to an end with the two opponents hewing at each other with their weapons.* From the testimony of Saxo Grammaticus and the *Saga of Ásmund the Champion-Killer*, we know that the Hildebrand of the legend does in fact kill Hadubrand,[31] and it is difficult not to assume at least a modicum of audience familiarity with a subject whose lasting popularity with the Indo-European world is attested by analogues in the Old Irish *The Death of Aife's One Son*, the Persian *Book of Kings*, and some forty Russian variants.[32] The assumption becomes especially tempting when we recall that the episode outlined here is part of the Cycle of Dietrich von Bern, which remained for centuries a favorite of Germanic audiences.[33]

Even if one wishes to set aside Matthew Arnold's version of the story[34] as unrelated to the present argument, the literary critic is thus provided with a familiar context within which to examine the subject matter of the *Song of Hildebrand*, and there is a statistical likelihood that Germanic audiences would at some point have shared that familiarity, though obviously not through the study of texts yet to be composed in languages other than their own. A similar argument may be advanced in respect to the theme of the story-teller performing in front of the live hero of his own story. Although the fact that a certain pattern occurs twice in an Archaic Greek poem, twice again in an Old

English poem,[35] and once in an Old German poem might conceivably be dismissed as purely coincidental, the additional fact that similar recurrences of patterns are by no means uncommon between these two linguistic and chronological areas[36] would seem to put the burden of proof upon the proponents of coincidence. Even though the scarcity of extant recorded documents necessarily makes reliable statistics out of the question, one may reasonably assume the probability of some kind of audience familiarity with an oral-formulaic theme which—once again barring the likelihood of conscious borrowing—seems to have exhibited enough vitality to remain in use within the same linguistic family for over a millenium and probably much longer. The factual presence of a theme within a poem, however, does not necessarily mean that it will be critically recorded by the scholar, the reader, or the listener, for recent investigation has demonstrated that consumers of literature tend to notice mostly those aspects of a given text which they are cued in to expect or to seek out.[37] In the case of the *Song of Hildebrand*, the scholar is cued in to expect formulaic elements with the opening statement—"Ik gihorta þat seggen" ("I heard that told") [38]—whose Old English equivalent has been shown by Magoun to be the most common oral-formulaic opening statement in the surviving corpus ("Oral-Formulaic Character," p. 453).

With these observations out of the way, we may now turn to the form under which the theme under consideration appears in the *Song of Hildebrand* and to its function therein. As my outline may have suggested, the narrator of the story within the story is Hadubrand, who answers a request for self-identification with a mini-epic (15a-29) about Hildebrand's wanderings and the cause thereof (18a-b), his loneliness (24b) away from the woman and little child necessarily left behind (20a-22a), his brave deeds in the service of Dietrich (22b-24a; 25a-27b), his fame among bold warriors (28a-b), and his having presumably met with death by now (29):

(15)   dat sagetun mi   usere liuti
          alte anti frote,   dea erhina warun,
          dat Hiltibrant haetti min fater: ih heittu Hadubrant.

(18)   forn her ostar giweit,   floh her Otachres nid,
          hina miti Theotrihhe   enti sinero degano filu.

(20)   her furlaet in lante   luttila sitten

            prut in bure   barn unwahsan,

(22)   arbeo laosa: her raet ostar hina.
            sid Detrihhe   darba gistuontun

(24)   fateres mines: dat uuas so friuntlaos   man.
            her was Otachre   ummet tirri,
            degano dechisto   miti Deotrichhe.

(27)   her was eo folches at ente: imo was eo fehta ti leop:

(28)   chud was her . . .   chonnem mannum.

(29)   ni waniu ih iu lib habbe.

[(15) Our people told me that—the old and wise ones who used to
be around here—that my father was named Hildebrand: I am named
Hadubrand. (18) He went east—he fled from Odoacer's hostility—away
from here with Dietrich and many of his warriors. (20) He abandoned in
this country a wretched young son at his wife's home, (22) deprived of
his inheritance: he rode east from here. Eventually Dietrich stood in
need (24) of my father. That was a man quite without friends; he was
utterly furious with Odoacer. The best of warriors with Dietrich, (27) he
was always at the forefront of the host: fighting was always dear to
him. (28) He was famous among bold men. (29) I do not think that he
is still alive.][39]

As in the case of the *Odyssey* and *Beowulf*, the initial situation
conforms to Creed's description, since the story-teller recounts the
hero's adventures in front of the hero himself; and, with two important
exceptions, the remaining circumstances likewise conform to the
paradigm which I have drawn from the Greek and English poems. For
the sake of convenience, I am listing each point of comparison in the
same order which I used above for these two texts.

1) *As in the other texts, the narrator within the German poem
composes his story orally*: we are told that "Hadubrand *spoke*" (14a).

2) *As in the other texts, the hero whose adventures are recounted in
the German poem has travelled far and wide and has only recently
reached the location where the recounting is taking place*: Hildebrand
has "wandered sixty summers and winters" (50a-b) since he rode away
eastward (19a; 22b), and the fact that the two warriors have just met

(2a-b) and do not yet know each other's identity (8b-10) makes it obvious that he has only now arrived on the spot.

3) *As in the other texts, the recounting in the German poem takes place in the presence of a substantial crowd*: specifically, in this case, "between two armies" (3b).

4) *As in the other texts, the hero in the German poem must face a challenge of physical strength soon after the completion of the story to which he is listening*: his attempt at conciliation by offering some precious rings to his antagonist meets with the intractable answer that gifts from treacherous old men can only be received "spear-point against spear-point" (38), and the result of this challenge is the mortal combat in which the two must face each other at the end of the poem (63a-68).

5) *As in the other texts, the occasion in the German poem has the makings of a joyful scene*: in a society that attaches importance to the relationship between father and son, few things are likely to give greater cause for joy than the unexpected reunion of the two after a long and cruel separation. *In contrast to the other texts, however, the meeting results in mortal combat rather than in joyful celebration.*

6) *Again in contrast to the other texts, the story-teller and the hero in the German poem are bound by the closest possible blood relationship, but the former nevertheless succeeds in including in his story a crucial piece of gross misinformation*: he states of the man to whom he is talking, "I do not think that he is still alive" (29).

I believe that the two differences mentioned here are central to our critical understanding of the function of the passage under discussion. Since (a) the several points occur in the order in which I have listed them, (b) Hadubrand does not actually challenge Hildebrand until eight lines after the conclusion of the story within a story, and (c) the mistaken statement that he assumes his father to be dead comes only with the very last line of the story within a story, an audience consciously or unconsciously used to the implications of the theme embodied here would initially expect a recognition followed by the joyful scene appropriate to the occasion. But an audience likewise familiar with the legend of Hildebrand would also know that the father must kill the son, and it would presumably be sensible to the dissonance between the facts of the story and the expectations created by the oral-formulaic theme. Unfortunately, I have no means of ascertaining exactly how the dissonance in question would have affected the Carolingian readers for whom the only extant text of the *Song of*

Hildebrand was copied down, and I know even less about the audiences for whom the ancestors of that text were composed.[40] As a teacher of literature, however, I know very well how this dissonance affects me in a way which I can communicate objectively to my students. By calling to my attention the unnatural character of the action, it stresses the deeply moving fact that what ought rightfully to be a joyful reunion between an old warrior of heroic stature and his brave son must turn into the ultimate separation of death, and the tension thus created remains unsurpassed in Western literature. Even before Hadubrand's challenge to Hildebrand, the depth of the separation between father and son is emphasized comparatively by the fact that, in pronouncing the former long dead, the latter makes us see that he knows less about him than his counterparts in the other manifestations of the same theme know about perfect strangers. These observations in turn alert us to a host of details which imply Hildebrand's separation from practically everything dear to early Germanic warriors and thus enables us to appreciate his situation against the emotion-charged background of the many Germanic poems in which a man or a woman must endure the bitter pangs of separation.[41] This is no place to defend the implied interpretation of the poem, but we must note that this interpretation is possible only if we supplement the completely hypothetical and practically nonexistent geographic and chronological contexts by the tangibly attested context of an oral-formulaic theme.

A word about my choice of an illustrative theme is appropriate at this point, for I have argued elsewhere that—contrary to what might mistakenly be inferred from the foregoing analysis—the central oral-formulaic theme of the *Song of Hildebrand* is, not that in which the story-teller must face the subject of his story, but rather one known as "the hero on the beach," which is probably the second most common oral-formulaic theme in Germanic poetry, is attested in both mediaeval English and mediaeval German, and has been so often investigated since 1960 that it no longer needs an introduction.[42] The reason for my choice of the less appropriate theme was my wish to suggest an additional respect in which the oral-formulaic context may prove of special importance to the literary tradition at the end of the twentieth century. As already pointed out, the respective dates of the extant recorded texts of the works which I have used to illustrate the critical implications of the theme span more than a millennium. If we wish to be somewhat less cautious and argue on the assumption that the

Homeric poems may have been composed around the seventh century, B.C., and that the only manuscript of *Beowulf* may have been copied down as recently as the tenth century A.D., we may then venture to say that our theme occurs over a period of about 1600 years in works which were vital enough to be the property of the general public rather than that of a few specialized scholars isolated from the mainstream of their respective cultures. If we also keep in mind that the texts examined here have come to us in three different languages used respectively in three different geographic locations, we are tempted to conclude that the oral-formulaic approach to relevant works of literature may provide us with an objective context while affording us a great deal of freedom from both geography and chronology. In respect to the Western World, my statement applies especially to scholars concerned with the Middle Ages and Antiquity, but I am not at all certain that these limitations are with us to stay. As David Bynum has reminded us in a recent book, the amount of oral composition that goes on daily around the world is much greater than we tend to assume,[43] and the random samples of research in oral-formulaic composition which I have listed toward the beginning of this essay allow us to entertain some reasonable hope that the joint efforts of field workers and philologists will eventually find objectively significant points of comparison between genetically unrelated dead and live traditions. Insofar as the oral-formulaic approach enables us to handle vast areas of literature, it offers us an alternative to the critical theories mentioned at the outset of this essay, but it differs from them in two essential respects. The first is that it provides a flexible but *specific* context whose integrity is readily ascertainable and against which we may in turn measure the integrity of a given text,[44] about which we are thus enabled to make reasonably objective statements. The second is that it provides us with the means for understanding certain aspects of ancient texts through legitimate comparison with more modern texts. In contradistinction, the critical theories which are gaining popularity today make it very difficult to examine ancient literature, which usually demands close attention to both text and context, and the fact is that nearly all the practitioners of these theories are dedicated modernists. Some years ago, Harry Levin remarked before an audience of comparatists that, "having taken all literature for our province, we need special bibliographies rather than an *omnium gatherum.*"[45] For the same reason, we need special techniques, and the techniques developed by the students of oral-formulaic composition and related matters are among those that may help us retain something of our rapidly vanishing literary tradition. For those who would agree with Cicero that a human being without a past is doomed to remain a child,[46] the work of Milman Parry, Albert B. Lord, and their followers may conceivably prove one of the few remaining means whereby literary education can contribute to the formation of culturally responsible grown-ups.

NOTES

[1]"Literature in the Reader: Affective Stylistics," *NLH*, 2 (1970), 140.

[2]"War in Heaven: A Review of Harold Bloom's 'The Anxiety of Influence: A Theory of Poetry,'" in Hartman, *The Fate of Reading and Other Essays* (Chicago, 1975), p. 41; this review, incidentally, is not totally uncritical of Bloom's methods. One might wish to note that Hartman's book has itself been praised for its "gleeful unintelligibility" in a review by Richard Poirier, *NYTBR*, April 20, 1975, p. 21.

[3]For discussions of the trends treated here, see, e.g., William H. Pritchard, "The Hermeneutical Mafia or, After Strange Gods at Yale," *HudR*, 28 (1975-1976), 601-610, who refers to the critical enterprise of Hartman and his colleagues as a "hermeneutical shindig" (p. 610) which "attempts to frisk students of their principles as naive or enthusiastic readers" (p. 601). In a particularly witty and brilliant essay, Gerald Graff, "Fear and Trembling at Yale," *ASch*, 46 (1977), 467-478, recognizes the importance of these trends but sees in them a "literary quarrel with the objective way of knowing" (p. 477). Michael André Bernstein aptly points out in the work of one practitioner a "desire to preserve uncertainty from any contamination by 'sense' or 'meaning'," in "Jonathan Culler and the Limits of Uncertainty," *Poetics*, 3 (1977), 593.

[4]"The Interpreter: A Self-Analysis," in *The Fate of Reading*, p. 14.

[5]"The Ideal Reader: A Critical Fiction," *PMLA*, 93 (1978), 463; an excellent bibliography of the subject is given on p. 473, n. 1.

[6](Cambridge, 1959). He calls attention to such things as, e.g., "about a hundred inconsistencies and errors in the first printing of Sinclair Lewis's novel *Babbitt*" (p. 19).

[7]Parry, *L'Épithète traditionnelle dans Homère (The Traditional Epithet in Homer)*, in *The Making of Homeric Verse: the Collected Papers of Milman Parry*, ed. by Adam Parry (Oxford, 1971) (hereafter *MHV*), pp. 1-190; *Les formules et la métrique d'Homère (Homeric Formulae and Homeric Meter)*, in *MHV*, pp. 191-239; "Studies in the Epic Technique of Oral Verse-Making. I. Homer and Homeric Style," in

MHV, pp. 266-324; "Studies in the Epic Technique of Oral Verse-Making. II. The Homeric Language as the Language of an Oral Poetry," in *MHV*, pp. 325-364; Lord, "Homer and Huso II: Narrative Inconsistencies in Homer and Oral Poetry," *TAPA*, 69 (1938), 439-445; Magoun, "The Oral-Formulaic character of Anglo-Saxon Narrative Poetry," *Speculum*, 28 (1953), 446-467.

[8]*The Song of Roland: Formulaic Style and Poetic Craft* (Berkeley, 1973).

[9]*The Bell and the Drum: Shih Ching as Formulaic Poetry in an Oral Tradition* (Berkeley, 1974), p. 128.

[10]*Spontaneity and Tradition: a Study in the Oral Art of Homer* (Berkeley, 1974), p. xxiv.

[11]"Formula and Theme in Old English Poetry," in *Oral Literature and the Formula*, ed. by Benjamin A. Stolz and Richard S. Shannon (Ann Arbor, 1976) (hereafter *OL&F*), p. 231.

[12]"Formula and Meter," in *OL&F*, p. 256. See further his *Comparative Studies in Greek and Indic Meter* (Cambridge, Mass., 1974).

[13]"*Imbongi Nezibongo*: the Xhosa Tribal Poet and the Contemporary Poetic Tradition," *PMLA*, 90 (1975), 187.

[14]"Oral Residue in Tudor Prose Style," *PMLA*, 80 (1965), argues, e.g., that "the oral elements . . . in Tudor prose are akin to those in the *Iliad* and the *Odyssey*" (p. 153).

[15]"The Literary Character of Anglo-Saxon Formulaic Poetry," *PMLA*, 81 (1966), argues that we may no longer have "any lingering suspicion that the relative percentage of formulas might be used to distinguish between oral and lettered productions" (p. 336).

[16]"Cædmon as a Formulaic Poet," in *Oral Literature: Seven Essays* ed. by Joseph J. Duggan (New York, 1975) (hereafter *OLSE*), p. 41.

[17]See, e.g., F.H. Whitman, "The Meaning of 'Formulaic' in Old English Verse Composition," *NM*, 76 (1975), 529-537.

[18]"Perspectives on Recent Work on Oral Literature," in *OLSE*, p. 24.

[19]Aristophanes, *The Wasps*, ed. by C.E. Graves (Cambridge, 1899), 11.338-339.

[20]Henry G. Liddell and Robert Scott, *A Greek-English Lexicon*, rev. by Henry S. Jones (Oxford, 1961).

[21]Geoffrey Chaucer, *The Miller's Tale*, 11. 3337-3338; this and all subsequent quotations from Chaucer are from *The Works of Geoffrey Chaucer*, ed. by Fred N. Robinson (Cambridge, 1957).

[22]"The Formulaic Expression of the Theme of 'Exile' in Anglo-Saxon Poetry," *Speculum*, 30 (1955), 205.

[23]"*Beowulf* and the Beasts of Battle," *PMLA*, 72 (1957), 566.

[24]"The Heroine on the Beach in *Judith*," *NM*, 68 (1967), 181.

[25]John Miles Foley, "*Beowulf* and the Psychohistory of Anglo-Saxon Culture," *AI*, 34 (1977), convincingly argues that "the traditional oral society educates its members—that is, it provides them with necessary information—through the repeated and collective experience of performed epic poetry, by presenting them time and again with a verbal montage of the group's poetic models and thereby with the data which these models encode" (p. 134), and again "the psychohistorical matrix which underlines and generates the epic narrative remains available to all members of the society through repeated oral performance" (p. 153).

[26]"Oral Poetry and the Germanic *Heldenlied*," *RUS*, 62 (1976), 52. From a totally different point of view, the relationship of the German poem to Old English poetic practices was first analyzed in Moritz Trautmann's influential study, *Finn und Hildebrand* (Bonn, 1903), pp. 67-131. I have reconsidered this relationship from the point of view of a central oral-formulaic theme in my "The English Connection Revisited: a Reading Context for the *Hildebrandslied*," *Neophil.*, 63 (1979), 84-87.

[27]According to Roger A. Pack, *Greek and Latin Literary Texts from Greco-Roman Egypt* (Ann Arbor, 1952), pp. 39-42, the earliest extant papyri of the *Odyssey* are dated in the second century B.C. The only extant manuscript of the *Song of Hildebrand* is usually dated in the early ninth century, e.g., by Elias von Steinmeyer, ed., *Die kleineren althochdeutschen Sprachdenkmäler* (Berlin, 1916), who places it "wahrscheinlich im zweiten Dezenium des 9. Jh." (p. 8). The only manuscript of *Beowulf* is usually dated in the tenth century, e.g., by Elliott Van Kirk Dobbie, ed., *Beowulf and Judith*, Anglo-Saxon Poetic Records, Vol. 4 (New York, 1953), who places it "at the end of the tenth century" (p. ix), although scholars generally assume it to be a copy of an earlier text which, as Stanley B. Greenfield writes in his *A Critical History of Old English Literature* (New York, 1965), "probably existed in the middle of the eighth century" (p. 82).

[28]Even if all three poets had known each other, we should keep in mind that modern views on imitation and originality are not readily applicable to poetry composed within an oral-formulaic tradition. As Lord writes in *Singer*, "the truth of the matter is that our concept of 'the original,' of 'the song,' simply makes no sense in oral tradition" (p. 101); even in cases where a story is the object of "direct transmission without any intervening period of time" (p. 102), the resultant text follows the original only "fairly closely in terms of basic story" (p. 102), so that "in a variety of ways a song in tradition is separate, yet inseparable from other songs" (p. 123). In reference to Old English traditional poetry, I have tried to argue in my "Originality, Influence, Imitation: Two Mediaeval Phases," in François Jost, ed., *Proceedings of the IVth Congress of the International Comparative Literature*

Association (The Hague, 1966), that "the concepts of imitation, influence, and originality have practically no value for the criticism of the oral-formulaic phase of mediaeval literature" (II, p. 741). One might, of course, argue the influence of Homer upon *Beowulf* through Virgil, since the case for the influence of the *Aeneid* upon the English poem has been given a new lease on life in Theodore M. Andersson's fine *Early Epic Scenery: Homer, Virgil, and the Medieval Legacy* (Ithaca, 1976), with a chapter entitled "The Virgilian Heritage in *Beowulf*" (pp. 145-159). Although Andersson's argument in favor of Virgilian influence is the most compelling which I have read in recent years, I retain on the subject of classical influences on *Beowulf* reservations which I have expressed in my "The Terror of the Dark Waters: a Note on Virgilian and Beowulfian Techniques," *HES*, 5 (1974), esp. 147-150.

29"The Singer Looks at his Sources," *CL*, 14 (1962), 44-52; rpt. in Stanley B. Greenfield, ed., *Studies in Old English Literature in Honor of Arthur G. Brodeur* (Eugene, rpt. 1963), pp. 44-52.

30All references to *Beowulf* and the *Odyssey* are, respectively, to *Beowulf and Judith*, ed. by Dobbie, and to *Homeri Odyssea*, ed. by Guilielmus Dindorf (Leipzig, 1899).

31Saxo Grammaticus, *Gesta Danorum*, ed. by Jørgen Olrik and Hans R. Roeder (Copenhagen, 1931), I, 204; *Ásmundarsaga Kappabana*, ch. 8, in Ferdinand Dieter, ed., *Zwei Fornaldarsögur* (Halle, 1891).

32For discussions of the relationship between versions in different languages, see, e.g., Georg Baesecke, "Die indogermanischen Verwandtschaften des Hildebrandliedes," *NAWG*, Phil.-Hist., n.F., 3 (1940), 139-153; Jan De Fries, "Das Motiv des Vater-Sohn-Kampfes im Hildebrandslied," *GRM*, 24 (1953), 257-274; and A. T. Hatto, "On the Excellence of the *Hildebrandslied*: A Comparative Study in Dynamics," *MLR*, 68 (1973), 820-838. A version with a different ending is recorded in the Middle High German *Jüngeres Hildebrandslied*, in Elias Von Steinmeyer, ed., *Denkmäler deutscher Poesie und Prosa aus VIII-XII Jahrhundert* (Berlin, 1892), II, pp. 26-30, and in the *þidriks Saga af Bern*, ed. by Henrik Bertelsen (Copenhagen, 1905), V, pp. 348-352 (Chs. 407-410).

33See, e.g., Georges Zink, *Les légendes héroiques de Dietrich et d'Emrich dans les littératures germaniques* (Paris, 1950), esp. pp. 225-268.

34Matthew Arnold, *Sohrab and Rustum*, in *The Poems of Matthew Arnold*, ed. by Kenneth Allott (London, 1965), pp. 302-331, is based on the *Book of Kings* and treats the materials of the *Song of Hildebrand* in 11. 1-508.

35Since Hrothgar subsequently praises Beowulf's deeds after the latter's victory over Grendel's mother (1700a-1784b) and we can later learn that he actually composed a song (2105a-2115a) on that occasion, one might conceivably wish to argue that the theme in question occurs implicitly a third time in the poem.

[36]In addition to those works of Lord's already cited above (e.g., the section on *Beowulf* in his *Singer*, pp. 198-202), see his "Beowulf and Odysseus," in *Franciplegius*, pp. 86-91. In a paper presented before the 1963 annual meeting of the Philological Association of the Pacific Coast, Michael N. Nagler pointed out thematic similarities between Odysseus' encounter with Polyphemus and Beowulf's encounter with Grendel's mother; a modified version of this paper is included in his "*Beowulf* in the Context of Myth," in *Old English Literature in Context: Ten Essays*, ed. by John D. Niles (London and Totowa, New Jersey: Boydell-Brewer and Rowman and Littlefield, 1980), pp. 143-56, 178-81. In my "Oral Theme and Written Texts," *NM*, 77 (1976), 337-346, I have tried to argue the presence of the same oral-formulaic theme in the *Odyssey* and two different Old English poems.

[37]E.g., Norman N. Holland, *Poems in Persons* (New York, 1973), discusses the ways in which "a reader recreates a literary work" (pp. 99-100).

[38]*Das Hildebrandslied*, in Wilhelm Braune, ed., *Althochdeutsches Lesebuch*, rev. by Karl Helm (Halle, 1949), pp. 72-73; the translation is from Haymes' "Oral Poetry and the Germanic *Heldenlied*," p. 50; subsequent translations are my own.

[39]My translation must perforce be arbitrary whenever the text is ambiguous (e.g., 1. 21a, where *prut* has been construed as either a genitive or an accusative), but my argument does not depend on the choice of one alternative rather than another in this passage.

[40]Scholars have argued in favor of ancestors in Old English (Trautmann, *Finn und Hildebrand*, with reconstruction on pp. 121-123), Longobardic (Willy Krogman, *Das Hildebrandslied in der langobardischen Urfassung hergestellt* [Berlin, 1959], with reconstruction on pp. 47-49), and Gothic (Richard H. Lawson, "The *Hildebrandslied* Originally Gothic?" *NM*, 74 [1973], esp. 339). The prevalent opinion is summed up by Hatto, "Excellence," p. 820, with the statement that the extant text is a "'Saxonized' version of a (scribal) Bavarian version of an original (oral) Longobardic lay."

[41]A documented discussion of this aspect of the poem will be found in my "Germanic Quintessence: the Theme of Isolation in the *Hildebrandslied*," in Margot King and Wesley M. Stevens, eds., *Saints, Scholars, and Heroes* (St. John, 1979), pp. 143-178.

[42]See my "The Armor of the *Hildebrandslied*: an Oral-Formulaic Point of View," *NM*, 78 (1977), 389-395. The theme of the hero on the beach was isolated and discussed by David K. Crowne, "The Hero on the Beach:

an Example of Composition by Theme in Anglo-Saxon Poetry," *NM*, 61 (1960), 362-372. Crowne's study has been followed by, e.g., my "Oral-Formulaic Theme Survival: a Possible Instance in the *Nibelungenlied*," *NM*, 65 (1964), 70-74; Fry, "The Hero on the Beach in *Finnsburh*," *NM*, 67 (1966), 27-31; "The Heroine on the Beach in *Judith*," *NM*, 68 (1967), 168-184; and "Themes and Type-Scenes in *Elene* 1-113," *Speculum*, 44 (1969), 35-45; Janet Thormann, "Variations on the Theme of 'The Hero on the Beach' in *The Phoenix*," *NM*, 71 (1970), 187-190; Carol J. Wolf, "Christ as Hero in *The Dream of the Rood*," *NM*, 71 (1970), 202-210; and James D. Johnson, "The Hero on the Beach in the Alliterative *Morte Arthur*," *NM*, 76 (1975), 271-281. The only theme more commonly attested is that of the Beasts of Battle, first isolated and analyzed by Magoun in his "The Theme of the Beasts of Battle in Anglo-Saxon Poetry," *NM*, 56 (1955), 81-90.

[43]*The Daemon in the Wood: a Study of Oral Narrative Patterns* (Cambridge, Mass., 1978), p. 35.

[44]In my "The Kassel Manuscript and the Conclusion of the *Hildebrandslied*," *Manuscripta*, 23 (1979), 104-108, I have tried to illustrate the extent to which the oral-formulaic context may occasionally enable us to ascertain the integrity of a given text.

[45]"Comparing the Literature," in Harry Levin, *Grounds for Comparison* (Cambridge, Mass., 1972), p. 89; this essay was originally an address delivered before the 1968 triennial meeting of the American Comparative Literature Association.

[46]Marcus Tullius Cicero, *Orator*, ed. by Otto Seel (Heidelberg, 1952): "nescire autem quid ante quam natus sis acciderit, id est semper esse puerum" (p. 76, XXXIV, 120).

Literary Art and Oral Tradition in Old English and Serbian Poetry

John Miles Foley

This essay confronts the much-debated problem of utility and aesthetics by reporting an analog to Old English poems like The Wanderer *and* The Seafarer: *the briefer Christian oral narrative poetry in Serbo-Croatian, especially as collected by Vuk Stefan Karadžić in the nineteenth century. Unlike the Moslem epic recorded and studied by Parry, Lord, and others, the Christian Yugoslav poems—written down from oral performance—reveal a combination of traditional structure and the kind of conscious artistic design customarily associated only with literate composition. In addition to arguing that such a combination of compositional modes can inform shorter oral genres and urging the comparison of the Christian Serbo-Croatian narratives and the briefer Old English poems, this article makes the larger point that studies in oral tradition must be prepared to recognize and understand a wide spectrum of poetic forms. Productive comparison and faithful aesthetic judgments will be possible only when we confront oral traditional art in its full richness and complexity.*

Reprinted from *Anglo-Saxon England*, 12 (1983), 183-214.

337

Forþon ic mæg singan ond secgan spell,
mænan fore mengo in meoduhealle
hu me cynegode cystum dohten. (*Widsith*, pp. 54-56)

Therefore I can sing and tell a story,
make known before a multitude in a mead-hall
how well-born ones would be generous to me with gifts.

... treći ćemer kljastu i slijepu:
nek slijepi po svijetu hode,
nek pjevaju i spominju Marka!

... the third moneybelt to the lame and blind:
let the blind walk about the world,
let them sing about and celebrate Marko! (*The
Death of Kraljević Marko*, pp. 110-12)

Oral literature research entered Old English literature through Albert
Lord's 1949 dissertation, eleven years later to become *The Singer of
Tales*, and Francis P. Magoun, Jr.'s ensuing essay, "The Oral-
Formulaic Character of Anglo-Saxon Narrative Poetry."[1] As I have
pointed out elsewhere,[2] these two scholars were not the first to identify
and discuss the recurrent phrase or "formula" in the poetry; German
Higher Criticism of the nineteenth century had analysed the use of
commonplaces of diction (or *Parallelstellen*) to try to determine
authorship and to establish the text of various poems. What Lord and
Magoun originated was the idea of an explicit and necessary connection
between the formula, defined by Milman Parry as "a group of words
regularly used under the same metrical conditions to express a given
essential idea,"[3] and a poem's orality. Following the lead of Parry's
ground-breaking analyses of Homeric epic and the Parry-Lord field work
on South Slavic oral epic, they and scholars following them reasoned
that the source of formulaic structure lay in a tradition of oral verse-
making and that formulaic phraseology was a kind of poetic idiom
fashioned over generations by bards responding to the continual pressure
of composition in performance. Only if his mind were well stocked
with phrases of metrical shape—if, in short, he had learned his poetic
language well—could an oral poet fluently tell his tale in the form of
traditional verse.

As has become apparent, these first approximations were, like all
pioneering statements, in need of elaboration and, in some areas, of

recasting. For one thing, the process of phrasemaking had somehow to be brought more into line with what has since been discovered about the inner workings of language, and the last few years have in fact seen the beginnings of co-operation between linguistic theory and oral studies from both the synchronic perspective of structuralism and the diachronic viewpoint of Indo-European reconstruction.[4] For another, the comparative method which led to many brilliant insights on similarities between and among oral literatures had to be refined to accommodate the inevitable differences in natural language characteristics, prosody, narrative form, and so on. Scholars have been rather slow to recognize the fundamental importance of this second area, but revaluations are beginning.[5] Thirdly, the key concept in Parry-Lord theory, the determining role of *utility* in the general development and individual use of formulaic language and other traditional structures, had in some manner to be reconciled with the obvious artistic value of the poetry. For within five years of Parry's famous 1928 doctoral theses[6] scholars were asking how an idiom which mechanically served the composing poet could also be an instrument employed by that same poet to aesthetic advantage.[7] How, they asked and are still asking, could metrical or narrative utility and art co-exist?

Homeric studies have often come to grief over this very problem, which, now that the existence of an oral tradition behind the *Iliad* and *Odyssey* has been proven beyond reasonable doubt, has in effect become the new Homeric Question. As the proceedings of a recent conference on ancient Greek epic, *Homer: Tradition and Invention,*[8] make clear, not all investigators will tolerate the Parry-Lord interpretation of Homeric oral tradition, principally because they believe it concentrates too heavily on the function of traditional forms and, correspondingly, undervalues the poet's and tradition's art. This view is perhaps most common among German researchers such as Alfred Heubeck, but it has long been espoused by many leading British and American classicists, such as G. S. Kirk, Adam Parry, Anne Amory Parry and Joseph Russo.[9] Fortunately, in the Greek area new discoveries in methodology have eased the tension between the opposing factions which we might style the Utilitarians and the Aesthetes,[10] but many an author still plants his feet firmly on one or the other side of the controversy and positivistically proclaims his allegiance.

The same sort of infighting has characterized research into the oral traditional nature of Old English verse, though with a somewhat different outcome. Apart from the reasons given above, Magoun's inflexible approach simply assumed too much: he claimed that "the recurrence in a poem of an appreciable number of formulas or formulaic phrases brands the latter as oral, just as a lack of such repetitions marks a poem as composed in a lettered tradition. Oral poetry, it may be safely said, is composed entirely of formulas, large and small, while lettered poetry is never formulaic."[11] This rather reductive view of oral structure stirred a good deal of controversy and outright antagonism against oral theory from the start, and it centred on Magoun's overemphasis on utility and function at the apparent expense of aesthetics. In the years that immediately followed, scholars were to reveal much which had not been known before about the structure of poetry, but the argument against orality would always go back to the same issue of utility versus artistry.[12] Many critics were unwilling, either intellectually or practically, to adopt the oralists' stance and thus to forgo the familiar and comfortable "critical canons," as Stanley B. Greenfield put it,[13] of the literary interpretation of poetry. This reaction was in large part neither obstinacy nor a failure to see at least some of the implications that oral theory held for Old English verse; it was in most cases an honest concern with preserving the poetry as poetry, and this meant, implicitly and unassumingly, as literary and literate rather than as oral poetry.

Then in 1966 an important article by Larry D. Benson, "The Literary Character of Anglo-Saxon Formulaic Poetry,"[14] seemed to sever the necessary connection between the density of formulaic expression in an Old English poem and its verifiable orality. Of course, the dissolving of the supposed link between structure and oral character also cast into doubt the conclusions of those studies which had found other sorts of oral patterns in the poems, such as Lord's "themes."[15] Benson's analysis of four poems—the metrical preface to Alfred's *Pastoral Care*, Riddle 35, the macaronic *Phoenix*, and the poetic version of the *Metres of Boethius*, all of which for external reasons seem likely to have been written—shows that these probably non-oral poems have approximately the same formula density as *Beowulf* and the Cynewulf canon, which have been assumed by some to be oral. Having thus revealed the formulaic test for orality to be inapplicable in the case of Old English, Benson argued for a poetry which is *both* lettered *and* formulaic: "From [the four poems mentioned above] we can see that not only can literate poets write formulaic verse, they can write it pen in hand in the same way any writer observes a literary tradition."[16] This explanation of the diction of Old English poetry has proved acceptable to a large number of scholars, particularly those who, as indicated above, felt the aesthetic value of the literature in danger of being explained away by oral theory.[17] Benson's final comments offer a new critical path: "Because Old English poetry is formulaic, our study of it must begin with the exciting and useful techniques developed by students of oral verse, but because this poetry is also literature, our study need not end there."[18]

Benson's article thus turned the current methodology of the oral theory back on itself; by denying the applicability of the test they had invented, he seemed to prove the oralists wrong on their own terms and to readmit Old English poetry to the family of written literature. The later studies of Donald K. Fry, one of the leading proponents of formulaic theory in Anglo-Saxon, and even those of Lord, would make no claims for the poetry's orality, although the element of tradition was never directly assailed. Laying aside for the moment any comments which could be offered on what might be termed the Oral Traditional Question,[19] let us consider what this sequence of events really meant. First, with the Magoun school championing orality on the basis of the Parry-Lord model, one alternative was moulded and firmly cast: either Old English conformed exactly not only to Homeric Greek epic but also more specifically to *the Parry-Lord theory of Homeric epic* or it did not; if it did then it was oral, but if it did not then it was written. Magoun and his followers, of course, implicitly assumed the former: that there was a complete and unambiguous equivalence between the two languages and traditions and that Old English emulated the Greek model. But they asserted this equivalence as an article of faith or a priori dogma, as if it were to be taken for granted that all oral traditions, genres, prosodies, and dictions are necessarily of a piece and necessarily follow the same rules. On the contrary, I would argue, such a simplistic assumption is quite likely to be a priori false; it cannot be true any more than that two languages or lexicons can be superimposed on one another without linguistic overlap.

The healthy corrective which Benson applied to a flawed act of initial assertions thus takes on a different character. In showing that poems probably written have about the same formulaic density as hypothetically oral poems, did he really deny orality to Old English verse? Do we question the findings of the Magoun school or must we first question an obviously imperfect method of analysis and evaluation? Our critique may proceed in two steps. The former has already been discussed: since a test developed in one tradition was administered without discernible "translation" to another, we can, for example, see the formulaic test as amounting to a search for Homeric Greek epic formulas in an Anglo-Saxon charm or riddle. For reasons which I have treated elsewhere, this is plainly a counterproductive procedure.[20] But there is also a second step, and it is one which would be viewed as heretical in some quarters. That step may be formulated as a deceptively simple question: is the Parry-Lord model of oral literature the only or the best available one to assist us in a comparative judgement of the possibly oral character of all Old English verse? The classic model, most fully described in *The Singer of Tales*, has illuminated dozens of literatures in new, exciting, and verifiably true ways: there cannot now be any question about its revolutionary effect on literary studies.[21] But is it the *only* model for oral literature? Does it explain *all* oral literature as completely and as accurately as it can be explained? Or are there oral traditions, or genres within oral traditions, which it does not or cannot explain?

These are difficult questions, now in the process of solution.[22] The reason that we need to know their answers, at least in a general way, is that we cannot in the present state of knowledge sensibly evaluate the work of Magoun and others who have contributed to scholarship on the oral theory in Old English. Quite clearly, if the Parry-Lord model turns out to be the only one available, then our task is to modify it to accord with the idiosyncratic properties of Old English poems and to develop a set of procedures for comparative work. I do not myself believe that formulaic density as a quantitative measure can alone prove either orality or its opposite, but at least the investigation could be conducted in terms that respect the integrity of individual languages and poetic traditions. If, however, another model or models might pertain more exactly in particular cases, then we must direct our attention elsewhere and develop a more pliable, pluralistic approach.

It is the purpose of this paper to report just such an alternative mode, one that diverges from the Parry-Lord orthodoxy on a number of issues, most significantly on the matter of utility versus aesthetics. What is more, this other model comes from the poetic tradition that forms the basis of prevailing theory, the Serbo-Croatian oral tradition. It offers an example of an oral narrative poetry which is highly formulaic but which also shows unmistakable signs of a poet who can consciously manipulate the oral traditional instruments, who can use his tradition to aesthetic advantage both as an individual artist and as a member of a tradition. In presenting this model, I hope to offer a basis for comparison with some of the shorter lyrics in Old English, not necessarily to suggest that they are "oral," for that elusive term needs some serious rethinking, but rather to establish an accurate and worthwhile avenue for a comparative investigation and to show that Old English poetry may display both "oral" character and "literary" art.

The model to which I refer is the Christian oral epic in the South Slavic tradition, as distinguished from the longer Muslim epic collected by, for example, Marjanović, Hörmann, and Parry, Lord, and Bynum.[23] It is, of course, the Muslim epic that Parry especially sought for his comparisons with the monumental poems of Homer and that Lord has made the primary and nearly exclusive comparand in his studies of ancient Greek, Old English, Old French, medieval Greek, and biblical material. They chose the Muslim tradition for two main reasons: (1) the average length of the poems more closely approximates the extent of the *Iliad* and *Odyssey*; whereas the Christian songs seldom exceed 200 verses (although there are examples that do), the Muslim songs recorded by Parry and Lord commonly run to 2,000 lines or even, as in the case of Avdo Medjedović's *The Wedding of Smailagić Meho*,[24] to more than 12,000; and (2) the story patterns of the Muslim epics correspond more closely to those of the Homeric poems, with the so-called Return Song in South Slavic and the *Odyssey* being of precisely the same generic type. Often the very same generic story appears in both Muslim and Christian traditions, but in the former it is customarily told at much greater length, with a good deal more of what Lord has called "elaboration."[25]

This then is the first point: the Parry-Lord theory is founded primarily on the longer Muslim material in the Serbo-Croatian oral tradition, largely to the exclusion of the shorter Christian poems. The second point to be addressed in presenting the Christian songs for analysis is the question of the texts, and this is a troublesome question which can at this point be only partially elucidated. Lord has always stressed the need for unambiguously oral material, preferably texts taken down from a singer either by audio apparatus or by dictation in an observed, documented situation. The unique archive of the Parry collection contains more than 1000 such song texts, contextualized by interviews with singers, by other songs in a given *guslar*'s repertoire, and by the local tradition of which he is a part. Many of the earlier collections of South Slavic narrative song were made under different and much less controlled conditions and, in fact, in many cases not much is actually known about the circumstances of collection. Such texts, some of which date from 100 or more years before the first Parry-Lord field trips and document areas not represented in the Parry archive, are precisely those against which Lord has argued.

If we choose to limit the sample from the living tradition in this way, we should be aware of the implications, for in doing so we patently eliminate the chance of any other model of oral narrative poetry. Logically, the choice of the sample upon which analysis will be carried out must always, to a greater or lesser extent, determine the results of that analysis. If, then, we use only Muslim oral epic recorded in the 1930s as the basis for comparison (whatever our motives in limiting the selection), we can discover in the compared poetry only those characteristics which exist in and define the source poetry. The problem is formally similar to the one sketched above in relation to the Old English formula: we can discover oral structures if and only if the oral structures we seek are understood as those observed in Muslim epic of the 1930s. If there is any discrepancy between our abstraction of "orality" and the sample we submit as the subject for analysis, then any and all comparative judgements that we base strictly on that sample are by definition invalid.

Now it is quite true, by the same token, that the earlier collections present us with manifold uncertainties, for, as Parry and Lord found in their field-work, not a few *guslari* were known either to have memorized or even to have copied out songs from commonly available *pjesmarice* ("songbooks"), taking the material from a published format and passing it off as traditional and genuine oral poetry. More serious than this disadvantage is the final, nagging question which must always be asked when we are dealing with a text of which we have a first-hand knowledge only as a written text—was it actually an oral poem or not? If it was not oral, was it perhaps transitional between oral and written and, if that is the case, exactly how is it transitional? It is a scholarly fact of life in oral literature research that we sometimes cannot answer these questions directly.[26] On the other hand, to look at the positive side for a moment, we must lose a great deal if we categorically dismiss all or a significant part of the earliest records of the oral tradition in

South Slavic in favour of restricting our study to Muslim epic songs recorded well into the twentieth century. However apposite the restriction of materials may prove in certain cases, it must mask explanation in other areas. Would it not be fairer at least to consider the older collections, and especially the Christian material in those collections, even calibrating their evidence to account for uncertainties if that proves advisable, before dismissing their importance? For we are engaged in formulating a theory of oral traditional literature which must serve not just Homer and not just longer epic of the Homeric kind, but whatever oral literature we may encounter.[27]

The particular material which I summon here as a comparand— selections from *Sprske narodne pjesme (Serbian Folk Songs)*, the famous collection of Christian oral narratives published by Vuk Stefan Karadžić between 1841 and 1862—is meant to illustrate a different kind of oral poem: not the monumental epic drama but rather the much briefer epic or lyric tale in the Christian tradition.[28] It may turn out that these selections from Vuk constitute a different genre or sub-genre from that represented by the Parry-Lord songs and it may turn out that we have two quite disparate types of literature distinguished along other than generic lines, but for the moment the important fact is that both the Vuk and the Parry-Lord collections contain oral epic poetry.

These Christian songs were chosen for publication by Vuk himself from among the many hundreds that were in his possession in manuscript form.[29] From what can be reconstructed of his activities, we know that these songs came from two sources. In the early part of his life Vuk took down the texts from dictation, but as he grew older he relied more and more on co-workers to do the actual collecting from singers. The only exception to this tendency was his continued interest in personally writing down songs from the best of his singers, whose work constitutes the major part of the published record. Although Vuk was apparently quite careful to instruct his helpers in what he considered a proper method of obtaining and documenting material, he did not himself follow these directions as rigorously, and so the circumstances of collection were not always noted. Another problem of identification, perhaps the most significant one, stems from his practice of destroying original manuscripts after copy was made ready for the printer. He followed this practice quite systematically, so that only a relatively small number of published songs survive in their original transcriptions. Živomir Mladenović, the co-editor of Vuk's unpublished works, explains the situation in these terms:

> Perhaps he destroyed them so that it would not be known how much he changed a text in the process of editing it for publication, although, as can be seen from the accidentally preserved manuscripts of edited songs, his emendations were always fully appropriate. But that which he did himself he did not permit others to do. He absolutely demanded of his coworkers that they change nothing while taking down the songs, adding that if anything needed setting straight or filling out, he alone would do it.[30]

Although my own inspection of the surviving manuscripts at the Archive of the Serbian Academy of Sciences indicated very infrequent emendation,[31] I believe it is important to note the typical reasons behind Vuk's editorial changes. First, he seems generally to have proceeded in two stages: an initial editing followed by a second group of modifications apparently made as the transcriptions were prepared for the publisher. All manuscripts show evidence of the first stage, which appears in a darker ink than that of the original; if there is actual notation of the second stage (and in most manuscripts there is not), it is in pencil. In both phases of the process, the single most common basis for editorial change is *metri causa*, adjustment of a word or words to a dialect equivalent or apocopated or syncopated form to make the line involved a regular decasyllable (*deseterac*). In "Djakon Stefan i dva andjela" ("Deacon Stefan and the Two Angels"),[32] for example, he changes MS *belu* to *belinu* in line 6 and MS *predje* to *pre* in line 17, both to eke out the ten syllables of the *deseterac* exactly:

| Te on seje *belinu* pšenicu | 6 |
| And he sowed white wheat | |

| Predje sunce i *pre* leturgije | 17 |
| Before dawn and before the service. | |

In addition to minor orthographical or syntactic adjustments, the latter of which seem designed to make the lines periodic and smooth, Vuk will on rare occasions add or substitute hemistichs or whole lines. Interestingly for our purposes, as a rule the hemistich changes replace a bounded utterance or formula with another at least equally common formula. In line 12 of "Ljuba Jakšića Šćepana" (Jakšić Šćepan's Love),[33] for instance, Vuk modifies

> Mitar skoči, *u planinu podje*
> to Mitar skoči *na noge lagane*
>
> Mitar jumped up, he headed for the mountain
> Mitar jumped up to his nimble feet

The even rarer whole-line additions customarily make the narrative progress more specific, but they do not "improve" the song in any other than a cosmetic manner. An example is lines 3-6 of "Djakon Stefan i dva andjela," lines 4-5 being Vuk's addition:

> Predje sunca i pre leturgije,
> Before dawn and before the service,
> One ne ide u bijelu crkvu,
> He didn't go to the white church,
> 5   Već on ide u to polje ravno,
> But he went to that level field,
> Te on seje belinu pšenicu,
> And he sowed white wheat.

Once again the added material is fully as formulaic and traditional as that which surrounds it. In general, the emendations introduced by Vuk into the texts of the songs that he published seem, on the basis of the evidence available, to be infrequent and slight; more importantly for our purposes, they seem also to have been insignificant with respect to the larger question of aesthetics.

My selections of illustrative passages from *Srpske narodne pjesme* have been made according to a number of criteria. First, to control as closely as possible the quality and homogeneity of the sample, I have used only songs taken from the initial four of Vuk's nine volumes, thus excluding the posthumous volumes which he did not himself prepare for publication. Secondly, I have limited the sample further to songs appearing in volume two, those which he labelled *pjesme junačke najstarije* (the "oldest heroic songs"); those chosen from this group all contribute to Vuk's verse portrait of the Serbian hero Kraljević Marko, or Prince Marko. Thirdly, since my purpose is to describe another kind of oral epic poetry, an oral poetry in which structure and aesthetics function together as complementary aspects of the poet's craft, I have intentionally selected songs in which the artistic value of traditional elements is beyond question but also, for practical reasons, briefly demonstrable. The examples drawn from the Old English poetic canon, whose ultimate origin is of course more obscure than that of the Serbian passages, have also been selected for their appropriateness to the present discussion. In this way I hope to have brought together some of the most memorable and important moments in these poems and to have illustrated the compatibility of oral structure and literary art.

As my first example, I refer to "Marko pije uz ramazan vino" ("Marko Drinks Wine During Ramazan"),[34] which with its ninety-eight verses is slightly shorter than the average song of the type I wish to describe. It concerns the problems raised by Kraljević Marko's actions during the Muslim holy time of Ramazan, a thirty-day period over the course of which, in this particular instance, Tsar Sulejman had ordered certain customary activities, such as wine-drinking, to be temporarily suspended. The situation is complicated by the fact that the action takes place in the later part of Marko's life, after circumstances have forced him into an uneasy relationship with the enemy Turks, in opposition to his Christian comrades. Other traditional assumptions not explicitly stated in the song are Marko's love of wine-drinking, which on occasion reveals a ritual significance,[35] and his legendary choleric nature. While other heroes might charge an adversary or at least issue a challenge, Marko often responds by tying up his horse Šarac and sitting down to empty his wineskin. When his moral or ethical values are impugned, however, he is just as likely to relieve the culprit of his head.

Against this background we encounter the still resolutely Christian hero flagrantly disobeying the tsar's four-point mandate against drinking wine, wearing a cloak, strapping on a sword, and dancing with women. The opening lines of the song set the structure and tone of the piece, with the command and Marko's defiance of it couched in formulaic terms:

Car Suleman jasak učinio:
Tsar Sulejman issued an order:
da s' ne pije uz ramazan vino,
that none drink wine during Ramazan,
da s' ne nose zelene dolame,
that none wear green dolamas,
da s' ne pašu sablje okovane,

that none strap on plated swords,
5   da s' ne igra kolom uz kadune;
that none dance the kolo with women.
Marko igra kolom uz kadune,
Marko danced the kolo with women,
Marko paše sablju okovanu,
Marko strapped on a plated sword,
Marko nosi zelenu dolamu,
Marko wore a green dolama,
Marko pije uz ramazan vino,
Marko drank wine during Ramazan.

Obviously these lines are formulaic; just as obviously they follow the classic pattern of "ring-composition" discovered in Homer and traced in many other oral literatures as well.[36] The sequence of order and defiance also conforms to other collections of South Slavic material and may possibly be explained as simply a symmetry induced by the utilitarian nature of formulaic composition. We may thus choose to see this grouping of lines as nothing more than a structural inevitability, given the character of the oral style, and we may even cling to that functional view of the poem's structure as the sequence recurs three times, with subtle variations, through the song. Though inherently questionable, this explanation would maintain Parry-Lord orthodoxy and ground the pattern in a traditional function.

It may, however, be more difficult to sustain this judgement as we approach Marko's own comments on his situation. Called before the tsar to account for his apparent flaunting of an official prohibition, he answers four questions founded on the very same sequence, as well as three items added by the tsar:

Poočime, care Sulemane,
Foster father, tsar Sulejman,
ako pijem uz ramazan vino,
if I drink wine during Ramazan,
70   ako pijem, vera mi donosi;
if I drink, my faith allows me;
ak' nagonim odže i adžije,
if I drive out the priests and pilgrims,
ne može mi ta obraz podneti
it is a breach of my honour
da ja pijem, oni da gledaju,

if I drink myself and let them look on,
nek ne idu meni u meanu;
so let them not come with me to the tavern;
75   ako l' nosim zelenu dolamu,
if I wear a green dolama,
mlad sam junak i dolikuje mi;
I am a young man and it suits me;
ako l' pašem sablju okovanu,
if I strap on a plated sword,
ja sam sablju za blago kupio;
I paid a good price for that sword;
ako igram kolom uz kadune,
if I dance the kolo with women,
80   ja se, care, nisam oženio
I have not, tsar, taken a wife
i ti s', care, bio neoženjen;
and you, tsar, were once without a wife;
ako kalpak na oči namičem,
if I pull my fur cap down over my eyes,
čelo gori, s carem se govori;
the forehead burns when talking with the tsar;37
što buzdovan uza se prevlačim
if I draw my mace closer to me
85   i što sablju na krilo namičem,
and pull my sword into my lap,
ja se bojim da ne bude kavge,—
I fear that there may be a quarrel,—
ako bi se zametnula kavga,
if a quarrel does break out,
teško onom tko j' najbliže Marka!
it will go hard on whoever is nearest Marko!

In the Parry-Lord epics of the Muslim tradition such lists of items and responses are common, but equally common is the omission of one or more items in the repetition. This phenomenon of omission, like Homer's famous narrative inconsistencies and other forms of supposed "nodding," has been convincingly explained as the result of the priority of "essential ideas" and other traditional structures over their actual expression in phraseology.38 To put it another way, in the longer Muslim epic a list of items can hardly avoid including supernumerary elements, at least from the traditional point of view; the individual performance is always contextualized by the other individual performances which make up a poetic tradition, and the "error" or "omission" is not as serious a literary problem as a missing paragraph or chapter in *The Bridge on the Drina* would be.[39] But in the passage just cited not only are the number and order of the elements preserved here as throughout the song, but the "map" is elaborated, the bare structure fleshed out, as the poet delineates Marko's character in fuller detail, but still within a traditional framework. We may trace his formulas and find his diction patterned and conventional; at the same time, however, we must admit the possibility of a singer in artistic control of his medium, one able to shape that medium, to answer his aesthetic sense of content and design.

Another indication of the poet's control comes in the last few lines of his song, after the tsar has been sufficiently impressed by Marko's threatening presence (and the absence of any of his own men for support) to excuse his offences and in fact to offer him a *pourboire* for services rendered. This motif of rewarding a servant or messenger with what is often called a *zahmedija* in the Parry Collection songs[40] is ubiquitous in the poetic tradition; it occurs frequently in songs about a hero's return from imprisonment, for example. But in this particular case, this highly traditional motif is employed as an extremely effective closure to a narrative that has profiled the uncomfortably unstable position of the Christian hero as the forced minion of the enemy:

> car s' odmiče, Marko se premiče,
> The tsar moved away, Marko moved forward
> dok dotera cara do duvara:
> until he drove the tsar against the wall:
>
> 95   car se maša rukom u džepove,
> the tsar thrust his hand into his pockets,
> on izvadi stotinu dukata
> he drew out one hundred ducats
> pa i daje Kraljeviću Marku:
> and gave them to Kraljević Marko:
> "Idi, Marko, te se napij vina!"
> "Go ahead, Marko, and drink wine!"

After the prohibitions of the tsar's original mandate and Marko's defiance, all couched in virtually identical formulas, and after the elaboration of that basic structure to allow the hero to characterize himself as well as to explain his situation, what is the outcome of

Marko's interview with authority? The tsar offers him a *pourboire* in direct contradiction to his own earlier command. Certainly this is a traditional motif, but just as certainly it is handled with an aesthetic sense of irony, an irony that tells us indirectly and engagingly of Marko's heroic character and of the survival of all that he represents as a stalwart Christian hero even in the camp of the Turkish enemy. The poet is not forced into this closure to his poem; rather he is able to mould his traditional materials with artistic craft.

An added example of the figure of ring-composition taking on an aesthetic as well as structural function is furnished by "Marko Kraljević i kći kralja arapskoga" ("Marko Kraljević and the Daughter of the Arab King"), recited by Tešan Podrugović, from whom Vuk collected a number of excellent songs.[41] In this case the ring consists of a typical series of questions posed to the hero by his mother, who wonders why he is building religious memorials:

> Pita majka Kraljevića Marka:
> Kraljević Marko's mother asked:
> "Ja moj sinko, Kraljeviću Marko,
> "O my son, Kraljević Marko,
> što ti gradiš mloge zadužbine?
> why are you building so many memorials?
> Il' si te ko bogu zgriješio,
> Have you sinned grievously against God,
> 5   il' si ludo blago zadobio?"
> Or have you come into unexpected riches?"

As often happens in this song cycle, Jevrosima's remarks launch her son on an adventure, here a reminiscence of an episode in past time. Marko tells of being captured and imprisoned by Arabs, his tale then following the classic Return pattern, which involves the intercession of a woman on his behalf. As Lord has shown, the Return story is an ancient one, probably deriving from a secularization of the myth of the dying god who is revived seasonally,[42] and so we may be sure that the basic story pattern is very traditional indeed. But in this instance, there occurs a striking departure from the conventional action: disgusted by the Arab girl who has freed him from prison, Marko slays her and goes home to his mother, bearing the wealth that the girl had given as an inducement to marriage.[43] As he later explains, it is exactly this *dénouement* which leads him to offer memorials:

85
Tu sam, mati, bogu zgriješio,
So, mother, I have sinned against God,
a veliko blago zadobio,
And come into great riches,
te ja gradim mloge zadužbine.
And thus I am building many memorials.

In this way the ring closes lexically and formulaically around Marko's reminiscence. At the level of the story itself, he feels he must offer appeasement to God for the untoward outcome of his adventure; at the deeper level of story pattern, the ring of formulaic language contextualizes a Return which is, as far as the integrity of the narrative pattern is concerned, never accomplished. But whatever level we choose to examine, we must note that the poet has echoed the opening questions posed by Jevrosima with the formulaic responses of Marko at the end of the song. Again the structure is beyond doubt traditional, both in the outer frame of ring-composition and in its formulaic expression, but the effect achieved by the singer's particular use of these materials must be understood as more than circumstantial or utilitarian; the effect is that of oral traditional art.

Another of Podrugović's songs, "Marko Kraljević i Arapin" ("Marko Kraljević and the Arab"), illustrates how the singer may deflect the usual action of a stock motif to describe a character and a situation. The pattern in question[44] entails a leader's search for a hero, often a substitute for the leader himself, to solve a problem recently arisen. In most cases the problem involves a foreign aggressor, here the Arab, who threatens the established order, often with an unlawful miscegenation as in the Podrugović song. The commander's procedure is typically to send out messengers offering a handsome reward for such a substitute; although their initial search is fruitless, very soon a hero who can and will help appears on the scene and rectifies the imbalance. This "theme" (in Lord's sense of a repeated narrative unit),[45] which for the sake of convenient reference I will call the "Search for a substitute," occurs relatively early in the song under consideration:

30
Kada vidje što mu knjiga kaže,
When he saw what the letter said,
stade care tražit mejdandžije,
the tsar began to seek combatants,[46]

obećava blago nebrojeno,
he promised uncountable riches
ko pogubi crnog Arapina.
to whoever killed the black Arab.
Mejdandžije mloge odlaziše,
Many combatants journeyed out,
al' Stambolu nijedan ne dodje.
but not one returned to Stambol.
35   Nuto caru velike nevolje!
This was great trouble for the tsar!
Veće njemu nesta mejdanžija,
And so he had no more combatants,
sve pogubi crni Arapine.
the black Arab had killed them all.
Ni tu nije goleme nevolje.
Nor was it serious trouble for [the Arab].
Al' s' opremi crni Arapine . . .
The black Arab armed himself . . .

After line 38 above, the conventional form of this theme would turn to the emergence of the willing and capable hero, Marko Kraljević in the present multiform. But—and I have added line 39 to the quotation to illustrate the point—the pattern does not hold; instead the poem continues not with Marko's but with the Arab's preparations for the ritual bride-stealing he earlier pledged and with a description of the wedding plans he forces the tsar and his daughter to accept. Do we read this sequence as a truncated pattern, one in which Podrugović "nods," so to speak, or do we question the significance and viability of an incomplete pattern for the song as a work of art?

Neither of these alternatives is satisfactory, and a brief look at events further along in the song shows why. First, the appearance of a suitable champion is not eliminated but only postponed; the theme of the "Search for a substitute" is not incomplete but, rather, elaborated. For example, the description of the Arab's arming and marriage demands gives way to the tsar's reaction: a letter to Marko pleading for help, or in other words an extension of the same "search for a substitute" theme taken a step further. As if to heighten the tension and represent the task as even more difficult of achievement, the poet also has the hero refuse a second letter of appeal written by the tsar's wife. Only when the daughter herself writes—that is, the girl who is the object of the Arab's nuptial quest—does Marko accede, and then the material rewards that she offers no doubt play a part in eliciting his grudging promise of aid. It is important to remember that all these actions, *particular* to the narrative situation in this story, are inserted by the poet into a *generic* structure with a momentum of its own. Podrugović has in a manner of speaking harnessed the traditional energy of the "Search for a substitute" and has used the narrative commonplace to bear the burden of story-specific information. Through the delay of what convention leads us to expect, we learn of the seriousness of the tsar's predicament, both through the frustration of his attempts to find a worthy and effective replacement and through Marko's clear and unabashed aversion to confronting the source of the trouble. We also learn that Marko is not merely a Diomedes who accepts all challenges immediately and, slashing through his enemies, proves over and over again his pure martial superiority. Marko is more like Odysseus: a wily planner who takes no direct action until he feels the time is right and the odds are in his favour, a sometimes reluctant hero who occasionally has to be enticed into battle by the promise of riches or the threat of embarrassment. What is more, we learn all these things by means of the poet's artistic manipulation of an oral traditional pattern. His control over the aesthetics of his poem could not be more apparent, and yet he is an oral poet employing a deeply traditional structure. There is, in short, no contradiction between the oral tradition he draws from and the literary work he creates; indeed, the absence of either oral traditional structure or aesthetic control would make the poem as it stands impossible.

With No. 73 in the second volume, Filip Višnjić's "Smrt Marka Kraljevića" ("The Death of Kraljević Marko"),[47] we come to the close of the Marko cycle as presented by Vuk. The hero who still cannot be beaten in combat, whose horse is still swiftest, and who, at least at the opening of the song, has no reason to doubt his continued success or even immortality feels Šarac stumble for the first time and hears a *vila* ("mountain nymph") explain the mis-step as an omen of his own approaching demise. After seeing his image, now aged and ready for a final peace, in the reflection of a pond, he prepares himself for death. Even in this very unusual narrative, certain traditional patterns ramify and provide impetus and direction. For instance, the conventional connection between Marko's and his horse's actions makes Šarac's stumbling at the start of the song a sure indication that his master will in some way follow suit. Just as the horse has often sensed danger and warned or tried to help Marko, or even as when the two comrades shared the ritual sustenance of wine-drinking before embarking on one or another adventure, so now the faulty step taken by Šarac foretells a weakness of some sort in Marko. The particular story content has changed, and radically, but the traditional generic structure remains active and dynamic in providing meaning to the narrative.

To take another example, we find the veteran of many battles responding to the realization of his mortality in what is finally a familiar manner. After viewing his reflection, Marko prepares himself for death by first killing the faithful Šarac and then destroying one by one the sword, lance, and mace which have served not only as martial accoutrements but also as symbols of his heroism. It is, in other words, as though he prepares for his last "battle" by reversing the customary procedures of arming; rather he prepares by "unpreparing," arms by disarming.[48] Instead of saddling Šarac, he dispatches him, ostensibly to prevent his falling into enemy hands, and instead of donning battle garb and gear, he renders his weapons useless and disposes of them. We cannot fail to see in this sad, funereal sequence of actions a heroic underlay: Marko performs the negative of each of the ritual oblations for battle, and the poet guides us through his personal obsequies along the traditional pathway of the themes of readying the horse and arming for battle. It says a great deal about Marko as a character that his preparations for death echo the ritualized pattern of his preparations for heroic adventure during his lifetime, and it says a great deal about the poet Višnjić and his poem that so singular an event as Marko's death is presented in so traditional a manner. For what is most satisfying about this very moving account is precisely that traditional way in which the pattern helps to explain as well as simply to present a reality otherwise hard to explain and accept.

I believe it is possible that this kind of poet, rather than either a singer of Muslim epic or a fully literate craftsman, composed some of the more finely-worked Anglo-Saxon poems, and in particular the shorter lyrics. Far from being a Parry-Lord *guslar* who cannot mould the material of his tradition into an artistic design because of the pressure of rapid formulaic composition in performance and the manifestly different genre of the longer epic,[49] this kind of poet might well have sung such carefully wrought poems as *The Seafarer, The Wanderer*, some of the more complex of the ninety-five Riddles (*Kunsträtsel*, as they were once called in opposition to *Volkrätsel*), *The*

Advent Lyrics, Deor and other Old English poems which display oral traditional structure in the service of an artistic sensibility. It is exactly this sort of poem for which the Parry-Lord model cannot account and which has seemed, given prevailing theory, to be an impossible creation. Since it would have been unthinkable and reductive to deny these poems' art, and since no model has been available that could explain both art and structure, it has until now been necessary to deny their orality. Perhaps even more crucially, it has as a result also been the fashion to undervalue their *traditional* character, and this practice has ironically led to undervaluing of their art. For, as I hope the examples drawn from the Vuk poetry have illustrated, not only is it a sin of omission not to recognize and interpret the oral traditional character of a poem, but it also bespeaks a decidedly misguided methodology. Simply put, if we do not consider all aspects of the aesthetic integrity of a work of art—and oral traditional structure is most definitely a telling quality of the Vuk and of many of the Old English poems—then we cannot be satisfied that we have produced a bona fide critical analysis of that work. Moving from the Serbian poetry to a few examples in the Anglo-Saxon verse canon, I hope to demonstrate once again how structure and aesthetics may go hand in hand; far from being mutually exclusive, it is only their combination that produces the finely-wrought oral traditional, and yet literary, poem.

In order to gain a perspective from which to view, for example, the *Seafarer* poet's achievement, it is first necessary to document the oral traditional nature of his diction and narrative structure. Jackson Campbell's "Oral Poetry in *The Seafarer*" is helpful in this regard, since it includes an analysis of the entire poem for exactly repeated formulas.[50] But I must agree with Wayne O'Neil[51] that Campbell's elimination of formulaic systems from the investigation, on the grounds that "some of these are often doubtful and difficult to verify,"[52] obscures the overall picture of formulaic structure; more seriously, I think, an insistence on verbatim repetition as the sole relevant evidence hampers our efforts to reach an understanding of the flexible and idiomatic character of traditional diction in Old English poetry. Since the present study seeks not to "prove orality" by assembling statistics but rather to appreciate the poet's art in handling traditional materials,[53] let us consider a few examples both of repeated phrases and of flexible systems in the opening lines of the poem.

As Campbell notes, there are four formulas in lines 1-7: *so ∂gied wrecan* (1b), *gebiden hæbbe* (4b), *atol yþa gewealc* (6a) and *æt nacan stefnan* (7b).[54] But a restriction of evidence to formulas alone masks the fact that all these phrases have other relatives, some near and others more distant, in the poetic wordhoard. For example, we find at *Beowulf* 3172a the verse *wordgyd wrecan*, obviously closely related to *soðgied wrecan*, with only the alliterating element in the *-gied* compound varying.[55] One could construe this pair of phrases as derivatives of the same formulaic system, using Donald K. Fry's generative model of traditional phraseology in Old English,[56] and this explanation would serve in the present case. In whatever manner the relationship among the phrases *wordgyd wrecan*, *soðgied wrecan* and *soðgied wrecaði*s described, however, we cannot fail to be aware of the suppleness of the diction; formulas are only one aspect of the phraseology and they cannot reveal its quality of multiformity.

The flexibility of the poetic diction becomes more apparent with the establishment of the traditional context of *The Seafarer* 6a, *atol yþa gewealc*, also found verbatim at *Exodus* 456a. Again the exact repetition tells only part of the story; to fill it out we need to take into account two additional phrases:

> Riddle 22 7a   *atol yþa gebræc*
> *Beowulf* 848a   *atol yða geswing.*

With vocalic alliteration in all four cases, there is no phonological or lexical pressure on the morph in final position, and so it varies freely (*-wealc* twice, *-bræc* and *-swing*) within a loosely defined semantic field. None of the traditional character of the diction is diluted by this variability, nor is the half-line system any less useful or appropriate than an invariable element; on the contrary, the flexible system enables the poet to compose more freely by affording him multiformity instead of frozen and therefore unwieldy phraseology.[57]

While the theory of the formulaic system can take the description this far, it cannot address certain other kinds of traditional structures. Campbell correctly finds *The Seafarer* 2-3, for example, entirely devoid of formulas; we may add that no true formulaic systems are to be located in these four verses, noting *hapax legomena* in 2b and 3a. And yet each of the four half-lines may be shown to be, each in its own way, an element of traditional diction. The table below places the verses in their respective phraseological contexts:

Verse	Traditional Context
siþas secgan (2a)	æþelu secgan (*R55* 8b) godspel secgan (*SnS* 65b) synne secga∂ (*Glc* 506a)
hu ic geswincdagum (2b)	in geardagum (*Bwf* 1b) on fyrndagum (*And* 1b, *SnS* 179b, etc.)
earfo∂hwile (3a)	earfo∂lice (*And* 514b, *SB1* 38a, *SB2* 35a, and seven others)
oft þrowade (3b)	leng þrowian (*And* 80b) for∂ þrowian (*Chr* 1632b)

None of the citations indicates a formula, and in most instances it would stretch credibility and definition to divine a formulaic system ordering the corresponding verses. Nonetheless, it is easily seen how *siþas secgan* is metrically, syntactically and in a general sense semantically related to its three phraseological kin. Verse 2b shares not only metre and lexical elements with the half-lines cited but also joins them in the poetic function of introducing a poem or section of a poem. This is not to mention the thirty-four additional verses which express the same "essential idea" even if they vary too much to be admitted to formulaic status. In the case of *earfo∂hwile*, an apparent coinage by the *Seafarer* poet, we find ten occurrences of the quite similar *earfo∂lice* as a context. Both words fill an identical metrical slot and perform the same syntactic function; although they are not properly construed as relatives within a single system, it is important to recognize that their similarity extends to sound patterning and beyond.[58] As for the last of the four verses, *oft þrowade*, there is no shortage of analogues: the problem is whether to stop with the two given in the table (examples of a monosyllabic adverb plus *∂rowian*) or to refer to the numerous occurrences of *oft* plus an unprefixed verb filling the verse.

It may be argued with justice that many of the correspondences listed above are simply predispositions within the poetic language as a

whole rather than true traditional elements, that they result from the
convergence of Old English syntax, prosody and habits of composition,
and that on these grounds we should distinguish them from formulas
and formulaic systems. While that partitioning may be the proper
taxonomic strategy, I would maintain that we must still take such
predispositions into account in studying the traditional character of the
poetic diction, for, although the phrases in question may be "non-
formulaic," they do respond to and take shape from habits of
composition; they are formed according to such patterns and, once
formed, they provide models for the making of verses like them.

Even from such a limited sample it becomes evident that the
diction of *The Seafarer* is in its various ways highly traditional. There
are formulas, to be sure, but on closer examination we also find
formulaic systems and, beyond the systems, less obvious relationships
which we may leave in the category of predispositions. The
phraseology is most productively understood not as a collection of
prefabricated units ready to hand, but as a living tissue of language with
genetic associations. These associations will not, nor should they be
expected to, submit tidily to one archetypal definition or set of
definitions; they manifest themselves as a spectrum of relationships
rather than as recurrences of a single type.[59] Only by viewing the entire
spectrum—verbatim formulas, flexible systems and predispositions—
can we come to appreciate the deeply traditional nature of Old English
poetic diction and its manifold possibilities for verbal art.

A poet in full and sensitive control of such a network of
interrelationships is no slave to his phraseology; rather he can, as we
have observed in the work of the Vuk singers, achieve the kind of
noteworthy stylistic effects for which we usually reserve the term
"literary" by manipulating the structures and associations which are part
of his poetic language. As one illustration of this literary recasting of
oral traditional patterns, let us compare the first few verses of *The
Seafarer* and its generic companion *The Wife's Lament* against the
background of our earlier analysis. Presented below are the initial
arguments of the two poems:

> Mæg ic be me sylfum   soðgied wrecan
> siþas secgan,   hu ic geswincdagum
> earfoðhwile   oft þrowade,
> bitre breostceare   gebiden hæbbe.
> (*The Seafarer*, 1-4)

> *Ic* þis *giedd wrece*   *bi me* ful geomorre,
> minre *sylfre si∂*   Ic þæt *secgan mæg,*
> hwæt ic yrmþa *gebad,*   siþþan ic up weox,
> niwes oþþe ealdes,   no ma þonne nu.
> A ic wite wonn   minra *wræcsiþa.*
>
> (*The Wife's Lament,* 1-5)

As the italicized elements show, there are many correspondences between the two passages, many more than could be expected unless there is some external reason for the similarity, such as one poet consciously echoing another poem or creating a work within a recognized thematic pattern or genre with certain lexical imperatives. For the present purpose, it is not necessary to advocate either position; in the one case the source of the verbal correspondence would be a deliberate artistic decision on the part of a literary craftsman, while in the other the echoes would result from the idiomatic use of words which have through convention attached themselves to the traditional theme of "exile."[60] What cannot be entertained is the hypothesis that the verbal repetition stems inevitably from the limitations imposed by traditional diction, the imagined phraseological fetters from which the captive poet cannot escape. For although, as I have demonstrated, these lines from *The Seafarer* are thoroughly traditional, the parallels now under consideration are not: the latter consist almost entirely of single words rather than patterns and do not correlate either syntactically or metrically. To put it another way, the parallels are neither formulas nor formulaic systems nor predispositions; they are verbal echoes that are achieved within traditional diction but do not depend upon that diction for their resonance.[61]

The phrase *so∂gied wrecan,* for example, shown above to be both a formula and a member of a system, correlates with *Ic* þis *giedd wrece* (*The Wife's Lament,* 1a), but their relationship in poetic diction is untraditional. The two verses may share a pair of roots, they may each individually belong to a formulaic system,[62] but they are not themselves phraseologically related in any discernible traditional way. They owe their reverberative presence in the opening lines of lyric elegies, as already suggested, either to direct imitation or to a thematic or generic constraint, and as single-word correspondences they exemplify the sort of echoic effect that is within the grasp of a literary poet in control of oral traditional diction.

Another example of the same phenomenon is offered by *The*

Seafarer, 1a and 2a, and *The Wife's Lament*, 2a-b. Here the repeated words (*Mæg/mæg, sylfum/sylfre, sipas/sið* and *secgan/ secgan*) are once again individually traceable to formulaic systems, but their relationship to these two poems is nontraditional and literary. The poets have used a group of words which are heavy with associations of elegy and exile, but they have done so without having recourse to metrically or syntactically parallel verses. These two opening passages are in fact dense with verbal correspondence but it amounts, if I may make the distinction, to a conscious *design* rather than an inherited *pattern*. Although each verse is itself constructed out of the materials which comprise the traditional wordhoard, and although we may find a thematic matrix underlying the ideas of each passage, the echoic elements themselves are prominently in the foreground. This kind of design, which puts traditional patterns to a new and individual use, must be the creation of a poet who can place his phraseological inheritance in the service of an artistic sensibility.

Within *The Seafarer* itself are found many similar verbal designs, none more important to the aesthetics of the poem than the echoic repetition of the word *dryhten*, designating at various points both the leader of the earthly comitatus and his divine equivalent. One of a group of keywords, first described by Greenfield as making for "a deliberate ambiguity of diction throughout the poem,"[63] *dryhten* assists in fashioning and maintaining a double focus for the reader by providing a verbal nexus for the two quite distinct narrative levels of the poem. The seafarer moves from the misery of having lost his temporal lord to the ultimate security of the heavenly comitatus—a *fæstnung*, as the *Wanderer* poet puts it—and both extremes of his journey from earthly to spiritual are imaged in the highly-charged ambivalence of this and other lexical fulcrums. The opening echo on *dryhten* (41b/43a) marks the beginning and end, and therefore the distance, of the journey and sets up a reverberation which will continue throughout the poem. At each of the other four occurrences, the double resonance enriches the momentary narrative meaning of the passage involved; even though all four are decidedly references to the Christian God, the *double entendre* persists in securing the ephemeral foil to the seafarer's spiritual voyage and experience.

Thus far we have been describing a literary technique, a kind of verbal echo not dissimilar to the lexical correspondences between *The Seafarer* and *The Wife's Lament*. But are the verses in question related in any manner other than their inclusion of the single word *dryhten*? Here are the lines under discussion:

41:	ne in his dædum to þæs deor, ne him his *dryhten* to þæs hold,
43:	to hwon hine *dryhten* gedon wille.
65:	*dryhtnes* dreamas þonne þis deade lif,
106:	Dol biþ se þe him his *dryhten* ne ondrædeþ; cymed him se deað unþinged.
121:	þær is lif gelong in lufan *dryhtnes*,
124:	ece *dryhten*, in ealle tid. Amen.

While no formulaic, metrical or syntactic relationship can be demonstrated among the six verses as a group, so that we must dismiss the possibility of a purely traditional echo and give the *Seafarer* poet himself full credit for this verbal figure, three of the six half-lines have formulaic relatives elsewhere in the poetic corpus.[64] Once more we glimpse an artist who apparently knows and can take advantage of the patterned diction while still embroidering its poetic fabric with his own personal design.

What kind of traditional poet can accomplish this feat of repeating certain significant words without resorting to identical formulas, flexible systems, and predispositions? The Parry-Lord theory offers no explanation for such an apparent anomaly. According to the model derived from Muslim epic, he must either depend entirely and exclusively on inherited verbal patterns, in which case close verbal repetition and other sorts of attention to detail typical of literary composition are impossible,[65] or be a literary artisan incapable of the formulaic technique; there is no middle ground. But we have observed in the *Seafarer* poet a craftsman who is able to do the impossible—to manipulate words and formulas at will, to use the traditional patterns in creating unique and engaging designs. The evidence from phraseology is straightforward: this is a poet very much like the best of Vuk's singers, one who balances formulaic craft and literary acumen and one who turns the expressive potential of the poetic tradition to an artistic purpose.

With this much established at the level of diction, let us now turn to the thematic structure of *The Seafarer* and consider the implementation of traditional narrative units in this manifestly literary poem. The common theme of "exile," first discussed by Greenfield and mentioned briefly above, involves four constituent motifs or aspects:

(1) status, (2) deprivation, (3) state of mind and (4) movement in or into exile.[66] As in most typical scenes in Old English poetry, there is any number of verbal solutions to the problem of presenting the exile figure and his dilemma; although some of the aspects seem to attract certain formulas and systems, there is, as Greenfield illustrates,[67] a good deal of freedom in the actual expression of core ideas.[68] The *Seafarer* poet, or for that matter any poet in control of this traditional pattern, is thus able to manipulate the conventional narrative structure to suit his purpose in the immediate context; in doing so he has the best of both worlds by simultaneously evoking a familiar chain of associations and expectations and managing nonetheless to direct the reader along a unique imaginative pathway. We are not ten lines into *The Seafarer* before our knowledge of the poetic tradition signals the thematic pattern of exile and prompts us to imagine a scenario or sequence of events, but at the same time the poet has already begun to weave his own verbal designs, such as the *dryhten* series, which will interact with the narrative theme to reveal a vision of earthly versus divine belonging which reaches far beyond either pattern or design alone. As in Višnjić's "The Death of Kraljević Marko," with its surpassingly heroic portrait of the hero disarming himself and embracing his mortality, literary art and oral tradition converge to yield a richly reverberative work, one which achieves its aesthetic effect by creating a seemingly impossible amalgam of convention and originality.

As a final example of the *Seafarer* poet's individual mastery of traditional patterns, consider the following two passages, both of them variations on the "joy in the hall" theme described by Jeff Opland:[69]

> Hwilum ylfete *song*
> dyde ic me to *gomene*, ganetes hleoþor
> ond huilpan *sweg* fore hleahtor wera,
> mæw *singende* fore medodrince. (19b-22)

> Ne biþ him to *hearpan* hyge ne to hringþege,
> ne to wife wyn ne to worulde hyht,
> ne ymbe owiht elles, nefne ymb yða gewealc,
> ac a hafað longunge se þe on lagu fundað. (44-47)

Apart from the narrative ideas of feasting, song and merriment in the mead-hall, Opland lists the recurrent words *dream, gamen, gleo, gyd, song/singan* (noun and verb), *sweg, hearpe* and *scop* as members of a lexical cluster which collectively assists in expressing this theme.[70] He locates the idea-structure of "joy in the hall," together with its typical verbal expression, at seven different junctures in *Beowulf*, interpreting each as a traditional multiform. In the *Seafarer* passages above there is the same combination of conventional narrative idea and, to different degrees, certain keywords, forming negative variations on the theme; these, by their reference to traditional values through a traditional structure, recall the feasting and camaraderie that the seafarer has left behind in the world of men. His is a *dryhtenleas* existence, as we have already been advised by the exile pattern and as the "deliberate ambiguity" of literary diction is to reinforce; now we learn that his only companions are the wild birds of the cold and comfortless sea, his only music (and poetic song) their strident cries. Because the *Seafarer* poet tells us of his protagonist's loss through manipulation of a theme which itself embodies all the light and life epitomized in and associated with the feasting-place, his portrayal of the desolate exile is that much more resonant and powerful. As with the other instances cited—the non-formulaic relationship between the opening lines of *The Seafarer* and *The Wife's Lament*, the echoic use of *dryhten* and the exile multiform—the theme of "joy in the hall" presents the poet with an oral traditional pattern which he artfully shapes into a literary design.

In summary, then, we have on the one hand incontrovertible evidence of Serbian oral poets who both knew and deftly used the poetic tradition that was their inheritance. Unlike the Muslim epic singers recorded and studied by Parry and Lord, they somehow managed to escape the exigencies of oral performance which bar the *guslar* from what we call literary composition. The best of Vuk's singers, notably Tešan Podrugović and Filip Višnjić, were able to weave together the patterns of oral tradition and the designs of literary art, and in the process to tap both reservoirs of meaning: their poems manifest both the reverberative depth of tradition and the finely worked surface of creative and original ideas. We cannot, as I have shown, ascribe the literary aspects of this material to the editing of Vuk Karadžić, since surviving manuscripts reveal that his emendations were slight and did not affect either the quality or the traditional character of the oral poetry to any discernible extent. In trying to imagine how such a poetry might be composed, we would do well to consider analogues in various African traditions,[71] that is, shorter oral poems whose entire texts could be committed to memory and revised on the palimpsest of a singer's rote memory. As Lord and others have suggested,[72] shorter narratives do not pose the same problems of large-scale composition as do the much more extensive forms such as the Muslim epic; instead of depending on the multiform treasures of the wordhoard to allow him to follow out a story pattern for thousands of lines in oral performance, the singer of the brief epic or lyric may have the opportunity to think carefully and even critically about both his subject and his means of expression as he makes his song. In the shorter genres, at least, he may be able to add his own contribution to the traditional canon by wresting a new and unique meaning from patterns of phraseology and narrative already heavy with connotation. He may, in short, create his own oral traditional text.

Could this also be the way in which some of the Old English poets, such as those responsible for briefer poems like *The Seafarer*, worked on their compositions? This possibility may seem logical enough, and it may explain the received text more felicitously than either the straight "singer thesis" or the unqualified hypothesis of a literate and literary artist, but it must remain a speculation. As for the nature of *The Seafarer* and its interpretation, however, we are on much firmer ground. As I have attempted to show, the poem exhibits the same combination of oral traditional elements and literary execution that typifies the best of the Vuk collection. The poet employs formulaic phraseology but is no slave to its constraints: he is free to set up a non-traditional system of echoes between poems or within a single work, a system which is wholly his quite literary creation. He can also harness the traditional energy of themes like "exile" or "joy in the hall" to serve his own ends, using the associations implicit in the narrative convention to reach beyond the immediacy of the moment. In either case the poet reveals both his passkey to the wordhoard and his literary craft.

Because of these fundamental correspondences between the two poetries, I would emphasize the need to incorporate the Christian oral songs collected and published by Vuk Karadžić into the model of oral narrative to be used for comparison with other literatures. The Parry-Lord model as it stands is apposite and incisive in certain cases, especially when one is dealing with extremely long works such as the

Iliad or *Odyssey*; it has told us much and will tell us more about oral traditions all over the world. But we must not restrict our basis for comparison to longer Muslim epic recorded in the 1930s, any more than the Italian sonnet of any given decade in the Renaissance should be forced to serve as the sole source for a description of Renaissance literature in general. Any model worth the name needs to be as adaptable—that is, as complete—as possible if we are to make meaningful comparative evaluations. The Vuk songs add a crucially important dimension to the comparison by illustrating how a poet can in fact combine oral traditional structure with a literary sensitivity to produce memorable poetry. The example of these songs, of their fusion of pattern and design, is essential to the understanding of many of the shorter works of Old English verse, whose obvious artistic value has been thought to be incompatible with oral tradition. By setting these precious remnants of Anglo-Saxon poetic tradition alongside the Serbian songs recorded in the nineteenth century, we can begin to grasp the nature, meaning and aesthetics of oral traditional art.[73]

NOTES

[1]Albert B. Lord, *The Singer of Tales* (Cambridge, Mass., 1960; rpt. New York, 1968, etc.); and F.P. Magoun, "Oral-Formulaic Character of Anglo-Saxon Narrative Poetry," *Speculum*, 28 (1953), 446-467, rpt., e.g., *The Beowulf Poet*, ed. Donald K. Fry (Englewood Cliffs, N.J., 1968), pp. 83-113, whose pagination is cited herein. For a complete history of formulaic theory in Old English, see my "Introduction: the Oral Theory in Context," *Oral Traditional Literature: A Festschrift for Albert Bates Lord*, ed. John Miles Foley (Columbus, Ohio, 1981; rpt. 1983), pp. 51-122. For more general accounts, see Edward R. Haymes, *A Bibliography of Studies Relating to Parry's and Lord's Oral Theory* (Cambridge, Mass., 1973); and Foley, "Oral Literature: Premises and Problems," *Choice*, 18 (1980), 487-496; and *idem, Oral-Formulaic Theory: An Introduction and Annotated Bibliography* (New York, 1984).

[2]For nineteenth-century interest in patterned diction, see "The Oral Theory in Context," pp. 51-59.

[3]This is Parry's original definition, given in "Studies in the Epic Technique of Oral Verse-Making. 1. Homer and Homeric Style," rpt. *The Making of Homeric Verse: the Collected Papers of Milman Parry*, ed. Adam Parry (Oxford, 1971), p. 272; I cite this volume hereafter as *MHV*.

[4]As an example of the synchronic approach see Michael N. Nagler,

Spontaneity and Tradition: a Study in the Oral Art of Homer (Berkeley, California, 1974); as an example of diachronic analysis see Gregory Nagy, *Comparative Studies in Greek and Indic Meter* (Cambridge, Mass., 1974); and *idem, The Best of the Achaeans: Concepts of the Hero in Archaic Greek Poetry* (Baltimore, Maryland, 1979).

[5]See, e.g., Patricia Arant, "Formulaic Style and the Russian Bylina," *Indiana Slavic Stud.*, 4 (1967), 7-51; and Foley, "Tradition-Dependent and -Independent Features in Oral Literature: a Comparative View of the Formula," *Oral Traditional Literature*, ed. Foley, pp. 262-281.

[6]Milman Parry, *L'Epithète traditionnelle dans Homère: Essai sur un problème de style homérique* (Paris, 1928), tr. Adam Parry as "The Traditional Epithet in Homer," *MHV*, pp. 1-190; and *idem, Les Formules et la métrique d'Homère* (Paris, 1928), trans. Adam Parry as "Homeric Formulae and Homeric Metre," *MHV*, pp. 191-239.

[7]Two early investigations of formulaic structure and aesthetics were George M. Calhoun's "Homeric Repetitions," *Univ. of California Publ. in Classical Philol.*, 12 (1933), 1-25; and *idem*, "The Art of Formula in Homer—ΕΠΕΑ ΠΤΕΡΟΕΝΤΑ," *Classical Philol.*, 30 (1935), 215-227, to which latter Parry replied in "About Winged Words," *Classical Philol.*, 32 (1937), 59-63, rpt. *MHV*, pp. 414-418.

[8]Ed. Bernard C. Fenik (Leiden, 1978).

[9]See, e.g., G. S. Kirk, *The Songs of Homer* (Cambridge, 1962); and *Homer and Oral Tradition*, ed. Kirk (Cambridge, 1976); Adam Parry, "Have We Homer's *Iliad*?," *Yale Classical Stud.*, 20 (1966), 177-216; Anne Parry, *Blameless Aegisthus: a Study of AMYMΩN and other Homeric Epithets* (Leiden, 1973); and J. A. Russo, "Homer against his Tradition," *Arion*, 7 (1968), 275-295. As Fenik puts the quandary ("Stylization and Variety: Four Monologues in the *Iliad*," *Homer: Tradition and Invention*, ed. Fenik, p. 90): "How shall we account for the not infrequent cases of carelessness and imprecision in Homer, set as they are against others where he demonstrates mastery of detail, conceptual penetration and architectural design? The ruling theory of the day (oral poetry) explains only half. The sheer quality of Homer remains an unicum in the body of oral poetry known to us."

[10]With evidence of both oral traditional structure and literary craftsmanship, many a critic would agree with Fenik ("Homer and Writing," *Würzburger Jahrbücher für die Altertumswissenschaft*, n.s. 2 [1976], 47) that "the dividing line between Mündlichkeit and Schriftlichkeit remains one that we still cannot accurately draw" [italics deleted].

[11]"Oral-Formulaic Character," p. 84.

[12]Cf. Robert P. Creed, "The Making of an Anglo-Saxon Poem," *Eng. Lit. Hist.*, 26 (1959), 445-454, rpt., with "Additional Remarks," *The*

Beowulf Poet, ed. Fry, pp. 141-153; and Stanley B. Greenfield, "Grendel's Approach to Heorot: Syntax and Poetry," *Old English Poetry: Fifteen Essays,* ed. Robert P. Creed (Providence, Rhode Island, 1967), pp. 275-284.

[13]"The Canons of Old English Criticism," *Eng. Lit. Hist.,* 34 (1967), 141-155.

[14]*PMLA,* 81 (1966), 334-341.

[15]Apart from Parry's brief mention of traditional narrative elements ("On Typical Scenes in Homer," *Classical Philol.,* 31 [1936], 357-360, rpt. *MHV,* pp. 404-407, itself a review of Walter Arend's *Die typischen Scenen bei Homer*), the first description of typical scenes as oral traditional elements was Lord's "Composition by Theme in Homer and South Slavic Epos," *Trans. of the Amer. Philol. Assoc.,* 82 (1951), 71-80; for earlier articles which touch on related aspects of oral composition, see his "Homer and Huso" series, *Trans. of the Amer. Philol. Assoc.,* 67 (1936), 106-113; 69 (1938), 439-445; and 79 (1948), 113-124. For fuller expositions, see his *The Singer of Tales,* where he defines themes as "groups of ideas regularly used in telling a tale in the formulaic style of traditional song" (p. 68); and *idem,* "Perspectives on Recent Work on Oral Literature," *Forum for Mod. Lang. Stud.,* 10 (1974), 187-210, rpt. *Oral Literature: Seven Essays,* ed. Joseph J. Duggan (Edinburgh and London, 1975), pp. 1-24. See, further, my "Introduction," pp. 79-122.

[16]"Literary Character," p. 337.

[17]As Fry puts it ("Cædmon as a Formulaic Poet," *Forum for Mod. Lang. Stud.,* 10 (1974), 228-248, rpt. *Oral Literature: Seven Essays,* ed. Duggan, pp. 41-61, at 41): "a consensus seems to be emerging that written Old English poetry used oral forms, but no reliable test can differentiate written from oral poems."

[18]"Literary Character," p. 340.

[19]See, esp., Fry, "Cædmon," and Lord, "Perspectives." Richard C. Payne ("Formulaic Poetry in Old English and its Backgrounds," *Stud. in Med. Culture,* 11 [1977], 49) argues that "given the evidence of deliberate composition and balanced literary design in Old English poems that many investigators of the problem have produced, it seems likely that most poems were produced by authors with pen in hand, though frequent communal reading of such works must be assumed to maintain the vitality of the formulaic tradition."

[20]See my "Formula and Theme in Old English Poetry," *Oral Literature and the Formula,* ed. Benjamin A. Stolz and Richard S. Shannon (Ann Arbor, Michigan, 1976), pp. 207-232. Of related interest are John D. Niles, "Formula and Formulaic System in *Beowulf,*" *Oral Traditional Literature,* ed. Foley, pp. 394-415; and Foley, "*Beowulf* and Traditional

Narrative Song: the Potential and Limits of Comparison," *Old English Literature in Context: Ten Essays*, ed. by John D. Niles (London and Totowa, N.J., 1980), pp. 117-136 and 173-178.

[21]A bibliography of writings on oral-formulaic theory published by Garland (see above, n. 1) contains more than 1800 items in dozens of literatures, most of which appeared after the publication of *The Singer of Tales* in 1960.

[22]Much new work is appearing each year from traditions all over the world: a telling example is Veronika Görög's enormous *Littérature orale d'Afrique Noire: Bibliographie analytique* (Paris, 1981).

[23]*Hrvatske narodne pjesme*, ed. Luka Marjanović, III-IV (Zagreb, 1898); *Narodne pjesme Muslimana u Bosni i Hercegovini*, ed. Kosta Hörmann, 2 vols. (Zagreb, 1888-9; rpt. Sarajevo, 1976); and *Serbo-Croatian Heroic Songs (Srpskohrvatske junačke pjesme)*, collected, ed. and trans. Milman Parry, Albert Lord and David E. Bynum, I-IV, VI and XIV (Cambridge, Mass., and Belgrade, 1953-1980).

[24]*Ibid.*, III-IV.

[25]See Lord, "The Theme of the Withdrawn Hero in Serbo-Croatian Oral Epic," *Prilozi za književnost, jezik, istoriju i folklor*, 35 (1969), 18-30; and Foley, "The Traditional Structure of Ibro Bašić's 'Alagić Alija and Velagić Selim,'" *Slavic and East European Jnl.*, 22 (1978), 1-14. For a bibliography of writings on the Return Song, see Foley, "*Beowulf* and Traditional Narrative Song," *Old English Literature in Context*, ed. Niles, p. 173, n. 6, to which should be added Mary P. Coote, "Lying in Passages," *Canadian-Amer. Slav. Stud.*, 15 (1981), 5-23, and W. W. Parks, "Generic Identity and the Guest-Host Exchange: A Study of Return Songs in the Homeric and Serbo-Croatian Traditions," *ibid.*, pp. 24-41.

[26]On some alternative quantitative methods for approaching these problems, see John S. Miletich, "Oral-Traditional Style and Learned Literature: a New Perspective," *Poetics and the Theory of Lit.*, 3 (1978), 345-356.

[27]This flexibility is one aim of much of Jeff Opland's scholarship; see, esp., "*Imbongi Nezibongo:* the Xhosa Tribal Poet and the Contemporary Poetic Tradition," *PMLA*, 90 (1975), 185-208, and *Anglo-Saxon Oral Poetry: A Study of the Traditions* (New Haven, Conn., 1980).

[28]Generic taxonomy is ever a matter of dispute in dealing with Serbo-Croatian oral poetry, and much of the Vuk material may just as convincingly be labelled "lyric" on the basis of its brevity. I choose, however, to maintain the label of "epic," the term favoured by many native investigators in spite of the songs' length, because of their epic subjects and phraseology.

[29]On the manuscripts, see Živomir Mladenović, "Rukopisi narodnih pesama Vukove zbirke i njihovo izdavanje," *Srpske narodne pjesme iz*

neobjavljenih rukopisa Vuka Stef. Karadžića, I, ed. Živomir Mladenović and Vladan Nedić (Belgrade, 1973), pp. i-cclxxix.
  [30]"Rukopisi narodnih pesama," p. iv (translation mine). See, further, Mladenović, "Vuk kao redaktor narodnih pesama," *Kovčežić,* I (1958), 64-93.
  [31]Vuk's editing amounted to one substantive change (a hemistich substitution or an added line) approximately every seventy-five lines. Most changes involved lesser matters, such as spelling, dialect forms, and morphology, as explained below.
  [32]Quotations from Vuk, with the exception of examples cited directly from the manuscripts, are taken from the edition of Vladan Nedić (Belgrade, 1969). "Djakon Stefan i dva andjela" is preserved in part (lines 1-19) as br. 8552/257, XXII, 5 of the Archive of the Srpska Akademija Nauka i Umetnosti in Belgrade.
  [33]"Ljuba Jakšića Šćepana," archive br. 8552/257, VII, 57.
  [34]In the standard edition of *Srpske narodne pjesme,* ed. P. Aleksić et al. II (Belgrade, 1958), in the "Beleške i objašnjena," p. 734, we find the following remark: "This song is not truly heroic, but more 'midway between heroic and lyric [women's] songs' (according to Vuk's distinction), like those in volume one. Vuk included it here because it tells of Kraljević Marko" (translation mine).
  [35]See, in Vol. II of Vuk's collection, "Marko Kraljević i Mina od Kostura," 193-194, where the drinking of wine acts as a restorative. On the context provided to an oral poem by its tradition, see Anna Caraveli, "The Song Beyond the Song: Aesthetics and Social Interaction in Greek Folksong," *Jnl of Amer. Folklore,* 95 (1982), 129-158.
  [36]See, e.g., Cedric H. Whitman, *Homer and the Heroic Tradition* (Cambridge, Mass., 1958; rpt. New York, 1965), esp. pp. 249-284; John D. Niles, "Ring Composition and the Structure of *Beowulf,*" *PMLA,* 94 (1979), 924-935.
  [37]*Čelo gori* ("the forehead burns") is a figurative way of indicating either shame, and therefore respect, before one's superior or impatience or possibly even anger. Both readings are supported by the passage and together present the dilemma of divided allegiance which Marko must continually confront as a Christian hero and yet a Turkish vassal and mercenary.
  [38]In *Homeric Formulae and Homeric Metre,* Parry explains various metrical flaws in the hexameter as the juxtaposition of formulas which, although each is metrically admissible by itself, create a flaw at their point of juncture. An example is the instance of short-vowel hiatus in "entha kathedzet' epeita Odusseos philos huios" (*Odyssey,* XVI.48), which he derives as a variation on the same model which produced "entha kathedzet' epeita periphrôn Pênelopeia" (*Odyssey,* XIX.59), among others

(p. 203). Inconsistencies at the level of the scene can result from an analogous juxtaposition of themes which by themselves are internally consistent, but which when placed alongside one another do not agree in certain details; see, further, Lord, "Homer and Huso II: Narrative Inconsistencies in Homer and Oral Poetry," *Trans. of the Amer. Philol. Assoc.*, 69 (1938), 439-445; *idem, The Singer of Tales*, pp. 68-98.

[39]See, further, Foley, "Narrativity in *Beowulf,* the *Odyssey,* and the Serbo-Croatian Return Song," *Proceedings of the IXth Congress of the International Comparative Literature Association, Innsbruck 1979. I: Classical Models in Literature,* ed. Zoran Konstantinović, Warren Anderson and Walter Dietze, Innsbrucker Beiträge zur Kulturwissenchaft, Sonderheft 49 (Innsbruck, 1981), pp. 295-301.

[40]See, further, Foley, "Epic and Charm in Old English and Serbo-Croatian Oral Tradition," *Comparative Criticism: Yearbook of the Brit. Comparative Lit. Assoc.*, 2 (1980), 71-92, esp. pp. 76-77.

[41]For a deftly drawn portrait of Podrugović see Svetozar Koljević, *The Epic in the Making* (Oxford, 1980), pp. 311-314 (this volume is a revision and expansion of his *Naš junački ep* [Belgrade, 1974]); also relevant are pp. 117-123. On p. 311 Koljević, quoting periodically from Vuk, remarks: "'He was clever and, for an outlaw, an honest man;' and it was at this time, when Podrugović was about forty, that Karadžić recorded twenty-two poems from him. 'I have never found anyone who knew the poems as well as he did. Each of his poems was a good one, because he—particularly as he did not sing but spoke his poems—understood and felt them, and he thought about what he said.' He had a large repertoire and knew, in Karadžić's opinion, at least another hundred poems apart from the recorded ones; moreover, Karadžić claims that if Podrugović were 'to hear the worst poem, after a few days he would speak it beautifully and in proper order which was characteristic of his other songs, or he would not remember it at all, and he would say that it was silly, not worth remembering or telling.'"

[42]"The Effect of the Turkish Conquest on Balkan Oral Tradition," *Aspects of the Balkans: Continuity and Change,* ed. Henrik Birnbaum and Speros Vryonis, Jr. (The Hague and Paris, 1972), esp. pp. 311-318. See also above, n. 25.

[43]In narrative terms, this is the result of the collision between the Return Song pattern, which must always end in a wedding or a reunion of husband and wife (a remarriage, from the folkloric viewpoint), and the particular case of Marko, for whom marriage never seems possible; see, further, in Vol. II of the Vuk collection, "Ženidba Kraljevića Marka" ("The Wedding of Kraljević Marko").

[44]Cf., in Vol. II, the champion Miloš in "Ženidba Dušanova" ("The Wedding of Dušan").

[45]See above, n. 15.

[46]*Mejdandžije*, translated here as "combatants," literally means "those who fight a duel," usually but not always as necessary replacements for their sovereigns, much as Gawain takes up the gauntlet for King Arthur in *Sir Gawain and the Green Knight*. The *mejdan* ("duel") itself is a common motif in many songs and customarily determines the disposition of disputed property or the betrothal of a maiden.

[47]Koljević describes Višnjić's achievement as "the richest evidence of the interplay of the formulaic, the formulopoeic and the unique" (*The Epic in the Making*, p. 340), indicating that this singer was able to combine stock epic phraseology and narrative design both with unique and with derivative language and scenes. See, further, his discussion of this blend of tradition and innovation in "Technique and Achievement," *ibid.*, pp. 322-343, the final section of which applies directly to Višnjić's songs.

[48]Compare the obvious parallel at *Beowulf*, 677-687, where the hero prepares for the battle against Grendel by disarming himself, a variation made more powerful by the traditional arming sequence which it reverses.

[49]It is important to recall at this point that the Muslim songs should not be criticized for their apparent lack of concern with such aesthetic issues as those discussed here, any more than the briefer poems should be taken to task for lack of development. The longer epic is simply a poetic form *sui generis* and operates on its own principles, as the writings of Lord and others have so well illustrated. We are dealing with a matter of genre, that is, with a taxonomic distinction: what is possible in a shorter and perhaps memorizable form is not possible in the much longer epic composed under the pressure of oral performance. The distinction is not, to put it another way, one of quality; it is one of genre.

[50]*Speculum*, 35 (1960), 87-96. Campbell allows minor morphological variants and substitution of function words within his conception of the formula.

[51]"Another Look at Oral Poetry in *The Seafarer*," *Speculum*, 35 (1960), 596-600.

[52]"Oral Poetry in *The Seafarer*," p. 91, n. 10.

[53]It may be worth noting that a poet who can consciously manipulate traditional style to aesthetic advantage has presumably freed himself from outright dependence on formulaic structure and so has disqualified himself from eligibility for the formulaic test. Cf. Geoffrey R. Russom, "Artful Avoidance of the Useful Phrase in *Beowulf, The Battle of Maldon*, and *Fates of the Apostles*," *SP*, 75 (1978), 371-390; Edward R. Haymes, "Formulaic Density and Bishop Njegoš," *Comparative Lit.*, 32 (1980), 390-401.

[54]All quotations of Old English poetry are from the collective

edition of George P. Krapp and E.V.K. Dobbie, *The Anglo-Saxon Poetic Records*, 6 vols. (New York, 1931-1953). Supporting evidence is drawn from *A Concordance to the Anglo-Saxon Poetic Records*, ed. Jess B. Bessinger, Jr.; prog. Philip H. Smith (Ithaca, N.Y., and London, 1978), with abbreviations as used therein: *soðgied wrecað* (*Vgl* 15b); *gebiden hæfdon* (*Exo* 238b), *gebiden hæbbe* (*DrR* 50b), *gebiden hæbbe* (*DrR* 79b) and *gebiden hæbbe* (*Bwf* 1928b); *atol yða gewealc* (*Exo* 456a); and *of nacan stefne* (*And* 291b).

55On this aspect of phraseology, see John D. Niles, "Compound Diction and the Style of *Beowulf*," *ES*, 62 (1981), 489-503.

56In "Old English Formulas and Systems," *ES*, 48 (1967), 193-204, Fry discusses the formulaic system, which he defines as "a group of half-lines, usually loosely related metrically and semantically, which are related in form by the identical relative placement of two elements, one a variable word or element of a compound usually supplying the alliteration, and the other a constant word or element of a compound, with approximately the same distribution of non-stressed elements" (p. 203; italics deleted), and the formula itself, which he then defines as "a group of words, one half-line in length, which shows evidence of being the direct product of a formulaic system" (p. 204). See further, above, n. 17.

57It is important to emphasize that this particular type of multiformity is a tradition-dependent property of Old English verse. As I have shown elsewhere (see above, n. 5), the Homeric Greek and Serbo-Croatian prosodies also prescribe idiosyncratic features in the phraseologies they support.

58Parry first described the operation of sound-patterning in oral traditional composition, calling it a form of "analogy" (e.g., "The Traditional Epithet in Homer," *MHV*, pp. 68-75). See, further, Lord, "The Role of Sound-Patterns in Serbo-Croatian Epic," *For Roman Jakobson*, ed. Morris Halle et al. (The Hague, 1956), pp. 301-305; *idem, The Singer of Tales*, pp. 54-58; W. B. Stanford, "Euphonic Reasons for the Choice of Homeric Formulae?", *Hermathena*, 108 (1969), 14-17; Creed, "The *Beowulf*-Poet: Master of Sound-Patterning," *Oral Traditional Literature*, ed. Foley, pp. 194-216.

59This is no less true of Serbo-Croatian and ancient Greek epic, in which traditional composition depends to varying degrees on exactly repeated phrases, flexible systems and phonetic patterns, all of which take shape under the aegis of prosody.

60See, further, Greenfield, "The Formulaic Expression of the Theme of 'Exile' in Anglo-Saxon Poetry," *Speculum*, 30 (1955), 200-206.

61On verbal echo see the early work of John O. Beaty, "The Echo-Word in *Beowulf* with a Note on the Finnsburg Fragment," *PMLA*, 49

(1934), 365-373; and later articles by Eugene R. Kintgen: e.g., "Wordplay in *The Wanderer*," *Neophilologus*, 59 (1975), 119-127.

[62]For *The Wife's Lament*, 1a, cf. *Beowulf*, 2446b: *þonne he gyd wrece.*

[63]"The Old English Elegies," *Continuations and Beginnings: Studies in Old English Literature*, ed. Eric G. Stanley (London and Edinburgh, 1966), p. 147. The other words involved in this design are *dream* (65a, 80a and 86b), *blæd* (79b and 88b), *duguð* (80a and 86a) and *lof* (73a and 78a).

[64]Line 65a: *dryhtnes dreamas* (*Glc* 123a); line 121b: *þa for lufan dryhtnes* (*Ele* 491b), *þæt hie lufan dryhtnes* (*Ele* 1205b), *ond mid lufan dryhtnes* (*Glc* 652b), *þæt hi lufan dryhtnes* (*Jul* 501b) and *ond a lufan dryhtnes* (*Jgl* 49b); and line 124a: *ece drihten* (*Gen* 112b) and eighty-seven other occurrences in the poetic corpus. Of the three remaining lines, all are verse-types beginning with unstressed elements, that is, those types most susceptible to changes through substitution of function words; in addition, lines 41a and 106a are hypermetric, the former also being part of a rhetorical series. Although it is beyond the scope of this article to discuss the phenomenon at length, parallels to various kinds of rhetorical series in *The Seafarer* can be located in the Vuk songs, so that we need not suppose such stylized figures the exclusive creation of the post-traditional poet.

[65]As an example of the controversy over formulaic structure and aesthetics, see Anne Amory Parry, "The Gates of Horn and Ivory," *Yale Classical Stud.*, 20 (1966), 3-57, versus Lord, "Homer as Oral Poet," *Harvard Stud. in Classical Philol.*, 72 (1968), 1-46.

[66]"The Formulaic Expression of the Theme of 'Exile'," p. 201.

[67]*Ibid.*, esp. pp. 201-205.

[68]Most investigators have sought to define Old English themes in terms of a recurring narrative pattern rather than actual verbal correspondence among instances. See, e.g., David Crowne ("The Hero on the Beach: an Example of Composition by Theme in Anglo-Saxon Poetry," *NM*, 61 [1960], 362-372), who defines this typical scene as "a stereotyped way of describing (1) a hero on the beach (2) with his retainers (3) in the presence of a flashing light (4) as a journey is completed (or begun)" (p. 368) and notes that "the regular content of this theme, then, consists not of a number of specific metrical formulas, but of a concatenation of four imagistic details" (p. 371). See, further, my review of scholarship on the theme: Foley, "Introduction," pp. 79-122.

[69]"*Beowulf* on the Poet," *MS*, 38 (1976), 445-453.

[70]On the roots of words as verbal correspondence among instances of a theme see Foley, "Formula and Theme in Old English Poetry," pp. 220-232; *idem*, "*Beowulf* and Traditional Narrative Song," pp. 122-134;

Lord, "Perspectives," pp. 20-24; Berkley Peabody, *The Winged Word: a Study in the Technique of Ancient Greek Oral Composition as Seen Principally through Hesiod's "Works and Days"* (Albany, N.Y., 1975), on "The Responsions of Thought," pp. 195-215. It is worth noting in this connection that not all themes in Serbo-Croatian answer precisely the same definition in terms of formulaic content and particular kinds of structure (see, e.g., Mary P. Coote, "The Singer's Themes in Serbocroatian Heroic Song," *California Slavic Stud.*, 11 [1980], 201-235), and so perhaps we should not expect all Old English themes to exhibit exactly the same features.

[71]Compare, for example, the panegyric material described by Opland (see above, n. 27) or the many shorter genres noted by Ruth Finnegan in her *Oral Literature in Africa* (Oxford, 1970). On the importance of matching genre in comparing oral poetries see Foley, "Oral Texts, Traditional Texts: Poetics and Critical Methods," *Canadian-Amer. Slavic Stud.*, 15 (1981), 122-145.

[72]See, esp., Lord ("Memory, Fixity, and Genre in Oral Traditional Poetries," *Oral Traditional Literature*, ed. Foley, pp. 459-461), who notes that "since memory may play a somewhat different role in different genres, it seems necessary to take genre into account in discussing fixity" (p. 459). Cf. James P. Holoka ("The Oral Formula and Anglo-Saxon Elegy: some Misgivings," *Neophilologus*, 60 [1976], 570-76), who argues that "in a short work . . . the factor of improvisation is much less operative. Certainly a skilled singer, one who could run on for thousands of verses without (we must suppose) serious breakdown, could easily enough hold in his mind, *in toto*, a set piece of some one hundred verses; he could review, polish, revise, rework until finally his method closely approximated that of his more educated counterpart. Thus, short, elegiac poems could conceivably attain a fixity indistinguishable from that of a written text" (p. 572).

[73]It is a pleasure to express my appreciation to the institutions that supported the research for this essay and the individuals who contributed to its development. The International Research and Exchanges Board, affiliated with the American Council of Learned Societies, together with the Yugoslav Federal Administration for International Scientific, Educational, Cultural and Technical Cooperation, provided a stipend for five months of research in Belgrade. Both the Odsek za jugoslovenske književnosti of the Filološki fakultet at Belgrade University and the staff of the Archive of the Srpska Akademija Nauka i Umetnosti were very gracious and helpful, the latter in allowing me direct access to the original manuscripts of Vuk Karadžić's collection. The first version of the essay was written during a 1980-1981 leave sponsored by the John Simon Guggenheim Memorial Foundation, and sections were later

presented to sessions on Old English poetry at the 1981 Medieval Institute and Modern Language Association. I am especially grateful to Professor Nada Milošević-Djordjević for her extensive discussions of the Vuk material.

Perspectives on Recent Work on the
Oral Traditional Formula
[excerpted]

Albert B. Lord

As the title, "Perspectives on Recent Work on the Oral Traditional Formula," implies, Albert Lord intended this essay as a sequel to his 1974 survey. Twelve years later, he sees fit to concentrate primarily on the structure, morphology, and implications of formulaic phraseology, but his comments once again treat a rich variety of oral traditions; the ancient Greek, Old and Middle English, Old Irish, Old and Middle High German, Old Norse, Old French, Hispanic, Russian, Latvian, Serbo-Croatian, Chinese, African, Asian Indian, Arabic, Persian, Mongolian, Kirghiz, Uzbek, and biblical traditions all come in for report and discussion. Lord also includes an extensive section on the history and application of the formulaic density test, the analysis that purported to establish the oral or written provenance of a given work by measuring its percentage of formulaic phraseology, and comes to the conclusion that "its evidence alone may not be sufficient to determine orality." He also offers examples of formulaic versus simply repetitive diction and further considers the kinds of "transitional" texts that may arise in various periods. As a carefully worded account of the state of oral-

Reprinted from *Forum for Modern Language Studies*, 10 (1974), 1-21.

formulaic studies in 1986, Lord's second survey (here excerpted) is an
ideal second bookend for the collection as a whole.

The history of the study of Oral Literature has been covered well by
John Miles Foley in his Introduction to *Oral Traditional Literature*
(1981b), and also in his Introduction to *Oral-Formulaic Theory and
Research* (1985), which includes a monumental annotated bibliography
to the subject. I do not intend to recapitulate what he has already done
so admirably; all the material is there, and his comments are even-
handed and exemplary. There are, however, several general observations
which it would probably be fitting to make at this juncture in the study
of Oral Traditional Literature, which is marked by the inauguration of a
new journal devoted to Oral Tradition.

Perusing Foley's works just mentioned, one is immediately struck
by the number of language traditions and cultural areas in which the
"oral theory" is now discussed and by the diversity of forms and
problems included in the study of "oral traditional literature." This is an
exciting development; it is also sobering, because it carries with it a
mandate to be clear in our notion of what we mean by oral traditional
literature. There are some who would stress the literal sense of "oral"
and include in "oral traditional literature" any literature which is
"performed" orally no matter what its original manner of composition
was.[1] Such an interpretation, it seems to me, overemphasizes
performance to such an extent that the peculiar character of what is
performed is obscured. We are told that in some cultures it is the
performance that is important and that the words of what is performed
are unimportant, even meaningless. If that is true, then there is no
literary content in such performances, and those of us who are concerned
with literature are left with an empty shell, which we should leave to
other disciplines. While there may be special cases where this is true,
namely, that the words do not count, they are special cases, and it
would be a mistake to generalize from the exceptional.

I hasten to affirm, however, that performance is indeed significant,
that context is important, and that without a sympathetic knowledge of
context the text may well be misunderstood and misinterpreted. There is
no doubt in my own mind that text and context are inseparable. To
consider the one without showing an awareness of the other is to miss
much. On the other hand, it is true that certain types of research may
concentrate either on describing context or on analyzing text, but this
should be done with the clear understanding that the other facet exists,

and that it must be called upon wherever the description or the analysis should be taken into consideration, because the study would otherwise be inaccurate or incomplete.[2]

Just as there are those who would overemphasize "oral performance," there are those would underemphasize, to the point of eliminating, the concept of "traditional." It seems to me shortsighted to ignore that aspect of oral traditional literature, which, I submit, is traditional by its origin and nature, which gives it the depth of meaning set into it at its origin by previous generations. Forcing oral traditional literature into the straight-jacket of synchronic observation is to distort it beyond recognition.

Turning to the last element in our subject, oral traditional literature, need it be said that we must be very clear about what we mean by literature? Must we spend time squabbling about whether "oral literature" is a contradiction in terms? Such controversy is a red herring, taking our attention away from the real issues. If we can but accept the well-recognized meaning of "literature" as "carefully structured verbal expression," then carefully structured oral verbal expression can surely qualify as literature.

This is not to say, however, that oral and written literature are indistinguishable! Let there be no doubt on this question either; for oral traditional literature without tradition is meaningless; and oral traditional literature without a clear distinction between it and "written literature" ceases to exist.

I would like to take this opportunity to bring up to date an article on "perspectives," which I wrote a few years ago, published in 1974 by Professor Joseph Duggan, entitled "Perspectives on Recent Work on Oral Literature." In it I expressed the opinion that we need more study of bona fide oral traditional literature. I am happy to report that there seems to be more attention being given to both collecting and studying oral traditional literature, even to the point of suggesting new models for comparative studies. If I speak mainly about epic, it is because my deepest commitment is there, but I do not mean to imply that other genres either do not exist or are unimportant.

It was my privilege last September to attend a conference at the University of Bonn on Central Asiatic epic. The specialists who participated, including Professor A. T. Hatto of London, who has edited and translated the Kirghiz epic *The Memorial Feast for Kökötöy-khan* (1977), as well as six scholars from Mongolia and China, were very impressive. It was a particular pleasure to become acquainted with the work of Professor Karl Reichl of the English Department at Bonn, a specialist on Old and Middle English, who has just published a translation of an Uzbek oral traditional epic about *RawŠan,* the grandson of Kurroglou (1985). In the introduction to it and in a recent article (1984), he has called attention to parallels in European medieval literature, especially Old French and Anglo-Saxon, and has suggested that medievalists might find in Central Asiatic epic another helpful model for comparative research in addition to the South Slavic songs. Parallels have also been drawn between Mongolian and medieval German epic by Professor Walther Heissig (1983a). Professor Heissig is the founder and prime mover of the Seminar für Sprach- und Kulturwissenschaft Zentralasiens der Universität Bonn. His recent monumental *Geser-Studien* (1983b) is especially valuable for comparative study of European and Asiatic epic. A new body of Mongolian Geser material was collected in 1972 and published with text and German translation by S. Ju. Nekljudov and Z. Tömörceren (1985). The abundance of Geser material from Central Asia which is now available in original and translation makes this one of the richest fields for research. The *Asiatische Forschungen* of the Seminar für Sprach- und Kulturwissenschaften at Bonn is the worthy successor to the tradition started by Radloff in the nineteenth century.

Earlier that same month, at the International Conference on Folk Epic in Dublin, I made the acquaintance of Dr. John D. Smith of Cambridge, who has collected Pabuji epic, long oral traditional songs, from western India. He has made a comparative study of passages from four different versions, with a view to investigating whether the texts are memorized or not (1977, 1981). Smith's paper at the Dublin conference was entitled "Use of Formulaic Language in Indian Oral Epic." Professor Stuart Blackburn of Dartmouth College has collected in South India, and he had a presentation on "A Folk Ramayana in South India: Textual Transmission and Local Ideology." I have recently heard also of a study of a South Indian poem, the 5082-line Dravidian epic, the *Cilappatikaram* (The Epic of the Anklet), in Tamil, by Dr. R. Parthasarathy, which treats the formulaic poetics of the poem. These texts and studies from the Indian sub-continent provide further opportunities to expand our knowledge of oral traditional poetry and to test our hypotheses on *remembering* structured phrases and lines rather than *memorizing* a fixed text.

Needless to say, at Dublin one heard of work being done on Celtic oral traditional literatures. Among recent works which stand out are Joseph Falaky Nagy's splendid study, *The Wisdom of the Outlaw* (1985) and Kevin O'Nolan's translation of the long Irish tale *Eochair, Mac Ri in Eirinn* (1982), which was central to his conference presentation on story-telling in Ireland.

The last decade has also seen the publication of Jeff Opland's study of Xhosa oral poetry.[3] Praise poetry is not epic, of course, nor is it essentially narrative, but it offers valuable examples for the study of true improvisation, as distinct from composition by formula and theme. It is, indeed, *sui generis*, and of considerable interest in its own right.

But there is epic in Africa too. During the last decade Daniel Biebuyck of the University of Delaware has published two more versions of the *Mwindo Epic* (1969) in *Hero and Chief* (1978), and John William Johnson of Indiana University has just published *The Epic of Son-Jara* (1985). In 1979 Johnson had published two volumes of the *Epic of Sun-Jata* from Mali, and the new book enriches the material available from the Manding tradition. Five years earlier Gordon Innes had published three versions of Sunjata (1974), and it is gratifying to have the available material for analysis increasing so strongly within a period of ten years. In 1973 Innes wrote an article on the manner in which the *griots* learn, compose, and perform the *Epic of Sunjata*. Foley notes in his annotated bibliography that this is "a study based on fieldwork by the author and others."

One should not leave the African scene without noting John W. Johnson's work on Somali poetry, which offers a very different body of material from the epic songs of Mali. In 1974 Johnson published a study of a kind of poetry called *Heello*. In 1980 he described the way in which Somali poetry is composed and transmitted and agreed with others that it is a completely oral and at the same time completely "memorial" tradition. This is valuable reporting from a scholar who has done extensive fieldwork in both Mali and Somalia. It is important to note, however, that the Somalis do not appear to have a tradition of long narrative poems. In the same year Johnson published a now well-known article "Yes, Virginia, There is an Epic in Africa," defending Africa against the allegations that it has no epic poetry. I should like to add one more little book to the African "report" because it was done by one of Harvard's first Ph.D.'s in Folklore, Clement A. Okafor of Nigeria. He has published in English some Tonga tales which he himself collected and studied for his dissertation under the title *The Banished Child* (1983).

There have been some fine studies of Arabic oral poetry. The work of James T. Monroe (1972) and Michael J. Zwettler (1978) comes immediately to mind. A study has just appeared of a body of poetry which has hitherto been neglected. It is by Saad Abdullah Sowayan and focuses on Nabati poetry, which he says is "the popular vernacular poetry of Arabia. Due to the great mobility of the Arab tribes, it is not easy to confine this poetic tradition to one particular locality; it is widespread throughout the Arabian peninsula" (1985, p. 1). Sowayan is critical of both Monroe and Zwettler, who dealt with Pre-Islamic and Classical Arabic poetry, in part because they go to alien, Yugoslav, poetry for a model for understanding composition and not to the native "continuator" of the earlier poetry, namely, the Nabati poetry. This is an interesting and valuable book, in spite of its native Arabic bias and its feeling of discomfort with the critical approaches of Westerners. It does provide a balance and deserves careful reading.

There is considerable activity going on at present in entering Latvian *dainas* onto computers, and several helpful analyses of formulas in the Latvian quatrains have appeared. The data from the entire nineteenth-century classical collection of Krišjānis Barons are stored at Massachusetts Institute of Technology and a very large selection, including all the sun-songs, is located at the University of Montreal. Among studies worth mentioning are the University of Michigan, Ann Arbor, doctoral dissertation in 1981 by Lalita Lāce Muižniece, "Linguistic Analysis of Latvian Death and Burial Folk Songs," and two articles by the Freibergs, namely, "Formulaic Analysis of the Computer-Accessible Corpus of Latvian Sun-Songs," by Vaira Vīķis-Freibergs and Imants Freibergs (1978), and "Creativity and Tradition in Oral Folklore, or the Balance of Innovation and Repetition in the Oral Poet's Art," by Vaira Vīķis-Freibergs (1984).

Thus there is a growing body of authentic source materials, and we can read new collections and up-to-date studies of oral traditional poetry and prose in Central Asia, India, Africa, Arabia, and Ireland. And there is the suggestion by scholars like Jeff Opland in South Africa, Karl Reichl in Bonn, and John D. Smith at Cambridge that the poetic traditions with which they work could serve as another model, in addition to or instead of Serbo-Croatian for comparative study in Old English and elsewhere. I welcome these suggestions, and have only one caveat, namely, that like should be compared with like. The non-narrative African praise poetry of the Xhosa or Zulus, for example, or the occasional or lyric poetry in Somaliland, may be helpful in studying the shorter Anglo-Saxon genres, or other true improvisations, but its usefulness for the study of epic would be very limited. For the epic, the Central Asiatic and Indian traditions, or the songs in Mali and the epics from Zaire, are much more apt and deserve further study in depth. I should like to add that I believe that comparatists would find the Russian and Ukrainian models also helpful, especially for Old English with which they share similar metrical bases. I am puzzled that more use has not been made of them than is the case.

*   *   *

Homeric and other ancient Greek, and Old and Middle English scholarship dealing with questions of oral traditional literature continues strong. Attempts to modify Parry's definitions of the terms formula, system, and theme have been given considerable attention, especially in Old English, and contextual studies of differing kinds are of great significance in both these areas. The following comments are intended to highlight some of what is being done in these two important fields.

In the scholarship devoted to ancient Greek and Homeric poetry there has been considerable activity in the publishing of works in which the force of oral tradition has been considered of great importance in its creation, without which it cannot be properly interpreted. One of the most outstanding books in that category is Gregory Nagy's *The Best of the Achaeans* (1979). By perceptively analyzing formulas in context in ancient Greek and other ancient Indo-Iranian traditional literature, Nagy reconstructs concepts of the hero which once characterized an entire epoch, and still have relevance today. Nagy's work is multi-faceted, profound, and far-reaching. Two recent articles by him, one "On the Death of Sarpedon" (1983) and the other on "Ancient Greek Epic and Praise Poetry: Some Typological Considerations" (1986), add further theoretical perspectives to his book. The first provides an extraordinarily apt additional illustration of principles previously set forth, and the second brings the praise poems of Pindar into the larger theoretical framework that also includes the Homeric poems. Nagy's methodology has inspired a number of others, of which I should like especially to mention Leonard Charles Muellner's *The Meaning of*

Homeric "eyxomai" through its Formulas (1976) as a worthy representative. The book on Theognis of Megara, edited by Thomas Figueira and Gregory Nagy (1985), should be added here.

Another important recent book is Richard Janko's *Homer, Hesiod and the Hymns: Diachronic Development in Epic Diction* (1982). One might also mention a very useful article of his, "Equivalent Formulas in the Greek Epos" (1981). His work uses an entirely different technique from Nagy's, but one that is also based on the oral traditional nature of the material, to establish a comparative dating for the early texts.

It is especially interesting to me that one of the most significant undertakings going on at the moment in Homeric studies is being carried on by scholars well acquainted with Parry's Homeric studies and not unsympathetic to the oral-formulaic theory. The project to which I refer, of course, is the multi-volumed commentary to the *Iliad*, under the editorship of Geoffrey Kirk, the first volume of which, done by Kirk himself, has already appeared (1985). While Kirk is not comfortable with the South Slavic model, nevertheless, if I read his work correctly, he accepts Homer as an oral traditional bard, the composer of the "monumental epic," a term which originated with him, I believe. Associated with him in the commentary are J. Bryan Hainsworth, the well-known author of *The Flexibility of the Homeric Formula* (1968), which is a landmark in Homeric studies after Parry; Mark Edwards of Stanford, who has written much on thematic structures in Homer (e.g., 1970, 1975, 1980); and Richard Janko, whose recent book I mentioned above.

Several other books of note have been published dealing in one form or another with ancient Greek and oral tradition, including a consideration of traditional formulas and themes. Two collections of essays by a number of scholars have appeared that are pertinent here: *Homer: Tradition and Invention*, edited by Bernard C. Fenik (1978), and *Homer: Tradition und Neuerung*, edited by Joachim Latacz (1979). Fenik has just published another book on Homer and the *Nibelungenlied* (1986). Finally, special mention should be made of the work of Mario Cantilena of the Università di Venezia, *Ricerche sulla dizione epica, 1. Per uno studio della formularità degli Inni Omerici* (1982).

Old English and Middle English studies reflecting the relationship of oral traditional literature to the extant Anglo-Saxon and Middle English poetic texts continue to flourish. Beginning in 1967 with an important article by Donald K. Fry and continuing in 1969 with Ann Chalmers Watts' significant book *The Lyre and the Harp*, followed by more articles by Fry, the questions about the formula in Old English were actively being raised and discussed. Jeff Opland's *Anglo-Saxon Oral Poetry: A Study of the Traditions* appeared in 1980, and it made extensive use of the Xhosa parallel, which was to be fully described in 1983 in his *Xhosa Oral Poetry*. Robert P. Creed, in addition to his concern for Anglo-Saxon metrics (1982), recently turned his attention as well to sound-patterning in *Beowulf* and the songs of Avdo Medjedović (1981a, b). John Miles Foley has also written on Anglo-Saxon metrics in "The Scansion of *Beowulf* in its Indo-European Context" (1982), and more generally on oral traditional literature, as in "Oral Texts, Traditional Texts: Poetics and Critical Methods" (1981c). Alain Renoir also contributed to the volume on *Approaches to Beowulfian Scansion* cited above, and has expanded his interests to include the *Hildebrandslied* (e.g., 1977). He has been especially attracted by the larger subject of context, as in "Oral-Formulaic Context: Implications for the Comparative Criticism of Mediaeval Texts" (1981). John Niles' book on *Beowulf* (1983) is the latest full-scale work on the subject, and Anita Riedinger's "The Old English Formula in Context" (1985), which appeared in *Speculum*, is the most recent article to come to my attention.

The Middle English *Alliterative Morte Arthur*, too, has been studied from the point of view of oral traditional literature. Among more recent works of importance are Jean Ritzke-Rutherford's two articles from 1981, and Karl H. Göller's article in the same publication, "A Summary of Research," is useful. Valerie Krishna's work on the *Alliterative Morte Arthure* (1982) has also kept the study of formula density very much alive.

In the Scandinavian field, among the studies that concern themselves with problems of oral tradition one should mention Lars Lönnroth's *Njals's Saga: A Critical Introduction* (1976), as well as several articles by him, most recently "Iorð fannz aeva né upphiminn. A Formula Analysis" (1981). Here too belong Peter Buchholz's *Vorzeitkunde: Mündliches Erzählen und Überliefern im mittelalterlichen Skandinavien nach dem Zeugnis von Fornaldarsaga und eddischer Dichtung* (1980), and Jesse L. Byock's *Feud in the Icelandic Saga* (1982), which analyzes the significance of traditional patterns of feuding in the sagas. The relationship of the Old Icelandic sagas and Eddic poetry to oral tradition is discussed in several of the chapters in the recently published *Old Norse-Icelandic Literature*, edited by Carol J. Clover and John Lindow (1985), especially that on Eddic poetry by Joseph Harris.

Old French studies in this area have been led by Joseph J. Duggan, two of his recent articles being of paramount importance, namely, "La Théorie de la composition des chansons de geste: les faits et les interprétations" (1981a) and "Le Mode de composition des chansons de geste: Analyse statistique, jugement esthétique, modèles de transmission" (1981b). Duggan is also at home in medieval Spanish, as is attested by at least two articles, "Formulaic Diction in the *Cantar de Mio Cid* and the Old French Epic" (1974b) and "Legitimation and the Hero's Exemplary Function in the *Cantar de Mio Cid* and the *Chanson de Roland*" (1981c). He is presently working on a much-needed new edition of the *Chanson de Roland*.

In medieval Spanish literature, Ruth Webber pioneered formulaic and thematic analysis beginning in 1951.[4] Recently she has returned to formulaic studies in connection with the *Mocedades de Rodrigo* (1980). In addition to stylistic studies of Spanish ballads, she has also written innovatively of their narrative structure (1978). One of her most remarkable articles (1981) has dealt with history and epic, particularly in regard to the *Cid*. In her latest paper, a discussion of the relationship between medieval Spanish and medieval French epic, she boldly suggests that together they formed the medieval Romance epic, the true "homeland" of each.

A recent long article on "The Crown-Bestower in the Iranian Book of Kings" by Olga M. Davidson (1985) brings to our attention one of the great epic traditions from the past, which still has importance today, namely, that of Persia, especially as represented by Ferdowsi's *Shahnama*, "The Book of the Kings."[5] In the first part of her study Dr. Davidson traces the elements of the Rostam narrative to Indo-European roots, and in the second she analyzes the traditional formulaic structure of parts of the epic.

The Far East is well represented by Ching-Hsien Wang's *The Bell and the Drum*: Shih Ching *as Formulaic Poetry in an Oral Tradition* (1974). Wang analyzed formulas and themes in a famous group of lyric poems from China's past. Among other articles, Alsace Yen also wrote in 1975 on "The Parry-Lord Theory Applied to Vernacular Chinese Stories" (1975).

Two or three additional areas deserve comment before we conclude this brief survey. What I have termed "the philosophical school" of orality has produced a notable book by one of its most distinguished practitioners, the Reverend Walter J. Ong, S.J., who not long ago published *Orality and Literacy* (1982). A Festschrift in his honor will soon appear.[6] A recent article by Franz Bäuml, a member of the same philosophical school, on "Medieval Text and the Two Theories of Oral-Formulaic Composition: A Proposal for a Third Theory" (1984), has some suggestions concerning the changing relationships between orality and literacy in the thirteenth century in Germany. In New Testament studies mention should be made of Werner Kelber's challenging book, *The Oral and the Written Gospel: The Hermeneutics of Speaking and Writing in the Synoptic Tradition, Mark, Paul, and Q* (1983). The work of Professor Susan Niditch at Amherst College brings to Old Testament studies the methodology of oral traditional literature. This can be seen in her recent book *Chaos and Cosmos* (1985).

Finally, there is one book which defies classification under any regional rubric, but which is comparative in a larger sense of the term, namely, David E. Bynum's *The Daemon in the Wood* (1978). It is a study of the motif of wood, both alive and dead, and its significance in story patterns through man's history and throughout the world. A learned and provocative book, it is in a class by itself. In 1974, Bynum's "Oral Literature at Harvard Since 1856" appeared, and in the same year he also published for the Parry Collection *The Wedding of Smailagić Meho*, by Avdo Medjedović (Lord 1974b, translation) and the original-language text, *Ženidba Smailagina sina* (Bynum, 1974b). In 1979 he edited Volume XIV of the same *Serbo-Croatian Heroic Songs* series, this one containing songs from the Bihaćka Krajina; the accompanying translation volume is now ready for publication. In 1980 Volume VI appeared under his editorship, containing three more texts by Avdo Medjedović, including the 13,326-line "Osmanbeg Delibegović i Pavičević Luka," the longest in the Parry Collection. The Prolegomena to this volume include studies of metrics and melodic changes in the performance of some of the singers, as well as comparative analysis of some of the versions.

In an article in 1974 I paid particular attention to the "theme" in oral traditional narrative song, specifically epic. It would be useful here to review some of the work on formulas over the years, because they have been the focus of the study of oral literature since Milman Parry's Sorbonne thesis, "L'Epithète traditionnelle dans Homère: Essai sur un problème de style homérique" (1928a) and his *thèse supplémentaire*, "Les Formules et la métrique d'Homère" (1928b). I should say at the beginning that I shall be talking about the formula as defined by Parry as "a word or group of words regularly employed under the same metrical conditions to express a given essential idea" (1930, p. 80), which does not include repeated passages, for which I use the term "theme." It is perhaps fair to begin with perspectives on my own previous work on formulas, and to comment especially on formula density, making clear my own views on the subject at the present time.

Formula Density

To the best of my memory, Parry did not mention "formula density," nor use it under that title as a test for orality, but he did make statements that implied that he was acquainted with the concept. For example he wrote (1930, p. 304):

We have found that formulas are to all purposes altogether lacking in verse which we know was written, and we are now undertaking the first step in showing the particular character in Homeric style, which is to prove that Homer's verse, on the contrary, has many. We are establishing the difference between many formulas and none.

Parry was interested in noting statistical data about frequency of occurrences of formulas in a text. On occasion he counted the number of formulas in a passage, as in the following statement, after presenting his chart of formulas in the opening of the *Iliad* and of the *Odyssey* (*idem*):

The expressions in the first twenty-five lines of the *Iliad* which are solidly underlined as being found unchanged elsewhere in Homer count up to 29, those in the passage from the *Odyssey* to 34. More than one out of every four of these is found again in eight or more places, whereas in all Euripides there was only one phrase which went so far as to appear seven times.

A little later in the article he wrote (p. 312):

> What we have done then is to prove that the style of Homer, so far as the repeated expressions go, is altogether unlike that of any verse which we know was written.

These statements, it should be emphasized, apply to Homer and ancient Greek literature rather than to medieval epic, and as medievalists we may disagree if they are imposed on medieval vernacular literatures, but the principle of formula density as a test of orality is clearly set forth in these quotations.

Parry did not write much on formulas after his Yugoslav experience, except for his article on whole-verse formulas in Homer and South Slavic (1933). When I ventured into medieval epic after Parry's death, I brought with me what I had learned. In my doctoral dissertation in 1949, entitled *The Singer of Tales*, I analyzed passages from the Homeric poems, *Beowulf*, the *Chanson de Roland*, *Digenis Akritas*, and the *Nibelungenlied*. This was published under the same title (which was originally Parry's), with revisions (1960), including the omission of the *Nibelungenlied*. Although I pointed out that there were many formulas and formulaic expressions in the passages analyzed, I did not speak of "density of formulas," nor, with the one exception noted above, did I reckon percentages. Such exact statistics, had, however, been figured for *Beowulf* by Magoun in his famous *Speculum* article (1953), and by Robert Creed in his unpublished doctoral dissertation at Harvard (1955).

During the fifties and sixties, in a seminar on Medieval Epic and Romance which I gave regularly in the Comparative Literature Department at Harvard, I began, with the help of the students, to count formulas in narrative poems in the several medieval language traditions with which they were acquainted in the original and to figure percentages. I believe that it was in this context that the term "formula density" came into being as a test of orality. We were experimenting, and the results turned out to be surprising because of the number of poems containing a high percentage of formulas or formulaic expressions. We worked not only with texts which, we were advised, might possibly belong to oral tradition, such as *Havelok the Dane* and *King Horn* in Middle English, and *Beowulf* in Anglo-Saxon, but also with those which we knew could not, such as *Sir Gawain and the Green Knight* and *König Rother*. The last two were clearly low in true formulas, as we had expected, and the first two were pretty high on the scale, but *Beowulf* was marginal.

The implication in our study of formula density at that time was that a poem which had many formulas was an oral poem and that one with few was not an oral poem. By an oral poem it was implied that it was a poem belonging to a tradition of oral verse-making—to use Parry's term—that is, to a tradition of singing and performing, and that the text before us was the product of a traditional singer dictating his song to a scribe. In retrospect, however, our thinking was too simplistic to cover the variety of situations in the medieval milieu. In *The Singer of Tales* I had argued against the existence of "transitional texts," a concept that constantly haunted us. That ghost has, for the moment at least, been laid to rest. There seem to be texts that can be called either transitional or belonging to the first stage of written literature. Does that mean, then, that our discovery that many medieval texts of written origin contained a surprising number of formulas was of no value, that that discovery is meaningless? Certainly not.

What we did show very clearly about the texts which we analyzed was *the degree to which they made use of the formulaic style*. Some were very close to it, some more remote, and others moderately formulaic in their manner of making lines. The formulaic style originated, as Larry Benson agreed in his well-known article (1966), in oral traditional singing of narrative verse. When people began to write Anglo-Saxon verse, as Magoun himself had indicated, they continued to use the same traditional style, because there was as yet no other available. A new style was to evolve in time. Our analyses of formula density demonstrated the degree of involvement of any given poem in the oral traditional style and conversely *its degree of involvement in a non-traditional style* if we could find a way of measuring that. Benson has himself admirably discussed the debt of the poet of *Sir Gawain and the Green Knight* to the traditional formulaic style (1965). Formula studies, *including intelligent statistical analyses*, are an important component in the investigation of medieval vernacular poetry.

We also learned in that seminar to adapt the concept of the formula to the particular tradition with which each student was working, to translate the general terms of Parry's definition to the specific metrical and rhythmic conventions of the several cultures involved. We learned too, that there were modifications needed in the idea of "exact repetition"; for example, metathesis was frequently found in the occurrences of the formulas, and we agreed to accept a metathesized form as an "exact repetition," as Wayne O'Neil had noted in 1960. He also remarked that "formulas, since they are made up of individual words, can be declined and conjugated and compared."[7] In the seminar we also struggled with the question of whether the repetition of a phrase within a few lines of another occurrence of it should count as evidence for formulicity. Our techniques were sharpened, as was our sense of what a formula was.

Although we did not succeed in the seminar in coming to grips fully with the problems of the "transitional" text, we were acutely aware that there was a problem. In the summer of 1981 I decided to return to the study of Anglo-Saxon poetry, which I had neglected for some time, and I prepared a paper for the Medieval Institute at Kalamazoo the following spring. I was engaged in comparing speech introductions in *Beowulf*, *Elene*, and *Andreas*. The paper was only a progress report, but it was well received. Since then I have written much more on the subject in manuscript. I for my part learned that the study of formula density is only part of a larger picture, and that its evidence alone may not be sufficient to determine orality. One might put it that formula density is a necessary criterion, a fundamental characteristic of orality, without which no testing would be complete or ultimately valid, but the concept of formula density needs to be expanded.

I mean by expanding the concept of formula density that it should be calculated not only on the basis of the number of the individual formulas, but it should also be reckoned in terms of larger syntactic and semantic units, such as the whole sentence, and within boundaries, therefore, that go beyond the single line, as needed to accommodate the syntactic requirements. Parry had to some extent foreseen this as an inevitable necessity when he spoke of the complexity of the formulaic style and noted that formulas would have to be adjusted to fit the constraints of the sentence: "The ways in which these formulas fit into the parts of the verse and join on to one another to make the sentence and the hexameter are very many, and vary for each type of formula" (1930, p. 126). His idea of the formula included, in the long run, its place not only in the metrical milieu, the line, but also in the syntactic milieu, the sentence, which often went beyond the boundaries of a line. Both Hainsworth (1968) and A. Hoekstra (1964) elaborated on this for the ancient Greek tradition in their studies on the flexibility of the

Homeric formula, and on the antiquity of some formulas in that tradition.

*   *   *

Differentiation between Formula and Repetition

One of the subjects that in retrospect I do not believe we have explored enough, that we seem to have taken for granted, or perhaps even to have forgotten entirely, is the difference between a formula and a repetition. Parry paid great attention to this (1930, p. 304).

> It is important at this point to remember that the formula in Homer is not necessarily a repetition, just as the repetitions of tragedy are not necessarily formulas. It is the nature of an expression which makes of it a formula, whereas its use a second time in Homer depends largely upon the hazard which led a poet, or a group of poets, to use it more than once in two given poems of a limited length. We are taking up the problem of the Homeric formulas from the side of the repetitions, but only because it is easier to recognize a formula if we find it used a second or a third time, since we can then show more easily that it is used regularly, and that it helps the poet in his verse-making.

What did Parry mean by "the nature of an expression?" The key to that is in the last clause in the above quotation. The formula "helps the poet in his verse-making." It is primarily for that reason that it is repeated. The "repetition," on the other hand, is a phrase repeated to call attention to a previous occurrence, for an aesthetic or other purpose. *Formulas do not point to other uses of themselves; they do not recall other occurrences.* It might be said that they embody *all* previous occurrences, and, therefore, not any one other single occurrence.

One of the changes that comes about in the "transitional" stage is that gradually *formulas*, no longer being necessary for composition, give place to true *repetitions*, which are repeated for aesthetic or referential reasons rather than for ease in verse-making. The true formula, extremely complex in practice, yet simple enough in concept, can be illustrated—if illustration be necessary—by epithets in Homer which provide a means of expressing an essential idea, such as "Achilleus," in all the places in the dactylic hexameter in which the ancient Greek traditional poet might have wanted to use it. I can illustrate "repetition" by turning to almost any modern poet in English. Here are lines 9-11 of Robert Frost's "An Old Man's Winter Night":

> And having *scared* the cellar under him
> *In clomping* here, he *scared* it once again
> *In clomping* off—and *scared* the outer night

Or from one of Carl Sandburg's poems:

> *Pile* the bodies *high at* Austerlitz and Waterloo!
> *Shovel them under and let me work!*
>   *I am the grass*; I cover all

> *And pile them high at* Gettysburg,
> *And pile them high at* Ypres and Verdun!

> *Shovel them under and let me work!*
> Two years, ten years, and passengers ask the
>   conductor
>   What place is this?
>   Where are we now?
>   *I am the grass*;
>   *Let me work!*

Or the last stanza of Robert Frost's "Stopping by Woods on a Snowy Evening":

> The woods are lovely, dark and deep.
> But I have promises to keep
> *And miles to go before I sleep*,
> *And miles to go before I sleep.*

A note to the above lines reads: "Frost always insisted repetition of the line in the last stanza was not supposed to imply death but only to imply a somnolent dreaminess in the speaker."[10]

It is clear, then, that the difference between formula and repetition is crucial to oral poetics, and one of the results of not having explored sufficiently the difference between formula and repetition has been that the lines between oral and written poetics have been blurred. There is a different attitude toward repetition in an oral poetics, where repetition is tied to verse-making, not to semantic or contextual reference, or to "aesthetics." In respect to repetition, oral poetics is different from written poetics *precisely* because in it one is dealing with *formulas*, not "repetitions."

In translating Homer, for example, exact repetition of the epithets, however desirous it may be, does not reproduce Homeric style except on a very superficial level, which does not take into account the *necessity* of the formulas in Homer and the *absence* of that necessity in the translation.

From Oral to Written: What are the Signposts?

In addition to the *density* of formulas in a *transitional* text, one has to consider also *their oral-traditionality* and the *oral-traditionality of the structures or systems* in which they belong.[11] Transition has meaning only if one passes from oral-traditional *diction* and oral-traditional *systems* of formulas to non-traditional diction and non-traditional structures. In order to assess this, however, one must know the traditional elements. The task, then, is to determine what the oral-traditional diction and systems are (or were).

We have enough information in the South Slavic material to make that determination. There is an abundance of pure oral-traditional verse extending over several centuries. With Anglo-Saxon, and some other medieval traditions, we are less fortunate. Nevertheless, there are some guidelines. We have indicated that what we were measuring in our analyses of formula density was not orality in the absolute, not whether any given text was a fully oral-traditional poem or not, although this was sometimes the case, but the degree of "orality" of that text, judging by its use of traditional formulas, which all seem to agree are characteristic of oral-traditional composition. We can, therefore, talk about formulas that are characteristic of oral-traditional composition in Anglo-Saxon, or any other tradition, only after we have determined a) which repetitions are formulas, and b) which formulas are oral-traditional, insofar as we can do so from the sometimes scanty evidence.

Conclusion

The study of Oral Literature has increased not only in quantity but also in quality. New collections in areas little cultivated by scholars except those in the particular discipline provide new models, some of which themselves represent a learned tradition of long standing. One can think of the Central Asiatic tradition, for example, from the time of Radloff to the present with Nekljudov, Heissig, and the members of the Bonn Seminar.

Formula studies, always an important ingredient for basic understanding of oral traditional poetry, have matured and become more sophisticated. And the way has been opened up to investigate the details of the creation and life of transitional texts. I have come to realize that, in fact, in such fields as Anglo-Saxon and other medieval poetries, we have been doing just that all along.

The time has come to deepen our comprehension of the role of *tradition* in oral traditional literature, lest its significance be forgotten in the present zeal for synchronic description of performance and contextuality, important though those elements may be. For it is tradition that imbues both the text *and* the context with a meaning profound and strong enough to demand persistence through time. The new journal *Oral Tradition* will provide a smithy on the anvils of which may be hammered out true perspectives on our present, as well as on our past.

NOTES

[1] I am referring particularly to Ruth Finnegan in her book *Oral Poetry: Its Nature, Significance and Social Context* (1977). She, however, does not by any means ignore text, as do many others in the essentially anthropological school.

[2] I am grateful to Professor Stephen A. Mitchell for providing me with the references to the recent text/context controversy in *Western Folklore*: Jones, 1979a; Ben-Amos, 1979; Jones, 1979b; Georges, 1980.

[3]1983. I am most grateful to Professor Opland for taking me last summer to hear praise poets in the Transkei and Ciskei.

[4]See also Webber, 1973.

[5]See further Davidson's forthcoming of formulaic structure in the *Shahnama*, to be published in *Oral Tradition*.

[6]The Ong Festschrift is the January 1987 issue of *Oral Tradition*.

[7]In "Oral-Formulaic Structure in Old English Elegiac Poetry" (1960, pp. 30, 38). His examples are 'fela feorhcynna,' *Bwf* 2266a and 'feorhcynna fela,' *Maxims I*, 14a. I owe this reference and quotation to Fry, 1967, p. 195.

[8]See below for a discussion of this distinction.

[9]See inter alia Russo, 1966 and Nagler, 1974, pp. 7, 11.

[10]The verses of Frost and Sandburg are quoted from Ellmann and O'Clair, 1973. The note on the last stanza of Frost's "Stopping by Woods on a Snowy Evening" is note 6 on page 205.

[11]We might add the element of artistic excellence, or aesthetics, because some scholars believe that this is a mark of the non-oral-traditional text. This is a separate subject, however, and should be treated separately as an argument to be discarded after discussion.

REFERENCES

Bäuml, Franz. 1984. "Medieval Texts and the Two Theories of Oral-Formulaic Composition: A Proposal for a Third Theory." *New Literary History*, 16:31-49.

Ben-Amos, Dan. 1979. "The Ceremony of Innocence." *Western Folklore*, 38:47-52.

Benson, Larry D. 1965. *Art and Tradition in Sir Gawain and the Green Knight*. New Brunswick: Rutgers University Press.

———. 1966. "The Literary Character of Anglo-Saxon Formulaic Poetry." *Publications of the Modern Language Association*, 81:334-341.

Biebuyck, Daniel P. 1969. *The Mwindo Epic from the Banyanga (Congo) Republic*. Ed. and tr. by Daniel Biebuyck and Kahombo C. Mateene. Berkeley: University of California Press.

———. 1978. *Hero and Chief: Epic Literature from the Banyanga Zaire Republic*. Berkeley: University of California Press.

Buchholz, Peter. 1980. *Vorzeitkunde: Mündliches Erzählen und Überliefern im mittelalterlichen Skandinavien nach dem Zeugnis von Fornaldarsage und eddischer Dichtung*. Skandinavische Studien, 13. Neumunster: K. Wachholz.

Bynum, David E. 1974a. "Child's Legacy Enlarged: Oral Literary

Studies at Harvard Since 1856." *Harvard Library Bulletin*, 22:237-267.

———, ed. 1974b. "*Ženidba Smailagina sina*, kazivao je Avdo Medjedović." Serbo-Croatian Heroic Songs, IV. Cambridge, Mass.: Center for the Study of Oral Literature.

———. 1978. *The Daemon in the Wood*. Cambridge, Mass.: Center for the Study of Oral Literature.

———, ed. 1979. *Bihaćka krajina: Epics from Bihać, Cazin, and Kulen Vakuf*. Serbo-Croatian Heroic Songs, XIV. Cambridge, Mass. : Harvard University Press.

———, ed. 1980. *Ženidba Vlahinjić Alije, Osmanbeg Delibegović i Pavičević Luka*. Serbo-Croatian Heroic Songs, VI. Cambridge, Mass.: Harvard University Press.

Byock, Jesse. 1982. *Feud in the Icelandic Saga*. Berkeley: University of California Press.

Cantilena, Mario. 1982. *Ricerche sulla dizione epica. 1. Per uno studio della formularità degli Inni Omerici*. Rome: Edizioni dell'Ateneo.

Clover, Carol J. and John Lindow, eds. 1985. *Old Norse-Icelandic Literature, A Critical Guide*. Islandica, 45. Ithaca: Cornell University Press.

Creed, Robert P. 1955. "Studies in the Techniques of Composition of the *Beowulf* Poetry in British Museum MS. Cotton Vitellius A. xv." Ph.D. dissertation, Harvard University.

———. 1981a. "The *Beowulf*-Poet: Master of Sound Patterning." In Foley, 1981a, pp. 194-216.

———. 1981b. "Sound-Patterning in Some Sung and Dictated Performances of Avdo Medjedović." *Canadian-American Slavic Studies*, 15, i:116-121.

———. 1982. "The Basis of the Meter of *Beowulf*." In *Approaches to Beowulfian Scansion*. Old English Colloquium Series, No. 1. Ed. Alain Renoir and Ann Hernández. Berkeley: Old English Colloquium, University of California. Rpt. Washington, DC: University Press of America, 1985, pp. 27-36.

Davidson, Olga M. 1985. "The Crown-Bestower in the Iranian Book of Kings." In *Papers in Honour of Mary Boyce*. Hommages et Opera Minora, 10. Leiden: E. J. Brill, pp. 61-148.

Duggan, Joseph J., ed. 1974a. *Oral Literature: Seven Essays*. Edinburgh and New York: Scottish Academic Press and Barnes & Noble, 1975. Rpt. of *Forum for Modern Language Studies*, 10, iii.

———. 1974b. "Formulaic Diction in the *Cantar de mio Cid* and the Old French Epic." In Duggan, 1974a, pp. 74-83.

———. 1981a. "La Théorie de la composition des chansons de geste: les faits et les interprétations." *Olifant*, 8, iii:238-255.

———. 1981b. "Le Mode de composition des chansons de geste:

Analyse statistique, jugement esthétique, modèles de transmission."
Olifant, 8, iii:286-316.

———. 1981c. "Legitimation and the Hero's Exemplary Function in the *Cantar de mio Cid* and the *Chanson de Roland*." In Foley, 1981a, pp. 217-234.

Edwards, Mark. 1970. "Homeric Speech Introductions." *Harvard Studies in Classical Philology*, 74:1-36.

———. 1975. "Type-Scenes and Homeric Hospitality." *Transactions of the American Philological Association*, 105:51-72.

———. 1980. "The Structure of Homeric Catalogues." *Transactions of the American Philological Association*, 110:81-105.

Ellmann, Richard and Robert O'Clair, eds. 1973. *The Norton Anthology of Modern Poetry*. New York: Norton.

Fenik, Bernard C., ed. 1978. *Homer: Tradition and Invention*. University of Cincinnati Classical Studies, n.s. 2, Leiden: E. J. Brill.

———. 1986. *Homer and the Nibelungelied: Comparative Studies in Epic Style*. Cambridge, Mass.: Harvard University Press.

Figueira, Thomas and Gregory Nagy, eds. 1985. *Theognis of Megara: Poetry and the Polis*. Baltimore: Johns Hopkins University Press.

Finnegan, Ruth. 1977. *Oral Poetry: Its Nature, Significance, and Social Context*. Cambridge: Cambridge University Press.

Foley, John Miles, ed. 1981a. *Oral Traditional Literature: A Festschrift for Albert Bates Lord*. Columbus, Ohio: Slavica Publishers, 2nd printing 1983.

———. 1981b. "Introduction: The Oral Theory in Context." In Foley, 1981a, pp. 27-122.

———. 1981c. "Oral Texts, Traditional Texts: Poetics and Critical Methods." *Canadian-American Slavic Studies*, 15, i:122-145.

———. 1982. "The Scansion of *Beowulf* in its Indo-European Context." In *Approaches to Beowulfian Scansion*. Ed. Alain Renoir and Ann Hernández. Old English Colloquium Series, No. 1. Berkeley: Old English Colloquium, University of California. Rpt. Washington, D.C.: University Press of America, 1985, pp. 1-17.

———. 1985. *Oral-Formulaic Theory and Research: An Introduction and Annotated Bibliography*. New York: Garland.

———, ed. 1986. *Oral Tradition in Literature: Interpretation in Context*. Columbia: University of Missouri Press.

Fry, Donald K., Jr. 1967. "Old English Formulas and Systems." *English Studies*, 48:193-204.

Georges, Robert A. 1980. "Toward a Resolution of the Text/Context Controversy." *Western Folklore*, 39:34-40.

Göller, Karl H., ed. 1981a. *The Alliterative Morte Arthure: A*

Reassessment of the Poem. Arthurian Studies, 3. London and Totowa, N.J.: D. S. Brewer and Rowman & Littlefield.

————. 1981b. "A Summary of Research." In Göller, 1981a, pp. 7-14, 153-57.

Hainsworth, J. Bryan. 1968. *The Flexibility of the Homeric Formula.* Oxford: Clarendon Press.

Hatto, A. T., ed. 1977. *The Memorial Feast for Kökötöy-Khan (Kökötöydün Aši): A Kirghiz Epic Poem.* Oxford: Oxford University Press.

Heissig, Walther. 1983a. *Westliche Motivparallelen in zentralasiatischen Epen.* Bayerische Akademie der Wissenschaft, Philosophisch-historische Klasse, Sitzungsbericht, Heft 2.

————. 1983b. *Geser-Studien, Untersuchungen zu den Erzählstoffen in den 'neuen' Kapiteln des mongolishcen Geser-Zyklus.* Abhandlungen der rheinisch-westfälischen Akademie der Wissenschaft, Band 69.

Hoekstra, A. 1964. *Homeric Modifications of Formulaic Prototypes: Studies in the Development of Greek Epic Diction.* Verhandelingen der Koniklijke Nederlandse Akademie van Wetenschappen, afd. Letterkunde, n.r., Deel 71, No. 1. Amsterdam: Noord-Hollandsche Uitgevers Maatschappij, rpt. 1969.

Innes, Gordon. 1973. "Stability and Change in Griots' Narrations." *African Language Studies,* 14:105-18.

————. 1974. *Sonjata: Three Mandinka Versions.* London: School of African and Oriental Studies, University of London.

Janko, Richard. 1981. "Equivalent Formulas in the Greek Epos." *Mnemosyne,* 34:251-64.

————. 1982. *Homer, Hesiod and the Hymns: Diachronic Development in Epic Diction.* Cambridge and New York: Cambridge University Press.

Johnson, John William. 1974. *Heellooy, Heelleellooy: The Development of the Genre "Heello" in Modern Somali Poetry.* Indiana University Publications, African Series, 5.

————. 1979. *The Epic of Sun-Jata According to Magan Sisòkò.* 2 vols. FPC Monograph Series, 5. Bloomington: Indiana University Folklore Publications Group.

————. 1980a. "Recent Contributions by Somalis and Somalists to the Study of Oral Literature." In *Somalia and the World: Proceedings of the International Symposium (held in Mogadishu, on the Tenth Anniversary of the Somali Revolution, October 15-21, 1979).* Ed. Hussein M. Adam. Mogadishu: Halgan. Vol. 1, pp. 117-131.

————. 1980b. "Yes, Virginia, There Is an Epic in Africa." *Review of African Literatures,* 11:308-26.

————. 1985. *The Epic of Son-Jara: A West African Tradition.*

Bloomington: Indiana University Press.

Jones, Steven. 1979a. "Slouching Towards Ethnography: The Text/Context Controversy Reconsidered." *Western Folklore*, 38:42-47.

⸻. 1979b. "Dogmatism in the Contextual Revolution." *Western Folklore*, 38:52-55.

Kelber, Werner. 1983. *The Oral and the Written Gospel: The Hermeneutics of Speaking and Writing in the Synoptic Tradition, Mark, Paul, and Q*. Philadelphia: Fortress Press.

Kirk, Geoffrey. 1985. *The Iliad: A Commentary*, Vol. 1. Cambridge: Cambridge University Press.

Krishna, Valerie. 1982. "Parataxis, Formulaic Density, and Thrift in the *Alliterative Morte Arthure*." *Speculum*, 57:63-83.

Latacz, Joachim, ed. 1979. *Homer: Tradition und Neuerung*. Wege der Forschung, 463. Darmstadt: Wissenschaftliche Buchgeselleschaft.

Lönnroth, Lars. 1976. *Njal's Saga: A Critical Introduction*. Berkeley: University of California Press.

⸻. 1981. "Ȝorð fannz aeva né upphiminn: A Formula Analysis." In Ursula Dronke et al., eds., *Speculum Norroenum: Norse Studies in Memory of Gabriel Turville-Petre*. Odense: Odense University Press, pp. 310-327.

Lord, Albert Bates. 1960. *The Singer of Tales*. Harvard Studies in Comparative Literature, 24. Cambridge: Harvard University Press, 1960. Rpt. New York: Atheneum, 1968 et seq. and Harvard University Press, 1981.

⸻. 1974a. "Perspectives on Recent Work on Oral Literature." In Duggan, 1974a, pp. 1-24.

⸻, trans. 1974b. "*The Wedding of Smailagić Meho*, by Avdo Medjedović." Serbo-Croatian Heroic Songs, III. Cambridge, Mass.: Harvard University Press.

Magoun, Francis P., Jr. 1953. "The Oral-Formulaic Character of Anglo-Saxon Narrative Poetry." *Speculum*, 28:446-467.

Monroe, James T. 1972. "Oral Composition in Pre-Islamic Poetry." *Journal of Arabic Literature*, 3:1-53.

Muellner, Leonard C. 1976. *The Meaning of Homeric "eyxomai" through its Formulas*. Innsbrucker Beiträge zur Sprachwissenschaft, 13.

Muižniece, Lalita Lāce. 1981. "Linguistic Analysis of Latvian Death and Burial Folk Songs." Ph.D. dissertation, University of Michigan, Ann Arbor.

Nagler, Michael N. 1974. *Spontaneity and Tradition: A Study in the Oral Art of Homer*. Berkeley: University of California Press.

Nagy, Gregory. 1979. *The Best of the Achaeans: Concepts of the Hero in Archaic Greek Poetry*. Baltimore: Johns Hopkins University Press.

————. 1983. "On the Death of Sarpedon." In *Approaches to Homer*. Ed. Carl A. Rubino and Cynthia W. Shelmerdine. Austin: University of Texas Press, pp. 189-217.

————. 1986. "Ancient Greek Epic and Praise Poetry: Some Typological Considerations." In Foley, 1986, pp. 89-102.

Nagy, Joseph Falaky. *The Wisdom of the Outlaw: The Boyhood Deeds of Finn in Gaelic Tradition.* Berkeley: University of California Press.

Nekljudov, S. Ju., and Z. Tömörceren. 1985. *Mongolische Erzählungen über Geser.* Asiatische Forschungen, Band 92. Wiesbaden: Harrasowitz.

Niditch, Susan. 1985. *Chaos and Cosmos: Studies in Biblical Patterns of Creation.* Chico, Cal.: Scholars Press.

Niles, John D. 1983. *Beowulf: The Poem and Its Tradition.* Cambridge, Mass.: Harvard University Press.

Okafor, C. A. 1983. *The Banished Child: A Study in Tonga Oral Literature.* London: The Folklore Society.

Ong, Walter J., S.J. 1982. *Orality and Literacy: The Technologizing of the Word.* London and New York: Methuen.

O'Neil, Wayne. 1960. "Oral-Formulaic Structure in Old English Elegiac Poetry." Ph.D. dissertation, University of Wisconsin.

O'Nolan, Kevin, ed. and trans. 1982. *Eochair, Mac Ri in Eirinn (Eochair, A King's Son in Ireland).* Told by Eamon Bourke, rec. by Liam Costello. Dublin: Comhairle Bhéaloideas Eireann, University College.

Opland, Jeff. 1980. *Anglo-Saxon Oral Poetry: A Study of the Traditions.* New Haven: Yale University Press.

————. 1983. *Xhosa Oral Poetry: Aspects of a Black South African Tradition.* Cambridge: Cambridge University Press.

Parry, Milman. 1928a. *L'Epithète traditionnelle dans Homère: Essai sur un problème de style homérique.* Paris: Société Editrice "Les Belles Lettres." Tr. by Adam Parry as "The Traditional Epithet in Homer" in *The Making of Homeric Verse: The Collected Papers of Milman Parry.* Oxford: Clarendon Press, 1971, pp. 1-190.

————. 1930. "Studies in the Epic Technique of Oral Verse-Making. I. Homer and Homeric Style." *Harvard Studies in Classical Philology*, 41:73-147. Rpt. in *The Making of Homeric Verse*, pp. 376-390.

————. 1933. "Whole Formulaic Verses in Greek and South Slavic Heroic Song." *Transactions of the American Philological Association*, 64:179-197. Rpt. in *The Making of Homeric Verse*, pp. 376-390.

Reichl, Karl. 1984. "Oral Tradition and Performance of the Uzbek and Karakalpak Epic Singers." In *Fragen der mongolischen Heldendichtung*, Vol. 3. Wiesbaden: Harrasowitz, pp. 613-643. With musical transcriptions.

————, ed. 1985. *Rawšan, Ein usbekisches mündliches Epos.*
Asiatische Forschungen, Band 93. Wiesbaden: Harrasowitz.

Renoir, Alain. 1977. "The Armor of the *Hildebrandslied:* An Oral-
Formulaic Point of View." *Neuphilologische Mitteilungen*, 78:389-395.

————. 1981. "Oral-Formulaic Context: Implications for the
Comparative Criticism of Mediaeval Texts." In Foley, 1981a, pp. 416-
439.

Riedinger, Anita. 1985. "The Old English Formula in Context."
Speculum, 60:294-317.

Ritzke-Rutherford, Jean. 1981a. "Formulaic Microstructure: The
Cluster." In Göller, 1981a, pp. 70-82, 167-169.

————. 1981b. "Formulaic Macrostructure: The Theme of Battle." In
Göller, 1981a, pp. 83-95, 169-171.

Russo, Joseph A. 1966. "The Structural Formula in Homeric Verse."
Yale Classical Studies, 20:219-240.

Smith, John D. 1977. "The Singer or the Song? A Reassessment of
Lord's 'Oral Theory.'" *Man*, N.S. 12:141-153.

————. 1981. "Words, Music, and Memory." In *Memory and Poetic
Structure: Papers of the Conference on Oral Literature and Literary Theory
Held at Middlesex Polytechnic, 1981.* London: Middlesex Polytechnic,
pp. 50-65.

Sowayan, Saad Abdullah. 1985. *Nabaṭi Poetry: The Oral Poetry of
Arabia.* Berkeley: University of California Press.

Viķis-Freibergs, Vaira, and Imants Freibergs. 1978. "Formulaic
Analysis of the Computer-Accessible Corpus of Latvian Sun-Songs."
Computers and the Humanities, 12:329-339.

————. 1984. "Creativity and Tradition in Oral Folklore, or the
Balance of Innovation and Repetition in the Oral Poet's Art." In
Cognitive Processes in the Perception of Art. Ed. W. R. Crozier and A. J.
Chapman. Amsterdam and New York: North-Holland Press.

Wang, Ching-Hsien. 1974. *The Bell and the Drum*: Shih Ching *as
Formulaic Poetry in an Oral Tradition.* Berkeley: University of California
Press.

Watts, Ann C. 1969. *The Lyre and the Harp: A Comparative
Reconsideration of Oral Tradition in Homer and Old English Epic Poetry.*
New Haven: Yale University Press.

Webber, Ruth H. 1951. *Formulistic Diction in the Spanish Ballad.*
University of California Publications in Modern Philology, 34, No.
2:175-277.

————. 1973. "Narrative Organization of the *Cantar de Mio Cid*."
Olifant, 1, ii:21-34.

————. 1978. "Prolegomena to the Study of the Narrative Structure
of the Hispanic Ballad." In *Ballads and Ballad Research.* Ed. Patricia

Conroy. Seattle: University of Washington Press, pp. 221-230.

———. 1980. "Formulaic Language in the *Mocedades de Rodrigo*." *Hispanic Review*, 48:195-211.

———. 1981. "Historicidad y tradicionalidad en el *Cantar de Mio Cid*." In *Actas del Septimo Congreso de la Asociación Internacional de Hispanistas (celebrado en Venecia del 25 al 30 Agosto de 1980)*: *Publicadas por Giuseppe Bellini*. Rome: Bulzoni, pp. 585-590.

Yen, Alsace. 1975. "The Parry-Lord Theory Applied to Vernacular Chinese Stories." *Journal of the American Oriental Society*, 95:403-416.

Zwettler, Michael J. 1978. *The Oral Tradition of Classical Arabic Poetry: Its Character and Implications*. Columbus: Ohio State University Press.